THE GALVESTON ERA
The Texas Crescent on the Eve of Secession

CUSTOMS HOUSE, at 20th and Post Office Street, Galveston, Texas. From a contemporary engraving by Theodore R. White for *Harper's Weekly*.

THE GALVESTON ERA

The Texas Crescent on the Eve of Secession

By EARL WESLEY FORNELL

Woodcuts by Lowell Collins

UNIVERSITY OF TEXAS PRESS   AUSTIN

PUBLISHED WITH THE ASSISTANCE OF A GRANT

FROM THE FORD FOUNDATION

UNDER ITS PROGRAM FOR THE SUPPORT OF PUBLICATIONS

IN THE HUMANITIES AND SOCIAL SCIENCES

International Standard Book Number 0-292-72710-0
Library of Congress Catalog Card Number 61-13316
Copyright © 1961 by Earl W. Fornell
Printed in the United States of America

First Paperback Printing, 1976

TO MARTHA

PREFACE

MANY WORKS have been written concerning the
Texas cattle country, the Great Plains, the cowboy, the famed Texas
Rangers, and other subjects related to the vast inland-orientated aspects of the history of the state. The story of the exciting days of the
Republic has also been the subject of numerous studies. In contrast,
little has been written concerning the sea-oriented areas of the state,
and a careful historical analysis has not yet been made of the period of
Texas history from the end of the Mexican War until the Reconstruction. In particular, one of the most neglected subjects of historical
study has been the Texas Gulf Coast in the formative period of the
1850's and the critical years of the War between the States.

At the outset this study was intended to deal with the Galveston
Coast during the period from statehood through the War; however, a
closer examination of the topic at the actual research level indicated
that this time delineation was too large for one book and that no satisfactory study of the Civil War period could be made without first
developing an analysis of the formative period of the late forties and
fifties. In fact, while the war years may appear to be more worthy of
study and perhaps more colorful, the decade before the war was actu-

ally much more important from the historical point of view because those were the years in which Texans determined the profile of their own future. It was during the decade of the 1850's that able and practical men on the Texas Gulf Coast, surveying the hundreds of square miles of rich bottom land of the state and being aware of the growing demand for cotton on the world market, realized that fortunes could be made there from the production of cotton.

In the late 1850's Texas was producing less than a half million bales of cotton per year on land that was capable of producing from 3 to 5 million bales according to the considered opinion of E. H. Cushing, editor of the Houston *Telegraph*, and Arthur Lynn, British consul in Galveston. Cotton for Texas in the 1850's possessed the same economic lure which oil, chemicals, natural gas, and sulphur do today. Fortunes were waiting to be made not only in the actual growing of the cotton but in related activities such as banking, the ginning and warehousing of the staple, transporting the cotton to market—a business of awesome potential, supplying the many services needed to support fiber production in this volume, and, certainly not least lucrative, selling labor for the basic production of the cotton. Since cities, seaports and towns all along the coast had a share in exploiting this new opportunity, merchants, editors, lawyers, school men, doctors, and even clergymen all saw in cotton a personal opportunity for themselves.

But standing in the way of cotton expansion in Texas were several formidable problems. One of these was lack of transportation; the cotton producer could be assured financial success only where he was assured a reliable means of transporting his product to market. Out of this need grew the monumental railroad struggle of the fifties; the issue was not whether or not Texas should have railroads but where they should run and whether or not they should be built by state or private funds.

Another prime question was labor and where to get it. Slave labor at that time was almost universally admitted to be the only type practical to use and acceptable in economic terms; free labor would be too costly and anyway it was not available. What Texan would work in the cotton fields for wages when he could, for a few dollars, have a piece of land of his own? But slave labor was very costly also and the supply was very short: a good prime Negro imported from the Old South cost from $900 to $1500. This high cost of labor presented a great barrier to the cotton expansion, but there was an alternative—the importation of Negroes from Africa. Labor from the dark continent could be put down on the coast of Texas for prices ranging from $150 to $300. The going rate was one dollar per pound. The difficulties in obtaining this type of labor were threefold. The trade was illegal, being contrary to both the federal and the Texas constitutions; there was a moral problem involved in opening up the African slave trade and thus defying the world wide movement to curtail the growth of slavery; and there was the political question of arousing the serious antagonism of large political factions in the North.

One interesting side issue of the labor problem was the famed filibustering campaigns toward Cuba and Central America whose participants hoped that these areas, once in the hands of Texas or other Southerners, could be used as way-stations for the African slave trade into Texas. In other words Texans' interest in filibustering was part of the movement to somehow find labor for the Texas cotton lands. A frontal attack on the barrier to secure labor was the very formidable attempt to legally reopen the African slave trade by repealing the prohibitions in the federal and Texas constitutions.

Thus, it would seem that the dominant political, economic and social drives affecting the Texas Gulf coast in the 1850's had their origins in the possible expansion of the potential cotton lands of Texas. There were, of course, other impulses active: the desire of the German immigrants for a "good life" and the interests of the small farmers from the central states who came to Texas for the same reasons that most Americans came to the frontier, but the main drive of those who brought money and political and social power with them arose from some aspect of cotton or supplying those who had an interest in cotton.

The 1850's on the Texas coast then must be studied in terms of the drive for cotton expansion, the filibusters and other attempts to open up the African slave trade, the need for better transportation, and the moral issue of slavery; all of these were profoundly influenced by how and by whom the great bottom lands of Texas were to be exploited. The fact that certain deep-South orientated factions won the struggle

ix

determined that Texas would join the Confederacy in 1861 instead of staying neutral, going back to the Lone Star status or actually staying in the Union.

The study of this struggle then is the theme of this book; there were, however, many minor aspects of life on the Gulf Coast in the mid-nineteenth century which are examined and while these may be of lesser importance in the major developments, yet the problems were very important to the persons involved and some, such as the banking controversy and the power struggle between Galveston and Houston, were related to the more important struggles and played their part in influencing the major decisions of this period of Texas history.

Once the decision had been made to make cotton production by means of slave labor the major economic enterprise of the state, a conflict with a Federal government which attempted to limit this slave labor was inevitable, and once the decision to secede had been reached, what happened to Texas during the war and reconstruction periods was beyond the control of Texans, being determined by events in a larger arena.

Galveston was chosen as the nucleus of the study rather than the Gulf Coast as a whole, because in terms of trade, banking, and journalism the Island dominated the coastal area. In fact, the city, the largest in Texas, was known as the "Queen City" of the Gulf.

This study does not pretend to be a complete history of Galveston in this period, rather the intention has been to focus on the major issues and major personalities that dominated life in the cosmopolitan metropolis in those critical years, 1845–1861.

ACKNOWLEDGMENTS

A STUDY SUCH AS THIS could never be successful without the aid, advice, criticism, and sympathy of many friends and associates of the investigator. To all of these I would like to express my appreciation.

I am first of all most grateful to Professor Edward Hake Phillips, formerly of Rice University and now on the history faculty of Austin College, for his assistance and advice in the preparation of this manuscript. I wish also to express my gratitude to Professors Hardin Craig, Jr., Katherine Fischer Drew, Chalmers Mac Hudspeth, Floyd Seyward Lear, William H. Masterson, Andrew F. Muir, William H. Nelson, and Frank E. Vandiver, all members of the Rice University faculty who read parts of the manuscript and assisted me in various ways during its preparation.

To Professor William B. Hesseltine of the University of Wisconsin I am greatly indebted for cogent and particular comment on the study during the early stages of my research, and to friends at Lamar State College of Technology—Dr. F. L. McDonald, President, Professor Lloyd Cherry, Director of the Lamar Research Center, Dr. Preston Williams, Chairman of the History Department, Dr. Irving Dawson,

Chairman of the Government Department, and Miss Julia Plummer, Librarian—for assistance in innumerable ways.

I wish also to express my appreciation to the artist Mr. Lowell Collins, Dean of the Houston Museum School of Art, for his interest in my work and for the illustrations of my book which convey the spirit of ante bellum Galveston as no words can do. I extend sincere thanks, as well, to my friend Mr. George Fuermann of *The Houston Post* for his interest, kindness and generous assistance on many occasions and to Mr. Thomas Rice of Galveston for his advice upon details concerning Galveston history.

All researchers are in debt to librarians and I am particularly indebted to those of the Rosenberg Library in Galveston, The University of Texas Library in Austin, the San Jacinto Memorial Library and the Houston Public Library. I am indeed particularly grateful to Miss Maxine Johnston, Reference Librarian at Lamar State College of Technology, to the former Reference Librarian at Fondren Library, Dr. James Phillips of Dallas, to Miss Pender Turnbull of the Fondren Library staff, and to Mrs. David Knepper, director of the San Jacinto Memorial Library.

For their interest and assistance in research and technical details Miss Mary Tod, Mrs. Rosa Tod Hamner and Mr. John Tod Hamner of Houston deserve my sincere gratitude. I further wish to pay tribute to Mrs. Alice H. Finckh, Editor of *The American-German Review* of the Carl Schurz Memorial Foundation of Philadelphia for her interest in my research concerning the early Germans of Texas.

And finally, to the departmental secretaries who faithfully delivered innumerable complicated messages, to the students who patiently endured desquisitions on Galvestoniana which somehow crept into lectures on the Texas Gulf Coast, to the colleagues whose passing and now forgotten comments or questions helped shape the course of my investigations, and to the multitude of other people who contributed to, or perhaps suffered through, the expansion of my interest in and knowledge of the history of the Texas Gulf Coast, my grateful thanks.

TABLE OF CONTENTS

ILLUSTRATIONS

PART
ONE

A Profile of Galveston

1. THE ISLAND CITY: AN INTRODUCTION

To Thomas North, the island city of Galveston—as he approached it by ship in 1861—appeared to be "a mirage" which floated as an "air suspension—a heavenward elongation" resting upon the glistening waters of the Gulf. Even as this sea-borne traveler drew nearer and the illusion blended into reality, the city still appeared in the shimmering sunlight as if it had been "painted by a fairy hand in spiritual shadows on the low extended horizon." Upon the traveler's

3

actual landing, the "romance" of the scene being "toned down by reality," the island city still remained "one of the finest and most beautiful cities in the South of her size."[1]

Another traveler, a European mercantile agent from Frankfort, declared upon visiting the Island that the city possessed one of the best commercial locations on the Gulf, that its harbor was superior to any other on the Gulf between Pensacola and Vera Cruz. "The city's proximity to the ports of the West Indies, Mexico, and the United States, enhanced by the fact that the Gulf stream at all times is at hand to sweep her vessels to the Eastern Atlantic" made Galveston's position for foreign commerce one of "immense value." Galveston Bay— the largest inlet on the coast, stretching thirty miles in length and about fifteen miles in width—provided, in the opinion of this maritime observer, a generous haven for seafaring vessels. The Island, which he estimated to be at that time about thirty miles long and three and one-half miles wide, provided a barrier which protected the bay area against the open sea. Although the average rise of the Island above the level of the sea was only five feet, thus providing scant protection from "northern wind tides," this maritime traveler nevertheless considered the Island an ideal site for the "surpassingly beautiful" city and gardens which he found there.[2]

An American traveler who, in 1859, approached Galveston Harbor from the landward side at the end of a long journey from Missouri, caught his first view of the Island as he crossed the sandy stretches on the way to Bolivar Point. He found the little maritime metropolis, which appeared in the hazy sky across the bay, a most pleasing sight: "We could see the towering lighthouse as it rose in majesty—with here and there the undefined outlines of the masts of vessels lying at anchor in the bay."[3]

[1] Thomas North, [*Journal:*] *Five Years in Texas: or What You Did Not Hear during the War from 1861 to January 1866. A Narrative of His Travels, Experiences, and Observations in Texas and Mexico*, pp. 53–54.

[2] "The City of Galveston," *De Bow's Review*, III (April, 1847), p. 348 (Sketches of American seaport cities written by an unidentified European traveler).

[3] Joseph Schmitz (editor), "Impressions of Texas in 1860" (an anonymous

Through the critical eye of the inland plainsman and trail blazer, Josiah Gregg, the physical characteristics of Galveston Island received a more cautious appraisal. While acknowledging that the harbor was a safe one—except during very high water—and that the city was "handsome, though too monotonous in appearance, being on an almost perfectly level prairie island," he, nevertheless, had serious doubts regarding the security of the city, due to "its lowness which makes it much exposed in flood tides." In Gregg's judgment, if the wind blew strongly for several days from the "south or southeast and a full tide happened at the conclusion," the sea would be apt "to rise over the coast." Yet even with these liabilities, wrote Gregg, Galveston seemed "destined to be the New York of Texas," since it was conveniently located "to command the trade with New Orleans and other ports of the United States." The Trinity River, upon which the interior traffic moved to the sea, emptied into Galveston Bay; so the city stood athwart the major waterway of the area.[4]

Galveston Bay, plus the Trinity and San Jacinto rivers, during the nineteenth century provided the most navigable water routes into the interior of Texas. There were, of course, other possible inlets on the Texas Gulf Coast some of which provided minor harbors for shallow-draft vessels. These, however—the entrances to the Brazos River or into Matagorda Bay and the Colorado River areas—were so impaired by sand bars during the mid-nineteenth century that many of the entrepreneurs of the time sensibly chose to exploit the virtues of Galveston Bay rather than other inlets along the coast.

There was, of course, some important water-borne traffic in these other areas, particularly at the entrance to the Brazos River and at Sabine Pass—the latter was a land and water route from New Orleans to Galveston. However, only at the Galveston Bay entrance was the channel deep enough to admit the larger ocean-going vessels. In fact, Galveston Bay was then and still is the finest natural harbor on the

---

journal of a trip to Texas during 1859–1860), *Southwestern Historical Quarterly*, XLII (April, 1939), 342.

[4] Josiah Gregg, *Diary and Letters of Josiah Gregg*, edited by Maurice Garland Fulton, I, 100–101.

entire Gulf of Mexico. The channel is not impaired by the drifting sands which often plague water inlets of shallow coastlines because the sea currents moving between Bolivar Point and the Island are so swift that the channel is kept clear of sand without the aid of dredging.

Also, once ships are moored at the wharfs on the landward side of the Island they are secure from all except the most severe storms. These natural advantages which made Galveston the best harbor entrance on the Gulf in the mid-nineteenth century still exist today.

The Gulf area of Texas is a long, low plain made up of layer upon layer of limestone, clay, and sand, originally deposited beneath the sea and later slowly lifted above the water. The gradually rising plain of land, which rises to remarkable heights in the northern high plains area of the state, emerges but a few feet above the water line for almost a hundred miles inland along the Gulf Coast, and the rivers moving toward the sea in this part of Texas are lazy and meandering.

Under the waters of the Gulf the low plains continue a smooth but somewhat steeper slope southward; thus, at a distance of 100 miles from the shores of Galveston Island the waters of the Gulf are more than 600 feet deep. The gradual slant of the Gulf-plain shelf reaching far out into the waters of this area accounts for the well-known roll of the Gulf, which innumerable passengers debarking from schooners and steamships at Galveston took occasion to curse or praise depending upon their natural gifts as sailors or the size of the roll on the particular instance.[5]

Perhaps the seamen best qualified to speak authoritatively concerning the Gulf waters in the vicinity of Galveston were the unfortunate crews who manned the gunboats which were anchored for months outside the port during the Union blockade of the city. The experience of these men indicated that the first few weeks of a blockading tour outside the port of Galveston were a continual "minor hell" of irritation and seasickness resulting from the persistent roll of the sea; however, after a time, when a seaman had learned to live with the roll, he found that the "soft swing of the sea" and the pleasing breezes of the Gulf made an evening's deck duty or the night's sleep aboard a

[5] Harriet Smith and Darthula Walker, *The Geography of Texas* (Boston, 1923), p. 10.

6

ship anchored in the Gulf second only to the pleasure enjoyed by a baby in a cradle.[6] Whatever may have been the effect of the wave of the Gulf waters upon seafarers, geographers agree that it was this movement of the water which formed the island of Galveston and Galveston Bay. Since the southwestern end of the Bay was shut off from the open sea, except to shallow-draft vessels, by the sand bars, there remained only one harbor opening—the pass between Bolivar Point and the Island. Galveston Bay, the water area enclosed between the long island and the mainland, thus provided a fine harbor which, except during extremely bad weather, enjoyed considerable natural shelter from the open sea.[7]

Since the eastern end of the Island, the tip nearest the deep-water pass at Bolivar Point, possessed the greatest elevation above the sea level, the city was constructed there, with wharves on the sheltered, landward side of the Island. The main throughfares of the town, which ran parallel with the length of the Island, were (in order) Water Street, the first street off the water front, Strand, Mechanic, Market, Post Office, and Church streets. The beaches of the Island were, of course, on the other side, facing the open sea, some three miles away from the wharf frontage, and passage to the beach front ran along short streets, numbered from first to thirty-third, which crossed the narrow eastern tip of the Island.

Actually, the city occupied but about one-eighth of the Island at the tip nearest to Bolivar Point; the long western end of the Island was vacant except for cattle grazing, small farming, and fruit growing. The far western end was in reality but a salt marsh covered with grass too coarse to be used even for cattle. Weather conditions prevailing in Galveston are determined now as they were then by the fact that

[6] W. F. Hutchinson, "Life on the Texan Blockade," *Soldiers and Sailors Historical Society of Rhode Island, Personal Narratives,* third series, No. 1 (Providence, 1933), pp. 5–42.

[7] Houston *Telegraph,* November 19, 1862; British Foreign Office Papers, Arthur T. Lynn (British Consul in Galveston) to J. W. King (Hydrographic Office, London), May 21, 1860, MS, (hereafter cited as F. O.); Max Hannemann, "Die Seehöfen von Texas, ihre geographischen Grundlagen, ihre Entwicklung und Bedeutung," *Frankfurter Geographische Hefte,* Zweiter Jahrgang, Hft 1 (1928), pp. 146–166.

the Island lies in a semitropical zone with an average annual rainfall of about forty-five inches and a mean average temperature of sixty-nine degrees; the mean temperature prevailing for January is fifty-four degrees and for July is eighty-three degrees.[8]

Although, in the 1850's, serious doubt was occasionally expressed as to the security of the city from high sea-tides, all visitors agreed that Galveston was a beautiful and pleasant harbor city. They also agreed that life in the city was both interesting and stimulating. Martin Maris, a French traveler, who visited Galveston in 1857, found the social atmosphere particularly "cosmopolitan." The seven thousand persons whom he found living there at that time appeared to him to present the most "heterogeneous" population he had ever encountered in any city. He conversed with persons who had recently arrived from Germany, Spain, France, Italy and Ireland, and the size and character of the German segment of the population made a particular impression on him.[9]

Another European visitor at mid-century noted the remarkably cosmopolitan characteristics of "the six to nine thousand" persons living in the city. He estimated that about half of the persons then living in Galveston were Americans; the rest were Germans and other Europeans. He found that the general citizenry enjoyed "an average quantum of intelligence above that to be found in most cities," and among the abler persons he noted "some decided talent." The visitor rode in a fine carriage down the "clean" and "spacious" streets and passed "a number of churches, a fine market house, town hall and offices for the municipal court and adjunct offices." He dined well at "very good American, German, and French hotels," and enjoyed delightful hospitality at "numerous smaller houses of entertainment." He saw several fine brick buildings and many other wooden frame structures in "fine architectural taste," all painted a gleaming white. The shops along the streets appeared to be well stocked with "every article demanded by the necessities and luxuries of man" and these items

[8] Smith and Walker, *Geography*, p. 10; Hanneman, "Die Seehöfen von Texas," pp. 146–166.

[9] Martin Maris, *Souvenirs d'Amerique: Relations d'un Voyage au Texas et en Haiti*, pp. 20–21, 89–90.

could be purchased at only slightly higher prices than those prevailing at Frankfort-on-Main. The leading citizens of the city, this visitor found, "lived in great comfort" enjoying "the most delightful residences" set amidst "surpassingly beautiful" gardens. Every variety of tropical shrub, flower, and tree seemed to grow with vigor and rapidity. The oleanders were "loaded with fresh and beautiful bloom."[10]

A Frenchman, Henri de St. Cyr, who for a time maintained a merchandising house in the city and also served as vice-consul for the French government, referred to Galveston in 1857 as "a charming, delightful little village, particularly remarkable for the greenest vegetables, good fishing, oysters and most profitable as a shipping center for merchants" trading in the Southwest. What the city needed, said Henri de St. Cyr, was a railroad bridge connecting the Island with the mainland. In that event, Galveston "would become a noble city accommodating 100,000 inhabitants and give wealth and prosperity to all."[11]

Most Galvestonians at this time agreed with the Frenchman's observation. They foresaw a large future for their city, visualizing their island as a potential Manhattan, as the funnel seaport through which the future commerce of the state must necessarily pass. *The New Texas Reader,* a textbook for young Texans, referred to Galveston as "the Queen City" on the Gulf,[12] and the Queen City's residents looked upon the landlocked inlanders on the mainland with the same patronizing reservations which metropolitans living on the seacoast have always maintained toward provincials. From the time of its emergence as the major seaport of Texas, Galveston carried an identity separate from the rest of the Lone Star State. The city's isolation arose from the fact that as an island it had a unique position of its own. The cosmopolitan characteristics of the port city separated it from the plantations, the inland hamlets, and the Great Plains by an intangible barrier much greater than the channel over which a causeway was eventually built in 1859.

[10] "The City of Galveston," *De Bow's Review,* III (April, 1847), 348.
[11] Houston *Telegraph,* May 13, 1857.
[12] E. H. Cushing, *The New Texas Reader: Designed for Use in the Schools,* p. 88.

But, although to her residents Galveston might seem a city destined for greatness, to the inland Texans of Houston, Austin, San Antonio, and other points west and north, the island appeared to be at most a useful appendage. They saw no certain destiny ordained by geography for the island city. Quite the contrary; those inland Texans who had acquired tracts of land and prospects in the areas around Houston and north, and westward toward Waco and Austin, lent their influence and imaginations toward the trade-route projects developed by the great promoters of the southern-routed transcontinental railroads. Some of these planners foresaw the trade of Texas rolling northeastward through St. Louis; others saw an eastward turning, beyond Houston, toward New Orleans; both bypassed the city of Galveston. Leading Islanders exerted valiant efforts to turn the trend of railroad building along the natural river drainage routes which led to the Gulf. For a time they almost succeeded, but in the end the combined interests of the great continental railroad builders and the speculators of Houston prevailed. In the opinion of this combination of entrepreneurs, the city of Houston, despite its unattractive surroundings, was better situated to serve as a base for both rail and sea transportation than Galveston Island.[13] The fact that during the Civil War Confederate military experts and state authorities decided that the Island was too exposed to permit a serious military defense, provided an additional argument in favor of the site at Houston. Two other factors which determined the eventual victory for Houston were the shortsighted policies of the Galveston Wharf Company and the very real fact that the Island stood in constant peril from the sea.

The relative arguments of the two cities in the race for command of the potential seagoing traffic out of Texas rested primarily upon their positions in respect to the key bays, bayous, and rivers in the Houston-Galveston area. The waterways in this region did not provide dependable arteries for the movement of transportation to the Gulf. The rivers, being long, meandering and subject to extreme variations of high- and low-water levels, did not afford trustworthy channels for shipping. What is more, since adequate dredging equipment was not

[13] W. A. Leonard (compiler), *Houston City Directory for 1866*, pp. 100, 104–105.

yet in existence, the shifting sand bars at the mouths of the rivers presented major barriers to river transportation. The only exception in this regard was the fortunate situation at Bolivar Pass, at the east end of Galveston Island. Here the channel was twelve feet deep and the water moved over a bottom of hard sand, so the usual hazard of shifting sandbars was not present. The combined harbor facilities provided by Bolivar Pass and Galveston Bay afforded a natural haven for Texas' sea-borne trade. Seen in conjunction with Galveston Bay, Buffalo Bayou, and the Trinity River, this water opening into the interior was enough to stir the imaginations of Texans entertaining an ambition to exploit river-boat transportation, as well as merchants engaged in seaborne trade. It was an accepted fact that Galveston Bay provided the state with an excellent harbor. The issue in question then, involved not the harbor but whether or not Galveston Island provided a secure site for a major harbor city. Galvestonians liked to compare their situation with that of Manhattan Island; however, the low sandy characteristics of Galveston Island did not provide such dry and sturdy foundation for a seaport metropolis as did the rugged and elevated aspects of the northern location.[14]

Unfortunately for Galveston, the combined force of men, events, and geography eventually turned the issue against the Island. On the eve of the Civil War the city of Houston had become the railroad terminal for the Texas empire, and almost before a transcontinental railroad had been completed the merchants of Houston began laying plans to move a part of Galveston's port trade to wharves along the Buffalo Bayou. Even before the Civil War ended "scientific engineers" in the hire of Houston merchants began to "calculate" the effort needed to complete a "ship channel so that ocean steamers could come

[14] The preceding analysis, as it relates to physical and geographical matters, is based in part upon the following: Edward Smith, *Account of a Journey through Northeastern Texas Undertaken in 1849*, pp. 15–19; "Notes on Texas," *Western Monthly Magazine*, I (September, 1858), 352; Andrew Forest Muir, "The Destiny of Buffalo Bayou," *Southwestern Historical Quarterly*, XLVII (October, 1943), 92–95; Railroad Papers, Report of Tipton Walker to James B. Shaw, October 31, 1855, MS. *De Bow's Review*, XXIII (July, 1857), 120; Lynn to King, May 21, 1860, MS, F.O.

up to Houston as easily as they could enter Galveston Bay."[15] During the fifties Houston men won the railroad battle; during the decade following the Civil War these men, profiting from the shortsighted policies of the Galveston men who controlled the Island port, set in motion a trend which won for them a port of their own on the major sea lane out of Texas.[16]

The events of the Civil War itself had a not unimportant influence upon the outcome of the contest. While the travail endured by the island city during the conflict exerted no apparently immediate curb upon its potential post-Civil War growth, the seaport strategy of the Confederacy nevertheless left the profound impression among leading Texans that Galveston was essentially indefensible in wartime—that the Island was, in military terms, expendable. The general Confederate strategy, dominated by land rather than naval concepts, was based on the tactic of retiring forces inland and using a defense in depth against the superior weight of the enemy. In the fall of 1862 Confederate policy in Galveston, one of almost total abandonment, enabled a federal force of less than 200 men to capture the city. Even the recapture of the city in 1863 occurred for reasons of political rather than military expediency. General John B. Magruder, a skilled and competent general suffering from grave misfortunes to his reputation on the Virginia front, had been exiled in Texas. He determined to recover Galveston Island from the federals as a means to recapture his fading military reputation. Since the Union Navy had made no serious preparation to hold the Island, Magruder won. The Island was then held by the Confederates for the rest of the war, not because the Confederate military was prepared to defend it, but because the Union was too occupied elsewhere to attempt the meager assault necessary to retake the Island. To be sure, intrepid Galvestonians such as

[15] J. M. Morphis, *History of Texas*, p. 502. In some respects, the growth of major railroad lines into the port of Galveston was stifled by the same trend in transcontinental railroad building which channeled southwestern and even northwestern potential trade away from the ports of the eastern Gulf, routing traffic northward via St. Louis, Chicago and points east, because these cities were the source of the railroad capital.

[16] *The Port of Galveston, U.S.A.*, pamphlet, pp. 4–15.

William Pitt Ballinger had spent their private funds to buy rifled cannon to defend their city. However even then Confederate officers, basing their strategy on Houston rather than Galveston, failed to mount the cannon and most of the weapons remained on freight cars for the duration of the war ready for sudden evacuation. All of these facts, well known to the land-oriented entrepreneurs of Texas after the war, tended to advise speculative money to consider Houston a safer place for long-term investment than Galveston.[17]

The balance in the fateful decision began to favor Houston when, during the war, such merchants as Thomas William House and William Marsh Rice began to shift their warehouse facilities from Galveston to Houston. House was a major figure in the daring, speculative blockade-running operations which carried goods into Galveston Harbor during the later years of the Civil War. He was also a financial godfather to the war effort on the Gulf Coast. Both he and Rice had always maintained large stores in Houston, but they had made Galveston their headquarters. Now, however, the critical circumstances of the Civil War made them decide to relegate the more vulnerable Galveston to the secondary position of an outpost, and to shift the center of their shipping and warehouse operations to a more secure location in Houston. House loved the city of Galveston and his beautiful home and gardens on the Island, but in his judgment, the colorful city was not a worthy site for the emporiums and warehouses of a major trading enterprise.[18]

That the island city still possessed a truly remarkable vitality and enterprising spirit is shown by the fact that, in spite of the forces and events lined up against it, the port enjoyed a phenomenal boom for a while following the Civil War. There were true Galvestonians, those of wealth or potential wealth, who loved the Island, who respected the

[17] Earl W. Fornell, "Confederate Seaport Strategy," *Civil War History*, II (December, 1956), 61–68.

[18] Edward Mandell House, *The Intimate Papers of Colonel House*, edited by Charles Seymour, I, 8–10; T. W. House Papers, MSS; Houston *Telegraph*, March 7, 1859; Richardson, Willard, *et al* (editors), *Galveston Directory, 1859–60*, p. 44; Galveston Historical Society, *Historic Galveston Homes*, pp. 2–39.

coastal city's mercantile life and culture, who, having a certain seacoast contempt for the inland city of Houston, tied their future to the Island despite the fact that it was threatened by the waters of the Gulf from time to time and that it was regarded as expendable in military terms. If their wisdom and foresight had been as great as their loyalty they might, perhaps, have succeeded in keeping their city as the prime port of Texas. However, although the tidal wave of 1900 may have dealt a final body blow to the city's economic life, and although its loss of power may have been greatly influenced by the growing importance of Houston as a railroad terminal, the real weakness which made it vulnerable to these attacks lay in the shortsighted policies of the very men who loved and fought for their city.

In spite of the shift to Houston of such men as House and Rice, there remained in Galveston many important firms and commission houses. Many firms—such as R. & D. G. Mills & Company; Ball, Hutchings, Sealy & Company; T. H. McMahan & Company; E. B. Nichols & Company; Hewitt, Swisher & Company; W. B. Sorley & Company; and others—operated as cotton factors and private bankers as well as exporters and importers during the fifties, and most of them continued to operate in Galveston during and after the war. The noted private banking firm of McKinney & Williams had been discontinued when Samuel M. Williams died in 1858, the good will and assets of this important firm having been absorbed by the private bank of Hutchings, Sealy & Company. The Galveston firm of R. & D. G. Mills & Company, the largest private bank in Texas during the fifties, was a partnership consisting of Robert Mills, David G. Mills, and John W. Jockusch. Robert Mills also held partnerships in the firm of Mills, McDowell & Company of New York City and in McDowell, Mills & Company of New Orleans. It was illegal in Texas at that time to issue bank notes. Nevertheless, this firm's private paper passed all over the lower south as "Mills money" in amounts estimated to have been over $300,000. "Mills money" was accepted everywhere as the equivalent of gold.[19] In addition to his banking and trading enterprises, Robert

[19] *State of Texas* v. *Robert Mills et al,* District Court of Galveston, January 12, 1857; Galveston *News,* January 15, 17, and February 3, 5, 1857; Houston *Telegraph,* January 16, 23, and February 6, 9, 18, 1857.

Mills owned and operated several large plantations in Texas. He was not only the largest slaveholder in Texas during the fifties, but also one of the richest men in the state.[20]

In addition to the private bankers and traders who invested their capital on the Island, there were hundreds of small merchants, professional men, and artisans who believed firmly in the future greatness of the Island's position. The dozens of smaller traders, the three fighting editors (Willard Richardson, Ferdinand Flake, and Hamilton Stuart), professional men such as William Pitt Ballinger, and social planners such as Lorenzo Sherwood, all supported the Island despite its liabilities.

Against this phalanx of financial, trading, and professional strength in Galveston, E. H. Cushing, the editor of the Houston *Telegraph*, confidently entrusted the victory for his city to the entrepreneurship of those "daring plungers of Houston and the Gulf, William J. Hutchins, Cornelius Ennis, T. W. House, Abram Groesbeeck, William M. Rice, William A. Van Alstyne, E. W. Taylor, Henry Sampson, and A. J. Burke."[21]

Considering the size of the financial interests which preferred to tie the Texas railroad system to the great transcontinental lines, it was a vain hope on the part of Galvestonians to insist in the 1850's that Galveston should be the apex of a "fan like" pattern of tracks all leading into the island city.[22] However, the loss of the seaport was another matter—this loss they could blame, at least to a considerable extent, upon the shortsighted and basically selfish policies of their own leaders.

The waterfront properties in Galveston prior to 1854 had been in the hands of several warehouse owners and shippers. At various times during the forties and early fifties, the following wharf companies operated facilities in the port: Kuhn's Wharf, Parson's Wharf, Bean's Wharf, Merchant's Wharf, The Brick Wharf Company, Central Wharf, Palmetto Wharf, and The Commercial Wharf. Some of these firms maintained active operations, but others were not kept in opera-

[20] *Robert Mills* v. *Alexander S. Johnston and David Dewbury*, District Court of Galveston, January 17, 1857.
[21] Houston *Telegraph*, January 17, 1859.
[22] Galveston *News*, April 22, 1856.

tion; their owners simply held the property for speculative purposes. In 1854 a group of entrepreneurs in Galveston joined together and acquired a monopolistic control over the wharf area of the port. On February 4th, 1854, the new wharf combine was chartered as a "semi-public company possessing a capital stock estimated to be one million dollars."[23] The Galveston Wharf & Cotton Press Company—the full name of the new firm—by a process of combination, absorption, and purchase united all the several wharf companies of Galveston into one unit. The directors of the new firm were M. B. Menard, Samuel May Williams, Stacy B. Lewis, J. S. LeClare, "and associates."[24] Some of the known associates in the combine were Henry H. Williams, John Sealy, Henry Rosenberg, J. L. Darragh, Isadore Dyer, J. G. Duffield, C. G. Wells, and Thomas Shearer.[25]

One third of the stock of this combine was held by the city, the remaining two thirds by the private members of the corporation. Since the Wharf Company was a semipublic enterprise the provisions of the charter granted to it by the state relieved the firm of the usual burden of taxation,[26] and as a city-owned corporation, at least in part, it was granted legal as well as actual control over all the usuable water front area.[27] Thus, in return for a minority share of the corporation, the city ceded to its leading private citizens a "monopolistic control by a private corporation of a necessary public utility."[28]

During the years between 1854 and 1859, three additional Galveston business men, Robert Mills, Henri de St. Cyr, and A. F. James joined the Wharf Company. By 1859, E. B. Nichols had taken over

[23] Richardson, *Galveston Directory, 1859–60,* p. 45; *Galveston City Company v. Benjamin Franklin and Henry A. Cobb,* District Court of Galveston, January 16, 1857.

[24] Richardson, *Galveston Directory, 1859–60,* p. 45.

[25] Homer S. Thrall, *Pictorial History of Texas,* p. 772; *The Galveston Wharf Company* v. *Laurence Frosh,* District Court of Galveston, January 2, 1861.

[26] *Charter and Bylaws of the Galveston Wharf Company;* E. L. Wall (editor), *The Port Situation,* p. 3. This study first appeared as a series of articles in the Galveston *News* in 1928. Hereafter cited as Wall, *The Port Situation.*

[27] *Charter and Bylaws of the Galveston Wharf Company; A Brief History of the Galveston Wharf Company,* brochure.

[28] Wall, *The Port Situation,* p. 1.

THE HARBOR AT 20TH STREET

From a contemporary photograph in the Historical Collection, John Winterbotham Room, Rosenberg Library, Galveston, Texas.

the presidency and Robert Mills, together with A. F. James, John H. Sealy, and Henri de St. Cyr comprised the directory.[29] William Pitt Ballinger, a leading attorney in the city, earned a legal fee of $6,000 for the year 1859 as a legal counselor for the Wharf Company. Ballinger was the attorney for A. F. James and later the trustee for his large estate. As trustee he transferred parts of the James' holdings into the lucrative wharf investment.[30] The declared earnings of the firm, which were paid out in dividends each month, amounted to $70,000 during the year 1859. It was acknowledged, however, that profits during this period were much larger, the major share being reinvested in wharf improvements.[31]

During the late fifties, when it was fully realized that a port monopoly in private hands had been created as the result of the charter, energetic attempts were made in public forums and in the courts to recover some control of the bay-shore property for the city.[32] The issue remained in the courts until April 1, 1869 when, with court approval, a compromise was achieved which gave the city a few more shares of stock but not an equal share in the matter of management.[33] Secure in the position which gave it control of the only major harbor in the state, the Galveston Wharf Company tended to take undue advantage of its position. Even as early as the 1850's the fees charged by the company aroused the ill will of shippers who wished to trade in the state of Texas. "For practical purposes," wrote one observer, it was not "an exaggeration to say that the Galveston Wharf Company owns the port of Galveston, since the business which goes to make the port moves almost entirely over terminal properties owned by the Wharf Company."[34] Texans not in sympathy with the Wharf Company often referred to the port of Galveston as the "Octopus of the Gulf."[35]

[29] Richardson, *Galveston Directory, 1859–60*, pp. 45–46.

[30] William Pitt Ballinger, Diary, MS. entries for April 26, 1860 and Oct. 28, 1861 (hereafter cited as Ballinger Diary); also see Ballinger Papers for 1859–1861.

[31] Richardson, *Galveston Directory, 1859–60*, p. 45; Ballinger Papers, 1859, MS.

[32] Wall, *The Port Situation*, p. 2.

[33] *Ibid.*, p. 3.   [34] *Ibid.*, p. 2.   [35] *Ibid.*, p. 5.

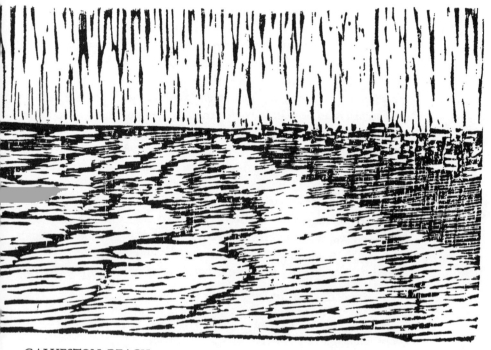

GALVESTON BEACH
From a photograph in the Historical Collection, John Winterbotham
Room, Rosenberg Library, Galveston, Texas.

In this situation, merchants and shippers in the area who were not associated financially with the Wharf Company began to look toward the possibility of developing a port elsewhere on Galveston Bay or on Buffalo Bayou.[36] The ensuing struggle for the control of the future trade channels of Texas was a prime mover of political combinations in Galveston and Houston during the decade of the fifties. In the long view, the conclusion of this issue proved to be even more important to the fate of Galveston than the issues behind slavery and secession.

It appears that the Galvestonian entrepreneurs employed their control over the port primarily as a device to build their personal fortunes rather than as a device to develop the Island and the adjacent mainland into a great seaport city. Their intent was to acquire personal wealth and security rather than to wield economic and political power. Occupying a geographic site which was threatened by grave risks from ocean storms, the Islanders expanded their facilities with a caution not in keeping with the dynamic aspects of the potential trade prospects then existing in Texas. Their expansion policy had many of the conservative characteristics usually associated with more mature port areas.

The entrepreneurs of Houston, buttressed as they were by the prospects of great transcontinental railroad building and by the possession of a situation secure from inundation by stormy seas, projected their investment policies along more dynamic patterns.[37] The pace was set

[36] Leonard, *Houston City Directory for 1866*, pp. 100–105.

[37] Houston *Telegraph*, January 17, 1859. The recent trend of modern traffic that has shifted the movement of freight originating in the area of the Middle West below Chicago from lines moving northeastward to lines moving southward toward the port of New Orleans may well foreshadow a similar shift in the Galveston area. The traffic renaissance in New Orleans occurred as the direct result of a recent port policy which evaluated profits in terms of expansion rather than revenue. The decision of interested parties, not long ago, to proceed with the development of the St. Lawrence Seaway project was in part a recognition of the fact that, except for the arbitrary establishment of previously fixed lines of transportation, the traffic moving out of the lower Middle West bound for Europe and the Middle East could pass as economically through the seaports of the Gulf of Mexico as through the great ports on the East Coast. The changes wrought by the development of modern highway trucking transportation have had a profound effect upon traffic customs originally fixed by the great railroad lines. Highway truck traffic, which by its nature is independent of the trans-

by the more venturesome policies of such inland men as those who were described by the editor of the *Telegraph* as "the plungers of Houston."

---

continental railroads, can, when it is desirable, follow the natural water levels rather than defy the transportation routes provided by nature. Exploiting this fact, truckers have revived the transport policies of the great French entrepreneurs, who, operating on the mid-continent during the seventeenth century, visualized the interconnected waterways of the St. Lawrence, the Mississippi and the Gulf as the logical route of communication. This logical artery may yet prevail over the artificial concepts of transcontinental railroads that were actually of political rather than economic origin. Thus the volume of future traffic moving over the wharves at Galveston or alternative wharves erected on Galveston Bay may be affected by the same factors which have increased wharf traffic at New Orleans. On a smaller scale, the apparent victory of the port of Houston over the port of Galveston may be reduced when transportation systems adjust to the natural drainage levels rather than defying them in order to comply with the political or imperial concept of transcontinental traffic.

2. FORMAL AND INFORMAL INSTITUTIONS

S INCE GALVESTON HARBOR was the most important seaport on the *Business and Professional Life*
Texas coast, most of the goods entering and leaving the state via the
sea passed over its wharves,[1] and it was this transmission of the imports and exports of the state, together with the many related activities,

[1] Sam Acheson, *35,000 Days in Texas,* p. 21; Hubert Howe Bancroft, *History of North Mexican States and Texas,* II, 567; "Galveston Sugar and Trade Statistics," *Hunt's Merchant's Magazine,* XXXIX (October, 1858), 729.

which served as the focal point for almost all of the commercial, industrial and professional life of the city. Of the 300,000 bales of cotton produced in Texas in the year 1860, over 200,000 were compressed and loaded for export at Galveston.[2] During the 1858 shipping season, 200,000 bales of cotton were shipped directly to Europe from Galveston wharves at an average selling price of fifty dollars per bale; thus the value of the port's cotton export to Europe amounted to over 10 million dollars.[3] The British consul in Galveston estimated that the 1861 cotton crop to be shipped out of Galveston would be almost 400,000 bales. In his opinion the potential cotton production of Texas could reach a total of from 2 to 6 million bales if the state acquired sufficient railroad transportation and field labor.[4] The consul also estimated that if the necessary transportation and labor were available in the interior areas of the state as many as 25 million bushels of Indian corn and 4 million bushels of wheat would be moving out of the port of Galveston. In actual fact, however, because of the lack of labor and transportation, only negligible amounts of these two potential crops were exported.[5]

The figures dealing with actual exports from Texas present a more modest picture than those projecting potential exports. Some estimate of the actual trade may be deduced from a few of the statistics available. During the year 1860, between January 1st and June 30th, 860 bales of wool left the wharves at Galveston.[6] The annual volume of a few other exports included 38 bales of deerskins, 1,227 bales of hides,

[2] Willard Richardson, *et al* (editors), *Texas Almanac,* p. 222; Arthur T. Lynn to J. W. King, London, May 21, 1860, MS, F. O.

[3] Galveston *Civilian,* October 5, 1858. This figure is higher than the sum usually quoted, but since the editor of the *Civilian* was also the customs collector, his estimate would seem to be a trustworthy one. E. H. Cushing, the Houston editor, estimated the cotton exports leaving Galveston between July 31, 1858 and July 31, 1859, to be worth 8 million dollars. Houston *Telegraph,* September 2, 1859.

[4] British Consulate Papers, Annual Reports of the British Consulate, Galveston, on Shipping, Navigation, Trade, Commerce, Agriculture, Population and Industries, 1860, MS (hereafter cited as Annual Reports of the British Consulate in Galveston, F.O.).

[5] *Ibid.*   [6] *Ibid.,* report for year 1861.

23

1,403,215 pounds of cottonseed and 7,075 pounds of tobacco.[7] The total value of all general exports from Galveston was estimated to be more than 11 million dollars.[8] Although cotton was Galveston's major export product, 15,000 barrels of sugar and 9,000 barrels of molasses from the Brazos plantations left the port during the year ending the decade.[9]

It is difficult to ascertain the total dollar value of goods annually imported into Galveston, but the volume varied from year to year, reflecting the increase or decrease of the general prosperity in the state as a whole. During years when the cotton yield was good and the price of cotton remained high, imports increased. An official report for the year 1857 fixed the value of imports at $2,163,504,[10] and the dollar value of a few particular items imported into Galveston during 1860 was:[11]

Liquors and wines	$ 26,664
Coffee	195,133
Salt	15,958
Groceries	16,093
Manufactures	27,677
Railroad iron	231,099
Bar, pig, and other iron	18,954
Sundries	12,511
Total	$544,089

The customs collector noted that during the slack second quarter of 1857 goods reaching Galveston were valued at only $448,664, but, he observed, "imports from New Orleans to Galveston usually run

[7] *Ibid.*, report for year 1858.   [8] *Ibid.*, report for year 1860.

[9] Ben C. Stuart, "Brief Chronology" and "Necrology," MSS, 1859–1860; Willard Richardson, *et al* (editors), *Galveston Directory, 1859–60*, pp. 84–85.

[10] Semi-Annual Trade Report and Return of Galveston Assessor and Collector, MS. This report lists the 1857 tax value of general consumer goods imported into the city by six leading merchants as follows: Block, Ware & Co., $75,000; Ball, Hutchings & Co., $51,000; Howard & Burckhardt, $45,000; J. Kauffman, $40,000; J. C. Kuhn, $57,000; and Lipmann & Korrel, $46,000. Forty-six others imported goods in lesser amounts.

[11] *De Bow's Review*, XXIX (December 1860), 783.

about one and one-half million dollars" during each quarterly period. He remarked that if the business interests in the city put more of their energy into the establishment of manufacturing enterprises the drain on Galveston capital to pay for imports could be eliminated.[12] But the development of such manufacturing was hindered by the prevailing opinion among businessmen in the city that the most profitable procedure for them was to "exchange their staple articles of cotton, wool and hides for the manufactured products of the Northern and Eastern states."[13]

One of the most lucrative of Galveston's enterprises was the provision of services for seamen and ships. Many vessels in the Gulf trade patronized Galveston's maritime service enterprises even though they had no cargoes for the port.[14] For example, Tatem & Reid, sailmakers in the port, operated a thriving business, and the Close & Cushman Company, as well as Morgan L. Parry Company, iron foundries, manufactured repaired marine engines. During the first three months of 1859, no less than 287 vessels carrying 4,194 seamen[15] were accommodated by the city's wharf services, lodging houses, and entertainment establishments. To the income from over 4,000 seamen spending their shore time on the Island was added to the trade derived from catering to the needs of the several hundred immigrants[16] and general travelers who entered and departed from the port. More than sixty-five vessels with capacity totaling 29,289 tons moved in a regular trade between Galveston and European ports. In addition a large number—483 ships with a combined tonnage of 247,504—moved in and out of the port in the coastwise trade.[17] Two years earlier a typical port day (January 9, 1857) found "2 steamers, 11 barks, 6 brigs, 8 schoon-

[12] Galveston *Civilian,* August 11, 1857. Hamilton Stuart, federal customs collector, was also the publisher and editor of this newspaper.
[13] Annual Reports of the British Consulate in Galveston, 1860, MS, F.O.
[14] Galveston *News,* April 28, 1857.
[15] Galveston *Civilian,* April 2, 1859.
[16] Joseph C. G. Kennedy, *The Population of the United States in 1860: Compiled from The Original Returns of the Eighth Census,* p. 490.
[17] Annual Reports of the British Consulate in Galveston, 1860, MS, F.O.; *U.S. House Docs., Misc.,* 47th Cong., 2nd Sess., XIII, 754–755, cites foreign tonnage moving in and out of Galveston in 1860 as 32,263 tons.

ers and 2 sloops in the harbor."[18] On April 11th of the same year, ten ships—including four steamers—entered and nine ships—including three steamers—left the port; in addition, thirteen vessels were in the process of being loaded or unloaded.[19] On Sunday, April 20th, five steamships entered and four steamships departed; "pretty brisk for a Sunday," was the comment of L. A. Falvel, the harbor master, on this occasion.[20] A year later, on December 15, 1858, an observer noted that "No less than 23 square rigged vessels are now in the roadstead outside Galveston bar, discharging their freight or taking freight. This is a large fleet."[21] But adequate port facilities were available to care for this fleet. "In the Harbour of Galveston ways have been constructed on which iron steamships or vessels of 150 tons burden may be repaired, but docks for building vessels have not yet been made."[22]

The importance of the port in military, economic, and political terms was indicated by the fact that in 1856 Congress appropriated $300,000 to be spent to erect fortifications in the bay,[23] and in 1857 appropriated $100,000 to build a new customs house on the Island.[24]

Galvestonians tended to exploit the fact that their port occupied a privileged position as the only good harbor on the coast, by levying heavier port fees than were actually required. The staff of officials, such as harbor masters, port wardens, pilots, inspectors, searchers, and others, was larger than the number usually needed for other ports of the same size. The persons holding most of these offices were leading businessmen in the city, so it is clear that the labor for which the fees were charged was not actually performed by the men holding the titles to the positions.[25]

Since railroad transportation was at this time just beginning in

[18] Galveston *Civilian*, January 13, 1857.
[20] *Ibid.*, April 20, 1857.   [19] *Ibid.*, April 11, 1857.
[21] Houston *Telegraph*, December 15, 1858.
[22] Annual Reports of the British Consulate in Galveston, 1860, MS, F.O.
[23] Houston *Telegraph*, March 10, 1856; *U.S. Senate Exec. Docs.*, 34th Cong., 1st Sess., VI, No. 5, January 28, 1856, p. 7.
[24] Galveston *News*, January 17 and May 2, 1857. The contract for erecting the structure was given to Clusky & Moore of Galveston.
[25] Annual Reports of the British Consulate in Galveston, MS, 1860, F.O.; Richardson, *Galveston Directory, 1856–75*, p. 40; *Ibid.*, *1859–60*, p. 37.

Texas, most communication still moved over water. Several shipping lines maintained regular service to Galveston. The Morgan interests operated the Galveston & New York Star Line, which kept four steamships and eight barks in regular service. This line also operated a bi-weekly steamship service between Galveston and New Orleans. E. B. Nichols & Company also had a line of sailing packets making regular trips betwen Galveston and Boston, and William Hendley & Company, agents of the Texas & New York Line, kept six ships in regular service. The United States Mail Line and the Mobile and Texas Steamship Line also made regular trips into the port. In addition to these maritime firms numerous irregular shippers such as T. W. House and William Marsh Rice maintained ships in both foreign and coastal trade.[26] The Galveston Bremen Line operated five vessels between Texas and European ports.[27] The fact that in 1856 eleven foreign nations maintained consular representatives in Galveston indicated the rising importance of the port in terms of foreign trade.[28]

Within the Gulf itself competition for passenger traffic between Galveston and New Orleans was very brisk, and the one-way fare seldom rose above five dollars.[29] The trip required twenty-five and one-half hours—sixteen by sea and nine and one-half by rail.[30] In 1857 when Vanderbilt opened a short-cut route via Berwick Bay, his competitors Morgan & Harris immediately acquired control of the railroad from Berwick to New Orleans and thus closed off this competitive advantage for a short while.[31]

In the early fifties before railroads were built the only transportation available to carry goods from the interior to Galveston moved over the rivers or over the ordinary dirt roads—the latter completely impassable during the wet seasons. Valuable cotton often rotted on the plantations waiting for the roads to dry or at points along the way when wagons

---

[26] *Ibid.*, *1856–57*, p. 42; Houston *Telegraph*, December 7, 1858 and January 7, 1859; Galveston *Civilian*, January 13, 1857; Galveston *News*, September 17, 1857.
[27] *Galveston Directory, 1856–57*, p. 42.   [28] *Ibid.*, p. 39.
[29] Houston *Telegraph*, June 10, 1857.
[30] Galveston *Civilian*, April 24, 1857.   [31] *Ibid.*

had become mired during wet weather.[32] Even when the roads were dry, hauling heavy goods by ox-wagons was a slow and laborious undertaking. The ox was suitable for short hauls from the plantation to the water routes or to the main roads, but he was not practical for the longer journeys to the seaports.

River transportation from the interior was, on the whole, more dependable and economical than land transport, even though the varying flood and dry seasons at times made this form of transportation also impracticable. Before the arrival of the river steamboats, enterprising men often created transportation by cutting timber near the Brazos River or along the shores of Galveston Bay and the bayous, and building log rafts to float cotton to the presses in Galveston. The cotton factors in Galveston provided the capital to finance these venturesome river raftmen who often moved more than a hundred bales[33] on a single raft from the interior to the port. These transport men who camped upon their rafts during the journey led "a free and happy life," snugly secure in their sleeping quarters between the bales of cotton. Louis Sterne, a partner in one of these transport enterprises with a large cotton factor in Galveston, stated that "the timber out of which the raft was constructed was nearly as valuable as the cotton." Once the raftmen had disposed of their goods—both timber and cotton—in Galveston they "slung their saddlebags across some mules and returned to the upper country for a fresh cargo of cotton."[34] The river rafts continued to be a part of the Texas cotton trade until the mid-fifties when the light-draft, flat-bottomed, stern-wheel steamboats, which could carry goods up as well as down the waterways, forced the raftmen to abandon their enterprises. By the end of the decade, with the causeway and the railroad to Houston connecting the Island to the mainland, the steamboaters, in their turn, were losing some of their trade to the iron-wheel carriages.[35]

[32] Louis Sterne, *Seventy Years of an Active Life,* p. 28.
[33] On the plantation cotton was stuffed into large burlap bags and tied with hemp or cotton rope into loose bales; however, when the material reached Galveston the cotton was repressed into firm bales of standard weights for shipment to Europe or to the East coast.
[34] Sterne, *Seventy Years,* p. 30.   [35] *Ibid.*

During the last half of the decade of the fifties, however, the river steamboats made active use of the waterways leading to the port of Galveston. Companies were chartered and financed; channels were cleared of obstructions; arrangements were made to store goods along the waterways so that full advantage could be taken of the high-water season. Persistent captains at the helms of flat-bottomed stern-wheelers pushed their boats up the rivers even "in places where there was not sufficient water" to float "an alligator."[36] By 1856 there were seventeen of the flat-bottomed river steamers carrying trade into Galveston from all points along the bay.[37] That year the Houston editor, Cushing, noted that there were three boats in the Houston-Galveston trade and that "all of them have as much as they can do."[38] A year later there were four regular steamers on the same run, two of them mailboats— the *Island City* and the *Eclipse*—which charged two dollars to carry a passenger between the two cities. A more luxurious service was provided by the steamers *Jenkins* and *Texas* which charged three dollars for the same voyage.[39]

During the wet season the Brazos River afforded an additional water route deep into the interior. In terms of distance and in terms of the fertile country through which this waterway passed, the Brazos appeared to offer richer prospects for transportation than the Galveston Bay—Buffalo Bayou system. One major difficulty impaired its use: even during the wet season the mouth of the river provided no natural harbor—no place to build loading docks or set up cotton-baling presses. In an effort to solve this problem and develop the river for traffic the Galveston Brazos Navigation Company secured a charter, on February 8, 1850, to construct a canal between West Galveston Bay and the Brazos River. This project was intended to join the channel of the river with the excellent harbor provided by Galveston Bay. The men behind this firm were leading business and political figures in the harbor city,[40] and the company was authorized to issue $150,000 in cap-

---

[36] *Ibid.*, p. 38.
[37] Richardson, *Galveston Directory, 1856–57*, p. 42.
[38] Houston *Telegraph*, October 20, 1856.   [39] *Ibid.*, September 4, 1857.
[40] The officers of this company were John Henry Brown, president; E. L. Ufford, secretary; and directors: E. B. Nichols, J. J. Hendley, L. M. Hitchcock,

29

FORMAL AND INFORMAL INSTITUTIONS

ital stock with the right to increase the issue to $300,000 if desired. By 1855 the four-and-one-half-mile-long canal plus the thirty miles of waterway passing through Oyster Bay and West Bay were completed. The canal, fifty feet wide and three and one-half feet deep, was large enough to accommodate rafts, hand-propelled boats, and steam vessels. The Brazos canal and waterways enjoyed some initial success but since efficient dredging equipment was not available at that time, the expense involved in keeping the water channels of the system open proved to be more than the profits of the firm could support, especially against the competition of the railroads and the steamer lines on Galveston Bay.[41] Capital which might have made the canal a success was attracted to more promising ventures in railroad building.

Perhaps if Galveston capitalists had recognized the fact that the future of their port would have been better served by a careful joining of water and potential rail transport than by the development of water facilities alone, they would have been in a better position to meet the rising competition developing in the inland port of Houston. Certainly it was clear at that time that the future belonged to the railroads. However, most of the needed miles of rails had not yet been laid down, so, during the critical decade of 1855–1865, the steamboats, churning their way up the meandering and clogged waterways of the Gulf Coast, provided the only major alternative form of transportation to the laboring ox-wagon.

Mail service during the fifties was closely associated with the Gulf and river steamship lines. A lucrative federal mail contract often provided an essential element in the operation of a profitable shipping line. Skillful routing of mails over the varied available means of transport across vast areas was a prime factor deciding whether or not a particular contract yielded a profit. Galveston was a major terminal in the well-known transcontinental mail line developed and maintained by

Captain J. Smith, M. B. Menard, P. R. Edwards, N. B. Yard, H. de St. Cyr, W. Hendley, W. Richardson and John Dean. (Richardson, *Galveston Directory, 1856–57*, p. 38.)

[41] Andrew Forest Muir, "The Destiny of Buffalo Bayou," *Southwestern Historical Quarterly*, XLVII (October, 1943), pp. 92–96; Railroad Papers, Report of Tipton Walker to James B. Shaw, October 31, 1855, MS.

the able mail contractor George H. Giddings of Texas. This carrier, called the "most experienced mail contractor of the plains," operated a service beginning in New Orleans, moving westward by sea to Galveston, and then overland to San Antonio, El Paso, and points west to San Francisco. The distance between New Orleans and the West Coast was covered in twenty-five days.[42] Other typical mail contracts prevailing in the fifties may be illustrated by the one held by J. A. Durant who carried the mails, via the sea, twice a week from Galveston to Matagorda, a distance of 114 miles, for a yearly payment of $10,000; or one held by John H. Sterrett and Frederick Smith who carried the mails by steamboat six times per week on a route between Galveston and Houston for an annual fee of $20,000; or another held by Fred W. Smith who carried the mails overland on a three-times-a-week basis from Galveston to Liberty, a distance of 110 miles, for $12,000 annually.[43]

The mail service was a constant source of complaint against the federal government and against the contractors. The active bidding for mail contracts often tempted inexperienced men to offer bids too low to support the service promised. In these situations the service suffered and the citizens had ample cause for annoyance. "Hardly a mail arrives but the service is under complaint," said E. H. Cushing of Houston, "yet no one can spot whose fault caused the delay."[44] The newspapers of the interior complained persistently that Galveston held a monopoly over the incoming mail from New Orleans. They charged that the publishers in Galveston, working in collusion with the postmaster, delayed sending the "exchange" newspapers into the interior until the two papers in Galveston had been given time to extract the newsworthy items thus scoring regular "news beats"[45] on the interior press. Galveston "sits on the mail and holds up the news" cried editor Cushing. The city of Houston must secure a mail service independent of "the bottle neck" on the Gulf, he insisted.[46]

[42] Galveston *Civilian,* March 30, 1858.
[43] *Ibid.*   [44] Houston *Telegraph,* June 10, 1857.
[45] Galveston *Civilian,* September 29, 1857. The *Civilian,* after quoting Cushing's charge, denied it vigorously.
[46] Houston *Telegraph,* March 24, 1856.

In addition to the regular mail services, there were private express companies—such as the famous Kyle's Texas Express Company and the Jones & Company Express—which carried mail as well as valuable packages among the cities of Texas. In fact valuable exchanges of money were more often entrusted to private carriers than to the federal mail contractors.[47] As to the delivery of mail in the city of Galveston itself, each citizen went to the city post office to collect his own mail. Individual boxes were rented to those who desired them for a fee of $10 per year. The rate for United States mail arriving in Galveston was fourteen cents per half-ounce letter, for mail to Europe, twenty-four cents per half ounce.[48] The Galveston post office annually sent approximately 30,000 pieces of mail from the port and received some 150,000 items. According to the postmaster, H. B. Andrews, the Galveston office earned one-fifth more money during the year 1859 than it spent, thus "making Galveston one of the few offices in the United States" which actually earned a profit.[49]

Closely related to the water transportation enterprises were the marine and fire insurance companies maintaining offices and agents at the port.[50] While most of the marine insurance was written by large foreign firms, a local company, the Union Marine & Fire Insurance Company of Galveston, did a substantial business in Texas. This firm possessed a capitalization of $500,000 and maintained a constant cash reserve in the city of $56,000 in gold and $144,000 in demand notes "secured by the best names in the city." Businessmen in the port, having considerable capital at their disposal, tended in part to underwrite their own risks.[51]

In addition to using their capital to underwrite their own risks the large cotton factors and private bankers during the fifties used it to

[47] Galveston *Civilian*, April 11, 1857.
[48] Arthur T. Lynn to George Hammond, October 27, 1859, MS, F.O.
[49] Richardson, *Galveston Directory, 1859–60*, p. 56.
[50] See *Ibid.*, *1856–57*, p. 59 for list of eight large foreign insurance firms maintaining agents in the city.
[51] *Ibid.*, *1859–60*, p. 48; Houston *Telegraph*, December 9, 1859. *John Burnett v. The Union Marine and Fire Insurance Company*, District Court of Galveston, January 13, 1860.

create prosperity in the port as well as to exploit it. The Houston editor, E. H. Cushing, remarked after a visit to Galveston in 1857 that property was "every day changing hands," that "speculation in real estate" was "astronomical" and the building boom "astonishing."[52] A year later he returned to Galveston and found that "many new and handsome three story brick buildings are quite the order of the day here, several new ones have gone up or are going up. The E. S. Wood and H. Rosenberg buildings display good taste."[53] The Ball, Hutchings & Company's new three-story building, "the finest in Galveston," was one hundred and ten feet in depth and possessed a thirty-one–foot front on the Strand, the entire front being "enhanced by a fine decorative iron front."[54]

These great iron fronts, fitted like picture frames two and three stories high over the faces of brick and frame buildings, were accepted during the late fifties in Galveston as a prime sign of progress. Some of these symbols of success were shipped into the port and others were molded from imported cast iron ingots by the two foundries in the city. In 1858 the Chamber of Commerce, under the direction of Joseph Kauffman, inaugurated a vigorous campaign to put an iron front on every store in the city.[55]

The size of the building boom during the later fifties may be seen in the fact that an average daily importation of lumber to "Messrs. Parsons, Labadie, Safford & Lidstone" amounted to 47,000 running feet plus 25,000 feet of wooden lath.[56] At about the same time (1857) the firm of Clusky & Moore began the construction of a new federal customs house at the cost of $100,000. To provide an avenue for the new iron store fronts the Strand was raised and shelled[57] until it presented a fine highway. This "splendid" thoroughfare was kept in a "cosmo-

---

[52] Houston *Telegraph*, May 25, 1857.

[53] *Ibid.*, December 17, 1858.   [54] *Ibid.*, January 21, 1857.

[55] Galveston *News*, October 27, 1858.   [56] *Ibid.*, April 27, 1857.

[57] Since good paving gravel was not available on the coast the streets of Galveston were often paved with oyster shells dredged up from the bays. On the Gulf Coast seashells are as abundant as is ordinary gravel in the interior of Texas. Galvestonians were very proud of their "shell paved" streets and of the fact that they were watered every day to settle the dust.

politan"[58] condition by the service of a "watering cart every day."[59] While the servicing of marine traffic in the port, and the banking and mercantile aspects of cotton exporting were major activities in the city, the actual baling and storing of cotton coming in from the interior also comprised an important industry. During the fifties in Galveston, before the invention of the hydraulic press, cotton was pressed into five-hundred-pound bales by wooden screw-presses. The arms of these great screws were turned by yokes of oxen. When the cotton had been pressed as much as the oxen-powered screw would permit, the bale was wrapped in "cotton lapp" and bound with rope. This process, which required much labor, provided employment for many persons both white and colored.[60]

In addition to the cotton and maritime trading enterprises there were in Galveston a few manufacturing concerns. Two iron foundries, those of Close & Cushman[61] and Morgan L. Parry, were able to "build any kind of engines for steamers" and "mills of as good workmanship as one would find in the North."[62] The Journeay & Aylott Cabinet Factory provided the port with a local source for millwork; the Ahrens Rope Factory produced 600 pounds of cotton rope daily to supply the needs of the cotton factors; the Cameron & Flynn Soap Factory supplied the detergent needs of the city; and W. B. Dunning & Co., bookbinders and book manufacturers, not only provided the commercial establishments with bound record books but also bound the books printed by the Civilian Job Printing Company and Willard Richardson & Company. In 1859 the latter firm published over 30,000 copies of the *Texas Almanac*, a volume of over 300 closely-printed pages, dem-

[58] To the Galvestonian of the time the word "cosmopolitan" meant citified or European, clean and serviceable. They spoke of making their streets, parks, and restaurants "cosmopolitan"—"like Europe."
[59] Houston *Telegraph*, May 25, 1857; Galveston County Commissioners Court, Minutes, 1856, MS, p. 70.
[60] Sterne, *Seventy Years*, p. 27.
[61] Every effort has been made to determine the first names or initials of all persons mentioned in this work; unfortunately in some instances this data was unobtainable.
[62] Galveston *News*, July 28, 1857; Richardson, *Galveston Directory, 1859–60*, p. 75.

onstrating that the publishing facilities then existing in Galveston were not inconsiderable.[63]

Providing and preserving the food necessary to feed the citizens of the port city was in itself a substantial undertaking. In the tropical climate of the Island food was preserved by salt packing, by dehydration in the hot sun, by canning in glass, and by the use of the "ice house." William Marsh Rice, a New Englander who had moved to Texas, operated an ice-importing business as one of his many enterprises. This enterprise was no mere novelty to provide iced drinks on the warm days, but a serious undertaking which operated on a large scale. On one day during the spring of 1859, "Rice's ice fleet" unloaded 540 tons of ice at Galveston for his Houston City Ice Company.[64]

The island city produced much of its own food. The more than 13,000 head of cattle pastured on the Island provided the base for both dairy and meat products.[65] The slaughtering industry was carefully regulated by city ordinances requiring that butchers rent stalls in the city-owned market for which they paid a yearly fee of $125. Meat was sold on a "warm kill" basis, that is, all fresh meat not salted or smoked had to be sold on the same day upon which it had been butchered.[66] Fish markets also were leased to merchants in the city-regulated markets for a fee of $40 per year; the regulations controlling sea food, however, were not so severe as those governing the handling of beef, pork and mutton.[67] Dried redfish was a "profitable article of trade out of Galveston," wrote E. H. Cushing one day in 1857, and "we know of several families who cure enough each season for a year's use."[68]

Persons visiting the Island or those who had newly arrived always expressed their surprise at the abundance and excellence of the food in the city. Thomas North, who visited the city in 1861, said that the "beef and table vegetables he found in Galveston surpassed any" he

---

[63] Galveston *News,* February 5 and April 28, 1857; Stuart "Brief Chronology," MS.
[64] Houston *Telegraph,* March 28 and August 12, 1859.
[65] Joseph Osterman Dyer (Dr. Dyer), "History of Galveston," MS, VI, 14.
[66] Galveston *Civilian,* August 10, 1858.   [67] *Ibid.*
[68] Houston *Telegraph,* June 15, 1857.

had seen elsewhere.[69] The Frenchman, Henri de St. Cyr, called the city "particularly remarkable" for its green vegetables, good fish, and oysters.[70]

The Island gardeners cultivated more than the ordinary variety of garden products. In 1857 Richardson wrote that "fruits peculiar to the tropics such as lemons, oranges, plantains, pomegranates, etc. have been cultivated this season by many on the Island with success, and in a few years, we have no doubt, will become generally and extensively raised by all."[71] Two years later Cushing noted that the bananas grown in Galveston were of a "superior quality," and he added that "a good deal of attention was being given to the cultivation of this fruit at the Island."[72]

An important adjunct to trade, industry, and banking on the Island was provided by the legal fraternity in Galveston. To the usual city and county legal practice available for attorneys was added that arising out of the sessions of the Supreme Court of Texas, the state district court, and the United States district court, all of which held sessions in Galveston. The legal and administrative talent needed to man these institutions brought together some fifty lawyers, an imposing legal colony for a city the size of Galveston in the 1850's,[73] far surpassing that to be found in any other city west of St. Louis or New Orleans.

In addition to such professional persons as the attorneys, Galveston possessed more than the normal number of representatives of the medical profession. Since the Island was situated in a tropical zone and was subject to severe fever seasons, the inhabitants entertained an extremely hospitable attitude toward medical men without being too critical of their qualifications. A comparison of the medical men in Galveston during the fifties with other leading groups such as the lawyers, bankers, traders, and merchants reveals that this profession, upon

[69] North, [*Journal*]: *Five Years in Texas: or What You Did Not Hear During The War from 1861 to January 1866. A Narrative of His Travels, Experiences, and Observations in Texas and Mexico*, pp. 56–57.

[70] Houston *Telegraph*, May 13, 1859.

[71] Galveston *News*, July 25, 1857.

[72] Houston *Telegraph*, October 17, 1859.

[73] Richardson, *Galveston Directory, 1856–57*, pp. 26, 42.

THE S.S. BUFFALO, in service from 1837 to 1848 in the Gulf area

From a contemporary engraving in the Historical Collection, John Winterbotham Room, Rosenberg Library, Galveston, Texas.

whose shoulders the defense against the fever plagues rested, was the least capable of bearing the responsibilities of its position. The city supported as many "doctors" as it did lawyers, and while some of these healers were men of the highest standing such as Dr. Ashbel Smith, who possessed an A.B., M.A., and M.D. from Yale, others were the crudest sort of quacks.[74] One "Doctor James Angell—Homeopathist," for instance, claimed to have twenty years' experience "with Southern diseases." This doctor offered, in a newspaper advertisement, to treat patients through the mails. Upon the receipt of a fee and a description of the illness the doctor undertook to send the medicine required to effect a cure.[75]

Honest doctors in Galveston, stirred to action by the events of the terrifying fever seasons when hundreds of persons died on the Island each month, and revolted by the usual malpractices of fraudulent medical practitioners, determined as early as 1848 that some means had to be found to regulate the profession in that city. In that year ten Galveston doctors of repute, headed by Dr. Ashbel Smith, asked the state legislature to grant a charter to a proposed Medical and Surgical Society of Galveston whose purpose was to advance medical and surgical skill, to aid in spreading medical knowledge, to raise standards, to establish a library, and to control quackery. The essence of the charter was the request for power to set up a board of censors to examine and license those who were to be permitted to practice in Galveston.[76] At that time there was no regulation of the profession. "We have, so far as I know," wrote Ashbel Smith in 1851, "no medical organization in our state." Each member of the "faculty is a separate independency, and sometimes adopts a sort of armed neutrality system."[77] But when the proposed charter for the Galveston society was subjected to the legislative process in Austin, it was changed to include the medical profession on a statewide basis rather than being confined to the city of Galveston. Medical men in other parts of the state, who did not like

[74] Pat Ireland Nixon, M.D., *A History of the Texas Medical Association, 1853–1954*, pp. 466–471.

[75] Galveston *News*, May 2, 1857.

[76] Nixon, *Texas Medical Association*, p. 5.

[77] *Fenner's Southern Medical Reports*, II, 458.

the prospect of a licensing board, exerted enough influence upon the legislators to defeat the bill.[78] This brought an end to attempts to set standards for doctors in Texas until after the Civil War.

In the 1850's a few local medical societies were organized, but none was granted authority to regulate the profession.[79] A meeting of medical men was scheduled to occur in Houston on February 9, 1857 in order "to establish a medical association." Galveston doctors were asked to attend, but none went. The Houston society as eventually organized was composed of Doctors J. S. Duval, W. H. Howard, Greenville Dowell, R. H. Boxley, and H. W. Waters; no member was to be admitted to this select group unless he had been graduated from a recognized medical school.[80]

In the last years of the decade, $20,000 was raised to establish a medical school in Houston to train young practitioners for the Gulf Coast area. "Dr. Ashbel Smith and four other teachers" were expected to comprise the faculty.[81] This institution, however, never actually opened.[82] It was not until 1865, when the Galveston Medical College was established under the direction of Dr. Greenville Dowell, that the medical profession on the Gulf Coast established an institution which could begin to set standards for the doctors in the area.[83]

Banks and Bankers

DURING THE EIGHTEEN-FIFTIES a clause in the Texas Constitution, as well as the state code, made the operation of a banking enterprise and the issuance of paper currency an illegal act.[84] Holding a Jacksonian point of view, Texans looked upon banks and bankers

---

[78] Nixon, *Texas Medical Association*, p. 6.

[79] Houston *Telegraph*, February 6, 1857; Nixon, *Texas Medical Association*, p. 6.

[80] Houston *Telegraph*, February 6 and March 18, 1857.

[81] *Ibid.*, March 12, 1858.　　　　[82] La Grange *True Issue*, April 11, 1861.

[83] Nixon, *Texas Medical Association*, p. 28.

[84] Oliver C. Hartley, *A Digest of the Laws of Texas*, p. 107, ". . . no person or persons within this state shall issue any bill, promissory note, check or other paper, to circulate as money." Also see H. P. N. Gammel, *The Laws of Texas, 1822–1897*, II, 130–134, 488–491.

with suspicion. General T. J. Rusk, speaking at the constitutional convention in 1845, pointed out that although a few fortunate individuals had been benefited by banks, "thousands upon thousands" had been ruined by them. A large majority of Texans agreed with Rusk that a bank in Texas would benefit only the few and would bring "ruin, want, misery, and degradation in its train" for the many.[85] Texans not only entertained the usual frontiersman's distrust of high finance, but also remembered unfortunate experiences with "money manipulations" during the days of the Republic. Some leading Galvestonians felt that bank charters and democratic constitutions were incompatible.[86]

Holding these beliefs a voting majority of Texans refused to permit their legislators to revise the code or the constitutional provisions which outlawed banks. The lack of banking services caused a nominal, if not real, inconvience to the smaller merchants and to the ordinary citizens. In particular, the lack of a legal paper currency sometimes necessitated the transportation of large amounts of specie between New Orleans and Galveston. In these circumstances there was always the danger that valuable shipments might be lost at sea. The steamer *General Rusk* docked at Galveston early in March of 1857 bearing $46,000 in specie under circumstances which gave concern to the underwriters of Galveston.[87] That same spring a friend of Cushing's arrived in Galveston with $3,600 in gold which he had carried in a belt for 350 miles. "Never again!" asserted this man. "Some may be fond of lugging gold. [I have] had enough of it."[88]

Legal paper money was the only way to relieve travelers from the need to carry gold, said Cushing. The Gulf Coast ought to "have

[85] *Debates of the Texas Convention* (Austin, 1846), pp. 278, 461.

[86] Houston *Telegraph,* April 29, 1837: William M. Gouge, *The Fiscal History of Texas,* pp. 60–61; Andrew Forest Muir, "Railroad Enterprise in Texas, 1836–1841," *Southwestern Historical Quarterly,* XLVII (April, 1944), 339–370; Avery Luvere Carlson, *A Monetary and Banking History of Texas from the Mexican Regime to Present Day, 1821–1929,* pp. 1–18.

[87] Houston *Telegraph,* March 4, 1857. If paper money was lost at sea there was no true loss since it could be replaced. If specie was lost the loss was real.

[88] *Ibid.,* May 11, 1857.

banks, but they must be safe ones." Both the Houston editor and Richardson of Galveston were in favor of legalizing banks.[89] Stuart, holding to the orthodox view of the Democratic party, was opposed and he used his newspaper to keep this point of view alive among Texans.[90]

In many respects the arguments over whether Texas needed chartered banks or whether paper money ought to be allowed to circulate were only academic prior to 1857. The commission merchants of the city who possessed some working capital were not hampered by the absence of a legal banking service. Few people carried large amounts of specie from place to place in order to conduct ordinary trade, despite the fact that Cushing and Richardson enjoyed citing occasional examples of the inconvenience entailed. Actually, since banks and the formal issuance of paper currency were illegal, the commission merchants were able to combine both of these services with their general commission business of buying and selling for planters and for smaller inland merchants. The two largest Galveston commission houses or "banks" kept more than a million dollars in paper circulating on the Gulf Coast, and this "currency" was accepted everywhere on a par with specie. These two firms, the Commercial and Agricultural Bank of S. M. Williams and the trading firm of R. & D. G. Mills, provided the Gulf Coat with adequate, and in some respects with superior, banking facilities for ordinary trading purposes. In addition to the two large firms, smaller commission merchants such as Ball, Hutchings and Company; W. B. Sorley and Company; Briggs and Yard; E. B. Nichols and Company; Hewitt, Swisher Company; T. H. McMahan and Company; and J. A. Sauter and Company, also allowed their "paper" to be passed around the city and the Gulf Coast as virtual currency.[91]

[89] Galveston *News,* January 15 and 17, February 3 and 5, April 30, May 5 and 21, 1857; Houston *Telegraph,* February 6, 9 and 18, May 11, June 3, October 19 and December 30, 1857.

[90] Galveston *Civilian,* April 29 and May 12, 1857; Lynn to General Accountant of Her Majesty's Navy, September 8, 1856, MS, F.O.

[91] *Robert Mills* v. *Alexander S. Johnston and another,* 25 Texas Reports, 324–329; also see Ballinger Papers for 1861, MSS, *Robert Mills* v. *John Nooman,* District Court of Galveston, January 2, 1857.

Although the laws might appear to be restrictive, the private bankers such as Mills, Williams, and the other lesser merchant financiers favored leaving the situation as it was because the existing practice permitted them to operate their money and mercantile enterprises with practically no government control at all. Their informal currency and their lending practices permitted them to expand or contract their capital as needed. Since the two major money sources in Galveston enjoyed and maintained very high financial stability and repute, the Gulf Coast had had a better and more flexible source of moderate sums of money than would have been available under a more formal banking system. (Needless to say, these firms were not able or not willing to provide the large risk capital needed for extensive railroad building.) The major criticism leveled against the money market in, Galveston did not concern lack of stability, but rather the high cost of money. The highest legal rate of interest which could be charged for money in Texas at that time was 12 percent, a rate almost twice as high as that charged in New York and New Orleans—the sources for most large loans going into Texas.[92] However, eastern and New Orleans banks would not loan money to Gulf Coast planters or Texas businessmen unless the advances were covered by very sound security, or if they did loan sound money on ordinary security such loans were never actually for rates as low as those charged by Galveston's informal bankers.[93]

According to Texas Supreme Court Judge James H. Bell, the commission business in Galveston had developed as an integral part of Gulf Coast agriculture and commerce and was as necessary to the development of the area as the planter and the farmer. The "enlightened courts" of the state, recognizing the fact, regularly awarded the commission merchants "a reasonable compensation for their serv-

[92] *Mills* v. *Johnston,* 23 Texas Reports, 310–311, 319 (the legal interest rate in New York was 7 per cent and in Louisiana 8 per cent); Lynn to Earl of Clarendon, January 1, 1857, MS, F.O. See also Samuel May Williams Papers, 1855–1858, MSS, and Ballinger Papers, 1860, MSS, for innumerable examples of interest rates and of the informal type of "paper money" in circulation at that time.

[93] *Mills* v. *Johnston,* 23 Texas Reports, 310–331.

ices in all cases where the issue had been tested in the courts." The question of the legality of a given commission did not depend so much upon whether the fee was contrary to the laws governing banking as it did upon whether the fee charged for money advanced was "reasonable" or "exorbitant." If money or goods were advanced to merchants or planters for long periods, even if the various fees charged for this service were similar to those exacted for a banking service, these facts did not necessarily mean that the fees charged were interest on money; they could be considered merely a charge for the commission merchants' "services"—a procedure which had long been an honored practice in Galveston and for that matter in many other states of the Union. Judge Bell stated that in these circumstances the question of usury or the infraction of the banking aspects of the law did not apply; rather, in these situations

the commission merchant advances the money not as a mere loan for the sake of interest; not ordinarily in the expectation that it will be repaid in money; he makes the advance as an incident to the general business which he has undertaken to do, and in the expectation that he will be repaid, out of the proceeds of crops or other goods, placed in his hands for sale.[94]

Thus, "banking" in Galveston was not considered to be the hiring of informal paper money but the hiring of service. In other Southern states of the Union this procedure was a common practice between the cotton factor and the planter, in Texas, however, since banking, at least in name, was illegal, the major commission merchants in Galveston financed not only the planters but also the minor traders and merchants of the Gulf Coast on the basis of "service" rather than on the basis of lending money as such.

In this situation the merchants in Galveston and in Houston were able to conduct their trading in goods and money with a minimum of regulation despite the fact that it was illegal to conduct a banking operation in Texas. The law, which on paper appeared to be a limitation, actually provided for a remarkably free market not only in goods but also in money and the astuteness and the integrity of the owners

[94] Judge J. H. Bell, commentary preceding his ruling in *Mills* v. *Johnston*, 23 Texas Reports, 324–326.

of the two large "banking houses" in Galveston prevented the "currency" on the Gulf Coast from deteriorating. The men behind these two institutions were by temperament and experience traders rather than promoters.[95] They were sharp trading business men, who charged as much for the credit they extended as the market would provide, but who never attempted to profit by the device of issuing paper which they did not intend to redeem in specie. "Mills money" and "Williams paper" were as respected as specie.[96]

Samuel May Williams, the elder of the two "bankers," began his mercantile career in Texas in 1822 when he landed in Matagorda Bay with a group of ninety colonists. Born at Providence, Rhode Island on October 4, 1795 of Welsh parents whose ancestors had migrated to Massachusetts in 1638, Williams received a good New England education followed by a brief apprenticeship in a Baltimore bank owned by his uncle. A little later he shipped as supercargo on a vessel trading with Latin America, and in 1815 he began work in New Orleans as a clerk for the trading firm of Morgan, Dorsey and Company. The valuable trading experience which Williams had acquired by the early 1820's recommended the young merchant's clerk to Stephen F. Austin who was at that time engaged in colonizing Texas in accord with the grant which he had received from the Mexican government. Austin engaged Williams as his secretary, and as public recorder, and director of the Public Land Office. Williams' association with Austin continued until 1834 when the two men broke off their connections because of a disagreement over the operation of the land office.[97]

[95] Lynn to Accountant General of Her Majesty's Navy, September 8, 1856, MS, F.O.; *State of Texas* v. *Samuel M. Williams and others,* 8 Texas Reports, 266th ff.; *Commercial and Agricultural Bank* v. *Jones,* 18 Texas Reports, 811–831; *Robert Mills and others* v. *The State,* 23 Texas Reports, 295; *Robert Mills* v. *Alexander S. Johnston and another,* 18 Texas Reports, 309; Houston *Telegraph,* January 20, 1856, January 16 and 23, February 5, 9, and 18, 1857; Galveston *News,* April 20 and May 21, 1857; Robert Mills Papers, MSS.

[96] *State of Texas* v. *Robert Mills, John W. Jockusch and David G. Mills,* District Court of Galveston, January 12, 1857.

[97] Ruth G. Nichols, "Samuel May Williams," *Southwestern Historical Quarterly,* LVI (October, 1952), 189–202; William Eckel to S. M. Williams, Feb-

In 1834 Williams formed a partnership with Thomas F. McKinney in an enterprise, which carried on mercantile operations in Brazoria, under the name of McKinney and Williams. The success of the partnership was due almost entirely to Williams' skill as a banker and merchant. When the Texas Revolution began, the firm, having valuable contacts in the United States, served as the principal agent of the Revolutionists in negotiating for the supplies and funds needed by the Texas forces. The two partners were reported to have advanced over $99,000 of their own capital to aid the cause. Apparently neither Williams nor McKinney was ever adequately repaid in monetary terms for the loans which they extended to the Republic of Texas.[98] After the Revolution, however, the two merchants transferred their trading and mercantile enterprise to Galveston. In a few years they had again accumulated enough capital to become one of the leading "banking houses" in Texas.

The R. & D. G. Mills and Company of Galveston was a stronger firm than the Williams' enterprise, both from the standpoint of management and of financial strength. The leading member in the company was Robert Mills, the most remarkable figure in Galveston during the fifties. Guy Bryan, a close friend of President Rutherford B. Hayes and a person of some consequence himself in Texas during the mid-nineteenth century, asserted that Robert Mills was not only the richest man in the state but also "the most influential merchant in Texas." In addition to his trading enterprises, which included an interest in firms in New Orleans, New York, Liverpool and Havana, and the ownership and operation of many sailing vessels and several steamships, Mills also maintained large sugar and cotton plantations in Texas and was the president and director of the Galveston and Brazos Navigation Company. Even though he disposed of many Negroes during the Civil War, he still retained over 800 slaves who were finally emancipated in 1865 as the struggle closed.[99]

---

ruary 11, 1832 and G. Dorsey to S. M. Williams, March 9, 1848, Williams Papers, MS.

[98] Nichols, "Samuel May Williams," pp. 189–202.

[99] Bryan to Hayes, March 13, 1887, in E. W. Winkler, (ed.), "The Bryan-

Robert Mills was born in Kentucky on March 9, 1808. During the years 1826 and 1827 he attended Cumberland College, and in 1830 he joined his older brother Andrew G. Mills in a mercantile enterprise in Brazoria, Texas. Andrew had charge of shipping operations while Robert managed the business of trading supplies for cotton and sugar. "In time, trains of [Mills] burros were exhanging goods across the Rio Grande for specie and bars of Mexican silver" which were "stacked like stovewood in the counting room."[100] When Andrew Mills died during the 1830's, Robert was joined by his younger brother David G. Mills. In 1849 they moved their main trading house to Galveston where John W. Jockusch, the Prussian Consul in Galveston, was admitted as a third partner in the firm. Robert managed the trading firm while the younger brother, David, remained on the plantations. During the fifties the four large plantations and other holdings owned by the Mills brothers comprised 3,300 acres under cultivation and 100,000 acres of unimproved land.[101] In 1860 the Robert Mills trading enterprise was reported to have been worth about 5 million dollars.[102]

Robert Mills' political convictions were in accord with those of the "old line Whigs." During the late fifties he had at first opposed secession in a moderate way; however, once Texas seceded Mills accepted the decision. Fundamentally, he was a trader rather than a politician or statesman. He was a man gifted with an extraordinary intelligence which manifested itself in his remarkable ability to accumulate wealth and his urbane facility for enjoying the good things of life which his possession of large sums of money enabled him to import to his Island home. To those Galveston families whom Mills favored he was a generous and charming friend; but in dealing with

Hayes Correspondence," *Southwestern Historical Quarterly*, XXVII (July, 1924), 61.

[100] Abigail Curlee Holbrook, "Robert Mills," in Walter Prescott Webb (editor-in-chief), *The Handbook of Texas*, II, 200; Abigail Curlee, "Robert Mills," *Dictionary of American Biography*, edited by Dumas Malone, XIII, 13–14.

[101] *Mills* v. *Nooman*, January 2, 1857; *James Baldridge* v. *Robert and D. G. Mills*, District Court of Galveston, March 31, 1857.

[102] *Mills* v. *Johnston and Dewbury*, District Court of Galveston, January 17, 1857.

THE BALL, HUTCHINGS AND COMPANY BUILDING
Note the wrought iron columns and arches of the store front (*ca.* 1900).

From a photograph in the Historical Collection, John Winterbotham Room, Rosenberg Library, Galveston, Texas.

some of his customers or with the gullible he sometimes turned his shrewd mind and his urbane manner to the purpose of shearing the simple of their wool.[103]

This aspect of the merchant speculator appeared in particularly sharp focus during the war years when Mills operated blockade-running enterprises into Texas from the ports of Liverpool, New York and Havana. The very character of his superb handwriting, the literary style of his correspondence and the ironic and at most times cynical attitude with which he indulged his love of sharp trading—an art that he seemed to love more as a game than for money profit—marked the character of the impact which this remarkably sophisticated, cynical, and urbane Kentucky-born merchant had upon the Gulf Coast of Texas during the fifties and during the war years. Mills was much loved by his family circle and by his friends. Over a period of years, however, his unusual skill in trading aroused a substantial number of persons who often took occasion to refer to him in terms somewhat less than friendly.

Being a speculative man by nature, Mills gambled his mercantile fortune in daring blockade-running adventures during the Civil War and lost. His wealth in plantations and slaves was wrested from him when the Confederacy fell. Yet, he was not an ardent Confederate patriot. At heart, he was a cosmopolitan trader whose attitude toward life made it impossible for him to acquire a dedicated allegiance to any cause. After the war, when he returned to Galveston from Europe and Havana, Mills was a man broken in spirit and in finances; during the 1870's he was a tragic figure barely able to earn a living and not even able to muster enough political influence to secure the position of Galveston's Customs Collector.

Even though Robert Mills' love of trading often caused him to drive bargains which may have been questionable, nonetheless, he maintained in many respects a code of honor in monetary affairs which was far above the custom of his time. The fact that he never abused the confidence that Texans placed in "Mills money," and the fact that when his firm was forced into bankruptcy after the Civil War he

103 *Ibid.*

placed his homestead mansion, his carriages, jewels, silver plate, and furniture, and his personal belongings on the public auction block in order to meet his creditors with clean hands presented a side of Robert Mills that ameliorated the reputation he had acquired for being a "sharp trader." For all his love of shrewd mercantile practices, he was also a man of unusual business integrity. The Texas homestead laws as well as the custom of the time would have permitted Mills to have kept large amounts of property beyond the reach of his creditors, but he refused to avail himself of this advantage presented by the laws.[104]

An indication of the pre-War financial strength of the R. & D. G. Mills organization and Samuel May Williams' Commercial and Agricultural Bank was demonstrated during the 1857 crash which shook northern financial institutions. The two Galveston banks had close to a million dollars in paper spread across the South, much of it in Texas. A majority of this paper was demand notes or "re-issue" notes. When news of the Northern panic reached the Gulf Coast, runs on the two banks in Galveston developed on the 19th and 20th of October, 1857. The Mills organization paid out on demand in specie during both days. Williams had some difficulty meeting the "run" which lasted for two days and for a few hours on the 20th he was forced to suspend payment. During that night some persons on the Island sold "Galveston paper" at a 25 percent discount. By the next morning, however, both banks were again paying in specie and those distrustful persons who had

[104] For further details regarding Robert Mills, see the following: *Mills* v. *Johnston and Dewbury*, District Court of Galveston, January 17, 1857; William Watson, *The Adventures of a Blockade Runner:* or *Trade in Time of War*, pp. 236–259; Ballinger Diary, *passim*, MS; Ballinger Papers, MSS; Mills Papers, MSS (this collection very limited); Joseph Kleiber Papers, MSS; Winkler, "Bryan-Hayes Correspondence"; R. H. Williams, *With the Border Ruffians*, p. 143; *Robert Mills and Others* v. *Fletcher C. Howeth*, 19 Texas Reports, 257; *Robert Mills and Another* v. *Thomas J. Walton* 19 Texas Reports, 271; *S. H. Summers* v. *Robert Mills and others*, 21 Texas Reports, 78; *Mills and others* v. *The State*, 23 Texas Reports, 308; Tax Assessor's Rolls, MSS; Census for 1850 and 1860, State Library, Austin, Texas; Houston *Telegraph*, January 17, August 14, 1850, January 30, 1852, March, 26, 1853, February 11 and 25, March 7, October 28 and November 4 and 11, 1857, January 13 and July 7, 1858; Galveston *News*, June 1, 1864, April 14, 15, 19, and 22, 1888.

sold their paper at a discount had cause to regret their transactions.[105]

Earlier in the year two of the "biggest business men of Galveston" had told Hamilton Stuart that in their knowledge "at least one half million in gold was kept available at all times in Galveston and could be had on any day at good security."[106] Cushing in Houston acknowledged that plenty of specie was always on hand in Galveston, but he wanted to know "how much of this could be had for less than 12%?"[107] One answer to Cushing's query was that although very little capital "could be had" at less than twelve per cent for speculative ventures, over $300,000 in gold had been allocated in low interest loans to be spent on building in Galveston during the first half of 1857.[108]

The agitation for or against banks had its origin in politics rather than in serious commercial considerations. The currency needs of the area were met by informal paper such as "Mills money." The paper of many lesser firms also served as money; and while some of this informal currency was of questionable value, it caused little serious harm to the economy because there was plenty of paper from Mills' or Williams' banks to be had for small trading. It was only after the two major "banks" headed by Mills and Williams had been curtailed by court action that informal money of a questionable character began to cause a serious disruption in the trading economy of the Gulf Coast.[109]

Some of the agitation for legal banks and for the enforcement of the state banking restrictions came from mainland merchants who resented the financial monopoly which "Galveston paper" exerted over Gulf Coast expansion. Also, Island and mainland politicians, for their own particular interest, found it expedient to be in opposition to the "financial colossus" existing in the port of Galveston. The major political issues of the late fifties, such as the legalization of the African

[105] Houston *Telegraph*, October 19 and 21, 1857; Galveston *News*, October 20, 1857.
[106] Galveston *Civilian*, May 12, 1857.
[107] Houston *Telegraph*, May 15, 1857.
[108] Galveston *Civilian*, May 12, 1857.
[109] See Ballinger Papers, for 1861, MSS.

slave trade, the issue of state-financed or corporate-financed railroads, the rise of Know-Nothingism and the fundamental question of secession, were all part and parcel of the "bank question" in Texas during the late fifties. Men sometimes associated themselves on either side of the bank issue for reasons which were far removed from actual financial considerations.

There were also legal purists who believed that, as long as the law prohibited banking enterprises, such institutions ought, as a matter of principle, to be curtailed. They were loathe to see powerful men such as Mills and Williams violate with impunity not only the Texas code but also the provision of the constitution.[110]

The effort to curtail the illegal banking activities in Galveston began in March of 1853 when "S. M. Williams, President, and J. H. McMillian, Cashier" of the Commercial and Agricultural Bank were tried in the District Court of Galveston before Judge Peter W. Gray "for issuing certain promissory notes, to circulate as money, in violation of the act to suppress illegal banking passed the 20th of March, 1848." Each of the notes in question were in the following form: "The Commercial and Agricultural Bank will pay one dollar to bearer on demand." Each note was signed by the president and the cashier.[111] The court action was the genesis of a series of litigations which finally forced the closing of Williams' bank and the curtailing of the issuance of "Mills money" during the last years of the fifties. During the years between 1853 and 1858 both firms continued to carry on as usual, believing, as did most Texans, that the courts would not strike down the "banks" or that if such action were necessary by the courts the legislature would intervene and provide some means to keep the banking operations of Mills and Williams within the law. A *rapprochement* between the "banks" and the law might have taken place much earlier than it finally did if the shattering political issues of the decade had not

[110] Houston *Telegraph*, February 6, 9, and 18, 1857; Galveston *News*, February 3, 1857.

[111] *State of Texas* v. *Samuel May Williams et al.*, District Court of Galveston, January 20, 1857; *Samuel M. Williams and others* v. *The State*, 23 Texas Reports, 291.

forced politicians and editors to harness the "bank question" for partisan purposes.[112]

Williams continued his banking operations while at the same time maintaining a dual line of defense in the courts. In the first instance Williams asserted that originally the firm of McKinney & Williams had been granted a charter by the Mexican authorities to operate a bank with a maximum capital of $1,000,000. This incipient institution, given the trade title of *Banco de Commercia y Agricultura*, was authorized to open when it had accumulated $300,000 in subscribed capital stock and had at least $100,000 in specie in its vaults. When Texas became a republic the Mexican charter was recognized by means of legislation enacted on December 10, 1836.[113] On the basis of this charter Williams maintained that he had a right to operate a bank despite the restrictions of Texas laws; he rested his contention upon the sanctity of contract principle which had been upheld in *Dartmouth v. Woodward*. The state on the other hand argued that since Williams had not actually opened his bank until after the state had enacted legislation which declared the operation of a banking enterprise to be illegal the original charter was null.[114]

Williams' second line of defense asserted that his enterprise was not a corporation, a company or an association in meaning of the state code and that therefore restrictions set forth in the code could not be applied to his operations. The Supreme Court of Texas thought otherwise. Williams' bank first lost its case in the lower court and after Williams' death in 1858 the Supreme Court sustained the penalty against the bank in 1859. The bank was closed and liquidated[115] immediately. The good will of the institution passed to Ball, Hutchings and Company established in 1854, which later became Hutchings, Sealy and Company, merging in 1930 with South Texas National Bank to become the Hutchings-Sealy National Bank of today.[116]

[112] *Mills and others* v. *The State*, 23 Texas Reports, 295.

[113] *State v. Williams*, 8 Texas Reports, 266; Gammel, Laws of Texas, I, 406; *Williams* v. *The State*, 23 Texas Reports, 264–292.

[114] *Ibid.*

[115] *State* v. *Williams et al.*, District Court of Galveston, January 20, 1857.

[116] Jesse A. Ziegler, "Bank Merger Recalls Early Methods of Galveston

In an effort to support the fiction that Williams' bank was not an "association," on May 14, 1857 the directors L. M. Hitchcock, G. H. Delesdernier, Andrew Moore, John L. Sleight, Jacob L. Briggs, and Allen Lewis resigned, publishing a formal announcement to that effect in the Galveston newspapers.[117] The possible fines which could have been levied not only against the bank but also against the directors could have amounted to well over $200,000. It was this possibility which prompted the directors to resign. The court, however, levied only a nominal fine against the bank. No action would have been taken in the first instance but for the fact that certain political elements in the state insisted "that men of great wealth" ought not to be above the law.[118]

Robert Mills, not having even a nebulous claim to a Mexican charter to legalize his banking operations, chose to exploit weaknesses in the law code. The devious procedure he used to "re-issue" "Mills money" rather than to issue it directly as Williams had unfortunately done indicated Mills' superior ability in conducting a successful banking enterprise in Texas despite the fact that such an undertaking was directly contrary to the law. By choosing to use the more indirect method of "re-issuing" notes drawn on out-of-state banks he avoided the appearance of directly violating the Texas law. The favorite technique of Mills was to countersign the notes issued by the Northern Bank of Mississippi located at Holly Springs. Without Mills' endorsement the notes of this "Wildcat" institution would have been practically worthless; however, once the notes were endorsed by the Galveston trader this paper became "Mills money" and thus acquired a respect equal to or even better than that accorded to specie. Mills

Firm," Galveston *News*, April 6, 1930; Nichols, "Samuel May Williams," p. 209.

[117] Galveston *News*, May 14, 1857.

[118] Houston *Telegraph,* January 16, 1857. For further details on Williams' bank see *Commercial Bank* v. *Jones*, 18 Texas Reports, 811–831; Williams Papers, MS; Lynn to the Accountant General of Her Majesty's Navy, September 8, 1856, MS, F.O.; Houston *Telegraph*, January 16, 1857; Galveston *News*, February 3 and 5, 1857.

depended upon the "re-issue" device to avoid the penalty against banking which had been written into the Texas code.[119]

The stability and flexibility of Robert Mills' operations rested upon the fact that he owned partnerships in trading firms outside of Texas. For example, he was the major partner in Mills, McDowell and Company of New York, and a second partner in McDowell, Mills and Company of New Orleans.[120]

He also maintained large trading accounts with foreign firms. This was particularly true during the war period. Single trading transactions which he negotiated with firms such as Pierce, Bacon, Hennings and Company in Liverpool, or Steussy and Blum and Company, a partnership operating in Matamoros and Frankfort, often amounted to over $100,000 in specie; Mills also maintained trading connections in Ireland as blinds to cover his operations during the war years.[121]

The conflict over the bank question in Texas reached its concluding and decisive stage during the years 1857–1859. Since even more serious questions of a political nature were also rapidly approaching a crisis during these years, it was inevitable that the decisions reached in the bank cases, which were first heard in the District Court and later in the Supreme Court, rested in part, at least, upon political rather than legal considerations.

In January of 1857 Judge Peter Gray, in the District Court of Galveston, handed down a decision against Mills which subjected the banking house to a fine of $100,000[122] if the Supreme Court failed to overturn or mitigate the verdict. This ruling taken in conjunction with the impending crisis also approaching for Williams' bank caused serious concern in the minds of persons who had an interest in sound

---

[119] Galveston *News*, April 30, 1857; Galveston *Civilian*, April 29, 1857.

[120] *Mills* v. *Johnston and another*, 23 Texas Reports, 310–311.

[121] Lynn to C. B. Malony (Ennis, Ireland), September 26, 1858, MS, F.O.; Mills to Thomas B. Powers (Liverpool, England), May 23, 1864, Ballinger Papers, MS; Joseph Kleiber Papers, letters, October 11, 1860 to July 10, 1877, MSS; Matamoros, Mexico, *Daily Morning Call*, December 9, 1864.

[122] *State* v. *Mills, Jockusch and Mills*, District Court of Galveston, January 12, 1857; *Mills and others* v. *The State*, 23 Texas Reports, 300.

currency.[123] Both Cushing and Richardson opposed the "shocking" implications of Judge Gray's action. While substantial persons in trading circles admitted that both "banks" were, perhaps, operating outside the law, nevertheless, these persons belived that the two institutions were providing a most valuable service to the state and therefore ought to be allowed to continue operations until an available legal banking institution could be provided.

Texans living in the Galveston area who were not primarily concerned with financial stability in a period when more dramatic considerations appeared to be the overriding ones, took the position that Judge Gray had demonstrated both courage and wisdom in the Mills case. The Mills were not above the law, proclaimed these persons; the public had long feared "that the great wealth of Messrs. Mills together with the influence which their extensive business connections gave them throughout the state would enable them to violate the constitutional prohibition of banking. But the public was wrong! A judge was found bold enough to enforce the law."[124]

Richardson, as spokesman for Galveston interests, demanded to be told why the state chose to prosecute Mills and Williams, while at the same time the state's attorneys allowed the house of Swenson and Swisher of Austin to carry on banking operations similar to that denied to the Galveston houses. Now that sound Galveston paper was being forced out of circulation, said Richardson, less stable currency from out of the state was flooding the area. The state government, he said, was "cutting off the sound money and aiding unsound money."[125]

Two days later Richardson again warned the interior politicians that since the threatening court action which had caused Mills and Williams to call in some of their paper, every boat from New Orleans was bringing large amounts of "Louisiana money" of questionable value; in fact, asserted Richardson, much of this imported money was actually counterfeit.[126] The editor's warning was well taken. As Galveston paper was gradually called in because of the pending court actions, the "paper

[123] Galveston *News*, January 15 and 17, 1857; Houston *Telegraph*, January 16, 1857.

[124] A letter from interested citizens, Houston *Telegraph*, January 23, 1857.

[125] Galveston *News*, February 3, 1857.   [126] *Ibid.*, February 5, 1857.

shortage" gave counterfeiters an opening which was not overlooked. The steamers from Mobile and New Orleans brought in dozens of "River Men," "gamblers," and "money artists" who exploited the vacuum caused by the withdrawal of "Galveston paper."[127]

Faced with a situation in which money of doubtful value was filling the vacuum left by the gradual withdrawal of Galveston paper, Gulf Coast merchants began to assert that they "would soon be without a paper dollar redeemable in this state;"[128] they pointed out that "Williams and Mills were strong and able men" and that "their banks were good" and their money as sound as specie; "perhaps, the law had been violated"; but, in any case, "the law had been a mistake." The Galveston banks ought to be allowed to operate until legal banks could be established.[129]

The $100,000 fine that Judge Gray had levied against Mills in the District Court was based upon the provision of the statute which permitted a fine of from $2,000 to $5,000 for each note issued in violation of the law. Severe as the $100,000 penalty was, if an actual count of the "Mills money" notes then circulating had been made, the possible fine which could have been levied against Mills would have been much larger. Faced with the severe fine set by the lower court, Mills appealed the case, trusting that the Supreme Court would reverse the sentence or at least reduce the fine to a nominal sum. Since Judge Gray's action rested in part upon political considerations, Mills, through his attorneys Ballinger and Jack, began at once to harness political as well as legal talent to reverse the decision of the lower court. At the same time Mills continued most of his usual banking operations; but in order to create the needed political effect he withdrew enough of his "Mills money" to demonstrate effectively the serious consequences which might ensue if all Galveston paper were forced from the market. When in October of 1857, a few months after the decision of the lower court, the panic of 1857 occurred, giving Mills an opportunity to demonstrate the extraordinary soundness of his firm by paying off

[127] *Ibid.*, May 5, 14, and 21, 1857; Houston *Telegraph*, February 6, 9, and 18, May 25, June 3 and December 30, 1857.
[128] Galveston *News*, May 21, 1857.
[129] Houston *Telegraph*, February 9, 1857.

steadily in specie during a two-day "run" on his bank, the "banker" scored a decided political as well as a financial triumph.

This incident, taken together with the influence of persons who had reason not to want to offend Robert Mills, caused the once popular decision of Judge Gray to lose favor. By 1859 when the appeal reached the Supreme Court the question of whether or not Mills had broken the law was seen in a "new light." "Abler legal minds" than Gray's— that is, the gentlemen on the highest bench—saw on a close examination that the statutes written in 1846 and 1848 which outlawed banking did not apply to organizations such as the Mills Company. The terms "companies" and "associations" referred to in the statute were intended to apply to larger aggregations of business men than the mere three-man partnership that comprised the R. & D. G. Mills Company. The Supreme Court, for these reasons, reversed the decision of the lower court leaving the Mills Company free to continue its operations.[130] Many other important events, however, were occurring as the year 1860 opened; within a few months "Mills money" was replaced by the many and varied classes of state and Confederate paper which marked the chaotic financial situation during the war years.

City Government

THE CITY OF GALVESTON during the fifties was governed by a mayor and a city council of aldermen. The mayor, who was elected annually by the qualified voters,[131] controlled the police department and had the power to fill all minor city offices. The legislative needs of the city were provided for by the twelve aldermen who were elected for two-year terms, four members from each of the three wards into which the city was divided. Galveston received its first city charter in 1839, a document afterward revised several times. Under the revised charter of 1856, the one still in force at the time of

[130] *Mills and others* v. *The State*, 23 Texas Reports, 295–309; Ballinger Diary for 1859 *passim*, MS; Ballinger Papers for year 1859, *passim*, MS; James D. Lynch, *The Bench and Bar of Texas*, pp. 412–416 and 267–272.

[131] All white males over twenty-one years of age who had lived in the city one year and had paid the taxes levied against them. Richardson, *Galveston Directory, 1859–60*, p. 36.

the Civil War, the council was permitted to incur an indebtedness up to $100,000 for improvements in the city; this limit could be raised only by the consent of two-thirds of the qualified voters.[132] This consent was secured in 1859 to construct the causeway to the mainland,[133] but, obviously, a city which gave as much care as Galveston did to public facilities must have had a more than adequate source of revenue.

A part of the city's expenses was met by tax assessments against real property, but the charter restricted these levies to one-fourth of one percent of the assessed value of the property and this only by a two-thirds vote in the council. In the year 1859 the tax yield on local property, assessed at a value of $8,681,176, was only $32,306.22.[134] The tax value placed upon the real property assessed that year was clearly only a fraction of the actual value.[135]

Most of the tax revenue was actually raised by an elaborate system of fees and special levies, the most profitable of which were license fees such as the following: $25 for each merchant plus $15 more if the firm operated a wholesale department, $25 for grog shops, $20 for each tenpin alley or billiard table, $25 for each boarding house selling liquor, $5 for each dray or carriage, $25 for each livery stable, $30 for each auctioneer, $25 for each cotton broker or real estate agent. In addition, there were many other similar levies assessed against hucksters, circuses, theatre performances and similar activities. The tax list indicated that the policy in force was to spread the burden in terms of citizens rather than in terms of property. The tax was collected by an agent, usually a leading political figure in the city, who was both assessor and collector, and who received a commission of five percent of all the money collected. The office was much coveted since it was very lucrative from several points of view.[136]

[132] *Charter and Revised Code of Ordinances of City of Galveston, Passed in Years 1856–57.*

[133] Ordinance Book, 1857–1865, MS, pp. 10, 17, and 40–41.

[134] These figures, taken from the actual tax records, exhibit a puzzling inconsistency. The tax collected amounts to not one-fourth of one percent, but a little over one-third of one percent of the assessed property value.

[135] Richardson, *Galveston Directory,* 1859–60, p. 36.

[136] Ordinance Book, 1857–1865, MS, p. 33.

The salary of the mayor was $800 per year plus the fees he received for granting licenses—an applicant for a license paid the regular fee plus a small required "gratuity" to the mayor of from $1 to $2. The secretary of the city also received a salary of $800 per year plus his "gratuities"—small fees for any papers which citizens might desire to have him endorse. The city marshal, who had charge of keeping the peace was appointed by the mayor and drew a salary of $1500 per year plus an allowance of $600 to pay for two deputies. In addition to his salary the marshal received a commission of two and one-half percent of all money he collected for the city. The marshal had another lucrative source of revenue in the following fee system of which he was the beneficiary: summons $1, warrants of arrest $1.50, writ of subpoena 50¢, commitment to jail $1, keeping prisoner 75¢ per day, release from jail $1, whipping a free person of color or a slave $1.50, if under sentence and at the request of the master $1. The several officers of the port of Galveston—who were actually officers of the Wharf Company—also enjoyed the benefits of an elaborate array of fees levied against the maritime trade moving through the port city. This myriad system of fees imposed upon all the commerce and trade in the port tended in the long run to cause the traders and merchants who were not in some manner or other on the receiving end of some of the fees to favor the city of Houston where this type of incumbrance was not so burdensome.

The offices in the city government of Galveston and in the Wharf Company were filled by a rotating system which, at one time or another during the decade, gave most of the leading men or the leading firms a share of the burden and perhaps the benefits inherent in the occupancy of the several important offices. Whatever the actual political system operating in Galveston was at that time, it could certainly claim to rest upon a broad base encompassing the shoulders of the leading men in the city. The only important Gulf Coast figures who appear to have been left out of the benefits were such men as House, Rice and Hutchins who eventually shifted most of their operations to Houston.[137]

[137] For information concerning the names of persons who held the important offices in the city of Galveston and in the Wharf Company see the pages of Richardson *Galveston Directory, 1859–60.*

The government of the city of Galveston was "as good as any on the Gulf of Mexico."[138] But when compared with older cities in Europe or on the eastern coast of the United States, it still left much to be desired. It's complex tax system, while bringing considerable income, was complicated to administer and burdensome to both citizens and visitors. The city fathers, while encouraging many physical improvements neglected other matters very vital to a tropical city, such as the improvement of sanitation and the enforcement of port quarantine. Although its citizens took great interest in "culture," the city did not support any schools adequate to produce educated individuals. Yet despite these weaknesses the city government had many admirable accomplishments.

Galvestonians were proud of their beautiful city and were much interested in preserving and increasing its beauty and convenience. They could be counted on to encourage such improvement as the beautifying of buildings, the maintaining of sidewalks, the paving of streets, the construction of bridges, and the installation of public utilities. During the year 1859 the city took positive action to pay for shell-paving the streets by levying upon each householder at the rate of $1 per front footage. To the $500 per block thus raised the city added $240 more, providing $740 per block to pay for shell-paving all the main streets in the city.[139] In 1858 the city council had appropriated $3,000 to pave a "shell-road-drive" along the bay to permit the citizens to enjoy the same "luxury of driving of an evening along the sea front as was indulged in by the better citizens of New Orleans."[140] In the same year the city fathers began to build along the Tremont Street drive a fine public park "similar to the ones we are told they have in Germany."[141] To provide more beautiful and useful sidewalks the city officials strictly enforced the ordinance requiring that all sidewalks must be "curbed and graded" by the 10th of May each year. "The

[138] Lynn to William Seymour V. Fitzgerald (Report to National Association for the Promotion of Social Science), August 8, 1859, MS, F.O.

[139] Houston *Telegraph*, February 4, 1859; Galveston County Commissioners Court, Minutes, MS, 1856–1870, p. 30.

[140] Galveston *Civilian,* November 10, 1858.

[141] *Ibid.,* August 31, 1858.

ordinance is a popular one; obey it or take the punishment," warned the editor of the *Civilian*.[142] The beautiful streets in Galveston also received the careful attention of "the watering carts" every day.[143]

Also in the interest of progress, the city council, on April 19, 1858, accepted the bid of Judge A. F. James to lay a system of gas pipes under the city's streets.[144] Within a few months the judge had organized the Galveston Gas Company, a firm with a capital stock of $120,000, and had begun to erect a large plant and storage tank designed to furnish the city with this new utility.[145] When the service began on December 1st, 1860, the charge for gas was $6 per 1,000 cubic feet plus a charge of 25 cents per month for the meter. Each consumer received a sheet of instructions from the gas company entitled "How to Read Your Gas Meter and Pay Your Bill."[146] Gas lights were used in the homes and for some very small cooking. Their main use, however, was for street lights and for stores. The merchants of Galveston were very proud indeed of their "Whitelighted Emporiums."

The new gas might be exciting and convenient but the wood stove, nevertheless, remained the primary means for household cooking and the major source for heat. It also remained, unfortunately, one of the major sources of fire in the city and in order to curb this danger the authorities vigorously enforced regulations pertaining to the use of stove pipes and chimneys. Every room in the city in which a fire was ever lighted had to be provided with a bucket kept full of two and one-half gallons of water—which, incidentally, must have provided a breeding place for the fever-bearing mosquito. As a further protection against fire the city made it unlawful for a citizen to store more than twenty-five pounds of gun powder in any one room in his home. So that there might be no confusion it was unlawful to ring bells in the city in a manner which would simulate the "fire bell."[147]

[142] *Ibid.*, April 30, 1858; Galveston *News*, November 19, 1857.
[143] Houston *Telegraph*, May 13, 1857.
[144] Galveston *Civilian*, April 27, 1858.
[145] *Ibid.*, November 30, 1858.
[146] Galveston Gas Company, [Broadside].
[147] Richardson, *Galveston Directory, 1859–60*, pp. 40–41; Ordinance Book, 1857–1865, MS, pp. 29, 35, 55.

A ring of this fire bell brought one or, if needed, all three of the Galveston fire-engine companies. The city's volunteer companies were organized into three units: "a water company," an "axe company," and "a hook and ladder company," each with its special duties in the case of a fire. Each of these units, manned by about thirty firemen, had a separate building, a fire chief, and other officers including a treasurer—who was usually one of the leading business men in the city.[148] The "axe company, a new experimental idea" was composed of carpenters "wielding axes, ropes, and leather ladders." The new principle developed by the axe brigade was "to destroy the roof before the fire gets started."[149]

Another duty of the axe company was to rescue children who had fallen into the numerous wells and cisterns in the city. Since the well water supply on the Island was both scarce and unsavory most citizens collected as much rain water as possible in mortar-lined cisterns which were usually sunk into the ground near their buildings. Small children were fascinated by these mysterious, dark caverns and each year several juvenile adventurers perished while investigating these cave-like cisterns. When a child disappeared it was the duty of the axe company to canvass the cisterns of the city in a search for the body of the missing child.[150]

In the latter part of the decade, the Island possessed an even more notable rescue brigade, the now-famous Galveston Life Boat Company organized on June 22, 1857 to provide the harbor city with a unit of men, trained and skilled in sea rescue operations, who were pledged to brave the rough waters of the Gulf to save persons whose lives might be imperiled by the sea.[151] The Life Boat Company came into being in the wake of the tragic wreck of the large steamer, the *Louisiana*, off Galveston Island on June 7, 1857. This disaster, one of the many which beset steamships in the Gulf on stormy nights, washed scores of bodies to the shores of the Island. The city had to form committees and even to commandeer citizens to secure the labor needed to gather

[148] Richardson, *Galveston Directory, 1856–57*, p. 27.
[149] Galveston *News*, May 19, 1857.
[150] *Ibid.*, May 5, 1857.
[151] Ordinance Book, 1857–1865, MS, p. 4.

POST OFFICE STREET, 1867

From a Galveston *News* reprint of a contemporary photograph. The reprint is in the Historical Collection, John Winterbotham Room, Rosenberg Library, Galveston, Texas.

the bodies together and to give the dead a decent burial. This grim task brought an unavoidable realization that if the city had possessed a rescue company equipped with boats and organized to provide immediate aid to a stricken vessel approaching the Bay, many of the dead from the *Louisiana* might have been saved. The Galveston Life Boat Company was chartered by the mayor of the city a few days after the wreck of the *Louisiana*. The city provided the boats and the boat houses while the personnel was composed of volunteers who knew the sea and understood the nature of the tasks they would suddenly be called upon to perform.[152]

Galvestonians, who were of a salt-water breed, always took good care of disaster victims. For example, a few days after the wreck of the *Louisiana*, resourceful Galvestonians induced a hardy survivor of the disaster "to render a discourse on the wreck to a crowded hall" and from this assembly collected enough money to provide clothes and homeward passage for the survivors.[153] Four months later, on the occasion of the crash of the steamships *Opelousas* and *Galveston* on Sunday November 17th, Galvestonians again demonstrated their willingness to care for travelers cast upon them by the stormy waters of the Gulf.[154]

This compassion for their less fortunate fellows was a strong characteristic of Galvestonians as a whole. In fact, except perhaps for their intense interest in the beauty and progress of their city, this brotherly attitude might be regarded as their most notable quality. The care of indigent persons who were residents of the city and the county was a burden that the Texas Code placed upon the county authorities.[155] In Galveston, however, cases of "destitution were generally relieved by voluntary contributions of the citizens and without reference to the nationality of the recipient."[156] Prior to 1850 many destitute persons, deposited in the city by ships entering the port, later became charges

[152] Richardson *Galveston Directory, 1859–60*, p. 41; Galveston *Civilian*, June 8 and June 10, 1857; Galveston *News*, June 6 and 25, 1857.

[153] Galveston *Civilian*, June 10, 1857.

[154] Houston *Telegraph*, November 23, 1857.

[155] Galveston County Commissioners Court, Minutes, MS, 1856–1870, p. 17.

[156] Lynn to Lord Lyons, November 19, 1859, MS, F.O.

upon the authorities. As a means of curtailing this expense the city induced the legislature on February 11th, 1850, to enact a law to compel every owner, or consignee, of any vessel arriving at Galveston to provide a $300 bond of five years' duration for each passenger deposited to ensure that no person would become a charge upon the state. Since a forced compliance with this law would have made the operation of a passenger service to Galveston almost impossible, an escape clause was included in a provision commuting the $300 bond by the payment of a fee of $1 per passenger within three days after the arrival of the vessel. This fee, taken in conjunction with a hospital fee of $1, which was also levied against every passenger entering the city from the sea, provided a substantial fund with which to care for the poor and the sick without considering whether they were resident or transient.[157] The British consul in Galveston, after having lived in the city for ten years, wrote in 1859 that he had "never known an instance where a pauper has been sent out of this city by municipal authorities."[158] While the Galveston city fathers were quick to levy a fee whenever possible, they were not lacking in a cosmopolitan largesse toward those in need. In fact, the care of the poor and the ill in Galveston was entered into as if the particular charity was one of a personal nature even though, in many cases, the funds came from official sources.

The lack of a bureaucracy in the city was reflected in an almost complete disregard for the maintenance of vital records. The only information about a citizen's death was that to be found in the church records, the sexton's books, or perhaps a mention in the newspaper. This lack of public records was the cause of numerous complaints to the city officials by foreign consuls in the city. "As no records of deaths are registered in this state," wrote Consul Lynn, "I have at all times found great difficulty in obtaining evidence of decease of persons whose relatives are non-residents of this state."[159] During severe fever epidemics in the forties and early fifties "men were frequently admitted

157 *Ibid.*
158 *Ibid.*
159 Lynn to James Murry, August 13, 1861, MS, F.O.

[to the hospital], died, and were buried whose names were un-known."[160]

Even more far-reaching than the failure to keep records was the government's lack of interest in matters of sanitation and public health. This was the one governmental function which, above all others, needed to be administered with a strong and impartial hand; yet, regarding this aspect of cosmopolitan living, both the government and the citizens were governed almost solely by the principle of *laissez-faire*. More care was taken in the shelling of the main streets and bay-shore drives or in erecting the great iron store-fronts than was taken in the draining of stagnant pools of water from the back alleys or in the enforcing of sanitary regulations concerning the privies stand-ing in rows behind the white-painted buildings framed by their deco-rated cast-iron fronts.

It was not until the beginning of the twentieth century that the methods necessary to control yellow fever in a tropical city were gen-erally known by hygiene experts; nevertheless, the enforcement of a sanitary code, the drainage of stagnant water near and in the city, and the strict enforcement of the maritime quarantine codes would have decreased the incidence of the fever. However, the enforcement of the needed regulations during the fifties was more than Galveston politicians cared to attempt even if they had been convinced that such measures would actually prove effective. There was a strong conviction, borne out by events, that the fever seldom struck the acclimated Gal-vestonian but was more likely to strike the newly-arrived. Since the newcomers lacked politician influence, their security interests carried little political weight.[161] Nevertheless, the arrival of the "Yellow Jack" on the Gulf Coast brought with it a terrifying fear.

When the fever epidemic season first arrived in either Galveston or Houston, the usual custom of the newspapers was to ignore the evil or to imply that the epidemic was one of minor porportions. The journals

[160] Lynn to E. M. Archibald (British Consul, New York City), September 24, 1860, MS, F.O.

[161] Richardson, *Galveston Directory, 1859–60*, p. 76; J. P. Cole to Gail Borden, November 19, 1853, Gail Borden Papers, MS; Galveston *Civilian*, October 5, 1858.

followed this practice because any other course would have been injurious to the trade of either city. But as the weeks passed, if the plague was a major one, rumor inevitably created the impression that the situation was even worse than the facts warranted.[162] Faced with this circumstance, the papers would then publish, at last, a long "Fever Report" which contained a list of all the persons in the city who had actually died of the fever. These lists, often containing well over one hundred names, were sobering indeed, but even so, they were always much smaller than the rumors had suggested.[163] Such "Fever Reports," when they were published in the newspapers, indicated the extent of the disaster endured.

The seriousness of the epidemics may be seen in the fact that the seven-week "fever season" in 1858 at Galveston took 373 lives. Other "fever seasons" took numerous lives as well: 400 persons died of yellow fever in Galveston in 1844 and 535 in 1853.[164] The personal aspect of these statistics may be seen in the fact that E. H. Cushing lost his wife and son during one epidemic; William Pitt Ballinger, the prominent Galveston jurist, lost four of his children to the fever; and the German editor in Galveston, Ferdinand Flake, lost five children during various epidemics. In fact, yellow fever, dysentery, and other diseases with which small children were afflicted, took the lives of almost one out of every two young Texans born on the coast during the fifties.[165]

The city maintained a hospital of sixty beds to care for indigent ill persons—usually fever victims. During the late fifties, an annual load of 1,760 patients received treatment at the hospital. "A large proportion of these, probably nine-tenths of those treated, were from abroad and strangers to our climate," reported the director of the institution.[166] A victim suffering an attack of yellow fever was usually

[162] Ballinger Diary, September 18, 1859, MS.

[163] Houston *Telegraph*, September 25, 1847, October 7, 1859; Galveston *Civilian*, October 5, 1858.

[164] Richardson, *Galveston Directory, 1859–60*, p. 76; Dyer, "History of Galveston," MS, VI, 17.

[165] Houston *Telegraph*, September 25, 1857; Ferdinand Flake, "Register of 1864 of the Male and Female Inhabitants of Galveston City," MS.

[166] Richardson, *Galveston Directory, 1859–60*, p. 76.

overwhelmed by the sudden ferocity of the disease. Death often came in two or three days. In order to provide assistance to destitute persons in such circumstances, about two dozen of the most substantial citizens of the city of Galveston organized a branch of the national philanthropic group called the Howard Association to care for the "indigent sick, especially in time of epidemics." The work of this ameliorative group was remarkable for its truly Samaritan and unselfish activity.[167]

Neither the authorities nor the citizens were of one mind as to what measures ought to be taken to guard against the fever. Some feared the night air, dogs, hogs, goats, mules, bad water, the fish markets, filthy streets, the slaughter houses, and innumerable other evils as the bearer of the fever. "Fill up the streets and purify them—filth makes fever" was a common cry as the "Yellow Jack" season approached; yet, not much was ever done in response to these warnings.[168] Conservative elder Galvestonians reiterated that "temperance, regular habits, cleanliness, avoidance of exposure to the heat of the sun and a composed mind [were] the best means of escape."[169] In an effort to reduce the incidence of fever and to follow all suggestions which would not cause too much inconvenience, the authorities occasionally destroyed stray unlicensed dogs in the city, threatened to kill all hogs, goats, mules, and horses found wandering in the streets, began to enforce the regulation of the fish markets, and hired a special deputy "to inspect all privies and report monthly to the hospital board."[170] The only measure which was successfully enforced, however, was one concerning hogs; in this instance it was provided that any citizen who saw a hog on the street after April 1st, 1857 could claim it as his own provided the finder caught and immediately fenced the animal on his own property.[171]

According to British sanitation experts who, for their own purposes,

[167] Galveston *Civilian*, April 17, 1857; Houston *Telegraph*, October 12, 1859; Richardson, *Galveston Directory, 1856–57*, p. 27.

[168] Houston *Telegraph*, March 16, 1857; Ordinance Book, 1857–1865, MS, pp. 5 and 34.

[169] Galveston *Civilian*, August 17, 1858.

[170] *Ibid.*, May 5, 1857.

[171] Houston *Telegraph*, March 25, 1857; Ordinance Book, 1857–1865, MS, pp. 5 and 34.

examined the situation at Galveston in 1859, the solution was not to be found in corralling hogs or in the avoidance of strong drink. They felt that the fever could be suppressed only by a complete enforcement of the sanitary code and the quarantine regulations—neither of which was actively applied in Galveston. Although completely adequate port quarantine regulations existed by virtue of city ordinances passed on March 31st, 1846 and February 1st, 1857, augmented by an act of the state legislature of February 11th, 1850, the existing regulations were completely negated by an escape clause whereby ship owners were allowed to pay a commutation of $1 per passenger and, as Consul Lynn said in 1859, "proceed to discharge cargo and passengers without hindrance; therefore, there is no law which subjects a vessel arriving at the port of Galveston to a quarantine, and no vessel has been put in quarantine during the last five years."[172] In the opinion of competent British observers the "general sanitary state of the city of Galveston" was as good as that of any other city on the Gulf; nevertheless, the lack of sanitary practices in certain of the food industries gave the fever in Galveston "a more malignant character" than would have been the case if better standards had been maintained. Some of the malpractices referred to were the condition of "the slaughterhouses to the south-ward of the city from which during the summer pestilential effluvia arising from putrified offal [was] disseminated by prevailing winds over the city;" tanks sunken in the streets for the purpose of obtaining a supply of water in the event of fire were in effect also reservoirs for stagnant putrid water, and the complete lack of concern for the general principles of drainage all contributed to making the port city a good host for yellow fever.[173] It was noted by these expert observers that the character of the climate in Galveston—hot during the summer and subject to sudden change to a very cold and even dry condition for short periods in the winter—tended to undermine the health of persons subject to pulmonary diseases, thus making such persons more likely victims of the yellow fever—which could be brought into the city at any time by persons entering the port since it provided no quarantine

[172] Lynn to Fitzgerald (Secretary of the British National Association for the Promotion of Social Science), August 8, 1859, MS, F.O.
[173] *Ibid.*

screen against the disease.[174] The political and commercial leaders in Galveston, however, were more concerned with the collection of the fee of $1 per passenger paid by ships' captains to avoid a quarantine than they were in keeping the fever out of Galveston.[175]

Schools

WHILE MANY OF Galveston's institutions were public or semipublic organizations, the schools of the city were all private, operated either as church functions or else as private enterprises. The state of Texas set aside, in January of 1854, a sum of 2 million dollars in United States bonds to be used to set up a public school system.[176] The chief justice of the county together with the commissioners were to constitute a school board, and each county was to receive school funds on the basis of a census of all white children living in the county between the ages of one and sixteen years of age. However, the money was to be used only for the payment of teachers' salaries; the buildings and equipment for public schools had to be provided by the county before the state money would be made available. In effect, these restrictions made it necessary for the county or the city to match the funds offered by the state.[177] In the year 1855 Galveston County, with a student load of 505 children, drew only $757.50 from the school fund; this sum was applied to educate children of the poor who could not afford to pay the tuition required at private schools.[178]

In the 1850's Galveston showed no interest in spending tax money to support public schools, although the citizens did demonstrate an interest in patronizing private schools and other institutions of an academic nature, such as libraries, lyceums, debating societies and musical concerts. Outside of the schools maintained by the Catholic church the quality of instruction offered and the character of support given to those who endeavored to organize respectable institutions in the city left much to be desired. On the one hand, the taxpaying

[174] *Ibid.*   [175] *Ibid.*

[176] Frederick Eby, *Education in Texas: Source Materials*, pp. 264–270.

[177] *De Bow's Review*, XIX (December, 1885), 695–696.

[178] Eby, *Education in Texas*, pp. 275 and 277; Galveston County, Commissioners Court, Minutes, MS, 1856–1870, pp. 72–73 and 118.

citizens were not ready to pay for a general public school, and on the other, the community was yet too young to have produced enough old and established families to underwrite a private school with funds sufficient to elevate the institution above the need to operate as a business enterprise struggling to please its "patrons" rather than to engage in the unpleasant task of disciplining the children of its "patrons."

The most successful primary school in the city was the Ursuline Academy for Girls established in 1847 by a group of Ursuline nuns from New Orleans. A school for boys was organized at the same time under the direction of the Oblates of Mary Immaculate.[179] Both of these schools accepted pupils of any faith either as boarding or day students. The only college in Galveston that actually deserved to be called an "institution of higher learning" was the University of St. Mary's founded in 1854 under the patronage of the Rt. Rev. J. M. Odin, Bishop of the Diocese. This institution was incorporated by the legislature in 1856 and was empowered to "confer academical degrees upon graduates, and likewise upon distinguished persons."[180] The year at this college consisted of two sessions of five months each, making one collegiate year from October 1st to August 1st. St. Mary's University accepted students of all denominations; however, "for the sake of good order all students were expected to attend church on Sunday."[181] The curriculum consisted of the Latin, Greek, and English languages, mathematics, calculus, descriptive geometry, mechanics and astronomy, chemistry and natural philosophy, history, poetry, rhetoric, surveying, botany, and mythology. Students boarding at the University paid the following yearly fees:

Tuition	$160.00
Washing	15.00
Bed and bedding	10.00
Physics fee	5.00
Music and drawing	40.00

[179] Galveston *News*, November 10, 1857; Galveston *Civilian*, August 4, 1857.
[180] Galveston *News*, November 10, 1857.
[181] Houston *Telegraph*, December 28, 1857.

Day students paid a tuition fee of three to five dollars per month, half-boarders—those staying at the college for dinner—paid an additional fee of $80 on an annual basis.[182] E. H. Cushing, the editor of the Houston *Telegraph*, a graduate of Dartmouth and a severe critic of education in Texas, wrote that "St. Mary's college at Galveston has a good reputation for scholarship. We commend it to the public."[183]

For a few years during the fifties the "Misses C. S. & E. M. Cobb" operated the Galveston Female Seminary with the blessing of the Methodist Church.[184] These ladies tried, under extremely difficult circumstances, to establish a successful school. Richardson of the *News* reprimanded the citizens of the city for failing to lend these two worthy teachers their assistance. "With the exception of the Catholic college and Convent," said Richardson, "there is not a building in the city fit to house a respectable school." The Misses Cobb were good teachers, he insisted; they deserved help. "In most other places wealthy men aid education, but not in Galveston." In this city, he said, the teacher is "left on her own to find the money and to build a school. Many able teachers have tried and failed. Teachers do not have the capital to set up good schools, therefore in Galveston we have poor schools or none." The Cobb sisters needed aid, he reiterated; they could not build a school alone. "Will Galveston lose another school?"[185] The answer to his question was "yes."

In 1847 the Galveston Female Collegiate Institute was organized by John McCullough in a very substantial building acquired for the institution by his brother, James McCullough of Washington, D. C. The Institute undertook to teach secondary and college-level subjects of a practical, scientific, and a classical nature. The faculty was composed almost entirely of members of the McCullough family. Despite the fact that it possessed a fine building and reserve capital the Institute was not able to survive the fever epidemic of 1854.[186]

E. H. Cushing—a graduate of Dartmouth as has already been noted,

[182] *Ibid.*; Galveston *News*, November 10, 1857.
[183] Houston *Telegraph*, December 21, 1857.
[184] Galveston *News*, June 18, 1857.
[185] *Ibid.*, May 21, 1857.
[186] *Ibid.*, October 22 ,1849; *Handbook of Texas*, I, 667.

a scholar possessing a substantial knowledge of classical subjects, a former school teacher in Galveston, a newspaper editor, and a publisher of school textbooks[187]—carried on a personal campaign, in the late fifties, to bring a semblance of integrity into the schools of Galveston and Houston. On this subject the pen of the editor flashed like the voice of an angry man. "We have," he said, "high sounding names and a great show of learning. We have degrees from universities, whose faculties are unable to converse with a university student in university language."[188] Colleges had been opened on occasion in Galveston and Houston, he said, in which "the president, the board of trustees, professors, and tutors were all comprised in one person, and he having no right to attach an A.M. or even an A.B. to his name." There was here and there, he said, a school taught by an educated person at which the boys and girls really learned what "they supposed they were learning"; but many schools had teachers who were too ignorant or indolent to do anything else; many were "loafers" who were actually only "profane" and "vulgar" but who by the "aid of humbuggery had made themselves well known as teachers." As to calling institutions directed by such persons "universities"—Cushing could only remark that to call a mere academy a university was to be ridiculous. All he hoped for was, at least, a fair academy to give the "boys and girls a first rate English education and a little knowledge of Latin and Greek." But even this was lacking in the common schools on the Gulf which presumed to call themselves "universities and colleges."[189]

One of the methods used by private schools in Galveston and Houston during the fifties to earn a reputation for excellence was to hold formal, public oral examinations in the evenings to which the patrons and townspeople were all invited. Various prizes were presented for the best answers given orally by students to the apparently difficult questions asked. The pupils always presented the appearance of remarkable achievement because "they had been drilled for months"

[187] Cushing published during the years 1863–1865 a textbook series called *The New Texas Series of School Books* which included the following titles: *The New Texas Primary Reader, The New Texas Reader,* and *The New Texas Grammar.*

[188] Houston *Telegraph,* May 4, 1857.   [189] *Ibid.*

previously on the exact questions they would be asked. The result was that "the school got the credit for doing wonders" and the students actually learned very little.[190]

Editor Cushing was particularly irritated by "this educating children in the art of humbuggery" and "giving great names to ordinary things." Yet, it seemed to him that public sentiment in Galveston and in Houston required it. People looked upon a school that did not "give a showy examination as unworthy of patronage."[191]

On one occasion during the late fifties Cushing had spent an evening discussing this matter with a visiting English naval officer who was a graduate of Cambridge. The Britisher, who had spent some time on the Gulf Coast and concurred with all of Cushing's remarks about education in Galveston and Houston, remarked that it was a strange situation "to send boys to a University to get a common school education." Yes, agreed Cushing, it was time "the legislature stopped giving college charters to common schools . . . Let us give up this art of shamming and come back to first principles."[192]

The condition of the schools was probably due to a fundamental flaw in the relationship of the teacher with his students and their parents. As long as the teacher was wholly dependent upon the whims of the parents for his livelihood he was free neither to exercise the kind of discipline nor to organize the kind of program which would lead to a sound education for his pupils. As one instructor explained, the children were allowed to abuse the teacher solely because the teacher had to live off their parents' fees. "A teacher ought to have the same rights as others," he insisted.[193]

This explanation of the situation was supported by a Galveston student who had just been graduated from a city school. He asserted that the sad state of the schools in the city was due to the fact that school-teaching in Galveston had "assumed the lowest form of demagoguism. The teacher must fawn upon each patron and also fawn upon the disposition of each pupil" if he expects to earn a living. The fault "was not the pupils, nor the teachers, rather it lay with the parents." "The teacher is told," said this student, "that I don't whip my children and

[190] Ibid.   [191] Ibid.   [192] Ibid.
[193] Galveston *Civilian*, June 9, 1857.

THE URSULINE ACADEMY, on Avenue N between 25th and 27th streets

From a contemporary engraving in the Historical Collection, John Winterbotham Room, Rosenberg Library, Galveston, Texas.

I don't suffer others to whip them." Each parent "must suggest some new idea in regard to the management of the school" and if these suggestions are not adopted some offense is given. "Thus," said this student, "pupils are sent to school licensed to do as they please"; girls at "14 and 15 are privileged characters." The system in Galveston was to have the pupil and not the teacher "govern the school." The end result of this system, said this student, would be "to drive from the schoolroom every teacher who has any professional dignity about him, and leave the schools in charge of men of no pride who permit themselves to be treated in any manner, by both patrons and pupils, solely on account of the small and trifling lucre to be obtained thereby." If Galveston patrons wanted good teachers, he continued, they would have "to give them authority and treat them like gentlemen." This student warned Galveston parents that "children have a very great deal of cunning, they pull the wool over the parents' eyes"; when "good teachers are driven away the city suffers much more than the teacher."[194]

The schoolteacher shortage in Galveston was very acute after 1857. Richardson of the *News* admitted that Galveston had long been more or less dependent upon New England for schoolteachers. This situation could be corrected, he said, only when Texas established her own "normal schools."[195]

However, not all of these northern schoolteachers gave satisfaction. On April 9th, 1857, a young man from Saratoga, New York, wrote to the postmaster in Galveston applying for a job in Galveston as a schoolteacher. The postmaster referred the letter to Professor Caleb G. Forshey, Director of the Rutersville Institute. The professor replied to the Saratoga applicant in a manner which, he said, was in accord with the sentiments of the citizens of Galveston. "The want" for good instructors in Galveston, the professor admitted, was very great but "the opportunity" for Northern teachers was gone because Galveston people had learned by dear experience that a very large majority of Northern people were "not to be trusted with institutions such as ours." Profes-

---

[194] Galveston *News*, September 17, 1857 ("a letter from a student").
[195] *Ibid.*, December 1, 1857.

sor Forshey wrote that it was painful for him to contemplate these facts, but since they were true, the people of Galveston were "compelled to act upon them." He admitted that this point of view was an injustice to many good Northern teachers, but even so, the officials in Galveston who might have occasion to contemplate hiring Northern teachers had no alternative but to refuse to do so for the reasons given.[196]

Churches

THE CITY OF GALVESTON, being a frontier area like the rest of Texas, had to draw upon the older communities of the Union for its spiritual as well as its educational leaders. However, perhaps because one cannot treat the welfare of the soul with quite the cavalier highhandedness which Galvestonians accorded to the development of the mind, these religious leaders occupied positions of influence such as no educator was able to attain.

The clergy of Texas had a varied origin; some were the products of the finest theological institutions, others were little better than charlatans who were looking for an easy living.[197] However the quality of the churches in such circumstances reflects the character and ethics of the clergy who direct them, and the cosmopolitan character of the Galveston population and the sophistication of the leading families made it impossible for incompetent or mountebank clergymen to gather a following on the Island. With one or two exceptions the behavior of the clergy in Galveston during the fifties was exemplary. In many respects the cosmopolitan character of the population also ruled out the utility of exuberant gospel as a means of mobilizing a congregation. The two most successful denominations on the Island were the Catholics and the High-Church Episcopalians, both of which employed formalism— that is, liturgical worship—rather than emotional extemporization as a means of attracting converts. The fact that these two were successful whereas their opposites failed to attract large numbers of converts on the Island indicates the prevailing level of social sophistication existing

[196] This correspondence printed in Galveston *News*, April 28, 1857.
[197] Galveston *News*, March 12, 1857.

even among the common people of Galveston during the fifties. For instance, the First Baptist Church in Galveston, which was organized in 1840 with only nine members, had not according to Willard Richardson, "developed in numbers with the other churches," during the twenty years between 1840 and 1860. It appeared that the "simplicity of its worship, and its entire freedom from those forms and ceremonies, which are so imposing and attractive in the worship of other denominations, may well be one of the reasons why this church is not popular with the masses" on the Island.[198]

All religious institutions on the Island profited from the steadying example provided by the Catholic and the Episcopalian churches. During the early fifties the dignity brought to religious worship by the Catholic Bishop John M. Odin and Episcopalian Rector Benjamin Eaton, both clergymen of the highest standards and training, had a very remedial and sobering effect upon leading Galvestonians who otherwise might have relegated the religious and cultural aspects of life to a lower place. Since the death rate in Galveston from the fever was particularly high during the fifties the Galvestonians had, at times, grave need for religious solace.[199]

The Catholic institutions in the city originated in 1841 when the Rt. Reverend John Marie Odin, later Bishop, aided by the Menard family and Doctor N. D. Labadie, began to build the first simple church structure. This frame building, the forerunner of the later St. Mary's Cathedral, was only fifty feet long and twenty-two feet wide. During the year 1844 two Vincentian priests, J. M. Paquin and John Brands, visited the Island lending considerable prestige to the new church. As the fever was particularly severe that year the two visiting fathers were given an opportunity to demonstrate the sincerity of their desire to serve mankind. Both men, by their Samaritan behavior, strengthened their church; in fact, Father Paquin died during that year of fever contracted while working with the sick. The relatives of this priest sent Father Odin one-half million bricks from Antwerp in the year 1845 to be used to build a larger church on the Island in his

---

[198] Richardson, *Galveston Directory, 1859–60*, p. 71. Houston *Telegraph*, August 12 and 28, 1859.

[199] Galveston *Civilian*, January 26, 1858.

memory. With this valuable assistance the erection of St. Mary's Cathedral was begun.[200]

This "fine Gothic church," completed in 1849 after an expenditure of "about $25,000," was 130 feet long and 75 feet wide. Its interior height was 60 feet and from the roof of the outer structure twin towers "extended far into the sky dominating the city."[201]

At this time, to assist Bishop Odin in conducting the affairs of the Diocese, two more priests arrived on the Island. These men, John Timon and Louis Chambodut, were in addition to Father Brands who still remained. Chambodut's particular duty was to conduct a boys' school at St. Joseph's Hall. In 1847 the Ursuline Sisters had already begun their school for girls, and as the decade closed the Galveston City Company, a Menard enterprise, donated a square block of land to the Church to assist in establishing St. Mary's University. On April 23, 1860 the Germans established their own Catholic Church and parish under the patronage of St. Joseph. Two laymen were hired to teach the young Germans in the boys' school at St. Joseph's Hall. Thus, as the decade of the sixties began, Bishop Odin had directed the creation of several influential spiritual and educational institutions on the Island.[202]

There were Episcopalians among the first citizens of Galveston even' in the early forties. Such men as Judge Robert Dabney Johnson (the first Chief Justice of Galveston County), Captain Lent Munson Hitchcock (the well-known ship chandler), Joshua Clark Shaw (proprietor of Tremont House), Colonel Charles Power (a Britisher and an Eton graduate), were but a few of the potential members for an Episcopal parish as the decade of the forties opened.[203]

The now venerable Trinity Church, founded in 1841 and directed

[200] Catholic Youth Organization, Diocese of Galveston, *Centennial, The Story of the Development of the Kingdom of God on Earth in That Portion of the Vineyard Which . . . Has Been the Diocese of Galveston*, pp. 39–40.

[201] Richardson, *Galveston Directory, 1859–60*, p. 64; Catholic Youth Organization, *Centennial*, p. 40.

[202] Houston *Telegraph*, December 21 and 28, 1857; Byrne, *Centennial*, p. 40.

[203] William Manning Morgan, *Trinity Protestant Episcopal Church Galveston, Texas 1841–1953*, pp. 19–23.

for several decades by Benjamin Eaton, was the most successful Protestant denomination on the Island during the mid-century.[204] Eaton, born in Dublin, Ireland in 1806, was from a distinguished family whose members had at various times distinguished themselves in the British army. It was reported, though not with certainty, that Eaton was a graduate of both Eton College of Windsor, England, and Trinity College of Dublin. In any case, upon his arrival in Galveston in 1841 as an Episcopalian clergyman, Eaton demonstrated that despite his gentle manner and his evident old-world scholarship he had the perseverance necessary to establish an influential institution reflecting his faith in the rising port of Galveston.[205]

Eaton, who preached his first sermon in the courthouse, nurtured the embryo Trinity Church through a transient period in which services were held in various rented quarters on the Island,[206] until, near the close of the year 1842, his congregation built a modest building of its own. By the end of the decade Trinity Church had not only "built up one of the finest congregations in the South," but, because of the generosity of General Nichols, had also constructed a fine new brick church at a cost of $40,000—a structure of "surpassing beauty and dignity" which could accommodate 800 Episcopalians at a single service.[207]

The large congregation of Trinity Church included such notable vestrymen as General Ebenezer Nichols, Willard Richardson, Henry Rosenberg, George Hall, John Henry Hutchings, Thomas Massey League, Christopher H. Pix, John Sealy, William Baylis Sorley and Arthur T. Lynn.[208] The religious, cultural, political and economic prestige of the Church was an important factor which had to be considered in the planning of civic leaders. Whether the gentle but persevering Eaton or the dynamic "Episcopalian benefactor" General

[204] Houston *Telegraph*, November 13, 1857 and May 9 and July 11, 1859.
[205] Morgan, *Trinity Church*, pp. 9–13; Richardson, *Galveston Directory, 1859–60*, pp. 71–72.
[206] Morgan, *Trinity Church*, pp. 19–23.
[207] Richardson, *Galveston Directory, 1859–60*, pp. 71–72; Ben Stuart, "History of Galveston," MS, IV.
[208] Morgan, *Trinity Church*, pp. 259–427.

Nichols actually dominated Trinity Church was sometimes a matter of conjecture by Galvestonians.[209] Certainly many of the lay members of the church were individuals possesssing extraordinary personal force; nevertheless, the long-term effect and remarkable continuity of influence demonstrated by Trinity Church under Eaton's directorship indicated that in his gentle way this churchman exerted a strong influence upon such independent personalities as Nichols, Richardson, Sealy, Ball, Hutchings, or others of the colorful leaders in Galveston.

Eaton's British background, his scholarly cultured demeanor—buttressed as these assets were by his artful employment of the beautiful Episcopal service to impress the more rugged Galvestonians with the finiteness of this life and with an awe for the ruler of the universe— gave Eaton instruments for exerting influence nearly as powerful as that possessed by the successful empire builders of this new frontier. In this regard the social pressure exerted by his fellow Britisher, the Cambridge-trained Arthur Lynn, was of considerable value in the service of God, the Episcopal Church, and perhaps incidentally of culture and other things Anglican.

The Presbyterian Church in Galveston, directed by John McCullough, received early assistance from W. L. McCalla, a missionary who helped to organize the Presbytery of the Brazos.[210] McCullough received a classical education in the secondary schools of Pennsylvania followed by two years of study at Princeton Theological Seminary. After being ordained by the Newton, New Jersey Presbytery in 1835, he eventually arrived in Galveston sustained by an annual salary of $200.[211] In 1849 McCullough and his two sisters established the Galveston Female Collegiate Institute,[212] but the school was forced to close in 1854 when it suffered from financial difficulties arising out of the fever epidemic in Galveston that year. McCullough was neither an effective administrator nor a dynamic speaker; rather, he "was a sound,

---

[209] Annual Reports of British Consulate in Galveston, 1858, MS, F.O.

[210] William Stuart Red, *A History of the Presbyterian Church in Texas,* pp. 61–69, 137–138, and 219.

[211] Roberts, Rev. Edward Howell (compiler), *Princeton Theological Seminary Biographical Catalog, 1815–1932,* p. 34.

[212] Galveston *News,* October 22, 1849.

scholarly preacher," who did not radiate "much magnetism in his manner." In fact, sometimes while he was preaching his thoughts appeared to wander and he seemed to be "about to go off into a laugh" during the most somber portions of his sermons.[213]

During the early fifties the Presbyterian Synod tried to develop a German church of that denomination on the Island. The Reverend Mr. H. P. Young corresponded with the Theological Seminary of Basal, Switzerland in an effort to secure German Presbyterian ministers, but this effort failed.[214] By the close of the decade, however, the Germans of this faith had provided themselves with both a clergyman and a modest church building.[215] In addition to the Catholic and the Presbyterian institutions already mentioned, the Germans living on the Island maintained congregations of both German Lutherans and German Methodists. The latter was a small group under the care of the Reverend Mr. P. Moelling,[216] but the Lutheran church, organized in 1844, was larger and more influential. The congregation erected a house of worship in 1844. They remained under the spiritual direction of the Reverend Mr. A. B. Guebner until 1851 when the Reverend Mr. Wendt and his young assistant minister J. C. Roehm assumed this duty. Roehm also conducted a school for boys in the German Lyceum building on Twenty-Fourth Street and Winnie. Leading Germans of the Island who were prominent laymen in this congregation included George Schneider, Sr., Louis Moser, H. Bohnenberger, Ferdinand Flake, and Adolph Flake.[217]

The original spiritual leader of the Jewish community was Isidore Dyer, a merchant born in Dessau, Germany, in 1813, who came to Galveston in 1840. In 1852 Dyer donated the land for two cemeteries in

[213] William Youel Allen, "Allen's Reminiscences," edited by W. S. Red, *Southwestern Historical Quarterly*, XVIII (January, 1915), 300 (hereafter cited as "Allen's Reminiscences").

[214] Red, *History of the Presbyterian Church*, pp. 106 and 143.

[215] Richardson, *Galveston Directory, 1859–60*, p. 71.

[216] Ben Stuart, "History of Galveston," MS, XII; Richardson, *Galveston Directory, 1859–60*, pp. 71–72 and 91.

[217] "Lutheran Church Rolls in Galveston," MS; Houston *Telegraph*, August 12, 1859; Ben Stuart, "History of Galveston," MS; Census Rolls, Galveston, 1850, MS.

which the Jewish citizens were privileged to bury their dead, and, beginning in the year 1856, the first actual public Jewish religious services in the city were held in his home, a special room there having been arranged and dedicated for that purpose. The congregation thus organized under the guidance of Isidore Dyer eventually became the B'nai Israel of Galveston.

Dyer was an outstanding businessman as well as a religious and civic leader. In 1861 he retired from his mercantile enterprise and assumed a more active role in the direction of the Union and Marine Fire Insurance Company of Galveston of which he was president. Dyer's sister, Rosanna, the wife of Joseph Osterman, also a a merchant on the Island, was particularly active in the Jewish religious community and donated funds and time to the organization of an orphanage and a home for the aged. Michael Seeligson, another member of B'nai Israel, was also active in religious and political life on the Island; he was an alderman during the years 1840 and 1848 and mayor in 1853. Still other Jewish businessmen who were active in the synagogue as well as in the affairs of the city were P. W. Frank, J. Rosenfield, I. C. Levy, Leon Bloom, L. Lieberman and L. Block.[218]

The Methodists on the Island were organized in 1840 under the leadership of Reverend Thomas O. Summers and Methodist laymen such as Joseph W. Rice, J. L. Briggs, John B. Jones, E. S. Wood, and J. J. Thompson.[219] Homer S. Thrall, a Methodist missionary trained in Ohio Wesleyan University, came to Galveston in 1842. The zeal and energy of this remarkable man contributed not only to the growth of the Methodist Church in Galveston and in Texas but also to the development of education and to the writing of history.[220] It was under Methodist sponsorship that the Misses Cobb established their good but financially unsuccessful Galveston Female Seminary. On the whole,

[218] District Court of Galveston, Minutes, 1857, pp. 9–12 and 1861, p. 218. Henry Cohen, David Lefkowitz, and Ephraim Frisch, *One Hundred Years of Jewry in Texas*, pp. 9–10 and 28–30; Richardson, *Texas Almanac*, 1870, pp. 57–58; Richardson, *Galveston Directory, 1859–60*, p. 71.
[219] Clarence Ousley, *Galveston in Nineteen Hundred*, p. 81; Richardson, *Galveston Directory, 1859–60*, p. 71.
[220] *Handbook of Texas*, II, 777.

while the Methodists were active in the interior of the state, their congregation on the Island was not particularly noteworthy during the fifties.[221]

The First Baptist Church of Galveston—despite its lack of popular appeal—served the Island community in many ways. During the twenty years referred to by Richardson, the Reverend Messrs. James Huckins, John F. Hillyer, R. H. Taliaferro, and J. B. Stiteler guided this congregation.[222] Reverend Mr. Huckins, a graduate of Brown University, was a man of more than ordinary clerical ability as he demonstrated when he helped to organize Baylor University. His wife, who was the daughter of a onetime governor of the state of Rhode Island, was accepted in the social circles of the city because of her "social spirit and extensive cultivation," despite the fact that her husband's church was not the one preferred by the mercantile families. The Baptists, none the less, possessed a few members of social prominence such as Mrs. William Pitt Ballinger and Mrs. John S. Sydnor.[223]

During the fifties the Negro slaves on the Island maintained a Baptist and a Methodist church. These churches were actually organized and the places of worship were built by the slaves themselves with some assistance from their white masters.[224] A local press notice in 1858 indicated that a fair was

to be held by the congregation of the Colored Methodist Church of this city on Thursday evening next in the rear of the Tremont Street house of Mr. Jordan, the baker, for the purpose of raising funds to complete their house of worship. At their last monthly collection they contributed $75 for this purpose.[225]

---

[221] Lynn to Lyons, October 19, 1861, MS, F.O.; Galveston *Civilian*, January 26 and June 25, 1858; Houston *Telegraph*, April 4, 1859.

[222] Galveston *Civilian*, January 26, 1858.

[223] Ousley, *Galveston in Ninteen Hundred*, p. 83; "Allen's Reminiscences," pp. 287–304.

[224] Richardson, *Galveston Directory, 1859–60*, p. 71; Ben Stuart, "History of Galveston," MS, XIV.

[225] Galveston *Civilian*, March 30, 1858.

LOOKING SOUTH from the corner of 20th and Strand, 1861

From a contemporary photograph in the Historical Collection, John
Winterbotham Room, Rosenberg Library, Galveston, Texas.

The colored Baptists were loosely associated with the white church of the same denomination. With the assistance of friendly white Baptists, the colored slave members of that faith

purchased two lots of ground and constructed a neat and pleasant house of worship which cost them ten or twelve hundred dollars. The building itself, and the manner of its construction are highly creditable to this people, and the condition in which they live, under our laws.[226]

This interest of the white masters in the religious activities of their slaves and the encouragement and aid which they gave to the development of colored churches is perhaps an indication of one of the rather striking contradictions produced by the peculiar economic situation of Galveston. In a city possessing a number of very pronounced social classes there was a unity of interest, a spirit of cohesion, a general sympathy which could hold the city together in the face of seemingly inescapable divisive forces.

[226] Richardson, *Galveston Directory, 1859–60,* p. 71; Proceedings of the Mayor and Board of Aldermen of the City of Galveston, 1849–1855, July 20, 1854, Office of City Secretary.

3. THE SOCIAL SCENE

S OCIAL LIFE IN GALVESTON was composed of several elements. At the summit was what might be described as a local aristocracy consisting of a number of native American families who drew their incomes from mercantile, banking, shipping, and transportation enterprises, as well as from large plantations like the several cotton-growing establishments owned by the Mills family. The incomes of still other members of this group rested upon the professions, politics, manufacturing, and newspaper publishing. These leading families, who ruled Galveston led a cosmopolitan life, moving in a rather closed circle, bound together by a custom of visiting and entertaining each other in the many fine houses set amidst the splendid oleanders and gardens in their small but wealthy city.[1]

A second closely-knit social group on the Island, one which maintained good trading relationships with the native leaders on the business level but remained isolated in its own sphere of intimate social relations, was the very large contingent of prosperous Germans who had made a society for themselves in the city.[2] Below these two classes was a sizable group of small traders, clerks, mechanics, laborers, and seamen, who comprised a large, heterogeneous, and often transient portion of the 9,000 persons living in Galveston during the late fifties.

Even though the leading families displayed their considerable wealth by maintaining very ample city homes and associated surroundings, they nevertheless enjoyed the loyalty and good will of the less fortunate persons in the city. In all of the city elections the voters consistently returned to office the representatives of the leading families.[3] This good will and *esprit de corps* between the leading families and the working groups, which was quite remarkable in Galveston during the fifties, developed because the tax burden and even the cost of the informal social institutions set up to care for the poor in time of need was not levied upon the average local Galvestonian but upon the transient persons, the trade, and the shipping, moving into and out of the interior. All the local groups had a vested interest in this situation and this interest held them together to a remarkable degree. No one faction had occasion to bear a serious grievance against any other group. Furthermore, since the leading families during the fifties enjoyed a large prosperity and were relieved of much customary taxation they were in a position to display a largesse toward the more unfortu-

---

[1] Ballinger Diary, February 20 and 24, March 6, April 18, March 30, May 1, 1857, and December 25, 1860, MS.

[2] The position of the Germans in Galveston will be analyzed later in the chapter.

[3] Richardson, *Galveston Directory, 1859–60*, pp. 33–34.

nate. This fact helped to create unity in a city which was actually sharply divided into several economic, social, and racial strata.

In Galveston the absence of provincial characteristics such as marked other Texas cities was due not only to the city's maritime aspects, but also to the fact that the trading firms in the city maintained commercial and even partnership agreements with associates in the eastern cities, in Europe, in the Indies, and in Mexico. The Mills firm, for instance, owned substantial interests in trading firms in New York, England, Havana, and New Orleans.[4] The trading and banking firm of McKinney and Williams maintained contacts almost as wide as those of the Mills Company. The mercantile enterprises of the fifties, being of a much more personal nature than in modern times, tended to contribute to the social as well as to the commercial life of the city.[5]

This tendency was particularly true in the legal profession where it was the custom in Galveston for rising young lawyers periodically to make journeys to the great eastern cities, such as New York and Philadelphia, in order to make contacts with the leading merchants of those cities and to secure their legal business in Texas. These large eastern firms, which often sent large shipments of goods through the port of Galveston, were much in need of able legal talent to handle financial exchanges and to collect funds due from traders in Texas, some of whom were careless about meeting their obligations to northern and European firms.[6] For instance, in 1854 Ballinger made an extensive trip through the East in order to secure eastern legal business. In New York he enjoyed a long and pleasant afternoon with the famed Manhattan merchant A. T. Stewart. He noted that "the great Stewart was more like Robert Mills [of Mills & Company of Galveston] than anyone I can call to mind." The young Galveston attorney was particularly impressed by the fact that A. T. Stewart & Company "employed 257 persons and had 2 million dollars in gold in the bank as a cash re-

[4] Robert Mills Papers, MS; Arthur T. Lynn to C. B. Malony (Ennis, Ireland), MS, F.O.; Ballinger Papers, 1860, MS.

[5] Lynn to John F. Crompton, January 31, 1855, MS, F.O.

[6] Dan Anislie, Limited, Edinburgh to C. C. Nichols, Galveston, June 1, 1860, "Texas enjoys no enviable reputation in connection with her pecuniary transactions," in Ballinger Papers, Bundle 46, 1861, MS.

serve." Ballinger also made a successful contact at Bowen McNamee & Company despite the fact that they "were a great abolition house." He called on all the large "Texas traders" in Philadelphia, as well. While in the Quaker city he "went to Independence Hall and up on the steeple to get a view of the city" and spent "much time in the Hall —a glorious old place."[7]

These contacts, which encouraged commercial intercourse, also provided an incentive for occasional journeys by eastern businessmen to Galveston. The visits of these travelers, plus the constant presence of officers from the many merchant ships and occasionally from naval ships of a number of different nations, added such universal leveling to the social life of the city as to prompt the French traveler, Martin Maris, to remark that he found the social life in Galveston particularly "cosmopolitan."[8] These associations with northern trading, banking and particularly insurance firms continued on a limited basis even in the years of Civil War, and during the era of the reconstruction these enduring contacts were to pay generous dividends enabling the port of Galveston to make a spectacular recovery.[9]

The Galvestonian aristocrats lived a life which was luxurious in the extreme. Some indication of the manner of their life is evident from the fact that during one typical year (1858) such odd items as 23 grand pianos, $2,490 worth of silver plate, 3,665 gallons of French wine, 786 gallons of French brandy and $3,201 worth of small musical instruments were sold in the city.[10] Arthur Lynn, the British Consul, complained to the Earl of Clarendon that the luxurious standards maintained by the average family of the mercantile class in the city was so high that he found it impossible to maintain any semblance of social reciprocity with these families. The standard of living "was dearer at

[7] Ballinger Diary, entries from July 19 to September 8, 1854, MS.

[8] Martin Maris, Souvenirs d'Amerique: Relations d'un Voyage au Texas et en Haiti, pp. 89–90.

[9] Ballinger Papers, Bundles 43 and 44, 1860, and Bundle 55, 1865, MSS; Ashbel Smith to Gideon Wells, June 1865, Ballinger Papers, Bundle 55, MS; J. Ledyard Hodge, 611 Walnut Street, Philadelphia, to Ballinger, May 25, 1861, Ballinger Papers, 1861, MS.

[10] Annual Reports of British Consulate in Galveston, 1858, MS, F.O.

LOOKING SOUTHWEST down Strand from the corner of 20th Street, 1861

From a contemporary photograph in the Historical Collection, John Winterbotham Room, Rosenberg Library, Galveston, Texas.

this port" generally speaking than at any other in the United States. The annual household expense of the Vice Consul of France was $6,500 and that of th Consul of Hamburg was $4,500; on such sums these two consuls also found it most difficult to sustain their social obligations, said Lynn.[11] The British Consul, representing Her Majesty in the city, was regarded by the citizens of Galveston as the foremost of the consular corps.[12] Yet, because of the lavish manner in which many of the leading families lived, Lynn found it impossible to keep the consulate "in an approximate position with the merchants and elite of Galveston" from whom he derived information valuable to Her Majesty.[13]

There were many beautiful homes in Galveston in the fifties; the Williams, Mills, Menard, Sydnor, Ballinger, and James families, as well as many others, possessed substantial residences. The British Colonel James Fremantle, who visited Galveston in 1861, found the city's large houses "well built, its streets long, straight and shaded with trees."[14]

While the styles of many of the homes reflected the varied origins not only of their owners but also of the artisans who built them, they all exhibited certain features in common. Most were two-story, high ceilinged buildings with wide opening doors, high windows, broad veranda doors opening from upstairs rooms, and wide stairways all designed to permit the greatest possible ventilation. Homes such as these on an island which enjoys the famed cooling breezes off the Gulf were remarkably cool even during the summer season. In fact, all the homes of Galveston had very many doors and windows. Another notable feature of almost all Galveston residential construction was the raised first floor—usually several feet above the ground—which offered protec-

[11] Lynn to Earl of Clarendon, January 1, 1857, MS, F.O.
[12] Galveston *News*, December 11, 1888; Trinity Church, Galveston, Vestry Minutes, 1857–1888.
[13] Lynn to Clarendon, January 1, 1857, MS, F.O.
[14] James Arthur Lyon Fremantle, *The Fremantle Diary: Being the Journal of Lieutenant Colonel James Arthur Lyon Fremantle, Coldstream Guards, on his Three Months in the Southern States*, edited by Walter Lord, p. 55.

tion from flooding during a storm and provided additional ventilation during the summer heat.

Most of these homes had walled gardens in front or at the rear, with luxurious hedges of oleander shrubs, poinsettias, bougainvillaea, palm trees, and other tropical trees, bushes, and plants. At the rear also were usually a number of small service buildings, such as stables, wash houses, kitchens and quarters for servants—in those days mostly Negro slaves. In fact, many of the street systems of Galveston were augmented by alleys lined with very modest buildings for Negroes or other servants and sometimes with homes for the laboring calsses.

Even among the less wealthy citizens a pride in the appearance of their homes was evident. Most of the more modest homes were built of clap-board sometimes nailed upright on the structure timbers and sometimes crosswise as siding board. Even the simplest houses were kept well white-washed with lime paint or in some cases with the more expensive oil paint. All travelers to the Island were impressed by the bright whiteness of the city, especially in the clear sunlight.[15]

Like the lovely homes, entertainment in Galveston tended to be lavish. On March 7, 1859 the Houston merchant T. W. House, who loved to entertain at elaborate and unusual balls, gave a "magnificent affair" which included a great dance on board a steamer docked beside a large Galveston wharf. Before the dancing began a "sumptuous supper was served upon the many tables arranged in the spacious warehouse" adjoining the brick wharf. "In the profusion and luxury of viands and wines, and the extent and style of the general preparations, this party exceeded any ever before given in Galveston. The credit was entirely due to the liberality of the great merchant."[16]

During the winter season it was the custom for leading citizens to give a ball now and then in honor of the "military" in the city. These

[15] F. T. Fields, *Texas Sketchbook: A Collection of Historical Stories from the Humble Way*, pp. 26–27. Works Projects Administration, *Texas: A Guide to the Lone Star State*, compiled by workers of the writers' program of the Works Projects Administration in the State of Texas, American Guide Series, pp. 272–280.

[16] Galveston *Civilian*, March 8, 1859; Houston *Telegraph*, March 7, 1859.

balls, given in the Tremont Hotel, represented a tribute by the sponsor to the officers and the men who made up the various militia units. At these social functions all classes of citizens joined in the festivities consisting of "fine food, speeches, and dancing."[17]

An afternoon tea with the "urbane Robert Mills" meant "fine talk of homes, books and trade" and often playing dominoes until dinner time and even on into the evening.[18]

Sometimes, there were more serious occasions such as the one which found Ballinger and his family in the Episcopal Church christening the newborn baby girl of his law partner Tom Jack. Ballinger and his wife Hally stood as sponsors. "Don't believe in the church," said Ballinger, "but I do in the baby, God bless her little soul." And that evening he dined at the home of Robert Mills; later they went downtown and, for the sport of it, had their "heads examined" by the phrenologist Professor Fowler.[19]

On a wedding anniversary, "Nannie, K, and Charlotte James got up a surprise party" at Ballinger's house. "Laura was in on the secret but none of the rest heard of it until near sun down." Cake, champagne, music and a great crowd enlivened this occasion. "It was the pleasantest party" Ballinger had ever attended.[20] The next evening Ballinger and "Uncle Jimmy" (James Love) locked themselves in the jurist's study where they talked quietly or slept most of the time in the easy chairs.[21] A few weeks later Ballinger and Uncle Jimmy were entertaining thirty-five guests at a three dollar dinner served at the Tremont Hotel in honor of Judge Peter W. Gray. It was a "splendid banquet, everybody gave fine toasts and enjoyed the talk."[22]

On New Year's Eve, 1859, Judge Thompson gave a party for his friends in the city, and on this occasion the colored servant created such a remarkable bowl of Regent's Punch that Ballinger asked for the recipe, which follows:

[17] Ballinger Diary, January 23, 1857, MS.
[18] *Ibid.*, February 27, March 6, and April 18, 1857.
[19] *Ibid.*, March 9, 1859.
[20] *Ibid.*, March 30, 1857.
[21] *Ibid.*, May 1, 1857.
[22] *Ibid.*, June 6 and 13, 1860.

3 tablespoons of currant jelly
1 quart brandy
1 quart whiskey
1 quart champagne
4 lemons
sugar
1 ½ quarts clear old green tea—very strong
3 slices of ripe pineapple which will impart a fine flavor[23]

On the same New Year's evening, another party was given at the Tremont Hotel by "a Texas cattleman." This gathering was also to be the scene of his wedding: fifty couples and a magistrate were assembled at the party and the wedding was about to be performed when it was revealed that "the bride was a young man and that most of the wedding presents were a variety of liquors" which made them most suitable for the occasion.[24] In the same spirit, the Houston Bachelor's Club gave "their First Grand Ball" in Galveston with the hope that the festivities would lead to a "reduction of their membership"[25]—and such may well have happened. But the bachelors for some reason passed by a very British young lady, Miss Elizabeth Pressnell, who had "come to Texas hoping to find a pleasant and a better life and also a man." As neither of these most desired expectations had visited themselves upon her, Miss Presnell desired most urgently to return to Britain, but by that time her funds were gone. She pleaded with Consul Lynn in Galveston to secure enough funds from Her Majesty to send a spinster, who had been disappointed by the "prospects" in the Lone Star Empire, back to the more genteel society of the British Isles. The good consul arranged the matter.[26]

What exactly comprised Miss Pressnell's grievance against Galveston was not explained, but perhaps an insight into her point of view may be drawn from the assertion made by editor Richardson that social life on the Island was "without any excess of that straight-laced blue-law puritanism which thinks itself pious when it is only bilious."[27] Cer-

[23] *Ibid.*, January 9, 1859.   [24] Houston *Telegraph*, January 7, 1859.
[25] Galveston *News*, December 3, 1857.
[26] Lynn to Elizabeth Pressnell, May 19, 1858, MS, F.O.
[27] Galveston *News*, May 28, 1857.

tainly Galveston in the fifties was a city in which the residents and the visitors enjoyed themselves. The Island was the mecca for fraternal conventions. Galvestonians supported chapters of most of the innumerable brotherhoods which were the fashion in the nineteenth century. Hardly a week passed without finding the city host to marchers, singers, and bands. The horse-livery business during the "season" was one of the most lucrative in the city. Driving "briskly" along the "shelled and daily watered" boulevards and through the oleander parks with an occasional pause to hear the German bands and to "partake" of German sausage and pretzels was reason enough for the brotherhoods to come to Galveston. It was the reason, too, why British sailors "so often jumped ship and decided to become Texans."[28]

Galvestonians loved festival days such as the Fourth of July, May Day, Election Day, and Christmas—the last being a most exuberant time on the Island. "Galveston is wonderful at Yule tide," wrote one correspondent during the Christmas week of 1859, "the four book stores are doing a big business in selling books from all over the world." Each of the four stores sold at least "$1,000 worth of books a day" and even the smaller dealers sold $250 worth of printed products a day. All the stores were open until nine at night and were "beautifully illuminated with gas." The gift and "book business [was] highly prosperous in Galveston."[29] The Lyceum theatre, during the Yule period, was "a flourishing success"; the "young men's association," a club with "large rooms including a library," was also a center of a continuing Yule tide spirit; the "streets were in a fine condition" for carriage racing; the "gardens [were] preparing for spring operations"; the big market house, "a neat and spacious structure," was aglow with candles and cheer; and the "eleven church edifices" were alight, as

[28] Lynn to J. O. Trueheart, Justice of the Peace in Galveston February 2, 7, and March 15, 1860, MS, F.O.

[29] Houston *Telegraph*, December 26, 1859. Richardson of the *News* noting, two years before, the large sale of books in Galveston, remarked that a large sale of books did not indicate a rising culture in the city, since many of the works sold were only "extravagant works of fiction which would not promote literary taste." These cheap works, he said, were selling at an "alarming" rate. Galveston *News*, November 5, 1857.

GALVESTON HARBOR, looking west from 20th and Strand, 1861

From a contemporary photograph in the Historical Collection, John Winterbotham Room, Rosenberg Library, Galveston, Texas.

well, with the glory of the season.[30] That was the Christmas when the Houston editor, Cushing, excited by a rare snowfall, exclaimed in delight, "Snowballing on Main Street, our fingers are tingling as in boyhood; all hands had a good time trying to run gauntlets" down the streets.[31]

Election Day was another exciting festival in Galveston. On no other day was there "greater activity in the streets," with "carriages incessantly passing and repassing to and from the polls all covered with the names of the opposing candidates displayed on banners or immense placards." The numerous "candidates and their friends, constituting a large portion of the population, commenced their labors early in the day and did not rest until the polls closed." Yet, despite the interest manifested, there were never instances of "disturbance or quarreling in any part of the city." Galveston had "a well deserved reputation for orderly elections."[32]

The laying of the cornerstone for a new building was always the occasion for a celebration; thus, on Sunday, June 7, 1857, Galvestonians turned out to christen a new fire-engine house. The three fire companies paraded in full uniform, the Masons in "full regalia" were close behind, and these were followed by most of the other brotherhoods in the city. After a speech by the postmaster, H. B. Andrews, "the city papers and other documents were placed in the cornerstone."[33]

The "May Day" festivities were the particular concern of the very young ladies of the city. As the lush spring in Galveston reached its fullest bloom at the approach of May, "the young misses of Galveston [commenced] their usual flutter in preparation for the anniversary of the Goddess of Flowers." The Morian Hall was to be converted into a great flower garden to display the beauty, not only of the flowers, but of the young ladies as well.[34]

The long wait between May Day and July 4th, during which no completely satisfactory excuse existed for a celebration, sometimes taxed the patience of the average Galvestonian; "there is nothing to

[30] Houston *Telegraph*, December 26, 1859 (Galveston Correspondent, "B").
[31] *Ibid.*, December 5, 1859.   [32] Galveston *News*, March 3, 1857.
[33] Galveston *Herald*, June 7, 1859.
[34] Galveston *Civilian*, May 5, 1857.

break the monotony of the bayside," wrote one citizen during the month of June, in 1857, "but the occasional backing off the wharf by a careless drayman, or the jumping overboard of an unruly steer, who is opposed to patronizing the Vanderbilt Line." June was the time, he said, "to take things leisurely" in Galveston.[35]

The grand festival of the summer season was the Fourth of July. The sum of $250 had been invested in fireworks for the 1857 celebration; "something grand may be expected" was the prediction, and this was not an exaggeration. At sunrise a 13-gun salute awakened the elders of Galveston—the children were already awake. By eight o'clock the "civic and military bodies began to form" and by eight-thirty all was ready for the "grand march." Every club in the city including "five temperance orders" was in the columns. More than 3,000 adults and 800 children paraded. As darkness began to fall toward evening, Captain Crawford's "pyrotechnic balls of fire went whizzing, hissing, and roaring" over the bay "in combinations of sulphurous light which were grand and fantastically beautiful." And later in the evening as the spectacle of the fire display began to pale the Galvestonians gathered "at Schmidt's saloon, in the garden where charming music and lively dance prevailed until the captain of the night watch struck twelve ominous strokes on the town bell announcing the close of our 81st annual national anniversary and the advent of another Holy Sabbath day." The two "magnificent German bands" put away their instruments and the exciting day closed with the moonlight still glistening on the flickering waters of the Bay.[36]

To enliven the dull interludes between the festivals the ordinary Galvestonian, who did not own a large house surrounded by an oleander garden or a carriage to ride along the beach or a boat to sail upon the bay, was sometimes tempted by the beckoning lure of the "dancing academies" in Galveston. To assist those willing to venture into an affair of social improvement and opportunity, a dancing academy was operated by the "Misses Rachel & Irene Ewing in Pix's Hall." These young ladies undertook to teach Galvestonians any of the newest

[35] Galveston *Herald*, June 11, 1857.

[36] Galveston *Herald*, July 1 and 7, 1857; Houston *Telegraph*, July 6, 1857; Galveston *Civilian*, July 3 and 5, 1857.

dances, such as the "Polka de salon, Redowa, Varsovia, Le Reine de Dance, l'Imperial, Mazurkas, German polkas, and a variety of dances." On the second and fourth Fridays of each month "The Misses Ewing gave cotillion parties"; the charge on these occasions was $1.50 per person.[37] The editor of the *News* asserted that "these young ladies are giving great satisfaction to all who patronize them; Miss Rachel and Miss Irene can teach both the young and the middle aged to dance." Miss Rachel, in fact, had just returned from New Orleans where she had learned "all the mazes and movements of the most fashionable dances."[38] As a result of this social training and the opportunity for lasting social adventure arising therefrom, "Mr. James E. Brown" placed an advertisement in the press stating that he "respectfully informed" any interested persons that his marriage would take place at Spence's Hall and that he invited anyone who wished to attend his wedding to do so for it would also include a supper and a "cotillion dance."[39] After the dance—or perhaps while it was still in progress —couples slipped out next door to enjoy special refreshments at "Lewis & Kemp's new Ice Cream and Sherbet Saloon" which had just opened on Tremont Street.[40]

There were, however, romances in the city which originated in more elevated surroundings than those provided by the dancing schools or ice cream parlors. In October of 1860, the wealthy widow of Michael B. Menard, the founder of Galveston and heavy stockholder in the Galveston Wharf Company, was wooed and won by Colonel J. S. Thrasher, a former United States Consul at Havana and sometime newspaper man. William Pitt Ballinger, attorney managing some of the Menard property, appraised Colonel Thrasher as "a man of ability but also an adventurer in politics and matrimony." The Menard family had had "a great row with Helen over the matter and are in a state of high excitement,"[41] he said.

The middle-class white-collar citizens and the mechanic groups had

[37] Galveston *News*, April 28, 1857.   [38] *Ibid.*, January 27, 1857.

[39] Houston *Telegraph*, June 15, 1857.

[40] Galveston *News*, June 18, 1857.

[41] Ballinger Diary, October 21, 1860, MS; J. S. Thrasher to Ballinger, September 21, 1862, Ballinger Papers, Bundle 46, 1862, MS.

some difficulty maintaining a respectable standard of living in Galveston where most "articles of use except meat" were imported. The "salaries of clerks in a merchant's office varied from $1,200 to $2,000 per annum."[42] There were labor organizations among the journeymen printers and the mechanics in Galveston and in Houston during the late fifties. Early in March of 1857, the printers in Galveston formed an organization in order to secure higher pay from the *Civilian* and the *News*. The secretary of the Union was W. Cherry; other leading members were A. M. Dunn, J. Helfenstein, A. O. Bade, O. F. Zinke, Louis Bernard and John Sleven. The stated purpose of the union was "to fix prices for their work."[43] The printers demanded a rate of "50¢ per 1,000 ems." Both the Galveston newspapers opposed the union's demands on the grounds that printers in Galveston could not "expect to get Northern prices." The prevailing scale in Galveston of $8 to $17 per week, depending upon the skill of the type setter, was, according to both publishers, the highest scale which sound economics justified. The organization of printers did not succed in raising their rate of pay; nevertheless, the editorial comment on the Gulf Coast as to the printers' right to organize was respectful and, in the case of the Galveston and Houston papers, cordial.[44] The mechanics in Galveston and Houston also held an organizational meeting in June of 1857 in order to consider "matters pertaining to their mutual aid." The members, after concluding that mechanics' reading rooms and clubs should be established in the two cities, appointed a committee, made up of J. B. Hogan, Andrew Daly, Frank Powers, W. Stansbury, Ralph Hooker and Andrew Gammell, to carry forward their program.[45] A few days later further meetings were held at the court house in Houston on June 25th and June 26th. James B. Hogan, who was elected as a marshal, again mobilized the Houston mechanics at a mass meeting on the evening of July 2, 1857, in order to arrange for a giant parade in the city on the Fourth of July.[46]

[42] Lynn to Clarendon, January 21, 1857, MS, F.O.
[43] Galveston *News*, March 7, 1857.
[44] *Ibid.*, March 7, 21, and June 16, 1857.
[45] Houston *Telegraph*, June 15 and 24, 1857.
[46] *Ibid.* It would appear that the purpose for the Mechanics' Association was

While Galvestonians enjoyed religious worship, economic prosperity, and social pleasures, they were continually fretful over what they conceived to be their intellectual shortcomings with regard to schools, libraries, theatres, lyceums, and debating societies. Although the various private homes and a few of the clubs, such as those maintained by the Germans, had substantial libraries for that time, the city of Galveston itself had no library. Actually, there was not a very great need for one since those among the social groups who had a serious desire to read could very easily have borrowed a variety of books from the libraries in private homes. Ballinger, for instance, had some 2,000 volumes in his personal collection by 1860, much of it representing the great works of Greece, Rome, Europe and England.[47] The city fathers and others during the fifties, however, made several efforts to organize a city library and a debating society. The results were not encouraging.[48]

The one outstanding contribution to "culture and intellectual achievement" and a satisfaction to the city was "the grand exhibition" of the graduates and the continuing students at St. Mary's College at the close of the August term. On these proud occasions a great crowd of citizens gathered at the college to witness "the extended proceedings" which included a "large distribution of premiums to the sons and daughters of many of the leading families in the city." Recognition was given to students who had shown a definite proficiency in such subjects as "Latin, Mathematics, Declamation, Philosophy, Astronomy, English Composition, Bookkeeping and Flute." A similar "grand exhibition" was held, as well, for the younger students in July at the Ursuline Convent. Usually a total of some 200 premiums were given out annually by the college and the convent. During these "extended presentations" the "German band opened the programs and played its customary exquisite music." On the day following these "inspiring

---

actually similar to that of a social or fraternal society rather than one to exert pressure upon employers for higher wages.

[47] Ballinger Diary, 1858–1865, MS, plus his papers for the same years indicate the size of his library.

[48] Galveston *News*, December 8 and 22, 1857; Galveston *Civilian*, December 15 and 23, 1857.

presentations" the Galveston newspapers always appeared to be less fretful over the lack of intellectual display in the city and appeared for the time being, at least, more assured that the younger generation was not going to grow up to be as illiterate as the editors had previously feared.[49] On the whole, however, this optimism was usually very short lived.

In addition to teaching the elements of the sciences and the arts, the schools of Galveston also endeavored to instill in the young a wish to live the good and moral life. *The New Texas Reader,* published by E. H. Cushing of Houston and used in Galveston, was designed to teach morals as well as reading. Narratives bearing such titles as "Honesty and Faith," "Go Regularly to School," and "The Frontier Boy" served to illustrate the "right way." A tale of "The Insolent Boy" provided an illustration of what might well be expected if a boy chose the "wrong way," and the tearful story of "The Little Flower Girl" made many young Galvestonians realize the good fortune they enjoyed by possessing a snug home on the Island provided for them by "their loving parents."

Another lesson, important during the war years, related to the tradegy of the fall of Galveston: "Thus the Queen City of the Lone Star State was surrendered to our Yankee foes." Following directly after this one, in the later editions, was a stirring narrative of the recapture of the Island. But the children of the city had been told, even before the realistically tragic lessons which the war brought, that life has its bitter side: they had all read many times the awe-awakening facts so fearfully illustrated in "Lesson Number 18—Little Willie is Dead." For children who lived on an island enduring a fearful child mortality, "Lesson Number 18" must have evoked a sobering pathos in many a Galveston school room.[50]

Unfortunately the volume of youthful traffic moving down the "right way" was not as large as it should have been. Editor Cushing, the stout advocate of discipline and of better schools on the Gulf Coast, pointed out that less than a third of the youth between six and sixteen

---

[49] *Ibid.,* August 4, 1857 and August 10, 1858; Houston *Telegraph,* September 2 and 9, 1859.

[50] E. H. Cushing, *The New Texas Reader: Designed for Use in the Schools.*

were in school in Galveston and Houston. "What is to be their destiny?" he asked.[51] Two years later, in 1858, Cushing still pressed his query, "Where are the youth of Houston?" They were not in school; the "most reliable data" indicated that there were at that time 1,000 to 1,100 school-age youths in Houston, but less than 200 were in school; the rest, he said, "get only a street education." The situation in Galveston was no better than in Houston; there was a sufficient number of schools and teachers in both cities. So "Why aren't the children in school?" Cushing asked the collective elders of the two cities.[52]

An attraction offered by one institution in Galveston to keep the young people off the streets was the "Big Baptist Fair at Morian Hall." "Go forth," said the notice in the *Civilian,* "with your pockets full and try the games of chance."[53] There were, however, in Galveston three "precocious rascals," who completely rejected the lessons provided by *The New Texas Reader* and who, not being appeased by the adventure provided at the "Big Baptist Fair," broke into "Mr. Kinkleday's confectionery" and committed "mischief in the sweet meats." Later the same evening, they continued their "precocious rascality" by "helping themselves to 'segars' and nine dollars at a restaurant near Briggs & Yard."[54]

There were Galvestonians, other than precocious juveniles, whose respect for the customs of accepted behavior left much to be desired. One shocking example was the "Reverend Scoundrel," a self-styled clergyman named Christopher Columbus Jones who had arrived in Galveston from Paris, in Lamar County, in 1856. This person, during a year on the Island, had at first "saved a lot of souls and then purchased a horse, carriage and everything else he wanted on credit." While it was acknowledged in the city that the Reverend Christopher Columbus Jones was "a most verbose man," this characteristic of his was endured as the necessary endowment of a person engaged in turning backsliders from the ways of sin. But when, one spring morning in 1857, it was discovered that "the Reverend" had "eloped with the wife of one of the most respectable citizens of the city," the astonished Galvestonians,

---

[51] Houston *Telegraph,* March 10, 1856.
[52] *Ibid.,* December 19, 1858.   [53] Galveston *Civilian,* June 9, 1857.
[54] *Ibid.,* October 5, 1858.

after catching their breaths, thereafter referred to the departed Jones as the "Reverend Scoundrel."[55]

There were also "lay" scoundrels who followed the call to the thriving port of Galveston; "every steam boat brings in more sharp traders" warned Stuart in the *Civilian* in 1858. Only yesterday, he said, "The Strap Game took a country man for $400." This visitation of "suspicious river men should be dealt with firmly," declared the editor.[56] But the "River men" moved fast and were often far ahead of the "discipline" pursuing them.

"Look out for counterfeit $50 notes on the Union Bank of Louisiana" warned Cushing in Houston. These counterfeit notes coming up the Bay from Galveston were "better printed" than the real ones.[57] A year later, in June, 1857, Houstonians were still wary of counterfeit money being brought in by the "sharp traders,"[58] and by December, "many Houstonians were being caught" by a very dangerous counterfeit which had "appeared on the Commercial & Agricultural Bank at Galveston."[59]

There were other "sharp traders" in addition to the "River men." Respectable citizens of the Island were being accused of "claim stealing"; some Galvestonians were "selling their souls for a little more land."[60] In 1859 an Englishman named Fred Ogden purchased a large amount of "land scrip" from men who represented themselves as Texans from Galveston. When Ogden tried to arrange to have the land surveyed he discovered that the scrip was all fraudulent, "a very common thing in Texas," he was informed by A. F. James of Galveston, the "finest land lawyer in Texas."[61] Some "land stealers" had at least a partial integrity. A squatter named Seaborn Hopper wrote to Oscar Farish, a fine old gentleman in Galveston who owned a nice piece of timber land at Pin Oaks, stating, "this is to inform you that I have built me a camp on the piece of land you own here." Hopper explained that he hoped Farish would permit him to buy the land as he

---

[55] Galveston *News*, March 12, 1857.
[56] Galveston *Civilian*, April 27, 1858.
[57] Houston *Telegraph*, April 9, 1856.   [58] *Ibid.*, June 3, 1857.
[59] *Ibid.*, December 30, 1857.   [60] Galveston *Civilian*, June 9, 1857.
[61] Lynn to Fred Ogden (Manchester), May 3, 1859, MS, F.O.

was "old and poor and without a home." The old squatter assured Farish that he would "not injure anything on the land until I hear from you."[62] Other squatters were not as ethical; "some men sneaked in and cut a lot of timber off our land," wrote E. C. Jones of Galveston to his lawyers, "what should we do about it?"[63] And sometimes even one's lawyers could not be trusted. "The most disagreeable portion of my duties at this consulate has been the investigation of administrators and acts of attorneys to whom authority has been granted by the heirs of estates," wrote Arthur Lynn from the British Consulate in Galveston.[64]

There were Texans in the interior who looked upon Galveston Island as a "den of sin aggravated by flagrant drinking." Inlanders of this persuasion could point to the case of Robert Galer, "a drummer," who, while stopping at the Tremont House in Galveston had committed "suicide in a fit of delirium tremens" and his body had tumbled off the high veranda.[65] Another similar case was that of "a Mr. A. C. Williams, a drummer for a plough company who died of delirium tremens" on the veranda of the same hotel.[66] In Houston a traveling prohibition lecturer, for the edification of his large and respectable audience, explained on "a scientific basis" what was actually befalling the Galvestonians who used excessive amounts of liquor. The same fate, he predicted, would surely befall reckless Houstonians as well. According to the professor, excessive use of alcohol turned "brains into a hardened substance." This chemical result taking place in the cranium of a drinking man "dries up all the fountains of generous feeling, petrifies all the tender humanities, leaving only a brain of lead and a heart of stone."[67] Unfortunately, Galvestonians failed to heed the warnings of the temperance society lecturers who tried to reform the "Queen

[62] Seaborn Hopper to Oscar Farish, September 22, 1860, Ballinger Papers, Bundle for 1860, MS.

[63] E. C. Jones to M. M. Potter, August 21, 1860, Ballinger Papers, Bundle for 1860, MS.

[64] Lynn to Charles S. Hughes, January 25, 1860, MS, F.O.; Lynn to Mrs. D. S. White, Clinton (De Witt County, England), March 31, 1860, MS, F.O.

[65] Galveston *News*, March 28, 1857.

[66] *Ibid.*, January 27, 1857.

[67] Houston *Telegraph*, March 4, 1857.

City on the Gulf." A jury in a trial held on the Island in 1859 decided that a citizen hauled into court for being intoxicated could not have been in that condition since he had been drinking only "lager beer." A Houston editor commenting on this decision observed that apparently lager beer was not an intoxicating beverage in Galveston; "drink a barrel of it, even if it makes you drunk you aren't drunk."[68] From the point of view of the inlanders, moral standards appeared to be deteriorating on the Island as the decade closed. They noted with considerable interest a spectacular murder which occurred on a hot August night in 1859. The victim in this affair was a rooming-house keeper, Mrs. Chamberlain. The lady, reported to be of questionable virtue, was killed by her estranged husband who immediately afterward committed suicide. The excitement resulting from these events in the boardinghouse caused such "a panic among the young lady roomers" that a public spectacle ensued. The inland newspapers reported the scene occurring in Galveston in phrases which raised some questions as to the standards of moral conduct prevailing in the Queen City.[69]

If the attraction of earthly pleasures had taken command of the attention of too many Galvestonians, as the inlanders alleged, this lamentable situation had not developed without arousing the criticism of the temperance societies on the Island. These organizations with the aid of the Methodist churches in Galveston brought "Dr. Ross, the great temperance lecturer" to the port in an effort to turn the interest of the wayward Islanders toward better things. Dr. Ross' "manner was bold and impetuous"; he took "strong ground and seemed to carry his audiences with him." This reformer spoke longer than "two hours from the heart at each address," and yet it seems he failed to purify the hearts and interests of the Islanders.[70] Even after the good doctor's exhortations some could still find it in their hearts to continue living their customary lives and to attend such scarcely uplifting "exhibitions" as the one in which "Miss Fanny Cottone appeared in a most

[68] *Ibid.*, January 14, 1859.
[69] *Ibid.*, August 17, 1859.
[70] Galveston *Civilian*, March 12, 1857.

captivating dance and was applauded to the very echo," and to watch "little Miss Ewing" in her "very successful" demonstrations of "the poetry of motion."[71]

Fortunately there was more elevating theatrical fare available on the Island, such as "Apollo Minstrels" who performed "before full houses" for several weeks in the city; and on December 17th at the height of the pre-Christmas season a memorable concert was given by this troupe "for Bones," the favorite minstrel with the Islanders.[72] On another great occasion "the famed Mountain Minstrels," a troupe of singers from the French Alps, gave "a grand concert assisted by Professor Zorn." These great "artists" had previously performed at the "Courts of England, France, Germany and Russia."[73] During the 1857 "season" a "traveling company" with a repertory of plays opened at Theodore Neitch's Opera House, under the management of J. Barry Strong. This aggregation boasted in the newspapers of the fact that their troupe contained "Lucy Cutter and Howard Athenaeum of Boston, Miss Lotty St. Clair, late of Memphis, Mrs. W. B. Chippendale, late of New York City, Miss Ella Farley, late of St. Louis, M. J. Barry of New York and Boston, and Mr. W. B. Chippendale, comedian, and graduate of Old Park Theatre, New York." The cost of the tickets to see and hear these artists was listed as follows: boxes—$1, dress circle —75 cents, and gallery—25 cents.[74]

William Pitt Ballinger attended the several attractions presented in the city during the "fifty-seven–fifty-eight season." Finally, on March 30th, 1858, he wrote a general evaluation of what he had seen for Stuart's *Civilian*. After noting that the theatre bills announced that the performance that evening would be the last of the season, Ballinger said that he reiterated this item "gratuitously and with pleasure." During the last three months, he wrote, "the performances at this resort have been a libel on the town and an insult to intelligent people." Any grand jury which could "sit in the boxes" of the Galveston Theatre

[71] *Ibid.*, December 5, 1857.
[72] *Ibid.*, November 24, and December 17, 1858.
[73] *Ibid.*, July 7 and 14, 1857; Houston *Telegraph*, July 20, 1857.
[74] Galveston *Civilian*, December 19, 1857.

"without judging a true bill against the whole concern as a nuisance would be unfit to perform their duty." The only "legitimate drama that we have had," he said, was "Donnetti's 'Acting Monkeys', and they were bad enough God knows." It was time, he asserted, that the people of Galveston "learned to frown upon these clap-trap clowns, and cease patronizing every humbug announced in flaming hand bills." Galvestonians, being a prosperous and pleasure-loving people, he wrote, were "emphatically a show-ridden people, and the dimes flow alike into the coffers of those who exhibit a monstrosity in the shape of a bearded woman or an equally unnatural burlesque of the histrionic art."[75]

The sorry exhibitions presented during the 1857–1858 season aroused a few men in the city who loved the theatre to endeavor to raise the standard of the offerings in the "Temple of Thespis" during the next season. Under the leadership of Willard Richardson, an avid theatergoer, and others likewise interested, "a small but good company of players" headed by Ada Logan presented a "stock company season" in the city. Other members of the organization were "Mrs. Bussell, Mr. Keene, Mr. Knowles, and Mr. Ferris." The opening performance, given on January 25, 1859 to "a large audience," received press notices praising the company as "quite passable" and the reviewer for the *Civilian* suggested that a successful "stock company" season could be expected. On February 1st, a rendition of Shakespeare's *Taming of the Shrew* with Miss Logan as Catherine and Mr. Ferris as Petruchio convinced Galvestonians that the company was even better than it had appeared to be the first week. On the strength of these successes more actors from New Orleans were brought into the company and the list of future offerings announced such plays as *Barrack Room, Young Widow, Rough Diamond, The Golden Farmer,* and *The Persecuted Dutchman.* As the "season" moved on, more plays were presented in rapid succession; among the titles seen were *Soldiers Daughter, Still Waters Run Deep, Perfection or the Maid of Munster, Lady of Lyons, The Hunchback, The Man Without a Head,* and *Lucretia Borgia*—the last-named being a "splendid performance" given to a "brilliant house"

---

[75] *Ibid.*, March 30, 1858.

which appeared to appreciate the political skill of this Venetian "stateswoman."[76] Later, Julia Dean also performed in the city.[77]

Sometimes the circuses came to the Island. One of these arrived on April 15, 1857. The animals and the company were debarked from the steamer at the brick wharf and formed into a parade of fifteen horses, three lions, two leopards, a zebra, a bear, a llama, James Robinson—the daring bareback horseman, a giant Indian, and "a fat girl who would yield about three barrels of No. 1 soap."[78] The next year, 1858, Buckley & Company Circus came to the city featuring the bareback "marvels, Robinson & Wood" performing in a "big tent which seated 2,500 persons."[79]

While the Germans in the city provided the Islanders with much music, traveling performers also displayed their accomplishments in the city. A pianist who presented her repertoire regularly at Morian Hall was Madame Sieminsky; "well known—no praise needed" was the reception usually given her in the press.[80] Sometimes "Morrison's Ballade Troupe" stopped at the Island on the way through to the interior and sang some "very laughable and entertaining songs."[81] There were evenings when "The Peak Family Swiss Bell Ringers" assisted by Madame Anna Bishop, "the world-renowned cantatrice," gave concerts in the city.[82] During the Christmas season the members of the Austin Singing Society often gave concerts;[83] and on Friday and Saturday evenings, September 28th and 29th, 1860, Mrs. Sally Reinhardt and Professor Joseph Schultze gave a "grand vocal and instrumental concert" for the Islanders.[84] At one time, in 1857, the well-known "Madame Louie & Troupe," a company of fourteen "very professional

[76] Galveston *Civilian*, January 18 and 25, and February 1, 8, 10, 15, and 18, 1859.

[77] Philip C. Tucker, "History of Galveston, 1543–1869," MS, VIII.

[78] Galveston *Civilian*, April 17, 1857.

[79] *Ibid.*, December 14 and 21, 1858.

[80] *Ibid.*, August 6 and 11, 1857.

[81] Houston *Telegraph*, March 21, 1859.

[82] Broadside announcing a concert on the evening of April 11, 1860, Texas History Center, Austin, Texas.

[83] Houston *Telegraph*, December 11, 1860.

[84] *Ibid.*, September 28 and 29, 1860.

singers," stepped off from the Mobile and New Orleans steamer to present a "flashing" concert that greatly entertained the Galvestonians. Yet, despite the artistry of these performers, it was the opinion of E. H. Cushing that the finest music he had encountered at the "cosmopolitan Queen City" was a company of three strolling musicians from the Mediterranean. This trio consisted of two harpists and one violinist who "discoursed in as sweet and beautiful a melody" as he had ever heard from those who made great claims to artistry.[85]

Culture and the arts were not the only intellectual activities which interested Galvestonians during this period. "Science" of one sort or another was also a fascinating subject. The vogue of spiritualism which swept across the nation during the fifties aroused some ardent devotees among those Islanders who possessed a speculative bent, a portion of gullibility, and a wish to ride in the vanguard with so illustrious, though abolitionist, a group as New England's Concord intellectuals. In 1857 the "adherents" brought "Mr. A. I. Ambler" to the city to deliver "a course of spiritual lectures." E. H. Cushing, who treasured an open though skeptical mind, noted that the "lecturer" was "highly spoken of by the adherents of this new philosophy"; however, Cushing refused to venture an opinion regarding this strange phenomenon until he had learned more about it.[86] Richardson of the *News* wrote of the great "phenomenon" as a matter best approached with a tolerant and benevolent good humor. To illustrate his adherence to Voltaire's great principle, he printed a long letter written to the *News* by the editor of the Lockhart *Watchman* vigorously supporting the veracity of those who claimed to be in contact with the spirit world.[87] For the most part, however, neither the *News* nor the *Civilian* opened their columns to the few ardent letter-writing Galvestonians who advocated a respectful hearing for the disciples of the approaching *rapprochement* with the spirit world. Facing this impasse the "advocates" flooded the office of Cushing's Houston *Telegraph* with long letters which were in effect dissertations; replies were written by "scoffing skeptics" and by angry fundamentalists who were aroused by the "new heresy."

[85] *Ibid.*, February 23, 1857.
[86] *Ibid.*, January 30 and March 16, 1857.
[87] Galveston *News*, February 14, 1857.

Finally, Cushing had endured enough; he published a notice stating that no more "pro & con" letter writing regarding the spirit world would appear in the *Telegraph*: "We beg to be excused from keeping our columns open to this discussion longer." These advocates, wrote Cushing, may be in nightly contact with the ancient Greeks, but he "begged to doubt it."[88] Cushing, nevertheless, kept a weather eye upon the "phenomena." While he had been revolted by the native Galvestonian devotees of spiritualism, he was none the less impressed by the activities of the young spirit-instilled maidens, such as Margaret and Kate Fox, who were then appearing in New York City. Cushing was particularly impressed by another young medium, a "Miss Cora Hatch," who, in May of 1857, was holding the attention of immense crowds in the great eastern cities. "She is young, about 17 years old, accomplished," and "very beautiful," wrote Cushing. There was, indeed, at least nothing lost by a pause to ask how it was possible for so youthful a maiden to hold the attention of great crowds in so cosmopolitan a city.[89] And two years later, in 1859, the learned jurist Ballinger paused to note in his diary that "Dr. Sims, a strong spiritualist, gave me a list of books to read on the subject."[90]

The late fifties in Galveston provided other illustrations of local reactions to the scientific, and intellectual renaissance sweeping the nation in the mid-century. The lectures on the subject of "Electro-biology" delivered by "Professor Hale" to audiences which filled the Third Presbyterian Church illustrated the city's interest in scientific phenomena. This new science, said the professor, put into the hands of its practitioners the power to "destroy the individuality of the human mind." The great danger to civilization confronting the modern world in this new and unprecedented situation could be seen in the fact that a practitioner wielding the tools of "Electro-biology" could "make strong men obey his slightest wish." The "scientific" world was faced with the sobering realization that "Electro-biology has . . . upset many fine theories on the individuality of the human mind."[91] Since

[88] Houston *Telegraph*, January 30 and February 4, 1857.
[89] *Ibid.*, May 20, 1857.
[90] Ballinger Diary, August 31, 1859, MS.
[91] Galveston *Civilian*, March 22, 1858.

the professor's lectures, which created an intellectual sensation in the city, aroused too much effervescence to remain confined within the modest walls of the Third Presbyterian Church, his "series" on the "scientific" aspects of "Electro-biology" was presented at various other halls in the city including the several oral dissertations which were delivered to distinguished gentlemen in the large public rooms at the Court House. In fact, the days intervening between the professor's opening lecture on March 22nd, to his memorable closing presentation on April 13, 1858, marked a period of most unusual intellectual discussion on the Island during a decade when such periods of "renaissance" were not at all uncommon.[92]

The mental ferment aroused in the city by Professor Hale had not even begun to subside when "Professor Smith from Kentucky" stepped off the steamer from New Orleans to deliver a series of lectures on the "philosophy of the Science of Animal Magnetism." These lectures opened the door to the "wonders of human electricity for the lovers of science in Galveston."[93] After finishing his series on this subject, the professor then consented to remain for a second series in which he explained the science of phrenology. The high light of this series was his examination of "Mr. Reed's skull"—an examination which proved to be "true to the letter."[94] The science of phrenology was not without continuing patrons thereafter in Galveston. In March of 1859 "Professor O. S. Fowler, the greatest phrenologist now living" was "called" to Galveston to deliver a two-week series of lectures on the subject. The public response on the Island was very great. Cushing came down from Houston to hear the professor and returned to declare that if the scientist could be induced to come to the inland city he would be assured of "full houses for the course."[95] It was during this professor's "series" that William Pitt Ballinger happened to dine at the home of Robert Mills in celebration of the latter's birthday, and the lush wines having created a festive and "spoofing" mood, the two gentlemen went to town and had their "heads examined by Professor Fowler."[96]

[92] *Ibid.*, March 30 and April 13, 1858.
[93] *Ibid.*, April 20, 1858.   [94] *Ibid.*, April 27, 1858.
[95] Houston *Telegraph*, March 4, 1859.
[96] Ballinger Diary, March 9, 1859, MS.

There were occasions in the city and on the Gulf Coast when "series courses" other than those concerned with the "new scientific" developments or with the new revelations in the realm of the spirit world commanded the attention of Galveston intellectuals; one of these was the memorable series delivered by Alexander Keech on the "History of Civilization."[97] Nevertheless, the calming and quieting fact that civilization had already been in existence for a few thousand years and perhaps might possibly continue to exist was blurred by the disturbing aspects of "Electro-biology" and "the wonders of human electricity" to say nothing of the strange manifestations which had recently protruded out of the "spirit world." And thrust into the midst of these apprehensions came the additional disturbances arising from the uncertainty regarding the approach of Donati's Comet. It was in these circumstances, according to the Galveston *News,* that a well-known German gentleman in the city but not named by the newspaper, "went crazy from apprehensions of danger from the comet."[98] The strain of living in the uncertain fifties had apparently deranged this unfortunate German's mind. A few days later, however, it was learned that the first report had been an exaggeration; the man had "regained his senses." It appeared that the disturbances which deranged his mind were not, as had been supposed, in the heavenly area of Donati's Comet, but rather had originated in his bowels.[99]

During the year of the Comet, on the night of August 31st, 1857, a loud crash was heard in the city coming from the direction of the Bay. This disturbance, which appeared to have arrived from where the "spirits" or "comets" come, frightened not only the horses and most of the "darkies" but also "some citizens." But the tranquillity of a calm August evening on a semitropical island returned to quiet the frightened ones as soon as the dray and livery wagons from the wharfs pulled up to the entrance of the Tremont Hotel with the news that "the steamer *Charles Morgan* had taken another crack at the T-head of the wharf" as she came in for a landing in the dark.[100] Except for

97 Houston *Telegraph,* April 27, 1857.
98 *Ibid.,* May 8, 1857.
99 *Ibid.,* May 11, 1857.
100 Galveston *Civilian,* September 1, 1857.

the tension prevailing during the year 1857, the predilection of the *Charles Morgan* to "take cracks" at the wharf would have frightened no one but the horses and the "darkies." The latter, having had a long association with beings not of this immediate world were more cognizant of the reasons why "pussons" living on an island such as Galveston might well entertain a wary concern over unusual "disturbances."

There were, none the less, persons numbered among the slaves who had seen long service on the Gulf Coast and who had acquired a philosophic attitude which placed them beyond the reach of comets, spirits or "Electro-biology." Such a man was "Uncle Moses," aged eighty years when he died on November 21, 1858. He had served in the Texas War as a valet to General Hoxey; in fact, Uncle Moses "was almost a member of the staff." Cushing, writing an obituary in the *Telegraph* to honor the passing of this venerable slave, declared: "Here was a man, slave as he was, who glided smoothly along life's uneven currents . . . leaving no enemies behind. Peace be with thee, Uncle Moses."[101]

Galveston Slaves

BY THE VERY NATURE of their station the fifteen hundred slaves[102] living on Galveston Island ought to have been considered the least privileged group residing in the city; yet, from many points of view, this was not the case, for the actual privileges enjoyed by a vast number of the more fortunate slaves on the Island were many indeed. The Negroes loved the Island life and were always loathe to leave it. Even though the major slave markets in Texas held their auctions on the Island, including those of such well-known slave dealers as C. L. McCarthy and Colonel John S. Sydnor, an Island slave could frequently expect special consideration. During the decade of the fifties, Sydnor, a former mayor of the city, not only operated the largest slave market west of New Orleans, but also served as his own auctioneer. His voice, which "was famous through the state," could always drown out the bid of an undesirable buyer who sought to purchase a Galveston slave of long and respectable residence.[103]

[101] Houston *Telegraph*, November 22, 1858.
[102] Joseph Osterman Dyer, "History of Galveston," MS, VI, 20.
[103] Houston *Telegraph*, May 25, 1857; "Galveston Sketches," MS.

Among the leading citizens on the Island it was considered to be a mark of gentility not only to take good care of one's Negroes, but also to allow them to indulge their love for "fancy clothes." In some respects it was not considered proper by the better mercantile families to display personally a "conspicuous consumption" upon the public thoroughfares; in a strange way the function of "public display" had been delegated to the fortunate slaves who served the mercantile classes. The maintenance of a large residential establishment and the indulgence of luxurious display among one's own friends while visiting their homes or entertaining friends in one's own home were the accepted practices on the Island; but a public display of carriages or personal dress while traveling on the "shell-watered" thoroughfares or while riding the bay steamers or the "cars" to Houston was considered to be bad form. A visiting British colonel, in 1863, was amazed as he observed the behavior of the whites and the blacks on a festive occasion, to see

innumberable Negroes and Negresses parading about the streets in the most outrageously grand costumes—silks, satins, crinolines, hats with feathers, lace mantles, &c., forming an absurd contrast to the simple dresses of their mistresses. Many were driving about in their master's carriages, or riding on horses which are often lent to them on Sunday afternoons. All seemed intensely happy and satisfied with themselves.[104]

While the May Day celebration was a most important festival for the very young white ladies in the city and for the clerks and the working classes on the Island, the Festival of May was also a great holiday for the slaves of the merchants of the city. The "women folks" of the trading classes took very little part in this celebration except for the "very young ladies" who were a part of the flower festival. However, the families of the better merchants were usually represented in the May Day parade by a display of their carriages and horses being driven by their slaves and carrying others of their slaves, who were dressed in the "last year's" finery of their mistresses and their masters. It was on some occasions suspected that a mistress, in order to insure that her Negroes looked at least as well dressed as those of her neigh-

[104] Fremantle, *Diary*, pp. 58–59.

bors, sometimes "cast off" raiment which, under other less pressing circumstances, she might well have retained longer for her own use, or perhaps never purchased at all. Thus, the "cullud Pussons' "[105] part in the celebration often provided an outlet for public display of wealth and gentility which custom had denied to the actual owners of these accoutrements.[106] While the mercantile families were certainly not accustomed to deprive themselves of luxuries nor to live the puritan's life, they nevertheless seemed to derive pleasure and prestige by permitting their slaves to enjoy the fruits of occasional carefree excursions. Perhaps they indulged in these contradictions to the customary non-Southerner's vision of the "slave system" in order to confound the traveling traders from New England who often visited the Island; or perhaps they treated their Island Negroes well in order to show their disdain for some of the crude planters on the mainland; they might also have indulged their servants because they knew that some of their own class were in the African slave trade. They may have felt a need to demonstrate the benefits which might some day await the progeny of the unfortunate passengers arriving along the coast via the clandestine slavers' ships. In any case there were good reasons why the position of the Galveston "city Negroes" was envied by the slaves in the interior.

When households in Galveston ceased to exist as a unit because of death or financial or social collapse, it was not uncommon for the better executors or more interested members of the mercantile families to take an interest in the security of particularly worthy Negroes involved in property liquidations. Often the executor of a will or an administrator of an estate exerted considerable effort to see to it that the Negroes involved were well placed. Sometimes wills contained direct instructions which looked to the security of certain slaves, thus actually giving them definite legal rights in those cases in which estates were administered by ethical executors. In such circumstances certain lawyers in the city, who customarily acted as executors in liquidating estates often became in effect the guardians of the "household" or "merchant-employed" slaves who belonged among the properties of

[105] Galveston *Herald*, May 5, 1857; Houston *Telegraph*, May 13, 1857.
[106] Galveston *Herald*, May 5, 1857.

their deceased clients. In situations where property was inherited by persons not living on the Island or by heirs who had no particular wish to be kind to strange Negroes with whom they had no particular concern or affection, the executors often became actual advocates for the rights of Negro slaves who had been protected by the stipulations of a will.[107] In this curious circumstance the "legal rights of slaves" on the Island were in many cases more to be desired than the legal rights enjoyed by free Negroes.[108] These particular rights were not "human rights" but rather rights which came to the slave primarily because he was property and thus had to be respected as such in accord with the provisions of a will. The legal rights of the free Negro were very few indeed, and his position so untenable during the late fifties that he sometimes chose voluntarily to reenter slavery. Peter Gautier, during 1859 in Montgomery County, was so afraid of being sold into slavery to an unfavorable master that he appeared before the county court in Montgomery and chose Charles L. Jones as his master rather than run the risk of continuing as a free Negro.[109]

Lawyers, such as Ballinger and M. M. Potter, who acted as trustees for estates, sometimes personally purchased favored Negroes who pleaded that they did not want to leave the Island, rather than subject them to the hazard of the auction block. In such circumstances a good Negro often represented a sound investment, for a dependable slave either male or female could often be hired out for $250 to $300 per year plus keep. At those rates a $1,500 Negro could pay for himself in five years.[110] Ballinger, for example, had hired out his slave Caroline to B. W. Eve. Caroline was not "too happy" in her "hired" situation.

[107] B. W. Eve to Ballinger, November 17, 1862, Ballinger Papers, MS; see Ballinger Papers in general and the A. F. James estate papers in the Ballinger collection for instances of the protection accorded to Negroes who were the property of estates on the Island.
[108] Galveston *Civilian*, August 31, 1858; Lynn to Clarendon, July 18, 1857, MS, F.O.
[109] Houston *Telegraph*, May 27, 1859.
[110] *Ibid.*, January 21, 1859; Thomas Wright to Ballinger, January 1, 1861, regarding Negro boys Sam and Steve hired to James Hageman, Ballinger Papers, 1861, MS.

In order to make her more contented Ballinger instructed B. W. Eve to "let her have all the wages she earns to buy what she wants; let Caroline enjoy [life] while she can."[111] Since Ballinger's practice brought him the custodianship of many estate Negroes and since he was a man with a judicious yet gentle nature, many Negroes on the Island had learned to trust him; when they were in need of advice they often came to Ballinger for counsel. Even though he was a professional man, apparently he sometimes owned as many as twenty to twenty-five slaves, most of whom he "hired out" in one way or another. He certainly believed in the "institution" as the only logical status for the vast majority of slaves in Texas. Nevertheless, he sometimes lent his legal talent to free a family of Negroes. In the "Major Murrows case" where this officer had freed a colored family in a manner contrary to the law, Ballinger accepted the case and tried to protect the rights of this Negro family. He wrote in his diary that "they are a fine family and I intend to secure their freedom if I can."[112] Ballinger gave his legal aid to the slave, Harriet Ladd, who had purchased her freedom in 1859 from her owner Frank Rownels.[113] Captain Thomas Chubb of Galveston, who occasionally "acquired" free Negroes and then sold them into slavery,[114] was detaining Harriet at Goose Creek. She had tried to assert her rights, but Chubb and the authorities had told her that she would have to remain in slavery until the end of the war, at which time her case might be considered in the courts. Knowing Ballinger's reputation for fair dealing with slaves, Harriet appealed to Ballinger. Writing to him in her own hand, she asked if it would be possible for him to help her claim the freedom which she had purchased; "please let me know," she pleaded in conclusion, "don't keep

[111] Eve to Ballinger, November 17, 1862 and attached memo in Ballinger Papers, MS.

[112] Ballinger Diary, January 13, 1865, MS; *State of Texas* v. *Theophilus Freeman*, District Court of Galveston, January 6, 1857.

[113] See paper certifying "Freedom given to my slave Harriet aged 35 years" signed Frank Rownels, at Fort Arbuckle on September 30, 1859 in Ballinger Papers, Bundle for 1864, MS; also see J. S. Murrow to Ballinger regarding Harriet, May 18, 1864, MS.

[114] Fremantle, *Diary*, p. 54.

me in suspense." It appeared that Ballinger told her to await the end of the war when he assured her that he would see to it that she received justice.[115]

The choosing of a Negro house servant was a matter of some concern, especially so in a modest establishment where such a choice represented a major purchase. During the late fifties, when it happened that Ballinger was "in the market" for a young Negro woman, he found one for whom he was asked $1,800. "Hally took her out home to try her," and at first she seemed to like the probationary slave.[116] But the young slave was not retained, for in August of the same year Ballinger arranged with "Dr. Nelson" to "try out" another young Negro girl whom the doctor had for sale. This young "female" was sent out to the Ballinger household on probation. Hally seemed pleased with the girl; she particularly "liked her face." The only factor against the girl Agnes, for that was her name, was that she was only "14 or 15 years old" and was already "in a family way." In these circumstances Hally refused to pay the $1,200 asked for Agnes. When Dr. Nelson dropped his price to $1,050, however, Hally purchased her and was pleased to get her at that price. Ballinger was pleased, also, to have found a girl who suited his wife, "but there was, of course, risk and uncertainty" involved in the purchase due to Agnes' condition.[117]

Agnes remained in the household until the Yankees threatened the Island in 1862. In this perilous situation Hally retired with the children to her relatives in Waco and Agnes was hired out with the prospect of purchase by Aaron Coffee who operated a plantation in the interior. While this arrangement may have been a war convenience for the Ballinger family, it was most displeasing to Agnes. Eventually, Aaron Coffee was forced to admit to Ballinger that Agnes was "unwilling for me to buy her—says she can't work in the field and wants to stay in town" on the Island. Agnes told her master-on-probation that the situation on the plantation was very much displeasing to her.

[115] Harriet Ladd to Ballinger, December 9, 1864, Ballinger Papers, Bundle for 1864, MS; also, see *Betzy Webster* v. *T. J. Heard, 32 Texas Reports*, 686, for Ballinger's defense of the slave Betsy.
[116] Ballinger Diary, January 13, 1860, MS.
[117] *Ibid.*, August 11, 1860.

She asked Coffee to tell Ballinger that if she had to be sold she wanted to be purchased by a city family. To put the matter bluntly, Agnes said that "she was surprised that Master William would sell her at all."[118] Agnes failed to comprehend the unusual circumstances which denied "Master William" the privilege of indulging his predilections toward gentility. Eventually, in spite of her protests, in 1863 Ballinger sold Agnes and her children to Aaron Coffee for $2,000 in gold.[119]

The Yankee threat and the eventual occupation of the Island for a few months during the Civil War forced the leading mercantile families to close their Island homes, to disband their households and to retire to the mainland. During such an unhappy undertaking the Negroes attached to these families were major victims. With the port blockaded and the sale of cotton in jeopardy the value of slaves dropped considerably in terms of real money, although their price rose in terms of Confederate money. A Galveston family which had before the war retained many Negroes was now suddenly forced either to dispose of them at a loss or to try to find "hire out" locations for their "city Negroes." The only two employment opportunities available for large numbers of Negroes at that time were on the plantations and as labor for the military. Since no one wanted to trust the custody of well-liked "house Negroes" to the tender care of the military, an effort was made to find places for the Island Negroes on the inland plantations. This source of employment, however, was curtailed since cotton planting was decreasing because of the blockade. Thus, the war years were hard years for the Negroes; they suffered losses in terms of both care and dignity. The war situation caused a serious reduction of their actual monetary value and this, in turn, reduced the importance of their relative position in total society.

Ballinger, a typical responsible citizen of the Island, "hired" out some of his Negroes on plantations and others he kept with him when he finally brought his family back from Waco and set up a "war household" in Houston. One of the house slaves Ballinger brought with him was a "boy" called Dave, who eventually became a most annoying

[118] Aaron Coffee to Ballinger, November 27, 1862, Ballinger Papers, Bundle No. 48, MS.
[119] Ballinger Diary, July 12, 1863, MS.

problem to "Master William." For a while Ballinger placed Dave with Aaron Coffee on the plantation at Haleyon, and later hired him out as a servant at "Camp Fort Bates." The boy's career with the military was blighted, however, when some of the soldiers, who had caught him stealing, proceeded to give him a whipping. Dave's reaction to this indignity was to run away to a ranch owned by Aaron Coffee's sister. Coffee found the boy there; "Dave is a favorite boy with me," Coffee wrote to Ballinger, "and I would like to use him as a carriage boy." But Dave wanted none of the life in the country; he returned to Houston and the city environment.[120] During the occasions when he would run away to the city he would sell the new work clothes which Coffee had given him. He explained this action by saying that "he didn't care a damn for such common field nigger clothing as Master William and Master Tom Jack would give him city clothing."[121] After enduring several of Dave's excursions into the city, Coffee finally told Ballinger that "Hereafter, I shall flog him" if he continues to run away and sell his clothes.[122]

About a week later on returning from Galveston "to get one of his sick Negroes" Coffee accidentally encountered Dave in Houston. The boy had run away again from the plantation. Coffee put Dave on board the train intending to take him back to the country. After they had traveled a few miles Dave suddenly "jumped off the cars under full speed and escaped and, of course, went back to Houston." Coffee then wrote Ballinger that "under the circumstances to please hire him off to someone else." If ever "a man tried to take care of your Negroes" Coffee wrote to Ballinger "I have"; but this boy "says he will not work on any plantation and will not live out of the city." Life on the Island had spoiled Dave; it seemed that he would never be happy any other place. Coffee said that it was "truly unpleasant" for him to have to suggest that the only solution was for "you and Mrs. B. to dispose of him" even though it seemed heartless to do so.[123]

[120] Coffee to Ballinger, January 9, 1863, Ballinger Papers, Bundle for 1863, MS.

[121] Coffee to Ballinger, January 17, 1863, Ballinger Papers, MS.

[122] Coffee to Ballinger, February 16, 1863, Ballinger Papers, MS.

[123] Coffee to Ballinger, March 2, 1863, Ballinger Papers, MS.

Despite the planter's advice, Ballinger could not bring himself to sell Dave; instead, he took the boy into his household again, now and then hiring him out in the city. It soon became apparent that Dave had lately acquired a habit of acquisitiveness unbecoming in a slave. By August of 1863, the question of how to deal with the change in Dave grew even more serious. Ballinger noted gravely in his diary: "Dave caught stealing specie from Hally's chest—must consider selling him."[124] But Hally and the children wouldn't hear of disposing of him. Secretly, Ballinger knew that, considering the way the war was going, it might be well to put as much of one's assets as possible into specie, land, or even cotton, and where possible one ought to dispose of slaves while it was still possible to do so; yet he accepted the fact that he would have to humor Hally and retain Dave.[125]

Occasionally, Ballinger hired Dave out for a few weeks at a time to a man named Ferguson who paid well for the Negro's services. Although Ballinger was not aware of it, Ferguson was an associate of the notorious Nicaragua Smith who had looted several Galveston homes left vacant when their owners retired to the security of the mainland. On one occasion Smith had possessed the effrontery to steal $350 in specie from under Mrs. T. C. Saunders' pillow and $250 in gold from Mrs. Croycroft's mattress while the good ladies slept[126] and then escaped to Federal gunboats blockading the Island.[127] Ballinger had thus unwittingly placed Dave in very bad company indeed.

When during the summer of 1864, the jurist noticed that several items of specie and jewelry were missing from the locked chest in his bed chamber, he was certain that Dave had "got into our trunk again." But how should one "catch him?" Ballinger determined to try. He secured his gold and silver specie in several woolen socks and sewed the open ends together with a "thread so fine that it would not be noticed, but anyone tampering with the specie would be forced to break the thread."[128] Five days later, Ballinger discovered that some of

[124] Ballinger Diary, March 2, 1863, MS.
[125] Ibid., August 5, 1863.
[126] Galveston News, July 7, 1862.
[127] Ibid.; San Antonio Semi-Weekly, July 10, 1862.
[128] Ballinger Diary, January 5, 1863, MS.

the specie had been taken from the woolen sock which he had locked in the trunk. In these circumstances the jurist acted at once.

"I called him in and charged him," Ballinger wrote in his diary.

At first he denied it. I tied his hands and stripped him, and was about to commence on him when he said he would tell all. He confessed to opening the trunk four times. Took sums of 50¢, $2.50, and $2.25 in specie. He used pieces of wire to take off the hinges which served as well as if he had possessed a key.

Dave told his master that he had been honest until he had been hired out to Ferguson, who had taught him to pick locks; " he had gone robbing with Ferguson, Nicaragua Smith and their gang many times —carrying the tools and holding the lantern, he told a very heroic narrative, blaming it all upon Ferguson." After his confession, Dave became frightened because he feared that Ferguson would surely kill him for the story he had told of their peculations. At one time, Dave said, Ferguson had tried to persuade him to steal all of Ballinger's specie and then escape to Mexico, but Dave had refused because he was afraid. On hearing the slave's confession Ballinger realized that he would have to sell him even though Hally was "attached to Dave." Ballinger still acknowledged that the boy had "many kind traits of character."[129]

Realizing that he was in serious trouble, Dave decided to run away. He stole "Tom's pistol, Hally's jewelry and [Ballinger's] specie and tried to escape via the cars to Henderson." His behavior on the train, however, aroused the suspicions of the authorities and they returned him to Houston where he was lodged in jail.[130] But after a brief rest, he broke "out of jail and was on the run for a few days, but was caught and is now going to the penitentiary."[131]

On Christmas Eve of 1864 "the sheriff carried Dave off to the penitentiary," wrote Ballinger. I have hired him out to the authorities there for $300 per year and keep. I am to be paid in cloth. The year begins Jan. 1st," 1865.[132] Since the state institution was not able to pay in specie for the services of a slave, it was more expedient to receive the

[129] *Ibid.*, November 15, 1864.   [130] *Ibid.*, November 28, 1864.
[131] *Ibid.*, December 10, 1864.   [132] *Ibid.*, December 24, 1864.

remuneration in cloth manufactured by the penitentiary than in Confederate currency.

A few weeks later S. B. Hendrick, the financial agent at Huntsville penitentiary, wrote Ballinger that he was forwarding the cloth which represented Dave's hire. "Your boy is a most enterprising fellow," wrote Hendricks. "He made an escape a few nights since but was happily recaptured a day or two afterward. He managed to get hold of a rope and let himself down from the top of the penitentiary and in this way obtained freedom and fresh air." He would not likely escape again, continued the prison official, because Colonel Carahen had put him in the foundry where he received the treatment of a regular convict. He told Ballinger that Colonel Carahen was complying with Ballinger's request that Dave be taught a trade so that he would not have to steal for a living when he returned to society in the status of a free man—which changing conditions now appeared to indicate would be the case.[133]

The secure and ordered life which Dave and many other Galveston "city Negroes" had enjoyed was exchanged in the "changing conditions" for the uncertainties and unkindnesses which foreshadowed the new freedom. While the full impact of the changing times did not arrive until the end of the war, the coming disintegration of the city Negro society was clearly recognizable in the confusion which began when, threatened by the occupation of the Island by the Yankees, the leading families liquidated their households and erected on the mainland mere skeletons of their former establishments.

The Germans in Galveston

BECAUSE GALVESTON WAS a seaport city, possessing the usual cosmopolitan characteristics found in a maritime trading community, the citizens were accustomed to associating with foreigners. During the eighteen-fifties this was particularly true, because in that decade the port was the entry point for large numbers of German immigrants. Since providing accommodations for entering newcomers and servicing the ships which brought them were lucrative enterprises,

[133] S. B. Hendrick to Ballinger, February 8, 1865, Ballinger Papers, MS.

the Germans received a warm welcome from those Galvestonians who were engaged in catering to this flourishing trade.[134]

While sublimer urges such as the search for religious or political freedom induced some Germans to come to Texas, most of them immigrated for the same reasons that motivated native Americans to come—because they believed that their own chances for advancement would be better in Texas than they appeared to be in the localities from which they had come. The prime motive of most of these immigrants was the desire to acquire the cheap land which Texas offered to the newcomer. The wish to enjoy more political freedom and to escape service in European armies was usually only a secondary consideration. One immigrant from the Duchy of Oldenburg wrote that his family had at first considered going to a northern American state, but that when his people had accidentally acquired a letter from a German in Texas—which praised the Gulf Coast area—his family decided to ship to the port of Galveston. The climate and the fruitful soil appealed to them and also

the republic government with unbounded personal and political liberty, free from so many disadvantages and evils of old countries. Prussia, our former home, smarted at the time under a military despotism. We were enthusiastic lovers of republican institutions, full of romantic notions, and believed to find Texas, before all other countries, the blessed land of our hopes.[135]

While most of the immigrants who came to Galveston harbor were peasant farmers and city craftsmen, there were a few families among the arrivals who were not merely in comfortable circumstances, but were unquestionably wealthy.[136] An editor in New Orleans during the year 1857 asserted that no state in the Union was receiving as many German immigrants as the extraordinary numbers then entering Texas through the port of Galveston. These immigrants, wrote this editor, were "a more industrious, enterprising and desirable population" than

[134] Galveston *News*, April 28, 1857.
[135] From note written by Robert J. Kleberg, Sr., in 1876, printed in Caroline von Hinueber, "Life of German Pioneers in Early Texas," *Southwestern Historical Quarterly*, II (January, 1899), 228.
[136] Marcus Lee Hansen, *The Atlantic Migration, 1607–1860*, p. 288.

those debarking at other ports in the Union; "the great body of these" immigrants were "well provided with this world's good, much more so" than was the case among the usual groups of immigrants entering the country. Every steamer leaving New Orleans for Galveston, said this editor, was "crowded with Germans of some wealth who are going to Texas to select a future home."[137]

In Germany the champions of *Deutschtum* encouraged the concentration of Germans in those areas of the United States where they might be able to develop political strength. The purpose was to keep sentiment for the fatherland alive by fostering churches, schools, and intellectual bonds, the homeland drawing profit from these commercial and cultural ties by maintaining active trade consulates in the German-American cities and ports.[138] These spirited advocates for the fatherland, aware that the American Union was moving toward a possible break-up, urged that the advantage which the fatherland might be able to secure in such circumstances ought not to be overlooked. A Berlin newspaper, the *Allgemeine Zeitung,* observed that if perchance the Union should fall apart some states would then be wholly Teutonic and free to determine their political destiny.[139] As early as the forties the British were concerned about the danger to Her Majesty's interest arising from "the strong German colony being formed in Texas."[140]

A number of other forces were also at work encouraging emigration of Germans, and, of course, other Europeans, to Texas. For one thing, the economic and political conditions which preceded and followed the revolutions of 1848 were such as would inspire many to seek greater freedom, opportunity, and security elsewhere. In particular, the persecutions to which they were subjected in Prague and Budapest following the revolution caused many Jews to migrate to Galveston because it was reported that the Texas island city offered them political, economic,

---

[137] New Orleans *Picayune,* quoted in the Galveston *Civilian,* July 28, 1857.
[138] Hansen, *Atlantic Migration,* pp. 288, 302.
[139] *Allgemeine Zeitung,* April 22, 1843, quoted in Hansen, *Atlantic Migration,* p. 288.
[140] Consul William Kennedy to Richard Pakenham, September, 1844, MS, F.O.

and religious freedom.[141] Several groups in Texas or elsewhere in the United States were active in developing and encouraging German settlers. For their own interest shipping companies printed guidebooks which recommended Galveston as a point of debarkation because a call at this port enabled their vessels to secure a return cargo of cotton.[142] What is more, during the fifties entrepreneurs in Galveston as well as capitalists in Germany found it financially profitable to promote this settlement. They organized emigration companies in Europe to capitalize upon the desire of Germans to come to Texas. An early enterprise of this character, the Fisher and Miller Emigration Company, failed because of poor management, but it was reorganized by its creditors under the firm name of The Texas & German Emigration Company[143] and operated thereafter very successfully.

Two Galveston Germans, Kauffman and Klocker, with the aid of Island City capital, contracted for the construction of the 700-ton ship *Iris* which was built in Bremen "especially for the emigration trade to Galveston." On her first voyage from Bremen, in 1856, this vessel carried "240 emigrants and all debarked in good health" on the Island. Editor Willard Richardson of the *News* was on hand at the wharf when the *Iris* was made fast for the debarkation of the newcomers. He was impressed by the character of the persons debarking and he asserted that the ship was "one of the finest vessels" he had ever seen.[144] The *Iris* earned a good record during the remaining years of the decade as a healthy immigrant vessel. Not all vessels carrying the "immigrant

[141] Guido Kisch, "The Revolution of 1848 and The Jewish 'On to America' Movement," *Publications of American Jewish History Society*, XXXVIII, Pt. 3 (March, 1949), 185–237.

[142] Frederick Law Olmsted, *A Journey Through Texas: or a Saddle-Trip on the Southwestern Frontier With a Statistical Appendix*, p. 299.

[143] Houston *Telegraph*, October 9, 1857; Galveston *Civilian*, October 7, 1857. See also *Henry Francis Fisher and Burchard Miller* v. *William Smith Todd*, in records of January 17, 1856 of the District Court of Fredericksburg, Texas. For more details concerning German emigration companies operating in Texas see *C. A. Muller* v. *Joseph Landa*, 31 *Texas Reports*, 265; R. L. Biesele, *The History of the German Settlements in Texas, 1831–1861*; Ella Lonn, *Foreigners in the Confederacy;* and A. E. Zucker (editor), *The Forty-Eighters*.

[144] Galveston *News*, December 17, 1856.

trade" into Galveston boasted the sanitary perfection achieved by Kauffman and Klocker's *Iris;* the bark *Weser,* for example, arrived from Bremen on June 3rd, 1858, with 221 passengers and certificates of death showing twelve persons buried at sea during the voyage.[145] Yet, despite the hazards of travel on board immigrant ships almost 5,000 newcomers debarked annually at Galveston.[146]

The immigration during the years 1857 and 1858, asserted the Galveston customs collector, was one of "our biggest imports" and "service to these incoming passengers" represented one of Galveston's "biggest exports."[147] One of the instruments of propaganda used to promote this industry was Richardson's famous *Texas Almanac.* During the last year of the decade, 100,000 copies of the almanac were printed in German and distributed in Europe. Many immigrants who came to Galveston carried it "like a Bible."[148]

By the mid-fifties, the more or less permanent population of Galveston was composed of from one-third to one-half Germans; they, in conjunction with the Germans passing through the port on the way into the interior, lent a strong Germanic tone to life in the city.[149] The other United States ports of entry for immigrants were usually great cities such as New York, Boston or New Orleans; there, a few thousand foreigners passing through the city or tarrying for a few weeks did not have a major impact upon the social scene. However, when a small port city, such as Galveston, was host to a large foreign immigration the influence of the newcomers was considerable.[150]

Large numbers of the immigrants entering the port of Galveston chose to stay in the city rather than venture inland. "The German citizen is not for the frontier," wrote editor Cushing in 1859, "he likes

[145] Houston *Telegraph,* June 6, 1858.

[146] Galveston *Civilian,* January 13, 1857.

[147] Houston *Telegraph,* November 4, 1858; Galveston *News,* August 29, 1857 and October 5, 1858.

[148] Stuart McGregor, "The Texas Almanac," *Southwestern Historical Quarterly,* L (April, 1947), 427.

[149] Ferdinand Flake, "Register of 1864 of the Male and Female Inhabitants of Galveston City," MS, pp. 34–44.

[150] *State of Texas* v. *Ferdinand Flake,* District Court of Galveston, October 7, 1848.

to live in or near a city and has little fancy for the society of the Indian."[151] The large numbers of metropolitan-oriented Germans who remained on the Island exerted a very important influence on Galveston; their ideas, tastes, and talents were brought to bear upon architecture, street and park construction, music appreciation, and to some extent upon the intellectual life of the city.

The impact of the trade skills of the German carpenters, masons, and mechanics upon the Island's architecture was very great.[152] These artisans who came to Texas to improve their position in society hired out as carpenters and masons in order to earn some cash funds before going inland to buy an "estate" or before establishing a business of their own in the city.[153] In this situation they offered their services to the native Galvestonians for very nominal wages—less, in fact, than that demanded by the local skilled day laborers. Thus their labor found a ready market.

Furthermore, since most of the European artisans were well-trained workers, skilled in their crafts, they were able to influence the methods of construction used in erecting new buildings or in the formation of masonry in Galveston. The dominating native American families on the Island, the cotton factors, private bankers, merchants, absentee plantation owners, and professional men might pay for the building but they had no particular desire to excel in the building arts. While construction in general was controlled by these local entrepreneurs, the actual architectural aspects, as far as they concerned the details of construction, were usually left to the craftsmen themselves and sometimes even to the judgment of particularly skilled slaves. In these circumstances the well-trained foreign craftsmen pouring into the city were a welcome addition to the labor ranks during the incipient building boom which began with the opening of the 1850's.[154]

In addition to the building craftsmen, other skilled foreigners such as tailors, shoemakers, and millers exerted an influence on the native

[151] Houston *Telegraph*, September 14, 1859.

[152] Galveston *Civilian*, August 31, 1858.

[153] *Ibid.*, January 13, 1857.

[154] Houston *Telegraph*, September 30, 1857; Galveston *Civilian*, April 27 and July 28, 1857.

citizens. For example, during a three-month period, October, November, and December, 1857, 999 persons (516 males and 483 females) arrived in Galveston from Europe. The heads of families or adult single men listed in this enumeration included 101 farmers, 18 carpenters, 15 shoemakers, 11 tailors, and 7 millers. Most of the farmers and their families, of course, moved into the interior, but the craftsmen and their families remained in the city adding to the marked "cosmopolitan" and "metropolitan" character of the population during the fifties.[155] The influence of these immigrant tailors and shoemakers, and of others who preceded and followed them, was "constantly in evidence on the streets of Galveston."[156] The preference of the Germans for wheat rather than corn bread plus the skill of German millers in the craft of milling and mechanics in the manufacture of milling machinery[157] hastened the shift of Gulf Coast eating habit from corn bread to wheat bread.[158]

In the ease with which the German created a place for himself among the activities of the city and in the skill with which he did his work, we may see a partial reason for the somewhat mixed acceptance he received from the native Galvestonians. To the aristocrats, the wealthy governing class, he was a worthy addition to the population. Not only was he a good worker—and one whose fees were not over-high—but he was also a solid and dependable character. Stuart of the *Civilian* remarked that "these orderly and industrious people" were making an important contribution to the progress of the island city.[159] In fact, all three of the "city" newspapers on the Gulf Coast employed the most flattering adjectives to praise the "sober and law abiding" German craftsmen who were entering the port in large numbers.[160] It is significant that when the secession crisis eventually arose and the

[155] Galveston *Civilian*, January 13, 1857.

[156] *Ibid.*; *State of Texas* v. *Adolph Flake*, District Court of Galveston, January 9, 1860.

[157] Richardson, *Galveston Directory, 1859–60*, p. 75.

[158] Annual Report of the British Consulate in Galveston, 1860, MS, F.O.

[159] Galveston *Civilian*, January 13, 1857.

[160] Houston *Telegraph*, September 30, 1857; Galveston *Civilian*, July 18, 1857; Galveston *News*, December 17, 1856.

Germans came under criticism because of their Union and free-soil sympathies, the native Galvestonians who demonstrated a vigorous anti-German, Know-Nothing attitude came from the artisan groups rather than from the mercantile families. During the crisis the wealthier among the secessionists demonstrated a remarkable tolerance for the Union sympathies prevailing among the Germans in the city.

For example, the editor E. H. Cushing, who was himself a strong advocate for the reopening of the African slave trade and for the institution of slavery, often defended the political attitude of the Germans living on the Gulf Coast despite the admitted fact that most of them criticized the institution of slavery. Cushing insisted that the often repeated assertion that Texas was "rapidly filling" with anti-slave Germans who were a threat to the cotton industry represented an exaggeration of the facts. This was not so, he replied, because "the New Braunfels *Zeitung* and the Galveston *Union* [were] both sound and orthodox on the slavery question." He pointed out that the "German Emigration Company, after having bought the farm Napon in Fayette County. . . . sent an agent to New Orleans to purchase a large number of Negroes."[161] The Germans, he said, were "peaceful and law abiding citizens, not thugs, nor brass knuckled gentry"[162]—the latter designations were those which Cushing usually used when he referred to abolitionists.

While some of the Germans who came to Galveston had belonged to intellectual and proletarian forty-eighter movements in Europe and thus perhaps held slightly radical political views, these same persons were actually a very dependable and sober group in the social sense. On the other hand, although the native American craftsmen in Galveston were politically conservative, their social behavior was not conservative; they were apt to indulge in the excessive use of alcohol, they often failed to meet their financial obligations, and they generally irritated the orderly mercantile leaders on the Island.[163] Thus, while

[161] Houston *Telegraph*, September 30, 1857.   [162] *Ibid.*
[163] Charles R. Williams, *Life of Rutherford Birchard Hayes*, I, 50–51; Solms-Braunfels Archives, L. 35–41, quoted in R. L. Biesele, "Prince Solms' Trip to Texas, 1844–45," *Southwestern Historical Quarterly*, XL (July, 1936), 21–22.

the German artisans who came to Galveston may have harbored a few intellectual and political ideas which would not have found favor with the heads of the leading Island families, nevertheless, their conservative, sober behavior, despite their traditional beer drinking, commended them to the native aristocracy. The Germans went to church; they paid their bills and their taxes; they were reasonably sober; they could read and write and cipher; they were not prone to fight and brawl; they were a more dependable class of persons than their native counterparts.[164] Since the Germans were used to showing deference to their social and financial betters in Europe it was an easy matter for them to follow the same flattering pattern in their dealings with the leading Americans in Galveston. Educated and wealthy Galvestonians received a sincere deference from the German artisan class. On the other hand, the native Americans of the illiterate, crude, small trading classes, as well as the native artisan or small planter-farmer classes about the city, a group which gave at best a grudging respect to those fellow Americans who were obviously of a higher social or financial class and which would naturally regard itself as the equal or superior of the "foreign" artisan, received not deference but arrogance from the Germans, who could read, write and cipher, and who could demonstrate a remarkable proficiency in the use of musical instruments—in particular, this musicianship inspired both admiration and chagrin among the native artisan classes on the Island.[165] It is not surprising that resentment, overt or suppressed, should be felt by members of the native group.

On the whole the Germans received better treatment generally in Galveston than they did on the mainland because of the more cosmopolitan nature of the Island's society; nevertheless the native working classes resented the newcomers because they represented an economic threat and because they tended to coalesce into an exclusive social unit supporting their own newspapers, churches, and social and cultural

[164] Houston *Telegraph*, September 30, 1857.
[165] Galveston *Zeitung*, August 19, 1855. Martha and Earl W. Fornell, "A Century of German Song in Texas," *American-German Review*, October-November, 1957, pp. 24–31.

clubs.[166] One such organization was the German Reading Room, occupying two floors of a large building on the Strand, which contained
a book collection of several hundred volumes serviced by a full-time
librarian.[167] Another German cultural society was the Casino Association which erected its own building in 1859. The cost of this structure at that time was reported to be in excess of $5,000—"a handsome
and commodious building for theatrical representations, with a stage
and appropriate scenery."[168] The Turner's Association of Galveston,
another German organization, also erected its own club house on the
public square in 1859. The estimated value of this building, at that
time, was $8,000.[169] "The Germans devote a commendable degree of
attention to intellectual culture," wrote E. H. Cushing, "as well as to
the moral and religious training of the youthful German population"
in Galveston.[170] On another occasion the editor remarked that the
Germans "manifested a remarkable zeal in behalf of the education of
their race."[171]

During the late fifties a working political arrangement developed
between the leading native politicians in the city and the German
leaders and voters. The key German in this alliance was the politically
skilled Justice of the Peace I. E. Rump, who acted as a "spoils broker"
making the necessary arrangements between the two groups.[172] The
voting franchise in city elections was granted to any male above the
age of twenty-one years, regardless of his nationality, if he had lived in
Galveston for one year and had paid all the taxes assessed against
him.[173] This meant that any German immigrant who had lived on the
Island for one year and had paid his taxes could vote in the city election—which, after all, was the only one that really mattered to a Galvestonian. The restriction of voting to those who had paid their taxes
eliminated many members of the native American laboring and artisan

166 Galveston *Zeitung*, August 19, 1855.
167 Richardson, *Galveston Directory, 1859–60*, p. 47; Galveston *News*, January 22, 1861.
168 Richardson, *Galveston Directory, 1859–60*, p. 80.
169 *Ibid.*   170 Houston *Telegraph*, August 12, 1859.
171 *Ibid.*, June 10, 1859.   172 "Galveston Sketches," MS, pp. 302–309.
173 Richardson, *Galveston Directory, 1859–60*, p. 36.

classes who were careless of such matters. The native American leaders soon learned that, in city politics if not in national and state politics, the German immigrant was a steady ally[174] who in return for a few favors cooperated in the Galveston practice of rotating the major political offices among the men of the leading families. The ordinary voter seldom presumed to run for office himself; custom limited his political role to that of choosing his favorites from a slate made up of men designated by the mercantile and professional men on the Island.[175]

In order to strengthen the voting coalition consisting of the Germans and the leading mercantile families, Justice Rump and the German editor Ferdinand Flake with the assistance of their native friends secured a ruling from the Texas Supreme Court at Galveston which sustained the right of the County Court on the Island to "receive declarations and issue letters of citizenship." This in effect gave the local authorities the power to raise or lower the volume of foreign voters they wished to see appearing at the polls. The large numbers of Germans casting votes in the city indicated the measure of trust which the city fathers placed in this class of citizens, who in turn gave the county and the city fathers an assured majority in all local elections.[176] There were, of course, exceptionally gifted foreigners who achieved, during the fifties, positions of leadership almost comparable to those held by the leading Anglo-Americans. Such men as Ferdinand and Adolph Flake,[177] George Schneider, Sr., Henry Rosenberg, J. A. Sauter, Moritz Kopperl, Herman Marwitz, Michael W. Shaw, and Justus Julius Schott accumulated political and economic power which could not be ignored.[178]

As long as the ruling mercantile families remained united the Germans enjoyed ample privileges and opportunities in the city. Even the

[174] Galveston County Commissioners Court, Minutes, 1856–1870, MS, pp. 49–96; Ordinance Book, 1857–1865.
[175] Galveston News, July 19, 1872; Ballinger Diary, October 5, 1865, MS.
[176] Houston Telegraph, March 10, 1856; District Court of Galveston, Minutes, 1856–59, 84–90.
[177] Houston Telegraph, February 20, 1857.
[178] "Galveston Sketches," MS, pp. 300–309.

divisive issue of the reopening of the African slave trade, which caused a slight fracture among the ruling families, did not seriously react against the Germans although many of their leaders actively opposed the reopening of the slave trade. It was not until the secession crisis, which split the leading Galveston families and made it necessary for the secessionist leaders to mobilize the native American mechanic and labor groups to overcome the Union sympathies of the conservatives and Germans, that the comfortable position of the Germans was seriously threatened by an awakening of the latent resentment against the foreigners which had long been smoldering among the native workingmen in Galveston.[179]

During the fifties the slave-trade issue and the incipient secession threat remained like an unlighted explosive charge amidst the social scene on the Gulf Coast. The great cohesion arising out of a booming and prosperous frontier area was constantly threatened by these two related issues. In this situation there were a few Germans in Galveston who advocated programs to keep the Germans of the city alert for incipient threats to their position in Texas and prepared to meet these dangers. A leader of this temperament and conviction was a Prussian named M. Buechner, the editor and publisher of the Galveston *Zeitung* during the mid-fifties.

On August 19, 1855, Buechner published a manifesto in the *Zeitung*, which was addressed to the Germans of Texas. He called attention to the fact that "the continual clashing between native laborers and the foreigners might easily come to a general eruption, which would result disastrously to the Germans, unless we consider in time the proverb that 'He who desires peace should prepare for war.'" Buechner asserted that in case of serious trouble the police might not be able to guard the Germans against the native mechanic classes. "In such a case," said the Galvestonian German, "we must depend upon ourselves to defend our families and property as is our right and duty." He pointed out that without an organization the needed defense would be impossible: "In the moment of an attack it will be too late; our duty is to organize before hand." Buechner submitted to the Germans

[179] Galveston *Die Union*, June 23 and July 7, 1859; Galveston *Zeitung*, August 19, 1855; Houston *Telegraph*, July 4, 8 and 13, 1859.

of Galveston and Texas a detailed table of organization which he recommended as the best means to protect Germans and Germanic ideas in Texas.[180] The fact that a few months later Buechner sold the failing *Zeitung* to Ferdinand Flake, who changed the name of the paper to *Die Union*, indicated that Buechner's manifesto and his point of view were too extreme to attract popular support among the Germans. Flake had been a marshal of the city, was a delegate of the Democratic Party to state conventions, and was in favor with leading native Galvestonians as well as among the Germans.[181] He was, nevertheless, opposed to the reopening of the slave trade and was an antisecessionist. He was a man who held to moderate political principles, and was vigorous and daring in his persistent support of them. He was a "militant moderate" who wanted no part of the African slave trade, secession, nor a "fatherland" army in Texas.[182]

The editor of *Die Union*, as well as most of the Germans in the city, accepted the fact that they had to adjust their principles to those prevailing in their adopted city. They justified whatever compromises they had to make by saying that their expediency was not a negation of principle but was rather a demonstration of their willingness to abide by the will of the majority in the city. It was on this basis that most

[180] Galveston *Zeitung*, August 19, 1855. Buechner's plan contained the following recommendations:

1st. To form in every town where there is sufficient German population one or more guard companies who shall furnish their arms.

2d. The uniform must be everywhere the same, to preserve equality. The uniform is necessary to prevent confusion and to distinguish our friends.

3d. The arms must be everywhere the same, and we recommend as the best the arms of the Turners and revolvers.

4th. A member of any company shall be recognized as a member wherever there be such a company formed. All the companies in the United States must be in connection with one chief or leader.

5th. The decade system is the most commendable, i.e., every ten members to constitute one decade, and make one leader, who in case of necessity can call together his nine comrades. The leaders, then, elect their officers. Five decades would be enough for one company.

[181] Houston *Telegraph*, February 20, 1857.

[182] Galveston *Die Union*, June 23 and July 7, 1859, November 13, 1860, January 5 and 8 and April 11, 1861.

Germans tolerated the institution of slavery and sometimes purchased slaves for their own use.[183]

By tradition and custom the Germans liked to take part in fraternal organizations through which they could indulge in their predilection for organized military drill, marching musical bands, and gymnastic exercises. The well-known Turner societies were but one expression of their love for organized physical and cultural activity. The Germans on the Island, however, were too astute to follow the socially irritating program recommended by M. Buechner. Men such as Flake, Sauter, and Rump had seen enough of American politics to learn the art of adjustment which was the lubricant for the friction generated by politics in America;[184] yet, a judicious caution advocated that foreigners practicing the principle of abiding by the will of the majority in a strange land might well organize in a friendly way against an unforeseen eventuality. Since fraternal militia companies were an accepted social practice in America, the Germans in Galveston indulged their love for military drill in the formation of "German Rifle Companies" in Galveston and Houston. These units equipped themselves with attractive uniforms and rifles of the most modern breech-loading varieties which they imported from Germany. In conjunction with their military units they maintained "splendid" German bands which were an important contribution to the cultural life of the Island. When the Galveston German Rifle Company held its formal parades the occasion was always climaxed by a military ball in the evening held at the Tremont Hotel to which members of the leading native families in the city were invited.[185] It was in this way that the Germans in Galveston practicing "cultural politics" and tempering whatever principles they may have held with a measure of expediency were able to find a *modus vivendi* with the native Texans even during the most trying times of a civil war —a conflict which the vast majority of Germans looked upon as suicidal madness.

[183] San Antonio *Alamo Express*, February 4, 1861.
[184] W. J. Kyle to Ballinger, February 17, 1862, Ballinger papers, MS.
[185] Galveston *News*, May 28, 1857; Galveston *Civilian*, May 18, 1858.

"We came here, sir," said George Schneider in 1859,

with an intense desire for freedom. We have long sought for the country which guarantees us that full share of political and religous liberty denied to us at home. We found that blessed country in this great Union, and this imposing Confederacy of several states, and we will cling to it forever. Do not talk to us of dissolution of the Union. We do not believe in a Northern and Southern Confederacy, but we do know, that if this Union is dissolved the great bulwark of liberty will be destroyed.[186]

Loving the Union, their island city, their adopted state of Texas, and their concept of human liberty, the Galveston Germans faced a heart-rending dilemma as the Civil War began.

[186] "Letter from a German," Houston *Telegraph*, July 13, 1859.

4. EDITOR-PUBLISHER POLITICIANS

THE FOUR EDITOR-PUBLISHERS of the Galveston Gulf Coast—
Willard Richardson, Hamilton Stuart, Ferdinand Flake, and Edward
Cushing—exerted a marked influence upon the area during a period
when the people and the primitive environment into which the new
Texans poured were in a remarkably malleable state. All of these editors, three Americans and one German, were men of culture by virtue of birth, training, and education; they were essentially intellectuals,
academicians, and were to a marked degree "romantics" rather than

"realists." They were men of ideas rather than of action, interpreters or even teachers rather than administrators. On occasion they could make or break a politician, but none of them ever actively sought an important political office. During a period when men of much lesser ability were accumulating fortunes, none of these four men accumulated much wealth. Yet, all four were sufficiently able business administrators to direct the only four successful major newspapers on the Gulf Coast and to hold these positions against innumerable attempts to set up competing papers. Richardson of the Galveston *News*, Stuart of the Galveston *Civilian*, Flake of *Die Union* and *Bulletin*, and Cushing of the Houston *Telegraph* usually spoke for the interests, particularly the economic and political interests, of their respective cities. But on occasion, also, they put their own particular interests or idiosyncrasies above the obvious wish of the majority. If at such times they appeared to be the organs of a particular faction, they wrote the music they played and they fashioned the tunes in their own tastes. In these instances none of the editors was above decorating his own brow with a shining halo which he righteously labeled "principle."

Hamilton Stuart and Willard Richardson established themselves as leaders in Galveston during the days of the Republic. Since they had arrived on the Island in the late thirties they were able by the mid-fifties to speak for their city with an authority arising from having edited and published the two leading English language newspapers almost since the inception of the island city's position as the leading port of Texas. The professional skill of these two newspapermen had been amply demonstrated. During this period the Island had earned a reputation as a "newspaper graveyard" because literally a score of papers which had attempted to compete with Stuart's *Civilian* and Richardson's *News* had failed to survive financially, yet the *News* and the *Civilian* continued to retain their positions as successful newspapers.

In fact, the *News* was much more than a powerful Galveston newspaper; it was also the most influential paper in Texas and was regarded as an all-Texas paper as much as a news outlet for the island city.[1] Its circulation on the mainland was larger than its city circulation.

[1] Arthur T. Lynn to Earl of Clarendon, January 15, 1855, MS, F.O.; Sam Acheson, *35,000 Days in Texas*, pp. 22 ff.

Born in Marblehead, Massachusetts, in 1802, Richardson had gone to South Carolina as a boy of sixteen years. There he attended State College at Columbia and became a firm follower of the political philosophy of John C. Calhoun.[2] In 1837 he happened to meet Mirabeau Lamar. The two men became close friends and shortly, with the encouragement of Lamar, Richardson came to Texas. In Texas during the late thirties and early forties he surveyed land and taught school, and, in 1843, through the contact and influence of Doctor Francis Moore, Jr.,[3] together with the aid of Lamar and B. F. Neil,[4] Richardson acquired control of the Galveston *News*, which, under the editorship of Samuel Bangs, was failing financially.[5]

Richardson had a sharp sense for news, and in some ways he anticipated the circulation-building techniques used by Dana, Pulitzer and Greeley. His journalistic style included a strong element of rapid dramatic narrative. His own personal tastes as well as his journalistic evaluation of the taste of his readers moved him in that direction; he loved the theatre, dramatic plays, and fast moving tales of mystery and intrigue. Through his personal influence, financial and otherwise, numerous theatrical companies included Galveston on their itineraries. In fact, his interest in the theatre was so great that he built an opera house to indulge his fascination for this aspect of metropolitan culture.[6]

The editor was a man of "enormous enthusiasms," but his opinions on most matters, political and economic, were very orthodox and in

[2] Ben C. Stuart, "Scrapbook," MS, p. 172; Richardson, *Galveston Directory, 1859–60*, p. 90.

[3] Stuart, "Scrapbook," MS, p. 172; Galveston *News*, August 2 and October 31, 1857, and June 26, 1910. Moore was at that time the publisher of the Houston *Telegraph*.

[4] B. F. Neal was a Galveston businessman who was later an advocate of filibustering and secession. In the late 1850's he became clerk of the Court in Brownsville and, in 1862, a representative to the Texas Legislature. Havins, T. R. "Administration of the Sequestration Act in the Confederate District Court for the Western District of Texas, 1862–1865," *Southwestern Historical Quarterly*, XLIII (January 1940), 304.

[5] Galveston *News*, June 26, 1910.

[6] "Galveston Sketches," MS, p. 279.

THE UNION PRINTING OFFICE

From an early photograph in the Historical Collection, John Winterbotham Room, Rosenberg Library, Galveston, Texas.

accord with the views of his times.[7] However, his ideas about public transportation and public improvements were strongly influenced by that truly amazing lawyer-economist, Lorenzo Sherwood,[8] who talked and wrote brilliant polemics advocating state-owned and state-financed public enterprises such as would, even today, startle many jaded advocates of socialization.[9] Sherwood's amazing grasp of the economic facts of his day made his influence invincible when applied to a man such as Richardson, unlearned in economics but more than willing to listen and possessing the mental capacity to follow Sherwood's involved presentations.[10] A man of Richardson's intellectual energy and imagination could not help but be fired by contact with an economic planner such as this. For five years Richardson publicized Sherwood's doctrines advocating the development of a system of state-owned railroads all leading "fan-like" into Galveston. The ideas came from Sherwood but the trumpet sounding the notes was blown by Richardson. He favored the plan partly because he owned a little property on the Island, but much more because he loved Galveston and wanted to see his city prosper. Richardson did not strive for personal wealth; he was much too romantic for that. He was an empire builder—not an ac-

[7] Richardson was a leading member of Trinity Episcopal Church. William Manning Morgan, *Trinity Protestant Episcopal Church, Galveston, Texas, 1841–1953*, p. 367.

[8] Sherwood was a Yankee intellectual, a lawyer-economist from New York State, who in the middle forties played an important part in rewriting the New York State constitution. His views had put him in serious conflict with the railroad and canal builders of that state. However, De Bow, who had great respect for Sherwood's intellectual capacity, published many of his articles. Through this Southern contact Sherwood decided to set up a law practice in Galveston. There Richardson and the New Yorker became acquainted. Henry O'Rielly, *The Slave Aristocracy Against Democracy: Statements Addressed to Loyal Men of All Parties; Antagonistic Principles Involved in the Rebellion*, pamphlet.

[9] See the collection of Sherwood newspaper clippings in the Rosenberg Library, Galveston, Texas.

[10] Ballinger Diary, March 26, 1863, MS; Galveston *News*, April 22, 1856; Lynn to Clarendon, November 17, 1855, MS, F.O.; Houston *Telegraph*, December 5, 1855 and August 4, 1856.

cumulator of wealth.[11] He visualized his city as the apex of a vast transportation center through which the wealth of a "new empire" would
flow to the world's markets; likewise, he saw the port as the ingress
channel through which would pass the culture and products of the
world to develop the vast interior. He saw Galveston as the "Queen
City" and the *News* as the voice of the "Queen."[12] In many ways he
was quixotic and impractical,[13] yet he was hardheaded enough to see
that the transcontinental railroad builders planned to by-pass his island city. Since this was true, the only hope for Galveston was Sherwood's plan to use the state's credit to build a great Texas rail system
leading to the "Queen City."

Although Richardson spoke for the property interests and for the
emotional affection held by most Galvestonians for their city, his support for state-owned railroads was not in accord with the interest of
those Galvestonian businessmen or lawyers whose financial adventures
were connected with the transcontinental railroad builders. In this regard he and Sherwood thrust a divisive element into the unity of interest which was otherwise so marked in Galveston economic, political
and social life. However, on all other matters, "Whity Richardson"
was "sound." He favored a reopening of the slave trade and Nicaraguan filibustering, he saw cotton and slavery as the key to the future
of Texas, and he was fearless in urging secession from the Union if
that action became necessary to achieve the ultimate destiny of Texas;
on these latter matters his views were in opposition to those held by
Sherwood.[14]

All during the fifties Richardson maintained a vigorous opposition
to Sam Houston personally and to all political combinations which the
General organized. The editor went to great pains to belittle Houston's
"heroism" during the battles for Texan independence. In fact, he employed many pages of the popular *Texas Almanac*, which he printed,

[11] Ballinger Diary, March 26, 1863, MS.
[12] Galveston *News*, April 22, 1856.
[13] *William Cook* v. *Willard Richardson*, District Court of Galveston, November 23, 1860.
[14] O'Rielly, *The Slave Aristocracy.*

to expose the "myth" that Houston was a great soldier. Since this publication, which reached a circulation of over 30,000 in 1859, exerted considerable influence among Texans, the General's political and personal position was seriously damaged by Richardson's animosity. Houston replied to Richardson's criticisms at every opportunity including speeches on the floor of the United States Senate. In fact, his farewell speech to that body was devoted in large part to a rebuttal to the Galveston editor's attacks upon him. On May 18, 1857, the general made a special trip to the Island, hired Morian Hall and there delivered a furious denunciation of Richardson and reply to his attacks.[15]

The other three leading editors on the Gulf Coast, Stuart of the *Civilian*, Flake of *Die Union*, and Cushing of the Houston *Telegraph*, took a more kindly view of the old soldier. In fact, Stuart was an ardent supporter and long time friend of the General. Flake supported Houston during the late fifties after the General had abandoned Know-Nothingism,[16] and while Cushing usually disagreed politically with Houston, he always treated the old man with a marked respect. Since Stuart and his *Civilian* took a strong position behind Sam Houston on almost every issue, it would appear that part of Richardson's purpose

[15] Galveston *News*, May 19, 1857. For details concerning the Houston-Richardson feud see Richardson, *Texas Almanac, 1859*, pp. 36–89; *1860*, pp. 18–35; Congressional Globe, 1858–1859, 2nd Sess., 35th Cong., February 28, 1859, 1433, 1438.

[16] The Know-Nothing party, a Northern semi-secret organization opposed to foreigners, grew out of the Order of United Americans about 1852. Its membership was divided into three classes; the first two were permitted to determine policy or be nominated to office; the members of the third class were pledged to vote for the party ticket and to reply "I don't know" to all inquiries concerning the party. The organization had considerable success for a time in some Northern states, but by 1855 its control had been captured by Southerners and the name changed to the American party. In 1856 the party nominated Millard Fillmore, who received 874,538 popular votes and 8 electoral votes. In the late 1850's Sam Houston, having lost the support of the secession and slave-trade Democrats sought and acquired the support of the American party in Texas, which ironically, he combined with support from his German friends there to capture the governorship. This was indeed a strange combination; however, by the time of the secession crisis the Secessionists had won back the support of many members of the American party.

in maintaining a continuing attack upon Houson was to assume a position opposing that taken by the *Civilian* in order to increase circulation and to arouse reader interest in his *Almanac* and in his newspaper. The two editors in Galveston learned early that a controversy was not only good politics but also good for circulation.

As the decade closed, the moderate-minded men began to lose control and Richardson's political influence on the Gulf Coast became greater because his flamboyant characteristics were more suitable for the temper of secession times. In 1859 the well-placed Galvestonian Guy Bryan, who was then out of the state, wrote to his friend Ballinger for advice about whether he ought to venture to run for Congress. Ballinger advised him not to run because Richardson [was] "the key man here" who controlled the issue.[17]

Hamilton Stuart, the editor-publisher of the *Civilian*, was not only a journalist but also a practicing politician; he served as mayor of Galveston during the years 1849–1852 and for almost a decade and half was federal customs collector on the Island, retiring from this office only after the secession of Texas from the Union.

Stuart was a native Kentuckian, born on a farm near Louisville in 1813. Twenty-two years later he was publisher and editor of the *Sentinel* in Georgetown, Kentucky. In 1837 he married the daughter of Colonel B. S. Chambers who together with John Chambers published the *Kentucky* Gazette at Lexington.[18] Stuart and his wife came to Galveston in search of a milder climate, but, while the warm Gulf Coast weather was undoubtedly suited to his temperament, the more rugged characteristics of some aspects of Texas politics often proved to be a burden to him. In fact, in 1838, on the occasion when Stuart first arrived in Galveston, he called upon Sam Houston to present his letter of introduction. The General immediately offered him a glass of champagne which had been cooled in a hogshead of ice that had just arrived by boat. Stuart declined the drink, "an extraordinary thing to do in Texas in those days, especially as Mr. Stuart had come to Texas from Kentucky." Sam Houston was amazed but he took no offense, saying, "Young man, I never insist upon anyone drinking with me. I some-

[17] Ballinger Diary, January 26, 1859, MS.
[18] Stuart, "Scrapbook," MS, p. 174.

times think I drink too much myself. Probably it would have been better for me if I had never acquired the habit."[19] With the aid of Doctors Levi Jones and R. A. Iron, Stuart began to publish the *Civilian* on May 8, 1838. He called his paper the *Civilian* as a "mild protest" against the mania which "most prominent men in public affairs in Texas" had for assuming titles such as "General," "Colonel," "Major" or "Captain," who "in the language of Shakespeare 'never set a squadron in the field, nor of the diversion of battle know aught than a spinster.' "[20]

In 1859 Richardson wrote that Stuart "wielded a powerful influence" over the "destinies of the state and especially of the Democratic Party" of which the *Civilian* was the "leading organ."[21] However, Richardson was often very critical of Stuart's principles which he said were at times so flexible that the *Civilian* editor's actions often rested upon expediency rather than principle. When Stuart shifted his editorial policy from advocation of the reopening of the African slave trade to opposition to this traffic because he feared it would split the Union, Richardson and Cushing both accused Stuart of changing his views in order to retain his lucrative post at the Customs House. Stuart, said Richardson, had "too much liking for public salaries" to be able to sustain firm convictions.[22]

The fact was, however, that Stuart suffered severely over the division which he saw arising in America over slavery. He loved his state, his city and the Union; his seeming expediency and vacillation were the result of sincere but divided loyalties. At heart he was not a daring man, but rather a gentle person of a philosophical nature. He usually tried to avoid conflict; and yet at one time he was so aroused over the secession issue that he virtually challenged an adversary to a duel.[23] On a matter of prime importance such as secession, Stuart held his ground, but on "secondary" considerations such as expansion of the slave trade,

[19] St. Louis *Globe-Democrat*, August 31, 1892; Galveston *News*, November 17, 1894. The details of this incident involving Sam Houston were related by Ben Stuart in 1892 to Walter B. Stevens.

[20] Stuart, "Scrapbook," MS, p. 174.

[21] Richardson, *Galveston Directory, 1859–60*, p. 90.

[22] Galveston *News*, March 19, 1857.

[23] See Ballinger Diary, August 22–31, 1860, MS.

abuses of the civil rights of free Negroes, or threats against the free speech permitted to Unionists, Stuart kept his true convictions under a cautious leash.[24] Rugged men, such as those who were actively engaged in Nicaraguan filibustering and the clandestine slave trade intimidated him. At times they forced him to condone affairs with the Customs House of which he did not morally approve; nevertheless, Stuart rationalized that the destiny of Texas during the mid-decades required more slaves, even African slaves, and that filibustering itself was a legitimate tool shaping that destiny; he was, however, too kind a man to enjoy the association with the rough and ready expansionists; nor could he condone the idea of permanent slavery. He saw the institution as a temporary expedient which, he believed, would gradually be reduced to the vanishing point during the twentieth century. Although he was not a member of any religious sect and made no public profession to religious faith, Stuart was essentially a very moral and religious person. A contemporary newspaper colleague referred to him as a man of "cheerful nature, philosophical and with a sense of humor"—everyone "liked him."[25]

The *Civilian* under Stuart's editorship did not engage in the sensational style of journalism which characterized the *News*; rather, Stuart's paper was very orthodox. Following the usual custom of the time his columns contained long dissertations about grave political, philosophical, and economic matters. In between the long ranks of weighty discussions were sandwiched a slight leavening of sprightly "editor's notes" and "local items" which revealed the more human side of the man behind the *Civilian*. On occasion an "indignation" editorial written by Stuart would rise to the heights of a blazing fire and arouse vigorous comments or refutations from other Texas papers—particularly

[24] *Ibid.*, September 1 and November 14, 1860.
[25] Ben C. Stuart, "Hamilton Stuart: Pioneer Editor," Galveston *News*, June 3, 1917. Ben C. Stuart was the son of Hamilton. Ben Stuart, a newspaperman himself, was in his middle teens during the Civil War. During the war and afterwards he worked for both the *Civilian* and the *News* at various intervals. It is interesting to note that the funeral service for Hamilton Stuart was conducted jointly by Dr. Carter, an Episcopal rector, and Dr. Cohen, a Jewish rabbi.

from the *Telegraph* and the *News*. But Hamilton Stuart, by nature, was not one who could find a congenial place for himself as an actor in a program of manifest destiny. He had none of the characteristics of the empire builder, nor the realistic drive of the accumulator of great wealth. At heart he was closer to the romantic academic and was most at peace when he was concerned with the realm of ideas. Thus, he was always a little uncomfortable in Galveston during the nineteenth century, but his wisdom, gentility, humor and on occasion his fierce bursts of integrity served the Island well.

The immigrant among the four Gulf Coast journalists was Ferdinand Flake, editor and publisher of the German *Die Union* and later of the English language daily *Flake's Bulletin*, one of the leading newspapers in Texas, during the reconstruction period.[26] The Marshall *Flag* in 1858 referred to *Die Union* as "a very widely circulated and influential newspaper."[27] The impact of Flake's "trenchant English prose" as well as his command of the German language was one of the hallmarks of the *Bulletin* and *Die Union*. Since the *News* and the *Civilian* divided between them the English reading Galvestonians, Flake's *Die Union* actually enjoyed a larger city circulation than either of the two English language papers. Thus, in the rising secession crisis, when the German vote could have been a factor, Flake's influence was considerable.[28]

Ferdinand Flake was born in Hanover on September 19, 1822. His father, a professional teacher and Lutheran minister, gave him an excellent education. After a short period of employment in the Goettingen banking house of Klettwig, Reibstein and Company, Flake, then only eighteen years old, embarked for America and arrived in Galveston in the early forties.[29] After a brief association with German colonists in the interior of Texas, Flake returned to Galveston where he

[26] Galveston *News*, July 19, 1872; Dallas *Herald*, January 22, 1870.
[27] Marshall, Texas, *Flag*, July 20, 1858.
[28] "Galveston Sketches," MS, pp. 302–307; Richardson *Galveston Directory, 1859–60*, pp. 8, 91; Stuart, "Scrapbook," MS; Joseph Osterman Dyer, "History of Galveston," MS, VI, Rosenberg Library; *Flake's Bulletin*, July 21, 1872.
[29] "Galveston Sketches," MS, pp. 302–307; *State of Texas* v. *Ferdinand Flake*, District Court of Galveston, October 7, 1848.

won the friendship of Colonel John S. Sydnor, native-born political leader, who served as mayor of Galveston for several terms, and who was famous throughout the state because of the large slave market which he maintained on Galveston Island. Hundreds of slaves changed masters at Sydnor's auctions—where the interest of both the slave and the purchaser was taken into account before Colonel Sydnor's blessing was bestowed upon a "new situation."[30] In addition to his fortunate contact with Colonel Sydnor young Flake established a political friendship with the German born justice of the peace, I. E. Rump, the ablest political broker on the Island. These two established political leaders gave Flake his first political and financial start on the Island by allowing him to be elected to the lucrative position of city marshal—an office which occupied a key position in the tax collecting procedure then in vogue.[31] The agility and flexibility of Galveston politicians during the fifties was demonstrated by the fact that forty-eighter style Germans, such as Flake, who were professed "lovers of republican principles," could nevertheless achieve a political *rapprochement* not only with the chief slave merchant in Texas, but also with the "free Negro elevating" German justice of the peace, I. E. Rump.[32]

The sincerity of Ferdinand Flake's rejection of slavery as a permanent labor system or his rejection of measures which would lead to the reopening of the African slave trade cannot be questioned, because even under duress he persisted in asserting publicly that slavery could not be condoned as a permanent labor system. He was willing to concede the temporary necessity of using slavery as a labor system, but he would not agree that slavery could be morally justified.[33]

While Flake was willing to accept slavery as an intermediatory labor system[34] and was willing to overlook the occasional "elevation" of a

[30] *Ibid.*

[31] Richardson, *Galveston Directory, 1859–60*, p. 91.

[32] "Galveston Sketches," MS, p. 302–307; Lynn to John Henry Brown, June 9, 1857; Lynn to J. E. Rump, June 11, 1857; Lynn to Governor Elisha M. Pease, June 13, 1857; Rump to Lynn, June 13, 1857, MSS, F.O.; *State of Texas* v. *Thomas B. Chubb*, District Court of Galveston, January 24, 1857.

[33] Houston *Telegraph*, July 4, 8, and 13, 1859; Galveston *Die Union*, June 13, 1859.

[34] San Antonio *Alamo Express*, February 4, 1861.

free Negro into slavery by the justice court of his mentor I. E. Rump, he held fast to his affection for the union of the American states as the only enduring hope for a demonstration of man's ability to govern himself; holding these views and possessing the temerity to express them, Flake was often in serious conflict with prevailing Anglo-American opinion on the Island.[35] Yet, editor Flake, like most Germans on the Island, held a profound belief that as a new convert to a republican system, he was morally obligated to abide by the will of the majority.

Edward Hopkins Cushing, editor of the Houston *Telegraph* and "voice of the mainland" was the fourth member of the quartet of journalists on the Gulf Coast. He maintained a constant vigilance to prevent the city of Houston from being "bound in economic servitude to the Queen City on the Island which held an octopus-like hold upon the commercial throat of Texas."[36] This loquacious son of Vermont, born in Royalton on June 11, 1829, was reared and educated in the New England Puritan tradition. He graduated from Dartmouth College in 1850 after having "evinced a partiality for literature and ancient languages," and directly afterwards journeyed to Texas where, for a time, he taught school in Galveston, Brazoria, and Columbia.[37] Cushing soon transferred his attention from teaching to publishing and editing; he first acquired the Columbia *Democrat* and *Planter*. Later, in 1856, he secured control of the Houston *Telegraph* and thereafter made the operation of that newspaper his chief occupation. His *Telegraph* was a strong voice calling upon all readers to marshal their energy for the commercial and economic development of the Houston environs and for the development of "sound" educational facilities in Texas.[38]

Although Cushing was born and educated in the northeast he was as Southern in his political convictions as any native of Dixie. No man on

[35] Galveston *News*, January 22, 1861; San Antonio *Alamo Express*, February 4, 1861; Ben C. Stuart, "Necrology," MS.

[36] Houston *Telegraph*, July 8, 1859.

[37] E. B. Cushing, "Edward Hopkins Cushing," *Southwestern Historical Quarterly*, XXV (April, 1922), 261.

[38] *Ibid.*, p. 263.

the Gulf Coast was a more energetic advocate for the institution of slavery, the reopening of the African slave trade, and eventually for secession, than was editor Cushing. Yet, on occasion he opened the columns of his paper to permit advocates of opinions in opposition to his own to voice their convictions. In some respects Cushing's paper was the most objective of the four major journals on the Coast.[39]

It was the custom for leading men in Galveston and Houston to write an occasional article for the papers expressing a particular point of view on public affairs. Although these dissertations were usually signed only by an initial, persons who kept abreast of events were cognizant of each writer's identity. William Ballinger, Judge James Bell, Judge Peter Gray, or Lorenzo Sherwood, to name but a few, often indulged in this form of public expression. Both Stuart and Richardson, and especially the latter, at times neglected to find room to print these self-volunteered essays—"Old Richardson didn't put in the articles as I asked him to do," Ballinger often complained in his diary—however if one handled Cushing with care it was easy to secure the publication of one's effort in the *Telegraph*.[40] While Cushing practiced a hard-hitting style of journalism he was usually willing to grant the opposition leaders the right to hold different views if they could present a logical argument for their positions. Richardson on the other hand, who was not tolerant of "unsound" views, was less apt to be objective. Richardson was also "a hard loser"; Cushing could face a lost election with charm and grace. Richardson was a very professional journalist; Cushing was actually more the literate gentleman who happened to like the publishing business than he was the professional newspaperman.

Although Cushing and Richardson differed over the railroad issue and over the matter of whether or not the port of Galveston exercised an unfair control of Texas sea-borne trade, they were close allies on

[39] Galveston *Civilian*, July 14, 1857; *Proceedings of the State Convention of the Democratic Party of the State of Texas, Which Assembled at Waco, Monday, May 4th, 1857*, pamphlet, pp. 1–21; Ballinger Diary, August 22–31, 1860, MS.

[40] Ballinger Diary, January 1, 1862, MS. Also see the Diary for years 1859–1863.

such vital questions as the slave trade, filibustering, and secession. For the most part Cushing and Richardson were in political opposition to Stuart and Flake who were of one mind on many issues. Their journalistic duels were at times very fierce, and demonstrated the vigor, resourcefulness, and originality of these four able journalists. Actually, the editors held a marked respect and friendship for each other despite their verbal conflicts. With one or two exceptions during the uglier moments of the secession crisis and the war period the four men enjoyed the cordial personal relations with each other which so happily marked the association of gentlemen during the mid-nineteenth century in Galveston and on the Gulf Coast.[41]

[41] Galveston *Civilian*, July 14, 1857; *Proceedings of the State Convention*, pp. 1–21; Ballinger Diary, August 22–31, 1860, MS.

PART TWO

Texas Crescent Cotton Expansion: *Avant-Garde* of Secession

5. THE RAILROADS: TRANSPORTATION
FOR COTTON

T*riumph of the Corporate Railroad Builders*
WO THINGS TEXAS NEEDED to exploit the millions of acres of
potential cotton land in the state: slaves and railroads. The slaves were
to be had by reopening the African slave trade; the railroads could
and would be built. According to editor Cushing of the Houston *Telegraph* nearly 18 million acres of Texas cotton land waited to be cultivated. It would be "criminal folly," he said, to deprive the state of her
greatness. These figures on acreage were an exaggeration; the United

States Department of Agriculture's Bureau of the Census shows that by 1900 Texas had 7,363,000 acres in cotton producing 3,438,000 bales of cotton. But even these later figures illustrate the actual potential inherent in Texas cotton production.[1]

It is no wonder then that businessmen and planters in the state were eager for a good supply of slaves and transportation and that they intended to acquire both. Arthur Lynn in his annual report for 1860 stressed the fact that once Texas had acquired railroads she would find one way or another to secure the needed Negroes and that if the federal union denied her these Negroes from a cheap source, namely Africa, Texas would no doubt take drastic measures to secure these slaves.[2]

Most Houston and Galveston newspapers kept up a constant agitation for railroads and African Negroes. The letters to the editors' columns were filled with long messages from leading citizens, businessmen, planters, lawyers, and clergymen, to say nothing of politicians, which kept up a drumfire of comment stressing the need of the state for these two items.[3]

The great political struggle in Texas during the 1850's over where the railroads were to run—that is, if they were to favor Galveston or Houston—was an internal power fight of considerable significance to local areas of the state; whether the railroads were to be privately-owned or state-owned was an important ideological matter to the persons concerned; but the fact of the need for the railroads was never in question. All Texans were agreed on that.

By 1860 the issue of where the roads would run and how they were to be financed and who was to own them had been settled; by then the pattern for the lines was set and the fact that they would be built was

[1] "Texas Cotton Acreage, Production and Value," (Source: U.S. Department of Agriculture, U.S. Bureau of Census). Printed in *Texas Almanac, 1958–1959,* The Dallas *Morning News,* 1960; Houston *Telegraph,* March 21, 1859.

[2] Annual Reports of British Consulate, Galveston, 1860.

[3] Houston *Telegraph,* March 18, July 1, 1857; January 31, February 7, 28, March 21, August 11, 1859; Galveston *News,* June 20, July 2, August 8, 22, December 3, 1857.

certain. According to the most reliable atlas of the time the state, by 1860, possessed about 400 miles of railroad. In some cases all the rails had not yet been laid, but completion was in sight. The names of these roads illustrate the extent of their coverage: The San Antonio and Mexican Gulf Railroad, The Buffalo Bayou, Brazos and Colorado Railroad, The Houston, Tap, and Brazoria Railroad, The Houston and Texas Central Railroad, The Texas and New Orleans Railroad, The Galveston and Houston Railroad. While these names may give an exaggerated picture of the actual size of the railroads of Texas in 1860, they do, however, illustrate the potential of the roads and this was what influenced Texans of the time. There were actual railroads in operation connecting such towns as Victoria, Alleyton, Brenham, Hempstead, Wharton, Richmond, Houston, Galveston, Beaumont, and Orange. Thus the vast cotton potential of the near Gulf Coast interior was connected to the sea for the sale of cotton abroad and to the Northern textile markets. The interesting factor, then, in the so-called railroad battle of the 1850's was not whether there should be railroads but who should build them and where they should go. This was the issue in the political power struggle between Galveston and Houston in the 1850's.[4]

This struggle, which reached a critical stage in the year 1856, arose out of three different points of view that eventually coalesced into three different policies for the construction of Texas railroads, known respectively as the State Plan, the Galveston Plan, and the Corporate Plan. Lorenzo Sherwood was the originator and advocate of the State Plan that envisaged a rail system built and owned by the state. He suggested that these lines ought to run toward the Gulf—that is, converge in Galveston; however, Sherwood was more an advocate of state-built

---

[4] *Transactions of the Texas Academy of Science*, IX (1907), pp. 42–74; *Atlas To Accompany The Official Records of The Union and Confederate Armies*, published under the direction of the Hons. Redfield Proctor, Stephen B. Elkins, and Daniel S. Lamont, Secretaries of War, by Maj. George B. Davis, U.S. Army, Mr. Leslie J. Perry, Civilian Expert, Mr. Joseph W. Kirkley, Civilian Expert, Board of Publication, Compiled by Capt. Calvin D. Cowles, 23d U.S. Infantry, Washington: Government Printing Office, 1891–1895, General Topographical Map Sheet, XXII, Plate CLVII (Texas).

railroads than of the absolute necessity of making Galveston the key rail center of Texas.[5]

Willard Richardson was the prime instigator of the Galveston Plan. He believed that the logic of geography dictated that all Texas rail lines must lead "fan-like" to Galveston; he used his newspaper to point out that adherence to a transcontinental system, a key feature of the Corporate Plan, would make Texas an economic vassal of either New Orleans or St. Louis. He was not unduly concerned over whether his plan was executed by private builders or by a state-owned or a state-directed organization.[6]

The Corporate Plan, sometimes also known as the State Loan Plan, was projected by railroad entrepreneurs who asserted that the transportation system for the state ought to be built by private promoters. In order to attract the capital necessary to finance a private system, the advocates of the Corporate Plan recommended that substantial grants of land and loans of money be offered to entrepreneurs who would undertake the risk of building rail lines across the state.[7] The promoters suggested that grants of sixteen sections of land and loans of from $6,000 to $10,000 be granted for each mile of railroad line actually constructed.[8] It was argued by the advocates of the Corporate or Loan Plan that land and loan assistance were needed to induce foreign and do-

[5] Sherwood Collection, Rosenberg Library, Galveston, Texas. This collection consists of a scrapbook of undated newspaper and magazine articles written by Lorenzo Sherwood. Since it is impractical to cite these items by date or page, this material will be hereafter referred to as the Sherwood Collection *passim.*

[6] Samuel B. Hurlburt to P. C. Tucker, November 30, 1852, printed in H. Bailey Carroll, "Texas Collection," *Southwestern Historical Quarterly,* XLVIII, 116–118; Galveston *News,* April 22, 1856.

[7] Houston *Telegraph,* August 22, 1859.

[8] Jonathan F. Barrett (of Boston, President of the Buffalo Bayou, Brazos, and Colorado Railway Company) to John Grant Tod (Commodore and Secretary of the Navy of the Republic of Texas), July 28, 1853, John Grant Tod Papers, MS, a private collection owned by Mrs. Rosa Tod Hamner and John Tod Hamner, Houston, Texas; Houston *Telegraph,* April 16, 1856 and August 22, 1859.

THE GENERAL SIDNEY SHERMAN, a railroad locomotive
used on the Gulf Coast in the 1850's. This particular locomotive,
built by the M. W. Baldwin Company of Philadelphia, was well
known on the Gulf Coast in the early days.

From an original drawing of the engine in the Glendale Cemetery
Association Collection in Houston, Texas.

mestic speculators to advance the additional funds needed to build the railroads.[9]

The entreprenuers behind the Corporate Plan were a loose coalition of transcontinental "paper railroaders"—eastern stockbrokers who expected to secure commissions on issues of Texas railroad paper floated in Europe or America[10]—and merchant capitalists in Houston who expected to profit from a Texas railroad system which connected their inland city with the great transcontinental lines then taking shape on paper and in the halls of the national Congress.[11]

The merchant bankers of both Houston and Galveston favored the Corporate Plan because they hoped to sell the railroad builders large quantities of merchandise;[12] however, the mercantile interests in Galveston faced a dilemma because they did not favor either a Houston-oriented rail system or a "state controlled" system such as that advocated by Lorenzo Sherwood, even though they were attracted by the "Galveston-centered" possibilities in his plan. The Island merchants would have favored Richardson's plan but for the fact that they viewed his idea as impractical because it seemed unlikely that the private capital necessary to develop this plan could ever be mobilized. In the end they chose the Corporate Plan as the lesser of two evils.[13]

As "railroad planning" in Texas progressed, Richardson saw that the Island mercantile support which he had mobilized for the Galveston Plan was being won away from his point of view by the sponsors of the Houston-Transcontinental railroad orientation. His *News* warned the Galveston merchants once again in even shriller notes that if Texas joined her rail system with the projected transcontinental lines the state and most certainly the Island would lose control of their own economic development. In the mid-fifties, however, Richardson had

[9] Houston *Telegraph*, April 16, 1856; Barrett to Tod, August 9 and 27, September 8, 1853; Barrett to Sidney Sherman, August 27, 1853, Tod Papers, MS.

[10] Houston *Telegraph*, August 22, 1859; Sherman to Barrett, July 13 and 22, 1853, Tod Papers, MS.

[11] Richardson, *Texas Almanac, 1868*, pp. 118–122, 134, and 220–221; Galveston *News*, June 4, 1857; Houston *Telegraph*, September 11, 1857.

[12] *Ibid.*, July 20, 1857.   [13] *Ibid.*, June 23, 1856.

to acknowledge the financial and political realities of the railroad situation and accept the fact that the Corporate or private builders had, of necessity, to plan in terms of transcontinental railroads if they were to attract the influence and the capital needed to push their projects forward. Thus, since "realities" precluded the possibility of securing private funds to promote the Galveston Plan, Richardson merged his hopes for a Galveston-centered rail system with Sherwood's plan for lines built and owned by the state.[14] The fact that Richardson, a powerful editor and a key figure in the Texas Democratic Party, decided to align his influence with Sherwood's State Plan rather than associate himself with the advocates of privately built railroads was of key significance in "railroad politics" in Texas at the mid-decade crisis. Richardson gave the State Plan very powerful support, and in the *News* Sherwood had an unequaled opportunity to present his arguments.

By originating and advocating the State Plan, which ran counter to the interests of very influential persons in the state, Lorenzo Sherwood of Galveston, lawyer, economist, writer, "agitator," and political nonconformist, became the man most maligned in the public prints of Texas during the years 1855–1860. Sherwood was born in New York State in 1808; during the late thirties and early forties he had served his native state as a legislator, as a member of the 1846 constitutional convention, as an effective foe of "canal and railroad promotion schemes," and as an ardent advocate for the direct harnessing of state credit for the building of railroads. He believed that the practice of allowing private promoters to charge the public large interest and service costs to finance, build, and operate the needed transportation systems represented an unnecessary expense. As a member of the Radical Democratic faction in the New York State Legislature, he exercised his particular professional proficiency in the field of railroad and canal finance. In matters of state-financed public improvements he was an associate of the famous Radical advocate of canal economy, Michael Hoffman of Herkimer. Sherwood's financial innovations exerted an influence upon the taxation and public loan provisions written into the

[14] *Ibid.*, April 16 and May 12, 1856; Galveston *News*, April 22, 1856; Richardson, *Texas Almanac, 1868*, pp. 118–122, 134, and 220–221.

contitutional amendments placed in the New York State fundamental law in 1846. He often assailed the practice of using the state's credit as an instrument to underwrite risk for private promoters. His remarkable gifts as an economist enabled him to uncover carefully hidden financial sophistries,[15] and he had the discourteous habit of employing the financial statements of the enterprises supported by his political opponents as an effective weapon in floor debates.

In 1846 Sherwood decided to move his law practice to the state of Texas. He packed up his large library, his "peculiar financial notions," his wife Caroline and his young son and transported them to Galveston. On the way he had acquired a legal assistant in North Carolina by the name of William H. Goddard, a young law student, who later became the minor partner in the firm of Sherwood and Goddard of Galveston. This firm earned the enmity of several powerful Texans because of the fact that it often accepted clients who had financial grievances against such men as Robert Mills, Samuel May Williams, and the several railroad-promoting combines in Texas.[16]

Although Sherwood was barely fifty years old during the decade of the fifties, he was known on the Island as "Old Sherwood." Ballinger, who had to compete with the New Yorker in cases being tried before the courts in Galveston, was often particularly annoyed by "Old Sherwood" who frequently won litigations against his merchant banker clients. "Sherwood is a rather mean old fellow to get along with," wrote Ballinger in his diary, "He doesn't act like a gentleman."[17]

Although Sherwood neglected to conduct his practice in accord with the accepted code of camaraderie which graced the Galveston bar, nevertheless, his legal talents were of sufficient quality to provide him with lucrative clients from among the foreign shipping firms which

[15] Henry O'Rielly, *The Slave Aristocracy Against Democracy: Statements Addressed to Loyal Men of All Parties; Antagonist Principles Involved in the Rebellion*, pp. 1–31; Census Rolls, Galveston, 1850, MS; Ballinger Diary, June 17, 1859, MS; De Alva Stanwood Alexander, *A Political History of the State of New York*, II, 90–113; Herbert D. A. Donovan, *The Barnburners*, pp. 74–89; *Summers* v. *Mills*, 21 Texas Reports, 78; Richardson, *Galveston Directory, 1859–60*, p. 27.

[16] See Texas Reports, 1850–1861.

[17] Ballinger Diary, June 17, 1859, MS.

carried trade into Texas. It was Sherwood who not only wrote the brief but also presented the oral arguments in behalf of Liverpool merchants in the famous *Peterhoff* case before the United States Supreme Court. Sherwood's victory in this case fixed the principle governing the practice of contraband shipping during war time which later became the accepted practice under international law governing contraband. This principle exerted a profound effect upon blockade and contraband policies which prevailed during the first World War.[18]

The key principle of Sherwood's general economic program for Texas was that the semipublic institutions of banking and transportation ought to rest upon the great natural wealth of the state. If the federal bonds in the Texas Treasury plus a careful and planned expenditure of the public domain were used to establish a sound credit base for banks and railroads, then low-interest foreign loans for railroads and sound paper for banking would follow as a natural consequence of economics, said Sherwood; but, he warned, "if our public lands, public money and later the public credit is exhausted piecemeal" then no one will gain except those who have managed to exploit the situation. The corporate system as it was developing in the mid-fifties, said Sherwood, was and would continue to be one of "disorder and conflict." A total system of finance for both banks and railroads, fixed by a constitutional amendment that would put the matter beyond the control of any single legislature, was the policy which could bring the "greatest degree of political morality into a situation which was already in serious disorder." He insisted that all corporate property ought to be forced to accept liability for the acts of its agents, that the individual liability of every stockholder ought to extend to "once or twice the amount of his stock." No man should be allowed to exploit the situation by the use of devices which put him out of reach of court action. Under his plan, said Sherwood,

state bonds would attain their highest value and have a home market. The people as well as the bankers would have the strongest motives to keep the credit of the state good and sound, as the currency and business interest

---

[18] *The Peterhoff*, 72 United States Reports, 28–62; Herbert W. Briggs, *The Law of Nations*, pp. 905–908; Austin *State Gazette*, June 20, 1863.

would require that it be kept so. The idea that capital would not associate for banking purposes under these restrictions [was] a simple fallacy . . .

Experience had already shown in other nations that capital would be very willing to associate itself with the stable conditions arising from such control. "To leave the whole subject to uninstructed legislative caprice," said Sherwood, "would be the height of folly, unnecessary as it would be disastrous."[19]

Support for Sherwood's plan came from Richardson's *News*, the rank and file of Galvestonians, and from many Texans in the interior who distrusted "promoters" or who were more interested in getting railroads running in Texas than in securing a profit or advantage from the actual construction of rail lines. Sherwood began advocating his State Plan in the early fifties by means of letters to Texas newspapers, by speeches at conventions, and by articles in *DeBow's Review*.[20] He vigorously exploited his command of the economic details of railroad finance and his skill as a debater on these subjects to attract support. He took a leading role in a railroad convention held in Galveston in 1852 which passed a resolution recommending that a large fund be accumulated out of state assets to build a line from the Island to the Red River. A delegation from this convention tried unsuccessfully to secure the support of Governor P. H. Bell.[21] The next year an address that Sherwood delivered before a large railroad convention in Austin on December 13, 1853, attracted wide notice. In this instance he warned that if the private promoters were given a free rein they would exploit the state's credit, deplete its school fund and acquire thousands of acres of Texas land in return for mere shadow railroads. One editor who had heard the speech observed that "Mr. S. is a gentleman of extensive information on his subject and is an able advocate of his peculiar views; but they will not, we think, be adopted by the state of Texas" because his ideas were not in tune with the leading railroad-

[19] Galveston *News*, June 4, 1857; Sherwood Collection, *passim*.

[20] See articles by Lorenzo Sherwood in *De Bow's Review*, XIII, 523 and XIX, 85 and 202; Sherwood Collection, *passim*.

[21] *De Bow's Review*, XIII, 523; Sherwood Collection, *passim*; *Texas Senate Journal, 1853*, pp. 17–18.

minded men in the state.[22] In the spring of 1855 Sherwood was invited to address a Texas Railroad Convention in Huntsville on the subject of the "State System of Internal Improvements."[23] By that time the New Yorker's ideas were being taken very seriously by Texans throughout the state.[24]

To implement the principles expressed in his writing and public speaking, Sherwood persistently injected his railroad ideas into the state legislative bodies at Austin and into the political campaigns. In 1850, for example, he induced John Dancy, a senator serving Travis, Fayette, and Bastrop counties, to introduce a bill in the Senate to authorize the use of the public domain and the school fund to build a state-owned trunk line railroad into Galveston;[25] and five years later when Sherwood himself had been sent by the voters of Galveston to represent them in the legislature he personally introduced another bill which proposed to set in motion a plan for building state-owned railroads.[26]

Another device employed by Sherwood and his allies was to endeavor to capture the governorship on the basis of the State Plan. In 1853 they ran Senator John Dancy for governor on a Sherwood platform without success. During the first term of Governor E. M. Pease (1853–1855), they tried to win him over to the State Plan, but this maneuver failed. Two years later Sherwood's group approached David C. Dickinson, the Know-Nothing candidate for governor in 1855, but he, too, refused to favor their plan. However, by campaign time in 1855 the rising popular interest in the State Plan induced Governor Pease to shift his position and run for re-election on a Sherwood platform; and when Pease won his second term, the State Plan advocates were on the verge of victory.[27] On November 5, 1855 Governor Pease outlined in great detail his proposed State Plan. He told the lawmakers

[22] Austin *State Gazette*, December 13, 1853; also see Sherwood Collection, *passim.*

[23] Clarksville, Texas, *Standard*, February 18, 1855.

[24] Seguin, Texas, *Mercury*, March 10, 1855.

[25] Alexander Deussen, "The Beginnings of the Texas Railroad System," *Transactions of the Texas Academy of Science*, IX (1907), 49.

[26] Houston *Telegraph*, May 14, 1856.

[27] *Ibid.*; Sherwood Collection, *passim.*

that the railroad situation was chaotic, that individuals had acquired and held "charters merely for speculation"; the governor, therefore, set forth a plan to build 1600 miles of railroads during the next fifteen years to be financed along the lines recommended by Sherwood.[28]

During the first half of the decade of the fifties the interests which favored the Corporate Plan and its companion piece the Loan Plan[29] grew increasingly concerned over Sherwood's ability to make his ideas acceptable to the Texas voters.[30] The Corporate promoters acquired two particularly valuable allies in 1855 when the two leading private bankers in Texas, Robert Mills and Samuel May Williams, joined in the active opposition to Sherwood. Although the New Yorker had been friendly to the bankers, in that he had supported measures to legalize banking and had upheld the proposition that the illegally operating "private banks" ought not to be forced to close until provisions for legal institutions had been established, nevertheless, such men as Mills and Williams saw very clearly that any banking legislation written by Sherwood or with his advice would result in "restraining" regulations and thus bring an end to the existing "free money market" in Galveston.[31]

The Corporate faction tried hard to negate the effectiveness of the New Yorker's propositions. "How much money do Sherwood and his disciples expect to get out of the State Plan?" demanded Cushing of Houston. The editor pointed out that the illustrations Sherwood used to prove his case—such as referring to the systems used in Europe—ought to be suspect by their very nature. "Do we want to be like the monarchies of Russia, Prussia and Austria?" Cushing demanded of those who might see virtue in Sherwood's economics.[32]

During the spring of 1856 the newspapers on the mainland issued

[28] Texas *Senate Journal, 1855*, pp. 20–31.
[29] The Houston *Telegraph*, May 30, 1856, gives a long discussion of the merits of the Loan Plan or Corporate Plan.
[30] Galveston *News*, June 4, 1857; Sherwood Collection, *passim*; Houston *Telegraph*, July 14, 1856.
[31] Sherwood Collection, *passim*; Houston *Telegraph*, July 14, 1856, and Galveston *News*, June 4, 1857.
[32] Houston *Telegraph*, June 23, 1856.

continual assertions that "Mr. Sherwood and his disciples [were] trying to push the State Plan on an unwilling people."[33] Cushing proclaimed that the Galveston Plan and the State Plan were schemes "to rule out Houston in favor of Galveston."[34] He argued that the "wiseacres" on the Island were trying to force "the rest of the state to build Galveston a railroad." The assumed "integrity" of purpose with which Sherwood decorated himself was a plain fraud, said Cushing.[35]

To aid in "exposing" Sherwood's "humbuggery," railroad meetings were held in many Gulf Coast churches. Leading merchants and "civic minded men" such as E. H. Cushing, T. W. House, W. M. Rice, H. Cone, G. M. Bryan, F. R. Lubbock and E. D. Nash traveled over a wide itinerary in a campaign to counteract the influence of Sherwood's "humbuggery."[36] It was pointed out that the apparent popular support for the State Plan did not rest on the merits of the plan itself but rather in Sherwood's ability to make black appear to be white. These speakers called attention to the fact that the able Galveston banker and merchant, Robert Mills, favored the plan to allow the Corporate Builders to borrow money from the school fund. This system of financing the railroads, designated the State Loan Plan, was presented by the itinerant speakers as an honest alternate to Sherwood's ideas. The statement of Robert Mills that the State Loan Plan would save planters "up to $1,000,000 per year in transport costs" was quoted frequently to counter the "false arguments" being uttered by "recalcitrant men" like Sherwood's disciples.[37]

In April a giant mass railroad meeting was held in Houston; a galaxy of anti-Sherwood, pro-State Loan Bill men such as Henry Sampson, J. J. Cam, J. H. Stevens, W. M. Rice, T. W. House, T. S. Lubbock, F. R. Lubbock, W. J. Hutchins, I. Berry, and W. W. Baker addressed this extended gathering. Resolutions were passed that favored grants of land and loans to railroads; it was asserted that Sherwood's policies

[33] *Ibid.*, April 16, May 7 and 14, June 30, July 7 and 11, and August 22, 1856.
[34] *Ibid.*, March 12, 1856.
[35] *Ibid.*, May 19, June 23 and 25, 1856.
[36] Houston *Telegraph*, April 9 and 21, May 7, July 7 and August 22, 1856.
[37] *Ibid.*, April 16, 1856.

would be "ruinous and if adopted and carried out, would result in oppressive taxation, an onerous debt, leading to corruption as [was] shown in the annals of the State of New York," that since the Loan Bill was constitutional, no amendment was needed for its implementation, and that each county in Texas ought to send a delegation to Austin to inform the lawmakers of its views.[38] The only "safe plan" for building railroads, said the "loan men" was for the state to provide a portion of the funds by means of loans from the school fund and by big land grants "with the state not owning a single share of any railroad."[39]

Working in the background to stop the State Plan and to put forward the Loan Plan was a group operating *sub rosa* in the corporate faction. Richard Kimball and J. H. Wells in New York and Ashbel Smith, W. P. Ballinger, Senator M. M. Potter, and Senator W. H. Palmer in Texas, to name but a few of these special "corporation men," laid plans to protect the legislators in Austin from the danger of following Sherwood's economic policies. A Mr. Valentine, an agent who represented the "very first names" in London and Paris banking circles, was brought to Galveston to "stabilize the situation."[40] The agent, "fine gentleman in Bond Street suits," came to Galveston, Houston, and Austin to assure wavering Texas businessmen that once the Loan Plan had passed very reasonable loans would be available in London and Paris banking circles. He tried to indicate that Sherwood's claims that the Corporate Plan would result in "high money costs" were not true. He also tried to convince Galveston business that a transcontinental system would not really by-pass the Island. Valentine failed in all three attempts.

Sherwood and Richardson very effectively countered the campaign. On April 22, 1856, for instance, the editor published a long edition of the *News* which was given particularly wide circulation throughout the state. The front page of this issue contained a large map outlining the good features of the Galveston Plan, and the inside pages sup-

[38] *Ibid.*, April 21, 1856.
[39] *Ibid.*, April 11, 1856.
[40] R. Kimball to Senator M. M. Potter, June 4, July 9 and 12, 1856, J. H. Wells to Ashbel Smith, June 2, 1856, Ballinger Papers, M.S.

ported the State Plan with lucid and spirited editorials pointing out once again the fallacy of any policy which would bypass Galveston in favor of New Orleans or St. Louis as exit points for Texas trade.[41]

Considering the development of events in the "railroad battle" as the summer of 1856 approached, the leaders of the corporate faction realized that unless Sherwood was stopped their Loan Bill could never be pushed through the legislature. There was also the additional danger that the State Plan might actually be written into the law by the next legislature. An effort had been made to win over Sherwood, but since he was a man who held profound convictions which were buttressed by a very strong ego—one of his most prominent characteristics—such attempts failed. It was admitted that because of Sherwood's knowledge of economics, public law, and the mechanics of railroad finance, together with his remarkable polemic and forensic talents, it was almost impossible to challenge his "propositions" in the public forum.[42]

There was, however, one area where Sherwood was vulnerable—he was not "sound" on the question of slavery. The New Yorker had stated publicly on various occasions that, although slavery could be condoned as a temporary labor system and endured until perhaps the twentieth century, the institution itself could not be accepted as a permanent labor system in a democracy, and for this reason, as well as for moral reasons, he opposed any attempt to reopen the African slave trade.[43] On the question of the right of secession, Sherwood took a position contrary to that held by "Southern men." He was also accused, though erroneously, of having been "wrong on the Kansas-Nebraska issue."[44] Thus Sherwood was "unsound" on railroads, slavery, secession, the Kansas-Nebraska issue, and the African slave trade.[45]

Sherwood's political position was similar to that of many Northerners who came to Texas in the late forties and early fifties. During this earlier period it was possible for persons who opposed slavery as a permanent institution to assert their beliefs publicly without attract-

[41] Galveston *News,* April 22, 1856; Sherwood Collection, *passim.*
[42] Arthur T. Lynn to Earl of Clarendon, November 17, 1855, MS, F.O.; Sherwood Collection, *passim*; Ballinger Papers, 1856, MS.
[43] Galveston *News,* October 30, 1855.
[44] Houston *Telegraph,* June 30, 1856.   [45] *Ibid.,* June 25, 1856.

ing particular notice or even encountering vigorous disagreement. In fact, at a political convention held in Galveston on January 31, 1848, Sherwood had been applauded when he declared that he had encountered only a few persons on the Island who pretended to defend slavery in the abstract. Most persons agreed, said Sherwood, that the institution was an evil which was not the fault of the present generation and that the only apology needed to explain its continuance was the great difficulty which would arise in the event an effort were made to abolish it.[46] While these remarks were accepted as commonplace in 1848, the same ideas expressed in 1856 or resurrected from the past could be used to arouse prejudice against the speakers.

Thus, when the "Loan men" found that the success of their ventures was threatened because of their inability to counter Sherwood's "economic polemics" they decided to answer him in political terms where he was vulnerable. The mainland newspapers began to refer to the New Yorker as "the Negro-loving abolition pensioned Sherwood, a low, cunning political viper." It was claimed that "his years of study had enabled him to tell lies with statistics"; and in any case, no matter how good his economic advice might be, said these critics, no Texan ought to listen to a man who failed to take "a sound Southern tone on the subject of slavery."[47] It was claimed that if Sherwood had his way every Negro male over twenty-one years would soon be voting.[48] Special "anti-Sherwood" meetings were held in Texas cities to "strip the false hearted pretentions to public welfare paraded" by a man who was "really a Negro-loving abolitionist."

Austin and Houston papers proclaimed that Sherwood had "disgraced the name of Texas," that he was in the pay of New York free-soilers. Editors and public speakers professed to be "astonished" that the citizens of Galveston, "a Southern city," had allowed an "incendiary" person such as Sherwood to usurp the important place "of a

[46] Galveston *News*, February 2, 1848.

[47] Houston *Telegraph*, June 25, 1856.

[48] Dallas *Herald*, quoted in Houston *Telegraph*, June 30, 1856; Clarksville *Standards,* December 29 and March 10, 1855; Lynn to Clarandon, November 17, 1855, MS, F.O.

public teacher." If the Islanders did not divest themselves of "the insidious machinations of Sherwood" on railroad matters, Texans on the mainland might well begin to distrust the Southern loyalty of Galvestonians.[49]

"You have made 'nigger politics' your tilting ground," answered Sherwood to these critics. "Will you tell the people what that has to do with the Internal Improvements Policy of the State?" But his critics ignored this type of query and continued calling Sherwood "a wiseacre and a nigger lover" and asserted that the people of Texas would never agree with him either on his "nigger politics" or on his "State Plan." They told Sherwood that "he had been kicked downstairs." "Can't you take a hint and leave?" Sherwood countered with the assertion that these critics were "Loan men" whose chief concern was in special legislation which would enable them to milk the state to make their worthless paper good.[50]

As the "railroad battle" approached a conclusion the corporate faction realized that the only sure way to defeat the State Plan and pass the Loan Bill was to eliminate Sherwood from the legislature and somehow to intimidate Richardson and force him to drop his vigorous campaign. The Loan men determined therefore to force Sherwood to resign from the legislature on the basis of the charge of abolitionism which had been increasingly made against him. If this move were successful, the Loan men reasoned, it would also negate Richardson's political influence with the legislature.

During the conflict Sherwood tried to answer his accusers. In the election campaign of 1855 prominent men of the American Party had declared that the New Yorker was actually an insidious abolitionist. Sherwood asked for an opportunity to state his case before a large gathering of the American Party assembled in Austin, but this request was refused. A week later, however, he was allowed to state his position at a Democratic Party Meeting. He told this audience that while he lived in New York he had always spoken in defense of states' rights;

[49] Houston *Telegraph*, August 4, 1856; Austin *State Gazette*, December 1, 1856.
[50] Houston *Telegraph*, May 19, 1856.

he had been an associate of the New York political leader Silas Wright
in this regard. Life in the South, said Sherwood, had convinced him
that there was much that was good in the institution of slavery; it was
neither all black nor all white. He reminded his listeners that he had
been a believer in the Kansas-Nebraska Bill and had made a speech
supporting that act in Galveston in 1848.[51] Sherwood's reply to his
critics in this instance had a telling effect. His enemies became even
more convinced that the only effective strategy to employ against him
was to see to it that he was not given an opportunity to speak at public
gatherings.[52]

In order to implement this decision a letter signed by John Henry
Brown of Galveston was printed and circulated. This letter asserted
that on November 16, 1855 Sherwood had made a speech to the Committee of the Whole in the Legislature in which he had said that he
regarded "slavery as a moral evil, a fleeting and temporary institution
destined to gradually give way to some other system." Brown, as a
member of the delegation from Galveston and an ardent slave and
cotton expansionist, declared that Sherwood's attacks upon "the divine
institution of slavery" must be silenced. "We must meet Northern
agrarianism, socialism and abolitionism in a steel-clad appeal to the
God of battles," said Brown.[53] A move was then set in motion to try
to force Sherwood out of the Legislature on the eve of the approaching
struggle over the State Loan Bill.

Sherwood replied to Brown by stating that the circulated version of
the speech to the Legislature was a gross distortion. Sherwood re-
quested the printers of the Legislative records in Austin to issue a true
copy of the speech so that the public might read what actually was
said. The printers refused to allow a copy of the speech to be made
public until the regular printing of the records was released. This
meant that the actual copy of the speech could not appear until after
the critical vote on the Loan Bill had occurred.[54] At this point the

[51] *Ibid.*, December 5, 1855.
[52] Lynn to Clarendon, November 17, 1855, MS, F.O.
[53] John Henry Brown to H. P. Bee (Speaker of the House), November 17,
1955, letter printed in the Houston *Telegraph*, December 5, 1856.
[54] Sherwood to Menard, Secretary of the Democratic Committee in Gal-

movement to force Sherwood to withdraw from the Legislature was initiated. A public meeting was convened on the Island and passed a resolution demanding his immediate resignation. During this time Richardson's *News* was still supporting the State Plan in an all out campaign, but the editor had been forced to move over to a defense of his own position, stating that his views on slavery were not in accord with those attributed, however falsely, to Sherwood.[55]

In an effort to counter the movement to force him out of the Legislature Sherwood and those of his friends who had not been shaken by the charges of abolitionism made against the New Yorker arranged to hold a public meeting in Galveston on the evening of July 7, 1856 to give Sherwood a chance to reply to his critics.

The supporters of the State Loan Bill realized that their interest required them to prevent Sherwood from making this public address. Since the announcements of Sherwood's scheduled speech first appeared in Galveston on Sunday July 6, his opponents were forced to move with great speed in order to prevent the New Yorker from being able to make a public address in the city the following day. They moved with dispatch.

On the morning of July 7th, 1856, a meeting of citizens was "convened to take into consideration the propriety of permitting Lorenzo Sherwood to address the people in defense of his course in the last legislature." Samuel M. Williams presided at the meeting; Alfred F. James and William P. Ballinger served as secretaries. After the citizens had been told why they were assembled, Ballinger read a draft of a letter that he had written to Sherwood which, with their consent, he proposed to deliver to "this intruder from New York." The letter was in effect an ultimatum which ordered Sherwood to resign from his position in the legislature.[56]

In the letter Ballinger told Sherwood that "neither you, nor anyone entertaining your views, will be permitted to appear before the community in a public manner"; he declared that Sherwood would not

---

veston, November 27, 1855, printed in Houston *Telegraph*, December 5, 1855; Austin *State Gazette*, December 1, 1856.

[55] Galveston *News*, June 18, 1856.

[56] Galveston *News*, July 9 and 11, 1856.

be allowed to touch on the subject of slavery "either directly or indirectly, by way of explanation or otherwise under the pretext of personal right of self defense"; and he further advised Sherwood to refrain, in the future, "either in public or in private" from "further abuse of the patience of a people with whom, on that question, you have no congeniality, and whom you wholly misunderstand." Ballinger took cognizance of the fact that Sherwood had asserted that he "has some supporters in this community . . . we trust not; but if the gentleman should care to test this matter by trying to discuss slavery before a Galveston audience" the citizens of the city "will make this evening the occasion for the definite and final settlement of that issue, both as to you and to them. . . ." Any remarks concerning slavery, he reiterated, would be "the prompt signal for consequences to which we need not allude."[57]

It had been decided privately by the committee that their interest would be best served by appearing only to deny Sherwood the opportunity to speak on the subject of slavery and thus leave the impression that on other matters his right of free speech was not being curtailed. This plan seemed likely to attract the most popular support.[58]

While the meeting was in progress W. P. Ballinger, P. R. Edwards, H. Stuart, Thomas M. Joseph, B. C. Franklin, S. M. Williams, F. H. Merriman, O. Farish, M. B. Menard, N. John, and J. J. Hendley spoke to the citizens. Finally, Hamilton Stuart rose and proposed that all those who opposed the action apparently being taken by the meeting should withdraw. As Stuart left, Joseph J. Hendley, Stephen van Sickle and some others followed him out of the meeting.

At this juncture a committee made up of Samuel M. Williams, Judge Benjamin C. Franklin, William P. Ballinger and Colonel E. McLean was appointed to deliver the letter personally to Sherwood. These men were instructed to tell the New Yorker that if he persisted in holding his meeting the members of the present gathering would convene at the same place where he held his meeting to prevent him from making a public address in Galveston.[59]

[57] Ballinger Papers, for 1856, MS.
[58] *Ibid.*; Galveston *News*, July 11, 1856.
[59] See draft copy and related correspondence in Ballinger Papers for 1856;

At the critical juncture of the public meeting to prevent Sherwood from exercising his right to speak Willard Richardson finally deserted his old colleague and friend; in fact, the editor for several days prior to the meeting had been on the defensive explaining to the public and to those who wanted to silence Sherwood that while he held views similar to the New Yorker on the railroad situation he did not agree with Sherwood on slavery. The editor was faced with a critical decision; he had long been an advocate of reopening the African slave trade as an adjunct to cotton expansion and he held these views as a matter of sincere conviction. Also, if he continued to defend Sherwood in this present crisis he would not only have injured the economic position of his paper but also his future influence in Texas politics and it was becoming very clear by this time that the pro-slave faction was in the ascendancy. This was a hard decision for Richardson to make, but it is clear that, being faced with a very practical matter of politics and economics, he took the pragmatic rather than the idealistic course.

The reaction of Hamilton Stuart in this same situation was quite different. While he had never been a supporter of Sherwood or his economics the editor was a man who had strong convictions in matters of personal freedom and free speech. Stuart was not a bold man and certainly not one to look for a fight; yet, when faced with an issue which challenged his firm moral convictions, he would stand and fight. It is significant that at the public meeting to silence Sherwood it was Stuart of the *Civilian* and not Richardson of the *News* who stood up to speak in the New Yorker's defense and who led a protesting delegation from the meeting. And it is still more significant that the broadside which carried Sherwood's explanation of his stand was printed and distributed not in the shop of his friend Richardson of the *News,* but in the *Civilian* press of Hamilton Stuart.

Faced with either capitulation or violence, Sherwood decided not to fight. In the broadside printed during the afternoon and distributed

---

also see Galveston *News,* July 7, 9, and 11, 1856. Frederick Law Olmsted, who traveled through Texas during the mid-fifties, was struck by the cavalier treatment accorded Sherwood in Galveston. In the appendix of the 1857 edition of his *Journey Through Texas* (pp. 505–506), Olmsted included an extensive newspaper account of the "silencing" of Sherwood in Galveston.

throughout the city he explained, "Yielding to the representations of my friends," he had decided not to address the meeting which had been scheduled. "You will not misconstrue my course," he pleaded,

if I waive, for the present, the vindication of myself against the attacks of M. M. Potter, Esquire; and that any sacrifice I make of my right of self-defense, for the peace and harmony of the community, will be duly appreciated by all, both friends and opponents. I have consented that the meeting called for this evening be indefinitely postponed.[60]

Thus, Sherwood was forced to resign from his position as a delegate from Galveston to the State Legislature.[61] By harnessing the slavery issue as a weapon against the chief exponent of the State Plan for building railroads, the Loan Bill advocates won a decisive victory and removed the most dangerous opponents of the Loan Bill.

A few days later in a futile countermove to force the Loan men in Galveston to reveal their "true purpose," Sherwood's friends circulated a petition on the Island demanding that Senator M. M. Potter of Galveston state publicly what his position was on the railroad issue.[62] This petition, signed by a large number of the voters in Galveston, placed Potter in a very difficult position because he had been elected on what had appeared to be his support of the Galveston Plan. Actually, he had been for several months secretly supporting the corporate railroad builders as a lobbyist who dispensed money in Austin in the interest of the Loan Plan.[63] These funds were furnished to him by the New York agents of persons interested in the State Loan Bill.

Senator Potter knew that eventually he would have to vote for the Loan Bill. To quiet the excitement caused by the petition and to prepare the way for this shift in his public position, he finally returned to Galveston from Austin. Consenting to face a public gathering of Galvestonians, he explained his position on railroad matters by telling the citizens that he had not yet made up his mind on the railroad issue. He

[60] Copy of this broadside in Ballinger Papers for year 1856.
[61] Tommy Yett (comp.), *Members of the Legislature of the State of Texas from 1846 to 1939*, p. 25.
[62] Houston *Telegraph*, July 14, 1856.
[63] James Love to Ballinger, undated letter, Ballinger Papers, 1856, MS.

asserted that he would vote according to what seemed best for Galveston and Texas when all the facts were placed at his disposal in Austin. He vigorously condemned the "petition" as merely one more "purulent" move by Lorenzo Sherwood. Senator Potter publicly forgave those of his fellow Galvestonians who had once more been deceived by "this man" and had signed the petition "never dreaming" the "real purpose of its design."[64]

Having made his "position clear," Senator Potter then left for Austin. Even before he departed the House of Representatives in Austin had passed the Loan Bill by a vote of 57 yeas and 27 nays;[65] and on August 13, 1856, the Loan Bill, having passed both bodies of the legislature, became part of the Texas Law.[66] Thus, it was determined that the railroads of Texas would be built by private corporations encouraged by generous state aid.[67]

Building of the Railroads

ALTHOUGH THE CONFLICT between the various transport planners and "paper railroaders" absorbed much of the human energy during the fifties, none the less, some actual railroads were built. Most of the progress, however, occurred after the defeat of the State Plan had opened the way for a more vigorous exploitation of the facilities available to finance the projects. The demand for transportation arose from the urgent desire of the planters to develop the rich cotton and sugar bottom land which was drained by the Brazos and Trinity rivers. The matter of actually providing the transportation engrossed the attention of the entrepreneurs, the "planners," and the empire builders. The plank-road enthusiasts, the canal and river boat entrepreneurs, and the numerous promoters of plans to build railroads all claimed to have the answer to the state's transport problem.[68] In

[64] Houston *Telegraph*, August 4, 1856; Austin *State Gazette*, August 1, 1856; Sherwood Collection, *passim*.

[65] Houston *Telegraph*, August 13, 1856.

[66] Richardson, *Texas Almanac*, 1860, pp. 132–134.

[67] *Ibid.*, pp. 129 and 221; H. P. N. Gammel, *The Laws of Texas, 1822–1897*, IV, 449.

[68] Barrett to Tod, July 28, 1853, Tod Papers, MS.

the early fifties the rail lines were mere "shadow" or "paper railways," but as the decade of the fifties closed, the actual pattern of the future railroad system which was to serve the state had been fixed.[69]

The water-minded men, who as early as the forties endeavored to utilize the rivers, bayous and bays as a means of transport, had managed to develop several waterway services, which were remarkably successful considering the unnavigability of the inland channels of Texas, and they had ambitious plans for the future.[70] Wide variations of flood and dry periods, however, made water transportation a mere seasonal facility at best.[71] Even under these handicaps, the "river men" sometimes pushed their flat-bottomed "paddle-wheelers" over almost dry river bottoms in order to move cotton and sugar to Galveston.

On land wagon and cart transport hauled by oxen and horses served well enough in dry seasons, but a day or two of rain at any season of the year could halt such transport dead in its tracks for days and even weeks at a time. It was clear that there were only two possible solutions to the transport problem in the Galveston-Gulf Coast region—plank roads or railroads.[72] Everyone at that time understood that the ultimate solution of the transport problem would be provided by harnessing the iron horse to haul the potential tons of sugar and the "millions" of bales of cotton from the bottoms to the wharves at Galveston. But, reasoned some of the more practical men of the time, how many years would pass before operating railroads would be actually moving across the flat lands of the Gulf Coast? Some impatient Texans recommended that plank roads or corduroys be laid from the cotton and sugar lands to the navigable waterways to serve until the time when the paper railroads materialized. A few plank-road companies were chartered by "practical" men, but these "practical" projects tended to remain as shadowy as the dream railroads because even the most pessimistic Texans understood that within a decade or two the railroads would

[69] Lynn to F.O., Annual Report, 1860, MS, January 1, 1861, F.O.

[70] Richardson, *Texas Almanac, 1868*, pp. 118–122; Barrett to Tod, August 9 and 27, 1853; Barrett to Sherman, August 27, 1853, Tod Papers, MS.

[71] *De Bow's Review*, XXIII (1867), 113–126; Richardson, *Texas Almanac, 1868*, p. 118.

[72] Texas *Senate Journal*, 1855, pp. 198, 227, 314, and 337.

be in operation. In these circumstances, the capital needed to build the plank roads was never available.[73]

The first railway built to move cotton and sugar to Galveston Bay was constructed by the Buffalo Bayou, Brazos and Colorado Railway Company, which was chartered and built by General Sidney Sherman, Commodore John Grant Tod, Jonathan Barrett, and their associates. The builders of this road, which began construction in 1851, had completed twenty miles of track by September, 1853—from Harrisburg to Stafford's Point.[74] It was their belief that if a paying road moving westward could be developed even part way, the capital and political influence necessary to carry the project to a conclusion could be mobilized. In these circumstances it was a paramount necessity to acquire the assistance of influential persons. Barrett had contacts with Horace Greeley who was eminently in a position to lend prestige to the Harrisburg-San Antonio project as a forerunner to a line from Galveston Bay to the West Coast. Greeley, however, appeared to be hesitant about giving the journalistic blessing to the project which would have greatly assisted the promoters in their efforts to sell Buffalo Bayou, Brazos and Colorado stock to foreign investors.[75]

During the spring of 1853, Tod and Sherman spent considerable time in Galveston in an effort to convince the merchant banker Robert Mills that it would be to his interest and to the interest of Galveston to encourage the development of Harrisburg as an auxiliary of the port of Galveston. They argued that any land traffic into Galveston Bay at Harrisburg would be an asset to the Island port. It was pointed out to Mills that a railroad terminal at Harrisburg would act as a checkmate to Houston.[76]

This estimate of the situation was accepted by Mills. However, dur-

[73] W. A. Leonard (compiler), *Houston City Directory, 1866*, pp. 100–105.

[74] Galveston *News*, September 2, 1853. A recent article by Andrew Forest Muir, July, 1960, "The Railroads Come to Houston, 1857–1861," *Southwestern Historical Quarterly*, LXIV, 42–63, is an excellent and detailed study of pre-Civil War railroads around Houston as well as of the auxiliary industries which grew out of this new enterprise.

[75] Barrett to Tod, July 28, 1853, Tod Papers, MS.

[76] Tod to Barrett, August 12 and 13, 1853, Tod Papers, MS.

ing the summer he went to New York and spent some time discussing western railroad matters with Horace Greeley. The two men argued at length as to whether or not Galveston would be better served by utilizing Harrisburg as its rail terminal or whether the Island ought to begin to develop a direct rail contact with the interior. They compared the situation then prevailing in New York between the Hudson River steamboat lines and the Hudson River Railroad in an effort to determine whether or not the situation at the Texas island port and Galveston Bay were analogous. The two men were unable to reach any definite conclusion as to the most effective solution to the transportation problem in Texas. Therefore, Greeley failed to aid Barrett, Sherman, and Tod in selling the stock of their railroad project, and Mills decided, in the light of what he had learned, not to invest his capital in Texas railroads.[77] However, even without the blessing of Greeley or Mills, by 1860 Barrett, Sherman, and Tod had cars operating on a regular service from Harrisburg to Alleyton on the east bank of the Colorado River.[78]

While the Buffalo Bayou, Brazos and Colorado Railway furnished some transportation for the interior communities, this road provided no service for the planters in Brazoria, Matagorda, and Wharton, and most of Colorado counties, an area whose rich crops of cotton and sugar cane demanded transport to Galveston. Therefore, the planters in these counties began, in 1856, to build their own line from Columbia northward to join the Buffalo Bayou, Brazos and Colorado line. This enterprise was known as the "Sugar Railroad."[79]

Houston merchants, also being aware that their city needed a connection with the railroad system then taking shape in Texas, promoted and built in 1856 a short "tap" line from Houston to form a junction

[77] Barrett to Tod, August 9, 1853; Tod to Barrett, August 12 and 13, 1853; Barrett to Tod, September 8, 1853; Barrett to Sherman, August 27, 1853; Sherman to Barrett, July 13 and 27, 1853, Tod Papers, MS.

[78] James Arthur Lyon Fremantle, *The Fremantle Diary: Being the Journal of Lieutenant Colonel James Arthur Lyon Fremantle, Coldstream Guards, on His Three Months in the Southern States*. pp. 49–50.

[79] Galveston *Civilian*, March 22, 1859; Richardson, *Texas Almanac, 1860*, p. 202.

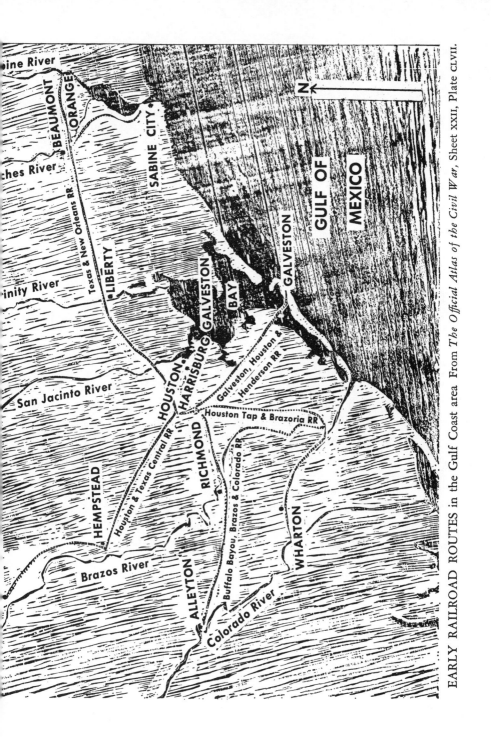

EARLY RAILROAD ROUTES in the Gulf Coast area From *The Official Atlas of the Civil War*, Sheet XXII, Plate CLVII.

with the other two railroads which were then moving goods toward Harrisburg and Galveston Bay. Since the "tap" line made a direct contact with the track coming northward from the sugar bottom lands, these two systems later became known as the Houston Tap and Brazoria Railroad when they were combined under one ownership and management in 1858.[80]

In the late forties and early fifties, Galveston merchants neglected to develop land-oriented trade channels from northeastern Texas into Galveston Bay. Attracted by the rich land wealth waiting to be exploited along the Brazos and the Colorado Rivers, they ignored the regions north of Houston and east of the Trinity River. In 1848 Ebenezer Allen had secured a charter for a line to be called the Galveston and Red River Railway, which was to begin on Galveston Bay and run northward to some point on the Red River. Allen's efforts to secure financial support in Galveston failed, however, because Island capital was more interested in the rich cotton and sugar bottom land than in the timber areas to the northeast.

In 1853, however, impatient farmers and planters living in the counties north of Houston, out of reach of waterways or good roads, began to agitate for a railroad. These northern farmers, led by Major Joseph Willis, decided to call a railroad convention at Chapel (at that time spelled "Chappell") Hill in order to find ways and means to secure a land transport system leading toward the city of Galveston. A few Houstonians led by Paul Bremond sent a delegation to Chapel Hill to take part in these deliberations and thus to protect Houston's interest in this situation. As a result of this meeting, these entrepreneurs acquired the old charter of the Galveston and Red River Railway and built a line which they renamed the Houston and Texas Central. Trains began operating on the line in October of 1856 over the twenty-five miles of track between Houston and Cypress; by 1860 the line had extended its services further northward to Hockley, Hempstead, and Millican.[81]

[80] Houston *Telegraph*, November 23, 1859; Richardson, *Texas Almanac, 1868*, pp. 130–132.

[81] *De Bow's Review*, XXIX (1860), 530–533; Galveston *News*, May 7 and October 8, 1857.

The threat to the port of Galveston arising from the growing importance of Houston's position as a rail center—a matter of continuing concern to Galvestonians[82] during the late fifties—became particularly acute when the projected Texas and New Orleans Railroad began to materialize in 1859. Originally this line had been chartered on September 1, 1856, as The Sabine and Galveston Railroad and Lumber Company by promoters who expected to use the line to exploit the lumber resources of East Texas. A. M. Gentry and I. S. Roberts, two promoters of this paper railroad in the middle fifties, had tried unsuccessfully to interest Galveston money in the project. The picture changed sharply in 1859, when New Orleans merchants finally realized that if the planned transcontinental railroads running southwestward from St. Louis *via* Houston were actually built they would divert the prevailing Galveston-New Orleans trade northward.[83] In order to protect their interest in the Texas trade, New Orleans merchants indicated that they were ready to assume the task of building the Louisiana section of the suggested Texas and New Orleans Railroad and induced the Louisiana Legislature to appeal to the Texas Legislature to encourage the building of a line between Houston and the Louisiana-Texas border. The New Orleans promoters pointed out to the Texas legislators that in the event of secession hostilities, good strategy required that the Southern states develop internal communications which would lie beyond the reach of Northern blockading vessels.[84] Although Galvestonian merchants and their delegates at Austin argued against this line of reasoning which, if heeded, would have diverted Texas trade from Galveston to New Orleans,[85] the majority of the members in the Texas Legislature gave every encouragement to the new railroad project.[86] By January 1st, 1861, officials of this line claimed that their railroad had been constructed and equipped to operate between Houston and Orange; this claim was an exaggeration, for the line never actually operated trains over the entire line. As the war years progressed, the entire road literally deteriorated and was eventually aban-

[82] Galveston *News*, November 7, 1857.
[83] *De Bow's Review*, XXIII (1857), 330–331.
[84] *Ibid.*, XXIX (1860), 530–533.
[85] Galveston *Civilian*, March 22, 1859.   [86] Texas *Senate Journal*, 1860.

doned.[87] The fact that the New Orleans promoters never completed their share of the project contributed to the failure of the Texas end of the system.[88]

The Galveston, Houston, and Henderson line, which eventually served as a vital link between the two major coastal cities of Texas during the war, was from the beginning a Galveston project; nevertheless, Houston merchants purchased token blocks of stock in the road. During the month of May, 1853, Willard Richardson, Hamilton Stuart, M. B. Menard, A. F. James, Lorenzo Sherwood and other Galvestonians attended a railroad meeting with such Houstonians as W. W. Baker, H. H. Smith, E. H. Cushing, W. M. Rice, and others. On this occasion the leaders of each city endorsed the proposition that interested parties in each of the two cities should attempt to underwrite $300,000 worth of stock in this railroad.[89]

During the year 1856, when the controversy concerning superiority of a state plan over a corporate plan was raging, the builders of the Galveston, Houston, and Henderson Railroad Company began the actual construction of their line at Virginia Point, a position on the mainland just opposite the Island. By the spring of 1857 twenty-four miles of the road had been finished; and by October, 1859, the line had covered forty miles, placing the terminal of the track practically on the outskirts of Houston. From October, 1859, until January, 1860, a tri-weekly train and ferry service accommodated freight and passenger traffic between Houston and Galveston Island. The ferry service was discontinued in 1860 when the bridge spanning the water between the Island and the mainland had been completed.[90]

Thus by the close of the decade, Galveston had direct rail contact with the Buffalo Bayou, Brazos and Colorado Railroad, and a potential contact with the Texas and New Orleans Railroad. Unfortunately, however, the Galveston, Houston and Henderson line had no direct

[87] George W. Randolph to General Louis Hebert, May 5, 1862, Ballinger Papers, for 1862, MS.

[88] Richardson, *Texas Almanac*, *1867*, p. 271 and *1868*, pp. 120–145.

[89] *Ibid.*, *1868*, pp. 120–123.

[90] *By-laws of the Galveston, Houston, and Henderson Railroad Company*, pamphlet, pp. 1–9.

track connection with the Houston and Texas Central which tapped the rich farming area north of Houston. A short line connecting these two roads was obviously most desirable. Although Galvestonian merchant capitalists had warily avoided actual investment in the other Texas railroads, such men as John Sealy, Robert Mills and David Mills readily provided the money needed to build the two-mile-long Galveston and Houston Junction Railway in order to connect the Island port with the rail line which served the area north of Houston.[91]

The greatest difficulty arising in the financing of Texas railroads was the matter of inducing foreign capital to invest in the projects. Foreign capital was essential, since the local merchants demonstrated no real desire to attempt to finance railroads. The local merchant bankers working in cooperation with the financial resources available to the state government could have financed a modest railroad system for Texas during the fifties. The merchants decided, however, that since foreign capital, state funds, and the resources available from state land would eventually be harnessed to finance the rail lines, the most profitable policy for them in these circumstances was not to be found in purchasing stock but rather in selling to the promoters of lines the various materials needed by the railroad contractors. Since the entrepreneurs of the new lines were most grateful for any credit extended by the merchants, the railroad purchasing agents were not as alert as they might have been in the matter of percentage mark-up on the goods they purchased. The merchants could not lose since, if the railroads paid, they made a good profit; if the railroads failed to honor the generous credit extended, the merchants, utilizing the favorable aspects of the law and the district courts, had ample protection for their advances in the land grant and in the school-fund assets of the early rail lines. In fact, the merchants stood to gain much more out of the receivers' courts than they would have if the railroads had been willing and able to meet their obligations,[92] when the railroads failed to meet the payments due on these obligations foreclosure proceedings to col-

[91] Richardson, *Texas Almanac, 1868*, pp. 120–123.
[92] Houston *Telegraph*, March 18, 1859; Richardson, *Texas Almanac, 1868*, pp. 129–133.

lect were instituted with unusual facility.[93] The service provided by the courts in these instances moved with remarkable dispatch; and as a result, the merchants soon acquired receivership control of the railroads which had been built in part by the joint enterprise of the state, county, city, and foreign capital.[94]

Consul Lynn was particularly angry over the fact that railroad promoters by means of false representations had given the impression to foreign investors that the British Consul's office at Galveston vouched for the accuracy of the promoters' claims as to the actual assets of Texas railroads. Lynn told Lord Wodehouse in 1860 that he had finally decided to refuse to lend further "assistance to speculators for the purpose of enhancing the value of lands associated with railroad schemes in this state, where parties interested sought the weight of [Lynn's] authority to effect loans from British capitalists on the security of the lands or the railroads." Lynn pointed out that the value of the land and railroad property in Texas presented as security for the foreign loans had been far from sufficient to provide security for the loans granted. In any case, said Lynn, neither the land nor the railroad property "have been made legally available for the redemption of the money loaned." Lynn explained that the "exaggerated character" of the promoters' statements to British investors "presented an appearance of fraud"; therefore, he said, that unless the Foreign Office gave him other instructions he would refrain henceforth from certifying any documents which were drawn up so as to create the impression that "a certification" represented an assertion to the effect that it was the consul's belief that the facts presented in the document were true.[95]

[93] Houston *Telegraph*, March 18, April 13, and November 23, 1859; Richardson, *Texas Almanac, 1860*, pp. 129 and 221 and *1867*, pp. 184–185 and 234; *Ibid.*, *1868*, pp. 118–145. *Robert and David Mills* v. *Galveston, Houston and Henderson Railroad*, July 1 and 13, 1859 and *Warren W. Buel* v. *Galveston, Houston, and Henderson Railroad*, June 21, 1859, and *Robert Pulsford* v. *Galveston, Houston, and Henderson Railroad*, June 30, 1859, all in the District Court of Galveston.

[94] Lynn to Lord Wodehouse, October 30, 1860, MS, F.O.; Houston *Telegraph*, March 18, 1859.

[95] Lynn to Wodehouse, October 30, 1860, MS, F.O.

Richard B. Kimball, the president and active promoter of the sale of stock in the Galveston, Houston and Henderson Railroad, in both the domestic and the foreign market, maintained an office at Number 4 Wall Street in New York City. One of his most active associates in the Texas Legislature was Senator M. M. Potter of Galveston. The sales agent in London and Paris, a stock broker named Valentine, occasionally came to Galveston with Kimball in order to impress upon Texas legislators that Kimball had men "of the very first names in London and Paris, men of influence and capital who stood ready to put money" in Texas railroads if the legislature would increase the land grants and keep the school fund open for loan purposes. The agents and the promoters looked for profit from two directions; in the one case they collected commissions for stock sold in Paris and London, and in the other instance they could hope to prosper if the rail line actually happened to earn a profit.

The promoters of the Galveston, Houston and Henderson Railroad and the Galveston merchants interested in the road as a mercantile asset calculated that once the line from Houston to Virginia Point had been built the taxpaying citizens of Galveston would readily agree to vote for a bond issue sufficient to build a bridge connecting the Island with the mainland terminal of the railroad.[96] It was estimated that such a bridge would cost about $100,000. According to this plan the city was to hold a temporary title to the bridge and lease it to the railroad for an annual rental sufficient to pay the interest and eventually to retire the bonds; a full title to the bridge would then be given to the railroad.[97] The promoters reasoned that once the bonds for the bridge were approved this fact could be used to attract more European money for railroad investment. The promoters also expected that the initial few miles of track which had already been laid in 1855 on the route between the two cities would generate enough interest in Galveston to insure the passage of the bond issue at a city election. Thus

[96] Texas *Senate Journal*, 1856, pp. 44, 55, 61, 64, 105, 381, 394, 605, and 619.
[97] Ordinance Book, 1857–1865, MS, pp. 10, 17, and 41, Office of Galveston City Secretary; Galveston County Commissioners Court, Minutes, 1856–1870, MS, pp. 10, 14, 55, and 72.

these entrepreneurs had as sources of capital the European investors, state money loans and land grants, and the taxpayers of Galveston.[98] The successful exploitation of one source increased the likelihood of securing more funds from the others in a kind of reciprocal action. At least that was the way the situation appeared to the promoters. They had, however, failed to anticipate the political contest that was to arise in 1856 in which the advocates of the Galveston Plan and Sherwood's State Plan almost removed the control of the building of the Texas railroads from the hands of the corporate promoters and their merchant associates. Although the promoters eventually defeated the State Plan, the "agitation" and suspicion generated by Sherwood's persistent queries into the operations of the railroad promoters aroused a sufficient wariness in the mind of the average Galvestonian voter to endanger gravely the passage of the bridge bond issues.

During the early spring of 1857 the Galveston *Civilian* kept up a steady press campaign in behalf of the bridge bonds. Meetings were held not only in the court house but also in the churches at which various speakers praised the benefits which would accrue to the city once the bridge became a reality. The Frenchman, Henri de St. Cyr, employed his well-known Gallic charm to explain in his cosmopolitan way that although the Island City was, in reality, then only a "delightful little village," once the Bay had been spanned Galveston would become "a noble city, accommodating one hundred thousand inhabitants" and giving wealth and prosperity to all.[99] Colonel John S. Sydnor, Judge Leslie A. Thompson and General Hugh McLeod spoke to gatherings in the churches, warning the good church people on the Island that they must not be persuaded by the fallacious questions about details, the particular pattern of calumny practiced by the lawyer Sherwood. Even Richardson of the *News* had finally "come around" to favor the bond issue.[100]

Richard Kimball, the New York promoter and the president of the railroad, spoke very gravely at public meetings explaining that "he

[98] Richardson, *Texas Almanac, 1860*, pp. 134–135.
[99] Houston *Telegraph*, May 13, 1857.
[100] Galveston *News*, May 12, 14, and 16, 1857; Galveston *Civilian*, May 11, 1857; Houston *Telegraph*, May 11, 1857.

needed proof that the city wanted the bridge if he was to get money from abroad to finish the railroad." He expressed his willingness to impoverish himself personally in the effort finally to join Galveston and Houston by a flourishing railroad; he pleaded with Galvestonians to lend him their good will; he asked no more.[101]

Lorenzo Sherwood in his turn warned the Islanders to proceed with "caution." He asked "eleven questions" of the "Bridge Advocates." In one of these queries Sherwood asked why the title of ownership of the bridge was to pass to the railroad when the bonds were eventually retired by the annual rental payments. Why should the city not own the title instead of a mere mortgage on the structure? No direct answers were given to "the Agitator's" questions. The charming St. Cyr, however, apparently replied effectively to Sherwood's queries by stating that, while "he held a most high regard for Mr. Sherwood's great legal talents," this was not the time for "bickering." Let the voters assist in the good effort to begin to build the bridge; there would be ample time to ask questions later.[102]

During these days of deliberation, "the friends of the Bridge" gave a "gigantic Railroad Party" at Virginia Point

for all Galvestonians young and old; the steamer the *Dr. William Smith* and several sloops were engaged to carry all who wished to come to the big party. Wines, cordials, and lemonades passed freely among the ladies, while gents helped themselves to various drinks of a stronger kind.[103]

The festivity was particularly enhanced by the fact that the cotton merchant James Sorley had composed a special "Bridge Song" for the festival set to the tune of "Wait for the Wagon." As the afternoon wore on and grew enlivened by the refreshments and by the rousing rendition of Mr. Sorley's composition by the German Band, it became clear that the result of "the Bridge Issue" was no longer in doubt.[104]

[101] Sherwood Collection, *passim.*

[102] Houston *Telegraph*, May 13, 1857; Galveston *News*, May 12 and 14, 1857.

[103] Galveston *News*, May 9 and 14, 1857; Galveston *Civilian*, May 12, 1857.

[104] *Ibid.*, May 16, 1857.

When the election was held a few days later, the Galvestonians voted for the bridge 741 to 11.[105]

The victory of the advocates for the bridge bonds, the eventual construction of the span, and the completion of the rail line connecting the Island with Houston was, in effect, a final incident of defeat for the original advocates of the Galveston Plan because these events determined that, although the Island might still remain as the water gate way for Texas, all hope of making Galveston the apex of a vast system of railroads had been surrendered.[106] The mainland city rather than the island city was destined to be not only the main railroad terminal of Texas but also the key center for a Southern transcontinental system. Although the Island port still dominated the sea lanes of Texas, in the matter of railroad traffic the Queen City was destined to remain a mere terminal of a spur line jutting off the main transcontinental line which passed through Houston.

[105] Galveston *News*, May 21, 1857.

[106] *Ibid.*, November 7 and 19, 1857; Houston *Telegraph*, January 12 and March 11, 1859.

6. THE PROBLEM OF SLAVE LABOR

Texans and the Filibusters

THE DECADE OF THE 1850's marked the high-water mark for filibustering expeditions launched from the ports of the Southern coasts of the United States. These ventures, privately organized and financed by adventurous and ambitious men, were sea-borne invasions launched into such poorly defended areas in the Caribbean as Cuba and Central America. The intention of the participants was to capture or to intimidate the governing authorities in these backward countries and set up

Anglo-Saxon governments there. Actually, filibustering was a form of private imperialism, another expression of nineteenth century Manifest Destiny imperialism on the part of expansion-minded Americans.

Since many politicians in the Southern states looked kindly upon the possibility of new slave-oriented states being eventually formed and admitted to the Union as the result of this unique form of expansionism the federal government at Washington was not in a position to deny the use of the ports of the United States as bases for launching these expeditions. Baltimore, Mobile, New Orleans, and Galveston figured most prominently as platforms for these exploits. Two famed leaders of these adventures were General Narciso López in the Cuban arena and General William Walker, the "grey-eyed man of destiny" in the Nicaraguan arena.

During the 1850's, filibustering campaigns into Cuba and Nicaragua received substantial support from the state of Texas. This support, however, was not a calculated effort in expansion designed to increase Southern representation in the national Congress; rather, filibustering expeditions were mobilized in Texas to achieve a more immediate objective. Practical men wished to establish independent slaveholding states—first in Cuba and more definitely later, when the Cuban effort failed to develop, in Central America—that could be used as local trading stations for a traffic in African slaves. The potential expansion of cotton planting in Texas during the 1850's presented an almost unlimited opportunity to acquire wealth. The only element lacking was an ample supply of cheap slave labor. On the domestic Texas market a prime field Negro cost from $1,200 to $1,500. Because a more reasonable source of supply had to be found if Texas cotton land was to be exploited, a large portion of the Texans living along the Gulf Coast in the last half of the 1850's had come to the reluctant conclusion that the reopening of the African slave trade was necessary. The leading newspapers vigorously urged a program which would lead to a reopening of this trade. Although, the high price of slaves had already induced adventurous men to run African slaves into the state from Havana and from Africa, a more readily available source was needed than these clandestine activities. Nicaragua was seen as a potential "way station" from which cheap labor could be quietly moved into Texas until such a time as the slave trade might be legalized. The Nicaraguan filibuster, General William Walker, attracted the attention and support of many enterprising Texans, especially those who were already engaged in cotton expansion, railroad promotion, cattle importation, and the domestic slave trade.

While Texas' aid to the filibustering expeditions to Cuba in the early 1850's was not in the substantial proportions of that given later to General Walker's armies in Nicaragua, the aid given to the Cuban adventure was more than a token. On July 12, 1850, a party of 250 armed Texans left the ports of Corpus Christi and Galveston to join an expedition being formed for the invasion of Cuba by General Narciso López.[1] In July, 1850, Governor P. Hansborough Bell of Texas delivered a public address in Galveston favoring the expeditions to Cuba and the annexation of the island to the Republic.[2] During August, 1851, Sam Houston of Texas addressed mass meetings in New Orleans organized to raise funds and soldiers for the Cuban expedition.[3] Even though the total defeat of the López expedition brought the execution of many of the participants, Texans continued to demonstrate an interest in the conquest of Cuba. Three years later, an expedition against Cuba was being prepared to sail from Galveston.[4] Although the waning of filibustering enthusiasm in other Southern states kept these armed Texans from ever actually sailing for Cuba, the armed preparations in Texas for further Cuban expeditions continued. In 1855 another expedition was being prepared to sail. The port of Galveston was "assigned as one from which the number of 600 men are to depart." These preparations were "conducted with great secrecy," and the obligation of secrecy imposed upon the initiated prevented the publication of details, but the "promised reward of spoilation" infused energy among the members.[5] Formidable bands of

[1] Arthur T. Lynn, to Sir H. L. Bulwer, British Foreign Office, May 13, 1850 and July 12, 1850, MS, F.O.

[2] Lynn to Bulwer, July 7, 1852, MS, F.O.

[3] Philadelphia *Ledger*, August 1 and August 6, 1851.

[4] Lynn to J. F. Crompton (British Minister to Washington), February 18, 1855, MS, F.O.

[5] Lynn to Crompton, February 18, 1855, MS, F.O.

men were expected to arrive in Galveston by steamboats. The Order of the Lone Star with its subordinate lodges made the necessary arrangements without exciting suspicion.

Although Texans were prepared to furnish their quota of men in a continued attempt to invade the island General López had failed to conquer, events occurring on the larger stage in 1855 precluded further expansion in this direction. The Democratic administration of Franklin Pierce, taking control in 1854, after the four-year Whig interlude, at first encouraged the exploration of various avenues which might lead to the acquisition of Cuba. It was, at that time, generally acknowledged in Washington that the "Pearl of the Antilles" ought to be acquired either by means of the "sword" or the "purse," and the Pierce administration therefore dispatched Senator Pierre Soule of Louisiana to Madrid, as minister to Spain, with instructions to pursue the Cuban policy. The minister's mission, however, produced only the abortive Ostend Manifesto,[6] which presumed to conquer the island of Cuba by the mere issuance of a joint statement to that effect. President Pierce and Secretary of State William L. Marcy gave up any further effort, for the time being, to acquire Cuba.[7] In this situation, Texan filibustering activities, which were still in motion, turned toward Central America.

At about the same time, during the early 1850's, General William Walker, who was later to become famed as the "Nicaraguan filibuster," had been experimenting with his particular kind of warfare by leading small expeditions against Mexican possessions on the Pacific coast. After failing to establish himself as the founder of a new nation on the Pacific coast, General Walker, in 1854, joined the side of the liberalist leader, Francisco Castellon, during the course of a political revolution then in progress in Nicaragua and soon rose to become commander in chief of Castellon's army. From that time until his execution in 1860

---

[6] A manifesto issued from Ostend, Belgium in 1854, by the United States ministers to Great Britain, France, and Spain, giving the grounds upon which the United States might seize Cuba in case of Spain's refusal to sell it. *U.S. House Exec. Docs.*, 33rd Congress, 2nd Session, No. 93, pp. 129–131.

[7] Thomas A. Bailey, *A Diplomatic History of the American People*, pp. 316–318; Graham H. Stuart, *Latin America and the United States*, pp. 324–327.

LOOKING WEST along 21st Street, 1885

From a copy made by H. H. Morris of an oil painting by J. Stockleth. The copy is in the Historical Collection, John Winterbotham Room, Rosenberg Library, Galveston, Texas.

he assumed the role which was to inspire his admirers to refer to him as "the grey-eyed man of destiny."

William Walker, a native Tennessean, perhaps should have been born in an earlier century; he was an authentic adventurer who had a grand notion of his own destiny. A shy person weighing less than one hundred pounds he had a strong personality able to command men twice his size. During the decade of the fifties he led an expedition into California and three into Central America. While all of these failed he nevertheless aroused much interest and some sympathy in all parts of the United States. His grand plan was to form a federation of Central America with himself as its leader. Free soilers in America considered him a mere front for slave expansion, the British saw him as a spearhead of American Manifest Destiny, and since Washington did little to interrupt his efforts this view may have had some validity. In any case, while his actions at times were cruel and ruthless, William Walker was certainly a soldier who knew and believed in his own destiny and followed it to his tragic end.

During this decade, Cornelius Vanderbilt, having secured from the Nicaraguan government a monopolistic concession to exploit the transportation potentialities then awaiting development across the isthmus to California, established the Accessory Transit Company, a combine of shipping, railroad and stage coach transportation, providing a practical route from New York to California. The New York and San Francisco agents of this system, Charles Morgan and Cornelius K. Garrison, wishing to wrest control of the concession from Vanderbilt, entered into a conspiratorial agreement with General Walker which provided that, in return for the general's transfer of the transit concession from Vanderbilt to a new firm organized by Morgan and Garrison, these shipping magnates were to furnish Walker the shipping he needed to move potential filibuster armies from the Gulf Coast states to Nicaragua.[8]

During July, 1856, Walker managed to improve his position by winning an election that made him the president of Nicaragua. By that time he had become a hero to a large portion of the general popu-

[8] Lynn to Crompton, February 18, 1855, MS, F.O.

lation of the Southern states; his expeditions and conquests were accepted by many as but a continuation of American expansion.[9] As early as March, 1856, E. H. Cushing, who was an ardent supporter of General Walker as well as an advocate of the reopening of the African slave trade, reported that Archibald Wynne had left Galveston for an inspection trip to Nicaragua. This "clever, high-toned gentleman of solid information and close observation," wrote Cushing, could be depended upon to bring Texans an accurate report concerning opportunities in "the Filibuster State."[10] A week later, the editor reported that, as a result of the opportunities beckoning in Nicaragua, many men were leaving the Gulf Coast for Nicaragua.[11] These men traveled upon the ships of the newly organized Garrison and Morgan line which had succeeded in wresting control of Nicaraguan transport connections from Cornelius Vanderbilt. Passage to the "new land of opportunity" could be purchased for as low as $35. Ships were scheduled to call at Galveston at eighteen-day intervals to pick up new groups of "emigrants."[12] A few days later, Dr. R. J. Swearingen of Chapel Hill, Texas, returned from Nicaragua where he had spent several months. On April 9th, this "well known" doctor addressed a gathering of citizens at the Galveston Court House concerning "the prospects in this land of promise." "Dr. S. is well known here and his statements will command confidence," was editor Cushing's evaluation of Dr. Swearingen's advocacy of emigration to Nicaragua.[13]

On May 24th and May 26th, two more public meetings were held in Galveston "for the purpose of giving expression to views" concerning the importance of lending aid to General Walker. The leaders of these gatherings were men prominent in public affairs. Judge David G. Burnet, ex-president of the late Republic, presided over the meeting. General Sidney Sherman, General Hugh McLeod, John Henry Brown[14] (the mayor of Galveston), Doctor William Carper, Oscar

---

[9] Lynn to Crompton, February 18, 1855, MS, F.O.

[10] Houston *Telegraph*, March 19, 1856.   [11] *Ibid.*, March 26, 1856.

[12] *Ibid.*, March 31, 1856.   [13] *Ibid.*, April 9, 1856.

[14] On November 25, 1857, John Henry Brown, member of the State House of Representatives from Galveston, introduced a joint resolution in the House recommending that all state officials be "instructed to press for a re-opening of

Farish, and Professor Caleb G. Forshey, director of Rutersville Military Institute, took an active part in the proceedings. Resolutions were adopted which recommended that aid be given to the "patriots in Nicaragua." A committee was empowered to charter a vessel and make arrangements for the transportation of emigrants from Galveston to Nicaragua to aid in wresting the isthmus from "the imbecile race" that controlled it.[15]

Many of the leaders of the filibuster organization in Galveston had occupied responsible positions during the Republic. These old patriots, who had been shouldered out of political power by younger and more astute men, appeared to be looking toward other avenues to regain a lost position, if not at home, then perhaps elsewhere. Other leaders came from among the younger men who were trying to rise to power at home or in the areas to the south; and still others looked toward developing a suitable source of cheap labor with which to exploit the enormous cotton-producing potential of Texas. While filibuster meetings were very well attended, the average citizen was certainly not yet ready to leave Galveston for Central America. The acquisition of Texas, however, as Consul Lynn observed, had taught "these gentlemen how to acquire territory by a cheap and facile method."[16]

During the month of June, several Nicaraguan meetings were held in Houston and Galveston.[17] At an anti-British, pro-Nicaraguan meeting held in Galveston on June 24th, eleven new recruits volunteered and $475 in cash was collected. The leaders expressed "regret at the apathy evinced by the large portion of our citizens, and the absence of large money contributions from many of our citizens known to be of ample means."[18]

---

the African slave-trade." *A Report and Treatise on Slavery,* a pamphlet printed by order of House of Representatives.

[15] Galveston *Civilian,* May 26 and 28, 1856.

[16] Lynn to Crompton, May 31, 1856, MS, F.O.

[17] Houston *Telegraph,* June 6, June 11, and June 26, 1856.

[18] Lynn to J. Saville Lamley, June 25, 1856, MS, F.O. In this dispatch Lynn included the names of the eleven volunteers and a list of 56 men who contributed money—among those names were such leading Texans as E. B. Nichols, F. R. Lubbock, W. Hendley, W. Richardson, J. S. Sydnor, M. M. Potter,

Actually, while a substantial minority of Islanders, especially those who favored the reopening of the African slave trade, looked with favor upon the filibusters, most Galvestonians were quite indifferent and some were revolted by the bravado and boasting of these adventurers. At times, however, when bands played and the men marched on board a ship to embark on a dangerous voyage, the people cheered and on occasion the ladies of a church society gave a supper in honor of the "boys going away." In general terms, these adventures eventually were looked upon with disfavor by many leading citizens and later when so many of the expeditions failed some citizens openly ridiculed the adventurous filibusters.[19]

During the first part of July that "high-toned gentleman of solid information," Archibald Wynne, returned to give Texans the promised report on opportunities in "the Filibuster State." He addressed a large gathering in Galveston on July 4, urging Galvestonians to lend their aid to General Walker.[20] On July 22nd P. R. Edwards acknowledged the receipt of $168 from one of the churches in Galveston to be used for the aid of General Walker.[21] During the latter part of August, 1856, Colonel S. A. Lockridge, one of General Walker's key officers,[22] wrote to E. H. Cushing advising him that he was "quartered at present in the pleasant village of Seguin" and would soon arrive in Galveston with about 250 men, who were to embark with him for Nicaragua on the third or fourth of September.[23] A part of Colonel Lockridge's command, composed of "200 men from Texas," actually left the port of New Orleans for Nicaragua on September 13th.[24] Late in November, Colonel Lockridge himself left the United States at the head of a company of 283 Texans.[25]

O. C. Hartley, Ex-Governor G. T. Wood, J. C. Shaw, M. Menard, and H. Stuart.

[19] Lord Lyons to Lynn, Nov. 16, 1860; Lynn to Lord Napier, April 25 and December 5, 1857, MS, F.O.

[20] Houston *Telegraph,* July 7, 1856.

[21] Galveston *Civilian,* July 22, 1856.

[22] William Walker, *The War in Nicaragua,* pp. 334–335.

[23] Houston *Telegraph,* August 25, 1856.

[24] *Ibid.,* September 19, 1856.

[25] New Orleans *Picayune,* November 26, 1856.

The reluctance of "emigrants" to venture themselves and their own capital in a journey to Nicaragua, despite the promise of $50 per month and a large grant of land, prompted the Morgan and Garrison Line to offer "free passage to Nicaragua for anyone who wished to emigrate" from Texas to the land of promise.[26] At the close of the year 1856, Fermin Ferrer, a transportation agent for General Walker, made a contract with William L. Cazneau of Texas that provided for the introduction of one thousand able-bodied Texan colonists to follow Colonel Lockridge's company into Nicaragua.[27]

The fact that armed expeditions destined for the shores of a friendly neighbor were embarking from the seaports of the United States confronted Washington officials with a clear violation of the federal neutrality laws. In these circumstances, Howell Cobb, the Secretary of the Treasury, upon whose office rested the responsibility to enforce these laws, dispatched instructions to Hamilton Stuart, the collector of customs at Galveston, "to keep a sharp look out" for the steamer *Fashion* "expected to return at once [to Galveston] for a second installment of troops for Nicaragua."[28] Despite these instructions, armed men continued to embark from Galveston for Central America.

In January, 1857, E. J. C. Kewen, Commissioner General for the Republic of Nicaragua, appointed Major W. C. Capers to serve as "Official Commissioner of the Republic of Nicaragua for the State of Texas." This official was authorized to solicit funds and raise volunteers for the army of General Walker.[29] The major had already collected a company of sixty recruits who arrived in Galveston with him. These men continued to Nicaragua. Later, in January, 1857, Willard Richardson, editor of the Galveston *News,* published a letter signed by twenty-nine members of the "Texas Rangers" in Nicaragua. These men, who were serving under the command of Colonel John Waters and Colonel Lockridge, wished to call to the attention of their fellow Texans at home the fact that Colonel G. W. Crawford, a fellow

[26] Houston *Telegraph,* October 10, 1856; "Trials of a Filibuster," *Harper's Weekly,* I (January 10, 1857), 23.

[27] New York *Herald,* December 25, 1856.

[28] *U.S. House Exec. Doc.* 35th Cong., 1st sess., No. 24, pp. 29–32, 49–56.

[29] Galveston *News,* January 3 and 6, 1857.

Ranger, would soon arrive in Galveston to raise another battalion of Texas Rangers.[30] As a recruiting inducement, the Galveston and Houston newspapers printed Nicaraguan stories listing the names of Texans who had achieved "promotion from the ranks" in General Walker's army.[31] These news stories referred to Colonel Crawford's Texas Rangers as a company of 240 men, and to Captain Higley's Company of Texas Infantry as 160 men.[32]

On February 16th the editor of the Houston *Telegraph* reported that within a few days Major W. C. Capers would be in Galveston with a company of 120 men en route to Nicaragua; other volunteers were urged to meet the major's unit at the port city.[33] Two days later, Colonel Crawford, "the Nicaraguan hero," attended a ball given by the Washington Light Guards. A company of Nicaraguan Volunteers from Austin was feted at this social gathering.[34] Colonel Crawford took this occasion to announce that each man in the Rangers would be mounted and equipped with a "Texas saddle and a Colt revolver." When this new contingent of men reached Galveston, it was greeted by a "grand reception" and a supper at the Methodist Church, followed by a ball at the Tremont Hotel. The hosts on this occasion were Francis Lubbock, C. F. Duer, Dr. Millan, Dr. Waters, J. A. Baron, and H. R. Runnels, who was elected governor of Texas the following December.[35]

The next day the steamer *Louisiana* arrived from Powder Horn with 104 men under the command of Captain Marcellus French and Captain Sam Jackson. This unit had been raised in San Antonio under the banner of the "Alamo Rangers." Before leaving the city, the company had been presented, by the ladies of the city, with a flag on which was inscribed, "Alamo Rangers, remember you are Texans." The enthusiasm "displayed on this occasion," reported a newspaper, "presented

---

[30] *Ibid.,* January 22, 1857.

[31] Houston *Telegraph,* January 23 and 26, 1857; Galveston *News,* January 22, 1857.

[32] Houston *Telegraph,* January 23, 1857.

[33] *Ibid.,* February 16, 1857.

[34] *Ibid.,* February 18, 1857.

[35] *Ibid.,* February 25, 1857; San Antonio *Texan,* August 20, 1857.

one of the proudest scenes that has ever been witnessed in San Antonio." Similar scenes, reported the same newspaper, were being witnessed in Austin and Gonzales.[36] At the same rendezvous in Galveston
a company of men arrived from Corpus Christi under the command of
Henry A. Maltby, the Mayor of Corpus Christi, who had resigned his
office to aid General Walker. "Mr. Maltby is an esteemed Texan and
a leader who will be an inspiration to those who go with him to
Nicaragua."[37]

Colonel Crawford's First Company, the initial unit of a new recruiting effort by this officer, was scheduled to form in Houston under
Captain Walker Maul on March 20th before proceeding to Galveston
on the 21st to join with Crawford's Second Company. This new "regiment from Texas," to be commanded by Colonel Crawford, was to be
"independent of all except General Walker." The unit was to be
equipped with its own hospital, munitions supply and provisions,
which it was maintained, would "render serving in it altogether more
agreeable."[38]

On the evening of February 24th, the same evening on which the
ball was held at the Tremont Hotel, a public meeting was convened at
the Court House in Galveston to honor the Nicaraguan Volunteers
and to raise funds for the cause. Francis Lubbock made the principal
address during which he declared that the men assembled in Galveston
were about to aid the cause of strengthening the institution of slavery
and to assist in securing a needed base for the African slave trade.[39]

On the subject of the African slave trade, the Quitman *Free Press*
in Wood County declared that the leading men in Galveston supported
Walker only because he promised to set up a base for the African slave
trade in Nicaragua. "Walker is not a liberator," wrote the Quitman

[36] Galveston *News*, February 24, 1857. An observer of the war in Nicaragua
recorded that in the middle of March, 1857, "a party of nearly 100 men styling
themselves the Alamo Rangers arrived in Nicaragua; they were a splendid
body of men commanded by Marcellus French," Franklin Gray Bartlett, "Expedition of the Alamo Rangers," *Overland Monthly*, New Series XXI (May,
1893), 517–523.

[37] Galveston *News,* February 24, 1857.

[38] *Ibid.,* February 26, 1857.   [39] *Ibid.*

SMALL BOATS AND BARGES in Galveston Harbor

From a contemporary engraving made by the German artist,
E. Schossig, in the Historical Collection, John Winterbotham
Room, Rosenberg Library, Galveston, Texas.

editor, "he is a slaver." This comment aroused the ire of Richardson of the *News* and he pointed to the *Free Press* "as an example of abolitionism in Texas. . . . If you agree to slavery," wrote the Galveston editor, "you must agree to the trade, for they are one. Those who are not for us must be against us. Those who deny slavery and the slave-trade are enemies of the South."[40]

On March 3rd meetings were held in Cypress City and in Houston to recruit men "to aid General Walker in reinstituting slavery" in Nicaragua. Committees were organized to conduct recruiting campaigns.[41] The new regiments were scheduled to sail in the following order: "First Company to leave April 2, Second Company to leave April 27, and Third Company to leave May 27."[42]

Then, late in March, word reached Galveston that Colonel Lockridge's Texas Rangers had suffered defeat. The situation became urgent. General Walker could "never succeed without the aid of our friend Crawford and his new band of gallant Texas Rangers. We hope they will take the field soon."[43] To meet the urgent need for additional men in Nicaragua, more meetings were held in Galveston and Houston. Francis Lubbock, Captain Walker Maul, Dr. Waters, Dr. Millan and C. B. Sabin campaigned vigorously in behalf of General Walker's cause.[44] Several "loosely organized" companies were mustered and shipped out en route to Nicaragua.[45]

During the month of April, 1857, the detailed news of the "disaster" which had overtaken Colonel Lockridge's Texas Rangers in the course of the Nicaraguan war reached Galveston. Lists of the known dead, as well as the names of "deserters," appeared in the Galveston newspapers; reports were printed that Colonel George B. Hall and Captain J. E. Farnham of Texas had been dismissed by General Walker for intemperance, that the Texas "Doctors Anderson and Richardson were absent without leave," that General Walker was dissatisfied with

[40] *Ibid.*, March 3, 1857.
[41] Houston *Telegraph*, March 11, 1857.
[42] Galveston *News*, March 10, 1857.
[43] Houston *Telegraph*, March 25, 1857.
[44] *Ibid.*, April 1, 1857; Galveston *News*, April 2, 1857.
[45] Lynn to Napier, April 25, 1857, MS, F.O.

Colonel Lockridge and had reduced his force to "100 men, 90 of whom were Texans," and that many Texan soldiers in Nicaragua were most anxious to return home.[46]

Then, early in May, "quite a number of Nicaraguans" from Lockridge's regiment returned to Galveston.[47] A few days later more Texas Rangers belonging to Captain French's Company reached the city "in a destitute condition." The editor of the *News* asked Galvestonians to contribute money and clothes for the relief of these men. Then Major James Bowie, of Eagle Pass, and Captain R. E. Stewart, of Anderson County, arrived and reported that in April they had been sent to the San Juan River by General Walker to contact Colonel Lockridge. These two officers said they had found the colonel's unit in a state of complete disintegration.[48]

A week later Colonel Crawford returned to Galveston after a trip to New Orleans. He at once published a long "card" in the Galveston *News* vindicating Colonel Lockridge's conduct, and stated that the fortunes of war had placed the colonel's command in a position so precarious that disintegration was unavoidable. Willard Richardson took the occasion to comment that many of the returning Nicaraguans supported Crawford's defense of Colonel Lockridge.[49] Colonel Crawford, however, had had enough of filibustering. He returned to Washington County to run for the State Senate.[50]

W. O. Scroggs, in his study of the war in Nicaragua, wrote that the term "Texan" was synonymous with the word "plunder" among the natives and that the Texas Rangers "quickly violated the confidence which had been placed in them by deserting, and proved to be a gang who had come to Nicaragua only for marauding."[51] This criticism should be read in conjunction with the obvious qualification that any defeated army retreating without the prospect of reinforcements or an

---

[46] Galveston *News,* April 4, 21, and 30, 1857; Galveston *Civilian,* April 27, 1857.
[47] Houston *Telegraph,* May 11, 1857.
[48] Galveston *News,* May 16, 1857.
[49] *Ibid.,* May 26, 1857.
[50] *Ibid.,* May 28, 1857.
[51] W. O. Scroggs, *Filibusters and Financiers,* pp. 243–244.

organized evacuation must, of necessity, live off the country. Not only the Texans, but also General Walker's whole army, which was disintegrating at the same time, abandoned the field of battle.[52]

Despite the admitted military talent displayed by Walker and his brilliant aide, General Charles Frederick Henningsen, a coalition consisting of Costa Rica, Guatemala, El Salvador, and anti-Walker Nicaraguans eventually defeated the filibusters. Vanderbilt assisted these "allies" by employing his facilities and agents to place a band of Costa Ricans arthwart Walker's line of communications. American shipping company agents on the isthmus had originally enabled Walker to conquer Nicaragua. Eventually shipping company agents in the employ of a competing transportation firm put him out.[53]

It so happened that at the time of Walker's debacle Commander Charles H. Davis was on patrol in Central American waters with the United States vessel *St. Mary*. Observing the desperate predicament of Walker's army, Davis arranged with the "allied" general to permit the filibusters to surrender to him. Eventually Davis transported the defeated men back to the United States.[54] For this humane act the commander was severely pilloried by the Texas press which accused him of using American naval power to drive Walker out of Nicaragua.[55]

The indefatigable General Walker, upon his return to New Orleans in apparent defeat, immediately began to organize another expedition with which to conquer Nicaragua. Two of his Texas officers, Colonel John Waters and Colonel Lockridge, arrived in Galveston in August to raise another force of Texans for the new venture. Colonel John Waters spent some time in Houston raising money and men while, at the same time, visiting his uncle, Colonel J. D. Waters, and his brother, Doctor Waters. Willard Richardson of the *News* gave the new recruiting program promotional assistance; the editor's view was that "the most conservative and prudent among our people are now convinced that the last hope of the South is in the Central American

[52] Houston *Telegraph*, June 1, 1857.

[53] Stuart, *Latin America and the United States*, pp. 328–330.

[54] *U.S. House Exec. Docs.*, 35th Cong., 1st sess., No. 24, p. 15.

[55] Houston *Telegraph*, June 1, 1857; Galveston *News*, August 8, 1857.

HANDLING COTTON on a Galveston wharf, *ca.* 1850

From a contemporary engraving, *Eigenthum der Verleger, Aus d. Kunstant. d. Bibliogr. in Hildbh.,* in the Historical Collection, John Winterbotham Room, Rosenberg Library, Galveston, Texas.

cause."[56] Hamilton Stuart, editor and publisher of the *Civilian*, who, as collector of customs, was under orders from the Secretary of the Treasury to assist in the enforcement of the federal neutrality laws, wrote in friendly terms of the fact that Colonel Lockridge was in the port city, "busily engaged in preparing an expedition for a return to Nicaragua."[57]

After a recruiting journey through the Gulf Coast counties, Colonel Lockridge passed through Galveston again on the way to New Orleans. He told Richardson that his influential friends in Texas had assured him that they would assemble several companies in Texas. They promised to mobilize "about 500 men" to embark on a steamer soon to be sent to Indianola for that purpose.[58]

Upon reaching New Orleans, Colonel Lockridge had a serious disagreement with General Walker and, as a result, the colonel published a "card" in the Galveston *News* stating that he had severed all "connection with General Walker's cause."[59] Despite this disaffection of a popular Texas officer, recruiting in the state proceeded vigorously. Captain W. R. Henry, a well-known frontier soldier, published a long "card" in the *News* urging that "all my old frontier comrades join me forthwith in the city of Galveston." Richardson supported the captain's appeal by supplementary editorials that likened Walker to Moses Austin and Lafayette. "We believe," wrote the editor, "that slavery must be seriously affected by events in Central America. We bespeak from our citizens a hearty welcome to Captain Henry and his men on their arrival, and urge that they may receive some accession to their members before leaving."[60] In Karnes County, C. K. Strubbling was "raising a company of 'emigrants' for Nicaragua," scheduled to leave Galveston on the 15th of October.[61]

Later in October Hamilton Stuart of the *Civilian* observed that "considerable Nicaraguan excitement" had prevailed in Galveston

[56] *Ibid.*, August 8, 1857.
[57] Galveston *Civilian*, August 11, 1957.
[58] Galveston *News*, August 28, 1857.
[59] *Ibid.*, September 5, 1857.
[60] *Ibid.*
[61] *Ibid.*, September 29, 1857.

during the past week. A "colony of some sixty prepared to leave today. Success to them. We of the South are in favor of the extension of slavery. We need more territory over which we can extend or maintain it." Stuart, however, criticized the organizers of the expeditions for failing to give "better assurances of subsistence and pay"; this failure, he said, kept many men from joining. He noted that Major J. R. Bostwick had arrived that evening on the steamship *Texas* to aid in the recruiting drive; perhaps the major would be able to provide the "necessary assurances."[62]

Whatever the conditions, Texans continued to volunteer. "There are now 500 men near Galveston ready to go to Nicaragua," reported the *News* on November 26th. "Captain Hal Runnels has 100 men in Houston, Captain McEachern 70 in Austin, Captain Phelps 40 in Brazoria, Captain Henry 75 men in Powder Horn, and Captains Perry and Strubbling have 100 men on the San Antonio River." It was also known that "Captains Mosely, McIlhenny, Moore and Keys" had companies practically ready to move. Willard Richardson wrote that he could personally vouch for the preceding statements.[63] General Walker's new expedition, said Richardson of the *News,* needed "a force of 10,000 men" to win and hold the country. The first venture had failed. This time the commander must be provided with the numbers needed.[64] Texans prepared to provide their share.

A few days later, the Houston *Telegraph* reported that a large body of men had left Galveston for Nicaragua via New Orleans on board the steamship *Mexico.*[65] "Large numbers" of young Texans were "lured" into the service by promises of large grants of land in Nicaragua. In order to have the necessary transportation available, the steamships *Fashion* and *Mexico* had been contracted for, through the agents J. Hasse and Company of Mobile, to make regular voyages

[62] Galveston *Civilian,* October 27, 1857.
[63] Galveston *News,* November 26, 1857.
[64] *Ibid.,* November 7, 1857.
[65] Houston *Telegraph,* December 7, 1857. While many of the claims made by the newspapers as to the size of the companies raised were exaggerated and promotional in character, there remains no reason to doubt that large bodies of men did leave the state to fight in Nicaragua.

during the winter on a route covering Mobile, New Orleans, Galveston, and ports in Nicaragua. On December 5th three companies of filibusters were waiting in Galveston for transportation to Nicaragua.[66]

While the Texans were busy raising men, General Walker, evading the federal authorities in New Orleans and Mobile, departed for Nicaragua on board the steamer *Fashion* with an army of 300 men, a part of which was made up of Texans.[67] Willard Richardson assured the friends of the Nicaraguan effort that this time General Walker would succeed. "President Buchanan will, of course, enforce our neutrality laws as a matter of duty, but is not disposed to embarrass Walker further than duty requires."[68]

During the second week in December Hamilton Stuart, received a message from the treasury department informing him that the steamship *Fashion,* which had recently taken General Walker and the army of volunteers to Nicaragua, was expected to stop at Galveston on her return trip to take on reinforcements. The collector was instructed to keep a sharp lookout for this vessel. If the ship put into Galveston, Stuart was told to "enforce the federal neutrality laws." These orders put the collector in a difficult position because, as editor and publisher of the *Civilian,* he had been a constant supporter of the Nicaraguan expeditions. However, since the federal government, in an attempt to tie up the *Fashion* at Galveston, had dispatched a special United States attorney to the city with instructions to take immediate action against the vessel, the collector was relieved of the necessity of having to act personally. In this situation, the "passengers" for the *Fashion* "departed quietly for New Orleans" on the regular mail steamers and avoided a clash with the special federal officials who were "on the alert to enforce the neutrality laws."[69]

When Commodore Hiram Paulding, commanding a United States naval vessel in Central American waters, learned that Walker had landed his "emigrants" near Greytown in Nicaragua, the commodore

[66] Lynn to Napier, December 5, 1857, MS, F.O.

[67] Galveston *News,* November 14, 1857.

[68] *Ibid.,* November 26, 1857.

[69] Galveston *Civilian,* December 15, 1857; *U.S. Sen. Exec. Docs.,* 35th Cong., 2nd Sess., Vol. 1, No. 13; Galveston *News,* December 3 and 12, 1857.

sent a force of marines ashore on Nicaraguan soil and ordered Walker to surrender. Although Paulding was exceeding his authority, Walker complied peacefully and allowed himself and his men to be returned to the United States. Paulding's interference with General Walker's emigration project was severely condemned by most Southern newspapers, including those of Galveston. Meetings were assembled in the Texas port and passed resolutions protesting against this "violation of the sovereign rights of Nicaragua."[70] Reacting to similar meetings held in many other Southern states, President Buchanan eventually admitted that Paulding had committed a "grave error."[71]

During the year 1858 General Walker appeared in Mobile, New Orleans, and other Southern cities arranging for future "peaceful migrations" to Nicaragua. In November, 1858, Walker wrote to a friend in Houston stating that a chartered vessel would leave Mobile on the 10th of November to carry "emigrants" to Nicaragua. He advised "Texas emigrants" to be in Mobile two or three days before the sailing date. The editor of the *Telegraph* pointed out that the new call for volunteers was "a legal operation and a great opportunity for Texans to go to the land of promise."[72]

A few days later it was reported that "Walker emigrants" from Texas were gathering in the Gulf ports.[73] These small groups occasionally sailed for Nicaragua from Mobile and landed at San Juan del Norte. While the federal government's half-hearted enforcements of the neutrality laws usually failed to prevent the armed travelers from reaching Nicaragua a few Texans en route were arrested and held for weeks in the custody of the authorities. Protests were made in Galveston and Houston against these "outrages."[74]

General Walker's failure to win a tangible victory in Nicaragua eventually reduced the enthusiasm of his supporters in Texas. Sam Houston, who in the early 1850's had addressed mass meetings assembled to raise money and men in support of filibustering expeditions,

[70] Galveston *Civilian,* January 12, 19 and 26, 1858.
[71] *U.S. House Reports,* 36th Cong., 1st Sess., Vol. 1, No. 74.
[72] Houston *Telegraph,* November 3, 1858.
[73] Galveston *Civilian,* November 9 and 24, 1858.
[74] Houston *Telegraph,* October 26, 1859.

had, by July, 1859, reversed his position. "I am no friend of filibustering as the term is understood," he said; "I am opposed to resistance to the laws, whether it be against the African Slave Trade Law, the Fugitive Slave Law or the Dred Scott Decision. When the laws are no longer regarded, liberty is at an end."[75]

Finally, in June, 1860, General Walker embarked personally on his last expedition to conquer the isthmus, carrying with him some of the recruits he had raised in Texas. Upon reaching Nicaragua, he attempted to mobilize other small groups of "emigrants" which had already been infiltrated into the country. This last effort, which was ill-planned, ended in disaster for his army and in execution for General Walker.

After that time the "Nicaraguan fever" subsided in Galveston. Consul Lynn reported that, since the defection of many of Walker's Texan officers during the previous months, and particularly since the execution of the general, "there has been a marked indifference to the appeals" of those advocating further migrations to Nicaragua. Lynn noted, however, the appearance of a new "expansionist" organization in the state called "The Secret Order of the Knights of the Golden Circle." This society was attempting to ally the old "Lone Star" spirit with a movement to penetrate into Mexico. It had no direct relationship with the expeditions led by Walker even though, in a general sense, the movement possessed similar aims and appealed to the same type of Texas citizens.[76]

The Texans who supported the filibustering expeditions had hoped by these adventures to gain personal wealth, to open the way to a lucrative trade in slaves, and to acquire cheap labor for the cotton plantations of Texas. A few of these adventurous men may have looked toward a greater Southern destiny and a larger representation in the national Congress. For the most part, however, the Texans were serving what they believed to be their own personal interests. In the same way, General Walker was pursuing what he must have ascertained to

[75] Sam Houston, *The Writings of Sam Houston, 1813–1863,* edited by Amelia W. Williams and Eugene C. Barker, VII, 262. Hereafter cited as Williams, *Writings of Sam Houston.*

[76] Lynn to Lyons, November 16 and 30, 1860; Lynn to Napier, April 25 and December 5, 1860, MSS, F.O.

be his own destiny. Vanderbilt, Morgan, and Garrison, the three financiers who actually manipulated the controlling factors in these adventures, exploited not only the "destiny" of the "grey-eyed" general, but also the predilection for adventure of the expansion-minded Texans.

Agitation for Reopening the Slave Trade

AGITATION FOR THE REPEAL of the laws prohibiting the African slave trade was a prominent subject of discussion in commercial and political conventions throughout the lower South in the last half of the eighteen-fifties.[77] The Texas delegation which attended a commercial and slave-trade convention in New Orleans in 1856 voted unanimously for action to legalize the trade.[78] Texas delegations voted the same way at similar conventions held in 1857, 1858 and 1859.[79]

An early Texas advocate for the repeal of the existing restrictions against the African slave trade was Hamilton Stuart, publisher and editor of the Galveston Civilian. Since Stuart was also the federal customs collector at the port and therefore responsible for enforcing the laws restricting the traffic, a conflict between duty and interest was clearly present at the customs office of the only major harbor in Texas. Due to the dynamic character of politics during these years, Stuart sometimes favored a policy of acquiring African labor even though to do so required the violation of state and federal laws and at other times he opposed the traffic so long as the laws made the trade illegal. Finally, in 1859 he opposed it categorically. He took the final position when he decided to support Sam Houston for the governorship rather than the proslave-trade candidate, H. R. Runnels.

Among the arguments Stuart had often marshalled in support of the move to bring African labor to the cotton fields of Texas were citations from the Holy Scripture which appeared to indicate that the savage Negro was ordained to be the servant of the Christian. To bring the "African to the plantation" was to save him, said Stuart. "Of course,

[77] W. E. Burghardt DuBois, *The Suppression of the African Slave-Trade of the United States of America, 1638–1870*, p. 169.

[78] Houston *Telegraph*, December 22, 1856.

[79] DuBois, *Slave-Trade*, pp. 169–173.

the opening of the slave trade is abhorrent to the pious feelings of the Boston abolitionist. To him the lowest half-baboon Negro in Africa is infinitely [better off] . . . than it is possible for a slave to be among the white folks 'down south.' " The "learned fools" of New England, wrote Stuart, "do not know what they are talking about; the whole continent of South Texas is going to waste for want of white intellects and Negro laborers." The Negro, insisted the editor, could never realize a better status than that which he could achieve under a mild system of slavery; in this state he could accomplish the most good for himself, as well as for his superior fellow, the white man, and thus he could assure that his posterity would live permanently in a Christian land. Stuart called the attention of Texans to a recent editorial in the London *Times* which had questioned whether or not the British government's policy of trying to restrain the African slave trade was not an impossible policy to pursue because of the enormous profits being made in the traffic. One slaver, reported the *Times,* had netted a profit of 37,000 pounds sterling on three trips. "Why not admit these facts," demanded Stuart, and accept the certainty "that the products of slave labor sustain the commerce of the world, civilization, and Christianity. When England gets to where she needs more cheap sugar and cotton for the spinners of Britain," argued the editor, "then, indeed, will the people of England sing out 'more niggers! We must eat and be clothed.' "[80]

Willard Richardson of the Galveston *News* endorsed the *Civilian's* position in a vigorous editorial. He pointed out that England's attempt to control the traffic had only compounded the cruelty of the trade. He cited the opinion of one slaver captain who had stated that in the "nine cargoes of slaves he had run, his shrinkage" had averaged more than 30 percent. The only solution was to legalize and then regulate the traffic.[81]

A few days later E. H. Cushing, editor of the Houston *Telegraph,* pointed to the fact that, although Texas was at that time producing less than one-half million bales of cotton per year, the cotton lands of Texas were "capable of producing three million bales. The only thing

[80] Galveston *Civilian,* June 20, 1857.
[81] Galveston *News,* June 20, 1857.

we want," he said, "is cheap labor; more cotton can be grown in Texas per acre than anywhere." Cushing insisted that Texas "may yet supply more than half the cotton of the world" if only some means were to be found to supply a "cheapened labor, so as to give the enterprise of our planters more scope." Cushing took an encouraging note from the fact that African Negroes were being brought into the British sugar islands as "apprentices for 10 years." Texas, he believed, ought to examine this method. "Apprentices, if not nominally slaves, are really so and it will be no cheating, if once we get them, to make slaves of them." The Houston editor urged Texans "to inquire into the practicability of using a little English shrewdness, so as not to offend the philanthropy of either Brother Jonathan or John Bull and at the same time give us what everyone knows ere long we must have." Cushing took precaution to emphasize that he was in favor of the apprentice system only as a means of increasing the number of slaves in Texas. "Let us replenish our fields with good, hearty, robust Negroes from the fountainhead," argued Cushing. "Let us take those black barbarians and make good Christians of them and raise them to the level of our Negroes. The work is one of philanthropy and patriotism."[82]

The next day, Richardson of the *News* published a commentary which praised the London *Times* for admitting, at long last, that sugar, coffee and cotton could be produced successfully only by employing slave labor. The Galveston editor, therefore, again urged the adoption of a policy allowing the importation of "Africans under some wise and humane system."[83]

During the late summer of 1857 those advocating the "new labor policy" found encouragement from the fact that the French government had originated a way to import labor from Africa to Martinique without appearing to be in violation of the general European treaties outlawing the traffic. Twelve hundred "free" Negroes were imported into the French colony to work under ten-year apprentice contracts. At the end of the "apprentice period," the Africans were to be returned

[82] Houston *Telegraph,* July 1, 1857.
[83] Galveston *News,* July 2, 1857. For other examples of proslave-trade editorials in 1857, see Galveston *News,* August 6, 8, 22, 29, and September 5; Galveston *Civilian,* October 6; Houston *Telegraph,* March 18.

to their homeland. Lord Palmerston, the British cabinet minister who had long been waging an almost personal war against the traffic—and who had instructed Consul Lynn, at Galveston, to keep him fully informed regarding "the traffic" in Texas—had questioned the French as to whether or not this "contract labor" policy was not in violation of existing treaties. The French authorities had assured him that it was not. Editor Richardson, after giving his Texas readers a detailed explantation of the new French policy, concluded that the "free labor," worked for ten years in Martinique, "would have cause to envy Texas Negroes." Few of the "Martinique-Negroes," said Richardson, would be alive after ten years on the French plantations.[84] He noted that during the fall months the ship *Phoenix*, of the French firm Regis and Company of Marseilles, had moved 296 Negroes from Africa to the colony at Guadaloupe on a 39-day voyage and had lost only fourteen out of the lot. Two more ships of the same firm, the *Stella* and the *Clara*, were engaged to carry 1,200 and 1,500 Negroes, respectively, to the French colony before the end of the year 1857. Losses on these journeys were expected to be negligible. Here, then, was an example of the humane benefits to be expected from a legalization of traffic.[85]

The advocates of a reopening of the slave trade recommended various proposals as the most expeditious ways in which to overcome the several legal barriers standing in the way—barriers such as the provisions of the federal constitution, the similar provision in the Texas constitution, and the general law codes of the two governing bodies. It was believed that if the restrictions in the Texas constitution and code which not only provided severe penalties for any person engaged in the African slave trade but also placed very encumbering punishments upon any parties aiding the immigration of free Negroes into the state were eliminated, the second barrier provided by the federal restrictions could eventually be undermined, if not repealed, since it would literally be impossible to secure a conviction, by a Texas jury, against any person accused of having been engaged in the traffic. As

[84] Galveston *News,* August 22, 1857; also see Galveston *News,* September 5, 1857.

[85] Galveston *Civilian,* October 6, 1857.

the situation stood in 1857, even though it was common knowledge that foreign Negroes were being imported into Texas and other Southern states, no slaver had been seriously hampered by the action of a federal court.

Looking at the problem from this point of view, John Henry Brown, many times the mayor of Galveston, partner of Hamilton Stuart in the Civilian Job Printing Company, and Representative from Galveston in the State House of Representatives, introduced into the Legislature at Austin on November 25, 1857, a "Joint Resolution in Relation to the Importation of African Slaves." In substance, the resolution was an elaborate polemic citing historical precedents, Biblical quotations, and classical literature in support of the institution of slavery. The paragraphs of the document also presented the proposition that the Texas governor and the members of the Texas delegation at Washington should be instructed to press for a repeal of the treaties and laws curtailing the African slave trade and that necessary laws be "enacted to make this trade more humane." The resolution was then referred to the Committee on Slaves and Slavery.[86] The resolution, however, was allowed to remain in the Committee because political expediency indicated that it would be an act of wisdom not to inject this issue into the current legislative program despite the fact that Sam Houston, who opposed the reopening of the traffic, had been defeated in the August election for the governorship by Hardin R. Runnels, an ardent filibuster and an advocate of a renewal of the foreign slave trade.

While this victory emboldened the proslave-trade elements to more vigorous action in 1858 and 1859, the result also aroused more conservative and moderate Texans to the realities of the situation and set the stage for the critical contest between the same candidates in 1859, at which time Sam Houston won the governorship and thus held the legal reins during the 1860 secession crisis. The major issue in Texas during these critical years was, in reality, the question of the slave

[86] Texas, *House Journal*, 1857. It is significant that the advocates of "legalization" appeared to be genuinely concerned about the inhumane aspects of the illegal trade then going on. They very clearly indicated their desire to correct that "acknowledged evil."

trade, although the states-rights Democrats struggled vigorously to maintain that the "labor question" was a nonpolitical question and therefore not an issue in the 1859 contest.

As was the case in other Southern states, the advocates for the reopening of the African slave trade received occasional support from the churches and clergymen. The Presbyterians in Galveston asserted that the slavers, who brought African Negroes into the United States and eventually converted them toward an adherence to Christianity, were actually engaged in "a missionary work." The federal fleet which occasionally intercepted a slaver off the coast of Africa was therefore actually impeding "God's work," said the Presbyterians.[87] A correspondent writing to the Houston *Telegraph* and signing himself "a Religious Man," maintained that "the opening of the African slave trade for a single year would civilize and Christianize more Africans than the combined efforts of all the sickly sentimental philanthropists could do or have done in a thousand years."[88]

The Methodist Episcopal Conference at Waco adopted a resolution to "memorialize" the next general conference of the church which was to meet in Nashville on May 1, 1858, urging that this meeting "expunge from the general rules the admonition against the buying and selling of men and women, with the intention to enslave them." The Texas conference "hoped that this obsolete prohibition" would be repealed.[89] Methodists in "Fannin county and others" who were opposed to the African slave trade attempted to organize a "M. E. Church North." However, the Methodists of Houston and Galveston convened a "mass meeting" which passed a resolution praising the attempts to reopen the slave trade and "gave all persons connected with said M. E. Church North, as itinerant preachers or Bishops or propagators of their views, 60 days to leave the state" or they would be dealt with "as hinted at in the above resolution."[90]

As the date approached for the 1859 meeting of the State Convention of the Democratic Party, the struggle for the control of the party

[87] Galveston *News,* August 29, 1857.
[88] Houston *Telegraph,* February 7, 1859.
[89] Galveston *Civilian,* January 26, 1858.
[90] Houston *Telegraph,* April 4, 1859.

and for the control of the state governmental machinery began to take definite form. The various leaders maneuvered to improve their respective positions. The moderate, pro-Union, antislave-trade factions, both within the party and on the outside, began to coalesce around a possible ticket headed by Sam Houston. Overriding the constant political factor created by the desire of various groups to control the seat of power was the immediate question of the slave trade and the potential issue of secession. These matters were vital and they infused unusual tension and political drama into the approaching Convention. Hamilton Stuart, tied as he was to federal government patronage by his office as customs collector, feared the loss of this lucrative position if the slave-trade–secession faction should capture control. Although the editor supported the institution of slavery, he was, nevertheless, a sincere Unionist, who dreaded the prospect of secession.

Viewing the dynamic political scene in this light at the opening of the year 1859, Stuart completely reversed his previous position on the slave-trade issue and thereafter used his newspaper, the *Civilian,* as an organ against the "African-traffic" and against the "Lubbock-Runnels-filibuster" element in the Democratic Party. He joined forces with Ferdinand Flake, the pro-Union, antislave-trade editor of the Galveston German newspaper, *Die Union,* who was a powerful leader of the Germans on the Gulf Coast. Allied with this faction, also, were such men as State Senator M. M. Potter and Lorenzo Sherwood of Galveston, and in the background as the potential standard bearer loomed Sam Houston; however, in early 1859 when Hamilton Stuart asked Houston to give him permission to tell his friends that "Old Sam" would consent to head a conservative Democratic ticket, the General refused.[91]

Nevertheless, Stuart made the critical decision to reverse his position on the African slave trade some time prior to December 28, 1858, for on that day he published an editorial in which he related the high price planters were getting for cotton to the high price of Negroes. "12 cent cotton" he wrote, "and $1200 Negroes" go together; if the price of Negroes were reduced, he reasoned, the price of cotton would fall.[92]

[91] Williams, *Writings of Sam Houston,* VI, 370.
[92] Galveston *Civilian,* December 28, 1858.

A few weeks later the editor condemned the illegal slave trade, asserting that the provisions of the federal constitution and the congressional act of 1808 "should be obeyed until repealed."[93] Willard Richardson of the Galveston *News* was very critical of Hamilton Stuart for shifting his position,[94] while E. H. Cushing, of the Houston *Telegraph*, declared that Stuart changed his views because of the office he held at the Customs House. The Houston editor asserted that he himself "would not change his principles for a pittance."[95] A week later Cushing wrote that "The *Civilian* stands alone as the enemy of cheap and abundant labor" for Texas; "legalize the trade and the greatest benefits will ensue," he said. Texas could produce 7 million bales of cotton annually as against the present 300,000. The industry, wrote Cushing, could not wait for the slow emigration "from the slave breeding states." To postpone "the greatness" of Texas by restrictions would be "criminal folly."[96] A few days later the same editor cited the capture of "a slaver in the Gulf off Florida" by the United States *Vixen* as an example of gross interference, on the part of the federal power, with the natural growth of Texas.[97]

Despite the fact, however, that vigorous opposition developed rapidly against the antislave-trade faction, the official Democratic County Convention of Galveston instructed its twenty-five delegates, who were appointed to attend the forthcoming state convention, to "oppose any platform resolution favoring the reopening of the slave trade."[98]

In this situation the Runnels-Lubbock, proslave-trade group realized the necessity to "prepare Texas thinking in these matters" prior to the meeting of the state convention. Richardson and Cushing once more launched elaborate journalistic polemics to support the slave-trade position. Richardson began his effort in February predicting that within a year there would be a "universal denunciation" of the federal pro-

---

[93] *Ibid.*, March 15, and 22, 1859.
[94] Galveston *News*, quoted in Houston *Telegraph*, February 28, 1859.
[95] Houston *Telegraph*, March 11, 1859.
[96] *Ibid.*, March 21, 1859.
[97] *Ibid.*, March 30, 1859.
[98] *Ibid.*, April 20, 1859.

hibition throughout the South. "The admonition that the slave trade is immoral is fatal to slavery," wrote Richardson; "every editor who holds this view condemns slavery and Texas whether he knows it or not." He pointed out that to develop the resources of Texas was the "deepest duty" of all Texans. "It will take two million slaves to people Texas" with the same relative proportion as possessed by the other Southern states. Should Texas, so well adapted to "slave products," asked the editor, "remain a wilderness for want of friendly legislation?" If it were not for the legal restriction, a slave might be purchased for $300. If prices were reasonable "the poor planter, who is now compelled to put all the menial labor of his household upon his wife, would have the means to put a Negro woman in her place and a man to help him in the fields; and the offspring of these Negroes would be a fortune for his children." The removal of these "trade restrictions" would save thousands of poor families in Texas from the hardships and sufferings of field labor. The assistance of even one slave per agricultural unit would compound the total production of the state at a rapid rate, said the editor; soon, new acres would be opened up, new roads would be made over the country, carpenters, blacksmiths and mechanics of every kind would be in demand; towns would spring up and an "impetus be given to improvements beyond all past precedent."

Richardson admitted that it would be difficult, as a matter of politics, to secure a repeal of the federal restrictions; yet this fact need not be a barrier to the growth of Texas. "We care not if every foreign slave trader in a Southern state shall be arrested by the colossal hand of the federal government," declared the editor, so long as "the state herself permits the citizen to trade in slaves unmolested—when the cases come before a jury, it will be the federal government and the rights of the state" at issue; no one need fear the result in such circumstances.[99]

Hamilton Stuart, who by that time had changed his position on the issue, argued that if the barriers impeding the slave trade were removed, the flood of Negroes entering the state would soon depress the price of cotton and wipe out any possible economic gain. This

[99] Galveston *News*, quoted in the Houston *Telegraph*, February 28, 1859.

would not be the case, argued a correspondent in the Houston *Telegraph*: "I have examined the difficulties and other circumstances concerning the trade," he wrote; "it is the long profit now which brings them in"; at $300 per Negro "there would be no flood; if we get too many we can close the trade again." White labor or European immigration wouldn't do. "You can't command it." In terms of a thousand acres, wrote this correspondent, the use of Negro labor was the only profitable way to work a plantation.[100]

Thus when the State Democratic Convention opened in Houston on May 4, 1859, the issue of the slave trade was the dominating factor upon which all else turned. Texans such as Governor Runnels, F. R. Lubbock and A. P. Wiley, who had also been among the engineers behind the movement to aid General Walker, were determined to take concrete action concerning the slave trade. They attempted to force the Convention to adopt a platform advocating the legalization of the traffic. Thus over the slave-trade issue, the heretofore strong Democratic party in Texas faced a critical division as the convention opened, and calmer party leaders strove to avert the breach. Two leading Democratic politicians, Judge John Henniger Reagan and Louis T. Wigfall, who had previously taken opposing positions on the issue, decided in the existing circumstances not to take an immediate stand either way because they realized that to inject the issue into the campaign would be to give a possible Sam Houston coalition of old Whigs and Know-Nothings a rallying item upon which to unite conservative pro-Union sentiment and thus capture the state government.

The leaders of the party kept the issue suppressed during the first two days of the meeting, but on the third day, Colonel Frank Bowden Chilton, of Smith County, forced the question onto the floor and criticized Judge Reagan for evading the issue. Captain C. C. Herbert, of Colorado County, urged that "it matters not whether it is constitutional or not, we must have more slaves, and we must encourage the trade by all means in our power." During the night session, P. W. Kittrell stated that "to call the African slave trade piracy was an insult to Southern men"; the matter, he said, ought to be left to the control of the states. Dr. Thomason, of Galveston, also spoke for a legalization

[100] Houston *Telegraph*, February 7, 1859.

of the traffic. The more moderate forces also had strong support. M. Aycock, of Falls County, maintained that the Democratic Convention was not a slave-trade convention and that, therefore, no resolution ought to be adopted. James E. Shepherd, of Washington County, added that, while it was his view that the federal law declaring that persons engaged in the importation of slaves were guilty of piracy was unconstitutional, he was opposed, nevertheless, to the resolution because it would split the party. F. S. Stockdale, a vigorous supporter of General Walker, said that "slavery was manifest destiny" and that "Africans would continue to be imported into Texas in spite of all laws and edicts." In the interest of party harmony, however, he was opposed to the resolution. Thomas Palmer, another ardent filibuster, took the same view.

Ferdinand Flake, a delegate from Galveston and the editor of the German newspaper *Die Union,* delivered an angry speech denouncing in vigorous terms the fact that the Democratic Party of Texas should even consider the possibility of legally reopening the African slave trade. At the conclusion of his remarks, Flake and Hamilton Stuart left the Convention hall, declaring that "the odor of the slave trade at the Convention was too strong for their nostrils."[101]

Shortly after this incident, the issue reached a vote in the form of a proposition that Colonel Chilton's proslave-trade resolution should be tabled. The vote was 228 to table, 81 not to table. Thus the wish of the majority was "that it would not be well to compel men to take sides at this time."[102]

At this juncture Stuart and Flake, realizing that the crucial issue had been suppressed only temporarily, approached Sam Houston once more and urged him to head an antislave-trade ticket. This time he agreed to run because, as he said, "I afterwards saw that to meet the issues of disunion and the African slave trade, I must face my foes and make the issue direct."[103]

The proslave-trade planters on the Gulf Coast who had supported the Runnels and Lubbock wing of the party in the hope of securing

[101] Houston *Telegraph,* May 6, 1859.
[102] *Ibid.*
[103] Williams, *Writings of Sam Houston,* VI, 370.

cheap labor, did not approve of the policy of conciliation adopted by the Houston Convention. These critics organized "States Rights Democratic Clubs" which proceeded to pass resolutions declaring that the laws restricting the slave trade were all unconstitutional. However, Horace Cone, a local political leader of the slave-trade faction, defended the Convention, declaring that Texas would get the slaves she needed without splitting the Democratic party over the issue.[104] Two days later Louis T. Wigfall delivered a public address in Houston in which he asserted that even though the federal law restricting the traffic was unconstitutional, the Houston Convention properly avoided making the issue a party matter. This was not "cowardice," he said; it was wisdom.[105] Two weeks afterwards, Cushing agreed that perhaps "it is better not to face the slave trade issue now. We can take care of it later,"[106] and a few days thereafter, Judge John H. Reagan and Wigfall reached a compromise by agreeing not to discuss the issue and to support each other.[107] Wigfall's decision was based on political expediency. Reagan sincerely opposed the reopening of the trade for he had previously denounced the traffic as "an evil piracy."[108]

The rising dissension within the Texas Democratic party was exploited by Hamilton Stuart, Ferdinand Flake, Oscar Farish, James Love and other conservative leaders to strengthen the Sam Houston ticket. "All the talk in Galveston is on politics," wrote William Pitt Ballinger in his diary, and the "general opinion in Galveston is that Houston will be the next governor."[109]

Ferdinand Flake asserted in his German weekly, *Die Union*, that Governor Runnels had lately consulted lawyers at New Orleans to ascertain "in what way the existing laws against the reopening of the slave trade could be eluded." The German editor accused "Runnels, Wiley, Lubbock and Co." of conspiring to undermine the constitution and their party to promote "their selfish interest in the African slave

[104] Houston *Telegraph,* May 16, 1859.
[105] *Ibid.,* May 18, 1859.
[106] *Ibid.,* June 3, 1859.
[107] *Ibid.,* June 20, 1859.
[108] *Ibid.,* July 18, 1859.
[109] Ballinger Diary, July 3, 1859, MS.

trade." He called the Democratic States Rights Clubs "slave trade clubs."[110] E. H. Cushing, of the *Telegraph,* replied by telling Flake that he was "selling out" his own Germans by supporting former Know-Nothing candidates. Flake, however, had already answered this charge by securing a letter from the former Know-Nothing, Sam Houston, in which the General stated categorically that "Know-nothingism is dead."[111]

Flake, in an effort to win the German vote for Sam Houston, continually called attention to the fact that A. P. Wiley, of Huntsville, had declared, in a speech before the Houston Convention, that "should the Germans of Texas declare themselves to be against the slave trade," restrictions ought to be set up to keep the German immigrants out of Texas. At the time the statement was made, said Flake, "not a delegate arose to correct or modify" this remark directed against the Germans in Texas. Wiley stated later that, since he had often defended the Germans against former Know-Nothings, he had a right now to expect the Germans to support him on the slave-trade issue.[112]

At about the same time, Sam Houston, delivering his only speech of the campaign, declared that he did not approve of filibustering. He was opposed to any resistance to the laws, whether it be against the African slave trade, the Fugitive Slave Law or the Dred Scott Decision. "When the laws are no longer regarded," he said "regulated liberty is at an end."[113]

During the summer Texans who were genuinely concerned over the political unrest that appeared to be arising out of the injection of the slave-trade issue into the already charged political atmosphere urged Peter W. Gray, a respected Houston jurist who occupied the position of judge of the Houston district of the Texas court system, to prepare and deliver a public address upon the slave-trade issue. Against the advice of his friends, the jurist complied. The "oration," which took three hours to deliver, presented the substantial arguments existing

---

[110] Galveston *Die Union,* July 7, 1859.

[111] Houston *Telegraph,* July 8, 1859.

[112] Galveston *Die Union,* June 23, 1859; Houston *Telegraph,* July 4, 1859.

[113] Williams, *Writings of Sam Houston,* VII, 362 (Speech at Nacogdoches, July 7, 1857).

against the reopening of the slave traffic. Although E. H. Cushing, editor of the *Telegraph*, "disagreed almost entirely" with the substance of the "oration," he, nevertheless, printed the address as a series in several issues of his newspaper as a public service.

Judge Gray asserted that the argument which held that the slave trade would Christianize African Negroes and which, for this reason, had won substantial support among "church going Texans," was a "double faced plea" resting upon self-interest rather than upon Christianity. He insisted that if Negroes were "made cheaper," all slaves would become less valuable and that their masters would provide them with less care; the native slaves themselves would be completely demoralized by the influx of cheap African labor.

"As a Texan," said Judge Gray, "I feel little complimented by the selection of this state as the field for 'special efforts' to revive this trade." Why was this done, he asked. "Because it is known that our vast territory, our spreading prairies, and rich bottom lands lie vacant and uncultivated. As our interest is supposed to lie that way," said the Judge, "our state is to be the theatre of this contest." Such "ideas are afloat," warned Gray; "how far they have been embodied for action I do not know, but that recent events indicate that definite steps have been taken for such action is beyond question."[114]

The division over the slave-trade issue was most trying upon those conservatives who believed in the "virtues" inherent in the "institution" as it then existed in Texas, but who abhorred the idea of legally accepting the African slave trade as an integral part of "the institution." The respected state senator, M. M. Potter of Galveston, journeyed to the neighboring city of Houston to advocate this point of view. He returned to the port city a saddened man. He confided to his friend, William Pitt Ballinger, that he was "thoroughly disgusted," because, for his effort, he had been "greatly slandered for want of good Southern principles." Ballinger himself was so revolted by the whole canvass that he refused to vote at all.[115] Hamilton Stuart became so involved in an exchange of "insults" over the "issue" with Tom

[114] Houston *Telegraph*, June 20, July 4, and July 13, 1859.
[115] Ballinger Diary, July 22 and August 1, 1859, MS.

Jack, a law partner and brother-in-law of Ballinger, that it took all the mediating skill of both families to avoid a challenge which might have ended in a duel.[116]

When the election was at last held on August 1st, Sam Houston received 36,257 votes and H. R. Runnels 27,500. The slave-trade men, nevertheless, carried the city of Galveston by a vote of 403 to 307, and Lubbock running for the office of lieutenant governor polled 436 votes as against 267 for his conservative opponent, Edward Clark.[117]

On contemplating the defeat of the slave-trade ticket, Cushing, editor of the *Telegraph,* professed to be genuinely surprised, because, he said, every English language newspaper in the state with one exception had favored reopening the slave trade. "Is it any wonder then," explained Cushing, "that with this showing of public feeling we were impressed with the belief that the people were in large majority in favor of these views." But, admitted the editor, the election appeared to show that many did not wish to see the trade opened legally. So, "let us be still a while, though we continue to hold the same views." White men, he repeated, ought to be freed from manual labor "by the ox and the Negro." To speak of the "dignity of labor," he said, was but to employ a "catch phrase of demagogues."[118] Later in the fall, Cushing had occasion to note, from the press exchanges, that a "cargo of Africans, numbering some six hundred," had recently been landed along the Gulf Coast near Florida. "We presume," the editor commented, "that they are now snugly ensconced on nearly as many plantations in the Southwestern states." No doubt "this new arrival of Southern laborers in our midst will cause expressions of worry from such nervous papers as the Galveston *Civilian,*" observed Cushing, as he further consoled "progressive Texans" with the assurance that, although "persons may rant and rave as much as they please about the 'sin,' if Texas needs more farm help she will get the help."[119]

The next attempt, however, to secure legal African labor was de-

[116] *Ibid.,* August 31, 1859.
[117] *Ibid.,* August 1, 1859.
[118] Houston *Telegraph,* August 19, 1859.
[119] *Ibid.*

layed by the issue of secession itself which dominated the two years between the 1859 election and the eventual Secession Convention, the subsequent referendum, and the withdrawal of Texas from the Union.

The Abduction of Free Negroes and Slaves

IN TEXAS during the eighteen-fifties, the demand for Negro labor often forced the prevailing selling price for slaves as high as $1500 for men and $1250 for women. Since a "likely" Negro could be hired out for $250 to $300 per season,[120] with the cost of his upkeep paid by the person employing him, many nonplanters acquired slaves merely as an income investment. In four to five years, even the most expensive Negro would, by his own labor, pay for his original purchase price.

The high selling price of slaves sometimes inspired acquisitive persons to kidnap or otherwise secure control over seafaring free Negroes, who might unwittingly present themselves as tempting prizes in Texas seaports. Titles to these acquisitions were usually obtained by fraud or by collusion between dealers and justices of the peace.[121] The latter procedure rested upon a semblance of legality, since a Negro charged with a real or an alleged crime could be sold into slavery as punishment in lieu of a fine or merely to pay for the cost of his maintenance during a jail term. Once the Negro had passed the line from freedom into even temporary slavery, his permanent status in the latter was almost a certainty. In instances where an apparent title was not obtainable, the acquired Negroes could be hired out to persons who would not ask embarrassing questions as to the actual ownership of the labor hired.

Captain Thomas Chubb, a Galveston shipmaster who later gained fame as the commander of the Confederate steamer *Royal Yacht* during the Civil War, employed a very direct device to acquire valuable Northern free Negroes. At one time, "he hired a colored crew at Boston, and then coolly [sold] them at Galveston."[122] Later, during

[120] Houston *Telegraph,* January 21, 1859.

[121] *State of Texas* v. *Theophilus Freeman,* District Court of Galveston, January 6, 1857.

[122] James Arthur Lyon Fremantle, *The Fremantle Diary: Being the Journal*

the Civil War, he was captured by the Yankees and condemned to be hanged as a pirate for having engaged in the slave trade; but, eventually, he was exchanged before the sentence was carried out.[123]

The kidnaping of an occasional "coloured lad" from the West Indies Islands, with the intent to sell the boy later as a slave in Texas, was a recurring source of irritation to British officials. As early as 1838, the British Foreign Office protested to Texas authorities against this abuse of her nationals and demanded the return of "some persons of colour kidnapped from" the islands.[124] More than a decade later, the Foreign Office was still aroused over similar kidnapings of British Negroes. Lord Palmerston wrote Arthur Lynn, then British consul in Galveston, that an organized system was being used to decoy "Young Negro lads on board United States vessels in Jamaica" for the purpose of "selling them as slaves in Galveston." Palmerston directed Lynn to exert all the means available in the law to "apprehend those engaged in this crime."[125]

Lynn endeavored to apprehend the perpetrators of this illegal trade and to rescue the victims, but with little success. "It is very hard to catch this kind of kidnaping," wrote Lynn to Palmerston a year later, "as it is kept in the dark and these slaves are closely watched." Although public laws and public opinion in Galveston did not sanction the kidnaping of British free Negroes, observed the consul, it was nevertheless true that neither public opinion nor the law would be of much practical help if one were to try to remedy the situation.

In December, 1854, however, Lynn did succeed in rescuing two

---

of *Lieutenant Colonel James Arthur Lyon Fremantle, Coldstream Guards, or His Three Months in the Southern States*, p. 54.

[123] *Ibid.* The above information was related to Colonel Fremantle when he visited Galveston during the month of May, 1863. Captain Chubb, according to Fremantle, was a well-known "character" in Galveston. *State of Texas* v. *Thomas B. Chubb,* District Court of Galveston, January 24, 1857. Chubb was indicted for stealing Negroes and all his property in Galveston was placed under bond to insure his appearance in court.

[124] William Kennedy to Earl of Aberdeen, May 30, 1843, printed in "British Correspondence Concerning Texas," Ephriam D. Adams, Editor, *Southwestern Historical Quarterly*, XVII (October, 1913), 200.

[125] Lord Palmerston to Lynn, December 5, 1851, MS, F.O.

West Indies colored boys. He notified Hamilton Stuart, customs collector in Galveston, that two British sailors of color, who had been brought into Sabine by Captain Hurd, "were about to be sold into slavery." Lynn demanded that the protection due British nationals be extended to them.[126] Stuart went to Sabine, ascertained the facts, and freed the two Negro sailors. He apologized to Lynn for the injustice done and promised to try to prevent further incidents of a similar nature.[127]

The position of the free Negro in Galveston was completely untenable, in both legal and social terms. Newspapers often complained about the "free Negro nuisance" and deplored the threat to the Texas institution presented by the fact that the neighboring states of Louisiana and Arkansas took a lenient view in regard to free Negroes.[128]

A free Negro could not legally reside within the state of Texas unless special permission had been granted in each case by an act of the legislature.[129] The testimony of a Negro, of whatever status, was not admissible in a court of law in any case where a white person was a party in the issue.[130] Consequently, a free Negro brought into court as a defendant on a charge by a white man could not testify in his own behalf. The same circumstances prevailed in cases where a free Negro appeared in court to determine whether or not a particular set of circumstances permitted his sale into temporary or permanent slavery. Such cases were decided on the basis of *ex parte* testimony unless some

[126] Lynn to Palmerston, January 17, 1852; Lynn to Lord Granville, February 14, 1853; Lynn to Lord Russell, February 4, 1853; Lynn to Earl of Clarendon, November 19, 1853; Lynn to Hamilton Stuart (Customs Collector, Galveston), December 4, 1854, MSS, F.O.

[127] Lynn to Stuart, December 25, 1854, MS, F.O.

[128] Galveston *Civilian,* August 25, 1857; August 31, 1858. For a comprehensive analysis of the position of the free Negro in Texas during the Republic, see Harold Schoen, "The Free Negro in The Republic of Texas," *Southwestern Historical Quarterly,* XXXIX (April, 1936), 292–308; XL (July, 1936), 26–34; (October, 1936), 85–113; (January, 1937), 169–199; (April, 1937), 267–289.

[129] Oliver C. Hartley, *A Digest of the Laws of Texas,* p. 783.

[130] *Ibid.,* p. 786.

white person chose to come forward to testify on the Negro's behalf.[131]

The fact that the Texas constitution and subsequent acts of the legislature made it a "penal offense for any shipmaster to bring a free Negro into Texas" presented the captains of British vessels with the serious handicap of not being able to grant shore leave to "British seamen of color" during a call at Galveston. The law required that colored sailors be kept on shipboard, or if brought ashore, they must be lodged in the county jail for the duration of their period in the city.[132] Lynn urged the Foreign Office to protest against this mistreatment of Her Majesty's seamen on the grounds that such oppressive laws were a violation of the general commerce treaties.[133] The Foreign Office, however, seeing little merit in this suggestion, warned Lynn to "act with caution in such cases." No clear remedy appeared in sight.[134]

The kidnaping of the young British mulatto boy, Charles H. Thomas, in Galveston during the year 1857, revealed some of the devices employed to acquire "likely" colored property. In November, 1856, Henry Johnson, master of the American schooner *Velasco,* which was then lying in the harbor of Port of Spain in the island of Trinidad, engaged Thomas to help unload a cargo. When the young Negro happened to express a desire to go to New York City, Captain Johnson told the boy that he could do no better than sign on as a member of the *Velasco* crew since New York would be her next port of call.[135] Contrary to the captain's assertion, however, the vessel sailed directly to Galveston, arriving there on December 12th.[136] Thomas was kept on board the *Velasco* while she lay in the harbour. A few days later, the vessel sailed to Pensacola. At that port, Johnson endeavored to sell Thomas as a slave, but was prevented from doing so by the mate. In February, the schooner returned to Galveston where the vessel was sold.

---

[131] Lynn to Clarendon, September 20, 1856; Lynn to George Hammond, March 14, 1857; Lynn to Earl of Malmesbury, April 6, 1858, MSS, F.O.

[132] Lynn to Clarendon, September 20, 1856, MS, F.O.

[133] *Ibid.*

[134] Lynn to Hammond, March 14, 1857, MS, F.O.

[135] Lynn to Clarendon, July 18, 1857, MS, F.O.

[136] Galveston *News,* June 23, 1857.

The members of the crew, other than Thomas and another colored boy, were sent north to Baltimore.[137] Captain Johnson attempted to "clear Thomas and another at the customs-house" in Galveston "as slaves" for shipment to New Orleans, but was denied the clearance because the slave status of the Negroes seemed doubtful.[138] Thomas was eventually "discharged in Galveston without any provision being made for him." The "other Negro" disappeared at the same time that Captain Johnson left the port.[139]

Thomas happened to encounter Charles A. Kleiber, a clerk who worked for Doctor N. D. Labadie, a lumber importer and drug merchant in Galveston. The colored boy asked Kleiber for directions to the British consulate. After learning why Thomas wished to contact a consular officer, Kleiber told the boy that, unfortunately, there was no such officer in Galveston. He took the occasion, however, to warn Thomas of the grave danger confronting a free Negro in Galveston. Faced with what was represented to him as an impending peril, Thomas signed a bond binding himself to Kleiber "for a term of 60 years, at the expiration of which" he was to receive "$5, a suit of clothes and three months' provision." The indenture document was drawn up by Judge Henry M. Trueheart and attested by "respectable witnesses." When these legal details had been completed, Kleiber "proceeded to exercise acts of ownership" over Thomas and offered "him for sale."[140]

Eventually when word came to Lynn of Thomas' indenture for sixty years, he began to make inquiries as to the whereabouts of the boy. A few days later, Thomas was brought into Justice I. E. Rump's court, charged with stealing $30 and a silver watch from a man named Barnett, who worked for Dr. Labadie. The result of this action in Justice Rump's court brought a sentence of thirty lashes for Thomas.

As this trial in the justice court made the actual existence of Charles Thomas in Galveston a matter of public record, Lynn asked the mayor

[137] Lynn to Clarendon, July 18, 1857, MS, F.O.
[138] Galveston *News,* June 23, 1857.
[139] Lynn to Clarendon, July 18, 1857, MS, F.O.
[140] Lynn to Clarendon, July 18, 1857, MS, F.O.

for a certified copy of the record relating to flogging of a British young man of color named Charles Thomas. Lynn demanded to know whether or not Thomas was punished as a Britisher or as a slave.[141] The mayor acknowledged the query, but evaded the issue. Lynn repeated his demand to the mayor[142] and, at the same time, called upon Justice Rump for a copy of the court record and demanded to know whether or not Thomas appeared in "court as a free man or a slave."[143]

Failing to obtain a satisfactory reply from Justice Rump,[144] Lynn wrote Governor Elisha M. Pease, informing him of "the outrage" which had been committed against Charles Thomas. The consul insisted that the governor ought to employ his high office in this instance to curb the abuse of power by local officials.[145]

The governor's eventual reply was a long analysis of the "case of Charles Thomas" by the attorney general of the state in which this officer maintained that "the courts of the county are open for redress of wrongs suffered by all classes of persons within their jurisdiction, whatever their conditions of life or of citizenship."[146] The consul's retort to this assertion maintained that the contrary was true, as "the courts of the state do not admit the evidence of persons of color against a white citizen, but only against Negroes, consequently any accusation which a free person of color kidnaped into slavery might prefer against a white man would be rejected by the courts."[147] In reference specifically to the Thomas case, the attorney general observed that "so far as it relates to kidnapping, it seems to have taken place under judicial sanction. It was the penalty affixed by the law for the offense charged. The presumption must be that it was deserved," since there was no testimony in the record "to rebuff" the charge against

[141] Lynn to John Henry Brown (Mayor of Galveston), June 9, 1857, MS, F.O.
[142] Brown to Lynn, June 10, 1857, and Lynn to Brown, June 10, 1857, MSS, F.O.
[143] Lynn to J. E. Rump, June 11, 1857, MS, F.O.
[144] Rump to Lynn, June 13, 1857, MS, F.O.
[145] Lynn to Governor Elisha M. Pease, June 13, 1857, MS, F.O.
[146] Pease to Lynn, June 23, 1857, and Lynn to Pease, July 2, 1857, MSS, F.O.
[147] Lynn to Clarendon, July 18, 1857, MS, F.O.

Thomas. Thus the conclusion must be that the boy was punished as a slave.[148]

A few days previously, however, Lynn had already tested the attorney general's suggestion that justice was to be found in the district court by presenting the case against Kleiber to a grand jury in Galveston. The jury refused "to find a bill of indictment against Kleiber." In these circumstances the case never received a public hearing.[149]

Soon afterward, however, Hamilton Stuart brought the case of Charles Thomas to public notice by printing an article concerned with the "kidnaping of Her Majesty's subjects." The editor wrote that he was "alarmed that a mulatto boy, C. H. Thomas, had been induced to sign indentures for 60 years."[150]

In these circumstances, Kleiber and Doctor Labadie, in order to get their versions of the Thomas case before the public, wrote letters to the Galveston *News*. Kleiber said that he found the boy starving in the streets. "Thomas," said this benefactor, "had got down on his knees and begged that he be allowed" to serve Kleiber "as long as he lived." In order to comply with the boy's plea, Kleiber took him before "respectable witnesses" and had the indentures drawn up. It was at this point, said Kleiber, that the British consul stepped in to meddle in the affair. Dr. Labadie corroborated Kleiber's version, adding that Thomas had insisted that "he would rather be a slave in Galveston than a free Negro in Trinidad."[151] In reply to these assertions, Lynn remarked that "the statement printed in the *News* was not true. No seaman would sell himself into slavery."[152]

In order to bring about what, from Lynn's point of view, was an acceptable conclusion to the Charles Thomas incident, the consul himself engaged in an act of kidnaping. On July 22nd, acting with the aid of Captain Parker, master of the American barque *Godfrey* of Boston, Lynn somehow got Thomas aboard Parker's vessel as she sailed for Boston. On board the same ship was a letter to the British consul

[148] *Ibid.;* also Lynn to Napier, July 18, 1857, MS, F.O.
[149] Lynn to Clarendon, July 18, 1857, MS, F.O.
[150] Galveston *Civilian*, June 16, 1857.
[151] Galveston *News*, June 23, 1857.
[152] Lynn to Clarendon, July 18, 1857, MS, F.O.

at Boston requesting him to give Thomas the aid to which he was entitled as one of Her Majesty's distressed seamen.[153]

A few months after the Charles Thomas incident, the legislature of the state passed an act "to permit free persons of African descent to select their own masters and become slaves."[154] Recognizing the effect which this legislation might have upon future incidents similar to the one involving Charles Thomas, Lynn wrote the state authorities in Austin requesting a copy of the act. After an ensuing correspondence in which polite discourtesies were exchanged, the consul was required to send two dollars in gold to the state treasury before a copy of the act was sent to him.[155] Lynn then sent the copy to the Earl of Malmesbury at the Foreign Office with an interpretation stressing the fact that in Texas "heretofore the forcible enslavement of a free person of color was a penal offense, now it is legal." The new act, wrote Lynn, applied to "all persons of African descent regardless of nationality" who entered the state.[156]

An illustration of the application of the act may be seen in an incident involving a young Portuguese subject named Joseph Vincente Suarez, who was initiated into the institution of slavery at Galveston in January, 1860. Suarez, at that time twenty years old, was a native of Goa, India. However, some months prior to his arrival at Galveston, while working in Calcutta, he had happened to encounter a theatrical troupe "styling themselves 'Negro Minstrels'." Since Suarez was a handsome young Iberian, possessing a pleasing voice, the minstrel company induced him to join them on a tour of American cities. It was in this role of a "musical artist" that Suarez arrived in Galveston. After spending a few days in the city in the pursuit of his vocation as a performing minstrel at the Opera House, Suarez was arrested and taken

[153] Lynn to Consul Edmund Grattan (Boston), July 22, 1857; Lynn to Clarendon, September 24, 1857, MSS, F.O.

[154] Lynn to T. S. Anderson (Secretary of State of Texas, Austin), March 6, 1858, MS, F.O.; Seguin County Commissioners Court Record, Volume A (1858), MS, p. 523.

[155] Bird Holland to Lynn, March 16, 1858, and Lynn to Holland, March 22, 1858, MSS, F.O.

[156] Lynn to Malmesbury, April 6, 1858, MS, F.O.

before a magistrate's court. The deputy sheriff of Galveston County asserted that the singer "had Negro blood and was residing in the city in violation of the laws of the state." The magistrate ordered the confinement of Suarez and directed that the young man be examined by a Galveston physician. The doctor advised the magistrate that "Suarez was tinctured with over an eighth portion of Negro blood." As a result of the doctor's report and the decision of the magistrate, the "hire" of Suarez was scheduled to be "auctioned off on the 30th of January, 1860 at the Court House" for a period of six months. The proceeds of the "hire," after deducting the cost of the proceedings and the expense of board and lodging for Suarez, were to be paid over to the singer to enable him to leave the state. It was acknowledged that the "minstrel artist's" earnings in his new circumstances would most likely not attain the sum required to cover "the cost of the proceedings and expenses" for a considerable number of months.[157]

At the time of the discovery of the singer's "tincture" there was no consular officer in Galveston authorized to look after the interest of Portuguese nationals. The nearest consular officer with such authority was in New Orleans. Arthur Lynn, however, entertaining a continuing interest in similar incidents, was an attentive spectator at the proceedings which "enslaved Suarez." Although Arthur Lynn had no authority whatever to interfere, he did presume to write to British Consul William Mure in New Orleans about the fate which was overtaking Suarez with the thought that, perhaps, Mure might be able to interest the Portuguese consul in New Orleans. The proceedings involving the singer, wrote Lynn, were held "without any trial by jury and without allowing Suarez to have counsel for his defense or to offer testimony to prove the truth of his statements, though such could easily have been obtained." Lynn suggested that if the Portuguese consul in New Orleans should think it proper to submit a protest "for this outrage" for Lynn said he could "view it in no other light"—and if the Portuguese government would pay "the costs and expenses" assessed by the Galveston authorities, the young singer might be liberated and sent to New Orleans. Or if an appeal action seemed to be desirable, Lynn

[157] Lynn to William Mure (British Consul, New Orleans), January 25, 1860, MS, F.O.

wrote, this procedure could be followed because the Supreme Court was then in session at Galveston. If Suarez was to be liberated, said Lynn, some action had to be taken before the singer was put up for auction on January 30th. Unfortunately for the minstrel singer, the Portuguese authorities did not wish to spend money to liberate traveling Portuguese artists who found themselves in difficulty.[158]

In August, 1860, an incident occurred involving the incarceration of a free British Negro taken from on board a British vessel lying in Galveston harbor by an arm of the federal government, engaged, it was asserted, in the act of enforcing a law of the state of Texas which made it a crime for any free Negro to enter the state.

Lieutenant Tennison, second in command of the United States revenue cutter in Galveston harbor, upon learning that the British vessel *Alma* had a colored cook on her crew, boarded the vessel, arrested the Negro and delivered him up to the county authorities. The lieutenant explained that he boarded the British vessel because "the *Alma* had a colored cook on the crew list contrary to the municipal laws of the state."[159]

Arthur Lynn immediately protested to Hamilton Stuart, the customs collector at the port. As soon as Stuart had ascertained the facts in the case, he had the Negro cook returned to the *Alma*. Stuart explained to Lynn that "this action of a United States officer in a purely state matter would not have taken place but for the great excitement" which at that time existed, "not only throughout the state, but in the city, owing to attempts recently made to incite the slaves to incendiary acts and insurrection." Stuart readily admitted that the lieutenant had exercised authority in a matter over which, as a federal officer, he had no jurisdiction.[160]

Lynn did not fail to comprehend the unspoken implication of Stuart's apology and explanation. He arranged for the immediate departure of the *Alma* in order to preclude a second boarding, this time by state authorities.[161]

[158] *Ibid.*
[159] Lynn to Stuart, August 17, 1860, MS, F.O.
[160] Stuart to Lynn, August 18, 1860, MS, F.O.
[161] Lynn to Lyons, August 30, 1860, MS, F.O.

239

The high price of slaves during the eighteen-fifties not only caused an increase in the number of free Negroes kidnaped, but it also caused an increase in another illegal means sometimes employed by Texans to acquire Negroes—the simple device of stealing a slave from his rightful owner and carrying the stolen property to another part of the state.[162] Some intimidation was needed in these circumstances to maintain control over the stolen property, since, unlike the enslaving of free Negroes, the theft of slaves did not have even tacit approval of the authorities. One such enterprise was carried on in the Galveston area by a Houstonian named Kuykendall and his associates, Wiley Bruton, a man named Dixon, and Kuykendall's Negro slave, Napoleon, an American African possessing great physical stature, a dominating personality, and an unusual facility in the art of persuading "likely" fellow Negroes that they ought to desert their masters and "escape to freedom" with him. Usually the persuaded ones, having been induced to commit the crime of "running away" and also the crime of stealing one of their master's horses, were afraid to offer an objection to their fate when the true state of the new situation became clear to them. Napoleon, Kuykendall, and their associates made the results of any attempted exposure graphically clear to those Negroes who had taken part in "a conspiracy with Napoleon."

The three white men, as well as the Negro Napoleon, were frequent visitors in Galveston and Houston during the two years in which they were engaged in this lucrative trade in Negroes. Legitimate dealers were unaware of the true nature of Kuykendall's operations. Finally in August, 1857, the governmental authorities discovered the truth and arrested the four men.[163] The traders, after having been made fast in "irons" and lodged in the Harris County Jail, became known as the "Kuykendall gang." On two occasions the foursome managed to escape from their confinement with the aid of some undisclosed outside assistance—in one instance by means of an iron file and in the other instance by the skilled use of "chisels and a bottle of nitric acid." On both

[162] *State of Texas* v. *Theophilus Freeman,* January 6, 1857 and *State of Texas* v. *Thomas B. Stubbs,* January 24, 1857, District Court of Galveston.

[163] Galveston *Civilian,* August 18, 1857; Houston *Telegraph,* August 17, 1857.

occasions, the four were recaptured. There was no third escape because the jailer then fastened his charges most securely; "they are now welded hands and feet in one inch irons," a prison official assured any who feared that the prisoners might again escape.[164]

Although the high price of slaves was a financial burden to the cotton planters, as well as a temptation that occasionally led some Texans to kidnap or steal Negroes, it was a blessing nevertheless to the slave class as a whole in Texas because it raised the standard of care which their masters bestowed upon them in return for their labor. A $1500 slave not only deserved good care since he was a valuable piece of property but, perhaps more important to the slave himself, his greater value gave him a higher standing in the total society, both slave and free. Most masters during the decade of the fifties in Galveston and Houston exercised a solicitous concern for the welfare of their slaves. The increased monetary value of their charges seemed to arouse an increased interest in the human qualities of their Negroes until, in many cases, the status of the Negroes appeared to be more like that of "charges" than of slaves.[165]

The African Slave Trade of the Texas Gulf Coast

THE DEMAND FOR NEGRO SLAVES in Texas resulted in a flourishing trade bringing in domestic slaves from the Old South to help work the new cotton lands; also, potential Texas plantation operators often brought Negroes with them. In any case, many Negroes from the Old South were arriving in Texas during the fifties. According to the 1850 census there were 58,161 Negroes in Texas at that time; by 1860 their number had risen to 182,566 or an increase of 124,405. Some of this increase, several hundreds and perhaps a few thousands, was the result of the illicit African slave trade.[166]

The revival of the clandestine African slave trade to Texas during

---

[164] Houston *Telegraph*, November 13, 1857.

[165] Ballinger Diary, for 1863–1864, MS.

[166] J. D. B. DeBow, *Statistical View of the United States . . . Being A Compendium of the Seventh Census . . .* , p. 83. Joseph C. G. Kennedy, *The Population of the United States in 1860: Compiled from the Original Returns of the Eighth Census, Under the Direction of the Secretary of the Interior*, p. 483.

the 1850's resulted from the urgent demand for the labor to exploit the immense areas of rich bottom lands lying uncultivated in Texas. To the men who controlled these "cotton mines," or who hoped to do so, the federal and state laws forbidding the importation of labor to work them could appear only as barriers to progress. These men employed a number of devices to circumvent the legal barriers, attempting not only to engage in a lucrative trade but also to pry a small opening in the legal restrictions with the hope that, sooner or later, the "prejudice" against their "legitimate right" to import labor could be removed by political and legal means.

While many ordinary Texans tolerated the clandestine slave trade because they believed that the political and economic development of the state depended upon an ample labor supply, the Texans actually engaged in the trade were in the enterprise primarily for its immediate profit. The fact that in the fifties a prime slave could be sold for as much as $1500 in Texas made the trade particularly attractive. The importers rested their merchandising adventures upon sound trading principles, since it was possible, even under adverse conditions, to deliver African labor to the coast line of Texas for about one dollar a pound, even absorbing the "shrinkage" that was an accepted cost of operation in this trade. Thus, the profit on a "likely boy" of say 150 pounds might be as high as $1350.

Although the number of African slaves imported into Texas during the days of the Republic and during the decades after 1845 was not large if measured against the total slave population of the state, nevertheless, when the price of domestic slaves rose as a result of the rising price of cotton, the illegal importation of slave labor sometimes amounted to several hundred slaves each year. At first traders used Texas merely as a way station, but by 1850 the state had become a major market for African slaves.

As early as 1817 smugglers were using Galveston Island as a base for running "black diamonds" into the United States. Jean Lafitte, the Bowie brothers (Resin, James and John), J. W. Fannin, Monroe Edwards, and Sterling McNeil were all, at various times during the first half of the century, engaged in running Africans into the United States via Texas. This trade was somewhat encumbered, in 1836, when the majority of Texans determined to outlaw the traffic by a provision of the Constitution of the new Republic,[167] but despite the positive legal restrictions Texas continued to be a base from which African Negroes were imported into the United States. "It cannot be disbelieved," said Sam Houston to a special session of the Texas Congress in 1837, "that thousands of Africans have lately been imported to the Island of Cuba, with the design to transport a large portion of them into this Republic,"[168] and, it may be added, into the states of the American Union.

The United States consul in Havana was also aware of the slave traffic moving into the waters around Galveston. He stated that complete cargoes of slaves "fresh from Africa were being shipped daily" to Texas in American vessels. In his view, many of these would be sold eventually in the United States.[169] According to one estimate, 15,000 Africans were imported into Texas during 1838. Many of these were "recovered" as fugitive slaves and were returned to the Southern states from which it was implied that they had escaped.[170]

In 1847 Lord Aberdeen, acting in accord with the general slave-trade policy of the British Foreign Office, directed William Kennedy, then the British consul in Galveston, to keep a close watch upon the slave trade moving from Havana into Texas. Kennedy reported that Monroe Edwards and his partner, Christopher Dart, openly debarked, from the American schooner *Shenandoah*, 180 "fresh African Negroes" on the coast of Texas at an inlet near the Brazos River. The schooner *Harriet,* in control of the same men, also had landed forty Negroes on the coast. Dart and Edwards continued this trade until 1838, when they had a disagreement over a debt of $35,000 owed to Messrs. Knight and Co. of Havana. The partnership was dissolved and Edwards was sentenced to prison for forgery by a New York court.[171]

[167] Eugene C. Barker, "The African Slave Trade in Texas," *Texas Historical Association Quarterly,* VI (1902), 145–158. Professor Barker's analysis deals primarily with the slave trade in Texas during the years 1817–1836.

[168] *Ibid.,* p. 155.

[169] Nicholas P. Trist to John Forsyth: U.S. *House Docs.,* 26th Cong., 2nd Sess., V, No. 115.

[170] DuBois, *Slave-Trade,* p. 165.

[171] Kennedy to Aberdeen, September 5, 1843, MS, F.O.

A Spanish trading partnership, Moro and Coigly, also operated a trade in African slaves with planters' agents whom they contacted at various places along the coast. The following locations and transactions were identified: 40 slaves at Caney Creek, 200 slaves at the mouth of the Sabine, 41 slaves near the Brazos, and additional smaller groups at other various points making a total of 540 Negroes in all.[172]

Another firm, this one composed of three British nationals, Charles Frankland, John Barnes and Richard P. Jones, operating as "Frankland and Company," also carried African slaves into the Galveston area during the 1840's. This firm, which owned the slave ships *Ellen Frankland, Caroline, Sarah Barnes,* and *Antoinette,* moved its Negroes through the Customs House at Galveston on the basis of a "Notarial Contract with Coloured Labourers." Consul Kennedy complained that it was "indeed mortifying to see the purchase and transport of slaves openly carried on by persons styling themselves British merchants and under British protection."[173] This "British Company" had maintained a plantation on the Brazos since 1842 which it used as a base for its slave trade. Although the men operating the plantation maintained that the Negroes brought in were "indentured apprentices" and not slaves, "the members of the firm of Frankland and Company were looked upon as slavers and nothing else." Yet despite the fact that these men did not have public opinion on their side, and also despite the fact that Texas law forbade the importation of even free Negroes into the area, no action was taken against these traders.[174]

Consul Kennedy's effort to prevent Englishmen from using vessels under British registry to engage in this illegal trade was greatly hindered by the fact that Captain Charles Elliot, a British special agent then representing Her Majesty's interests in the Republic of Texas, did not want Kennedy to report slave-trade incidents to the Foreign Office since doing so might upset the captain's pending negotiations concerning other matters. Kennedy, however, told Elliot that since he was under instruction from Lord Aberdeen to report directly on the slave trade, he would continue to do so unless the captain was prepared to give him

[172] *Ibid.*
[173] Kennedy to Aberdeen, July 6, 1843, MS, F.O.
[174] Kennedy to Aberdeen, July 10, 1843, MS, F.O.

written orders not to report. This, of course, Elliot was not prepared to do. Kennedy then arranged to take action against Frankland and Company slave ships which were lying in the Galveston harbor under British registry. The members of the trading firm promptly declared their intention to become Texas citizens and transferred their vessels to Texas registry, thus placing themselves and their vessels beyond British control. As the closing thrust, Kennedy took sworn depositions from J. M. Allen, then mayor of Galveston, and William Bollaert, one-time passenger aboard the *Caroline,* stating that the vessels of this firm had often carried slaves into Galveston. These documents the consul forwarded to the Foreign Office.[175]

During the late forties and early fifties, enterprising men continued to exploit the trade in "black ivory" whenever the demand had raised the price of this commodity high enough to justify the risk. One such adventurous trader, Captain Richard Drake, asserted that between 1847 and 1853, a joint stock company in which he was an active member, operated a branch slave farm in Texas at which was maintained a constant supply of "about 1600 slaves in good condition." At this trading station the firm's agents were kept busy "receiving and shipping constantly." These Negroes, who had been previously "seasoned and instructed" at training farms probably located on some of the coastal islands were brought into Texas in small sailing boats. Since no "squad contained more than a half dozen" it was easy to move them into the interior "without discovery and generally without suspicion." The blacks, who had already been taught to "gabble broken" English, were accustomed to discipline and were well-fed and well-treated.[176]

[175] Kennedy to Aberdeen, July 6, July 10, and July 17, 1843, MSS, F.O. See also copies of James H. Cocke (Collector of Customs at Galveston) to Kennedy, June 27, 1843; Kennedy to Messrs. Frankland, Jones and Company, June 26, 1843; Cocke to Kennedy, June 26, 1843 and reply, also June 26, 1843. All the above are in the Foreign Office correspondence.

[176] [Captain] Richard Drake, *Revelations of a Slave Smuggler: Being the Autobiography of Capt. Richard Drake, an African Trader for Fifty Years, from 1807–1857,* reprinted in George Francis Dow, *Slave Ships and Slaving* (Salem, 1927), p. 253; DuBois, *Slave-Trade,* p. 111, refers to Drake's work as highly colored and thus untrustworthy, but perhaps correct as to essential facts.

At the approach of the mid-century, the British Foreign Office came under the direction of Lord Palmerston, a persistent foe of the African slave trade even though leading commercial interests in Britain at that time were advocating a relaxed policy. Noting reports that the "African traffic" appeared to be thriving on the coast of Texas, Palmerston instructed Kennedy to maintain a careful scrutiny over all vessels of British registry moving in and out of Galveston to insure that British ships were not, through the consul's negligence, either bringing Africans into Galveston or using the port facilities to equip and supply for the slave trade.[177]

A few years later during the early fifties, Galveston was reported to be a port that not only equipped slave ships, but also offered no actual resistance to the importation of Africans. Special dispatches from the Foreign Office were sent to Arthur T. Lynn, who had replaced Kennedy as consul, to instruct the officials at the Galveston Customs House not to permit ships entering under British registry to take on board equipment that could easily be used to convert a ship into a slaver. The customs officer was directed to exercise careful vigilance over cattle boats since this type of vessel could easily be converted into a slaver. The Foreign Office was concerned over the fact that certain vessels of British registry under nominal if not actual Spanish and Barzilian ownership were believed to be smuggling Africans into Texas near Galveston. It was to be understood that such vessels were not to be accorded the port courtesies customarily granted vessels entering under British registry.[178]

The suspicion entertained by the British Foreign Office during the mid-fifties that an active slave traffic was then developing on the Texas coast was in accord with the facts. A trustworthy observer living in the area pointed out that the circumstances existing on the Texas coast presented advantages to the trade not available anywhere else in the South. It was logical to assume that these opportunities would be exploited. No slave trader would engage in the folly of importing "fresh African Negroes" directly into a port as large as New Orleans since this would arouse not only the ire of the federal government but

[177] Palmerston to Kennedy, March 19, 1847, MS, F.O.
[178] Crampton to Lynn, February 17, 1854, MS, F.O.

also the vengeance of the "whole sect of philanthropists and Negro-philists" as well. The method used was to import Negroes into the "quiet places," evading the law, and at the same time, creating a popular demand for more "cheap Negroes." There were a multitude of such "quiet places" on the Texas Gulf Coast, and in the interior close by were millions of acres needing only the "cheap Negroes" for their development. The end result was a virtual reopening of the slave trade by gradual stages.

The new phase of the trade, which began when the price of the slaves rose to such heights, had been opened when bold men had begun to import "Negroes slowly at first, but surely" into a "deep and abrupt pocket or indentation in the coast of Texas, about thirty miles from Brazos Santiago"—a spot which afforded remarkable seclusion for such operations. "Into this pocket a slaver could run at any hour of the night, because there was no hindrance at the entrance, and here she could discharge her cargo of movables upon the projecting bluff, and again proceed to sea inside of three hours." The "live stock" thus landed could be marched a short distance across the main island, "over a porous soil which refuses to retain recent footprints." The Texas islands, covered as they were with thick bushes and grass, afforded "an inscrutable hiding place for the 'black diamonds'." Such landings were actually frequent occurrences on the Gulf Coast. It was notorious, said this observer, that the slave trade had existed on the Texas coast for years. It was also notorious that the trade was carried on chiefly by Northern citizens; the vessels engaged in the traffic were fitted out in New York, Boston, and Portland. Between 1840 and 1859 over fifty slavers had been captured and brought into the port of New York, nearly all of which were fitted out with Northern capital. Yet the number of vessels captured were but a small number of those fitted out in Northern ports. "The slave fleet which leaves New York, Boston and other sea ports in a single year consists of about forty vessels of various sizes, ranging from one hundred to five hundred tons, capable of carrying from four to six hundred slaves each." The whole capital invested was not more than four million dollars upon which "a profit of something like eleven million dollars is realized annually." The records of the United States courts in New York City "stand as incontrovertible evidence of the existence of a sizeable slave trade moving into the Gulf Coast," but since no governmental authority was interested in curtailing this traffic, said this observer, "the landing of slaves continued without the danger of detection."[179]

The United States consul at San Juan, Puerto Rico, expressed the belief that the rising Gulf Coast slave trade could not be checked "while such great percentages are made in the business. The outlay of $35,000 often brings in $500,000." The consul stated that at the Congo River the prices asked for "slaves were $34 for prime men, $17 for women, and $10 for boys." On this basis, he said, a Negro worth $1000 to $1200 in the United States could be put ashore near the United States for a cost of not more than $106.[180] A British naval officer stated that the slave trade was flourishing in Havana due to the high price paid for Negroes in Texas; one Havana company in this trade operated a fleet of fifteen slavers and employed an agent in New York, A. T. Smolly, to purchase and equip its vessels. Another group

[179] R. B. Kingsbury Papers, TS; New York *Herald,* August 5, 1860; Galveston *Civilian,* March 23, 1858. Kingsbury, a personal friend of Gordon Bennett, publisher of the New York *Herald,* was at various times an editor of small newspapers on the Texas Gulf Coast, a United States postmaster handling the mails at seaport towns, and sometimes a correspondent for the *Herald.* Kingsbury and Bennett exchanged an interesting correspondence during this critical decade. Kingsbury's observations were corrobrated in British correspondence on the slave trade which reflected a persistent concern over the number of slave ships equipped in Eastern seaports. "In the past 18 months 85 vessels" equipped as slavers "sailed out of United States Eastern ports," Russell to Lyons, September 10, 1860, printed in U.S. *House Exec. Docs.,* 36th Cong., 2nd Session, Vol. IV, No. 7, pp. 455–456. In the above correspondence Russell estimated that from 12,000 to 15,000 Africans were landed in Cuba annually. For other commentary upon the size of the slave trade at that time, see the Galveston *Civilian,* June 9, July 14, July 21, October 6, 1857 and also January 5, June 15, August 3, and October 26, 1858. The editor of the *Civilian* estimated that during the first six months of 1857 forty slaving expeditions had been fitted out in Cuba, Galveston *Civilian,* August 4, 1857. The editor of the Galveston *News* observed at about the same time that "Cuba is becoming of very considerable importance" as a transfer point in the slave trade, Galveston *News,* February 3, 1857.

[180] Consul C. De Ronceray to Lewis Cass, August 22, 1860, U.S. *House Exec. Docs.,* 36th Cong., 2nd Sess., Vol. IV, No. 7, p. 450.

of financiers had purchased the 600 horse-power steamer *Garcaloua* and were preparing to put the steamer into the trade. The owners planned to "dress her men in white, fly an American flag and pass as an American Man of War." The commander chosen for this vessel was "a Lt. Hardy" who formerly had commanded the United States ship *Preble*. According to the Britisher, the lieutenant had been "cashiered out" of the navy during the Mexican War for "having called out one of the American generals." He carried a commission signed by President Polk that was either false or void, yet "he walks about Havana wearing an American uniform and apparently has plenty of money."[181]

Hamilton Stuart, as customs collector in Galveston during the fifties, was charged by law with the duty of enforcing federal regulations against the foreign slave trade. Yet in his capacity as an editor he had often insisted that the restrictions against the importation of African labor curtailed the economic growth of the state. Thus Stuart was caught in a direct conflict of interest. In addition to this dilemma he was trapped as well by the fact that in urging the repeal of the slave-trade restrictions and in lending his support to the several filibuster movements he had become associated with daring groups of men on the Gulf Coast who, by 1857, were clearly suggesting that unless they were permitted to import the labor they needed to develop the Southwest they would be forced to carry the state out of the Union. While Stuart sometimes had the high temper of a sensitive man, he was actually a very gentle person who despised violence. Only with difficulty could he find a common ground with the filibusters, the advocates for the reopening of the slave trade and the potential secessionists; yet in each instance, because he wished to advance the political and economic position of Texas he continued to be associated with these daring groups. Only when they approached what seemed to him to be dangerous violence—then he eventually drew back. Some of his friends suggested that perhaps he was afraid to clash directly with those

[181] Commander John Vesey of H. M. Steamer *Styx,* to the Secretary of the Admiralty, May 8, 1858, U.S. *House Exec. Docs.,* 36th Cong., 2nd Sess., Vol. IV, No. 7, pp. 103–104. Vesey advised that when the *Garcaloua* left Havana "I shall endeavor to follow her." Apparently she was too fast for him.

whom he had often aided but who were now failing to respect his position as the customs collector.[182] In any case it is clear that Stuart, a man of conscience and honor, was troubled by the conflict which engulfed him. Occasionally he expressed his frustration in the *Civilian* by reprinting in bold type the clause of the Texas Constitution outlawing the importation of African slaves into Texas, followed by the remark that "no more comment ought to be required." On another occasion, after noting that the British appeared to be capturing many Yankee slave traders en route from Africa, Stuart remarked that the revival of the slave trade was the work of the "Yankees of the North and East."[183]

A few venturesome Southern capitalists, however, belatedly moved into this profitable trade. In 1857 a New Orleans newspaper editor noted that "within the last sixty days quite a brisk trade has been going on in this port, in the purchase and fitting out of small, fast sailing vessels for the 'blackbird' trade on the coast of Africa." The trade had been so active that more vessels would have been fitted out for the traffic if a larger number of suitable craft had been available. No attempt was made to conceal the activity. "The usual cargoes for the trade" were put on board without interference and "the manifests at the Customs House" were "made as if the implements and outfit were of the most legitimate and regular character."[184]

A short time before the slave-trade activity in New Orleans, a Captain Whelden sailed the American schooner *Boquet,* "a fine fast ship of 100 tons," into Galveston with the single cargo of one thousand dollars worth of cigars; "she had already dropped a cargo of slaves from Cuba on the Texas coast. The master had some trouble at customs," but the vessel soon cleared again for Cuba.[185] A few months later the schooners *Merchant* and *Will-O-Wisp,* and the barques

[182] Lynn to Russell, August 31, 1860, MS, F.O.; also see an address delivered by Lorenzo Sherwood (of Galveston) at Champlain, New York, October, 1862, printed in pamphlet by Henry O'Rielly (New York, 1862); and see the Ballinger Diary, January 28, 1863, MS.

[183] Galveston *Civilian,* June 9, 1857 and August 3, 1858.

[184] Galveston *News,* May 5, 1857, quoting the New Orleans *True Delta* of May 3, 1857.

[185] Lynn to J. T. Crawford, February 24, 1857, MS, F.O.

William Lewis and *Jupiter,* four vessels that had frequently been in Galveston waters, were seized on the high seas as slavers.[186]

A combination of slave traders which included two brothers, J. A. Machado of New York City and Bernardo José Machado of Portugal, and two lesser traders, Thomas Watson and Mrs. Thomas Watson, was engaged in running slaves into Texas. The Machados provided the capital; the Watsons were among the many active seafaring people who manned the ships for the Machados.

The Machado Company was represented in New York by the respected law firm of Benedict, Burr and Benedict. These advocates protected the interests of the combination in the many conflicts their slaving fleet had with the British government. The Boston shipping firm of Ellis and Cobb also maintained business arrangements with these traders.[187]

During 1858, Captain Thomas Watson traded in slaves as master of the schooner *Lydia Gibbs* and Mrs. Watson sailed the fast, 348-ton schooner *Thomas Watson.*[188] On October 16, 1858, Mrs. Watson

[186] Galveston *Civilian,* June 9, July 14, and July 21, 1857; Galveston *News,* August 29, 1857.

[187] Nicholas Pike (United States consul at Oporto) to Cass, March 12, 1857; G. M. Dallas to Cass, May 11, 1858; Malmesbury to Dallas, May 6, 1858; British Consul Robert Bunch (Charleston) to Malmesbury, June 1, 1858; Thomas Savage (United States consul at Havana) to John Appleton (Assistant Secretary of State), June 18, July 13, 1858; J. A. Machado to Cass, June 23, 1858; Cass to Dallas, July 20, 1858; Dallas to Cass, October 12, 1858 (this correspondence printed in U.S. *House Exec. Docs.,* 36th Cong. 2nd Sess., Vol. 4, No. 7). Slave ships of the Machado combine, which appeared at various times in the Galveston coastal waters, were the *Locomatara, Thomas Watson, Lydia Gibbs, Nancy, Caroline, Lyra* and *Mary Varney.* Other persons who appear to have been members of the Machado firm were Antonio Reiz Vieria, Joao da Cunha Ferreira, R. C. Welling, Bradford Gibbs, Captain Dickey, Captain Williams, Don Ramon de Guerediaga. William Percher Miles (Member of House of Representatives from South Carolina) represented Thomas Watson's and Mrs. Watson's interest in negotiations at the State Department regarding Consul Lynn's "mistreatment" of the *Thomas Watson* in Galveston harbor.

[188] Malmesbury to Cass, March 8, and April 30, 1859. Captain Watson died of yellow fever at Whydak, Africa, on July 15, 1858. The *Lydia Gibbs* had been captured with the slaves on board by a British naval ship. The above

entered Galveston harbor with a deckload of eighty-nine camels at a declared value of $9,561.[189] This intrepid lady who, in the manner of Jefferson Davis in 1856, appeared to be attempting to introduce an ancient form of transportation to the coastal plains of Texas, had the misfortune of entering the port during a period when the city was infested by an epidemic of fever.[190] In order to protect the health of Her Majesty's Empire, Consul Lynn had determined to refuse to grant clean bills of health to vessels wishing to leave Galveston for British ports. The consul was burdened not only with an unusually firm habit of official compliance with Her Majesty's regulations, but also with a strong moral distaste for anyone who might be engaged in the African slave trade. The consul did not entertain the admiration expressed by Galveston newspapers for the enterprise shown by the venturesome Mrs. Watson in trying to introduce the "ships of the desert" to the coastal plains of Texas, for the travel-wise nose of Consul Lynn suspected correctly that some cargo other than "foul smelling camels" had been in the holds of the *Thomas Watson* while she had sailed leisurely along the Gulf Coast before putting into Galveston. Her Majesty's agent determined to impede Mrs. Watson's slave-trading enterprise in a skein of British red tape.[191]

The lady applied in the usual manner at the consul's office for clearance papers to sail to the British port of Liverpool. Knowing that Mrs. Watson's declared intention to sail for Liverpool was but a ruse to cover her real destination—the slave-trading port of Havana—Lynn refused to give the *Thomas Watson* a clean bill of health. Although the failure to secure this document would have caused the vessel no

---

correspondence printed in U.S. *House Exec. Docs.,* 36th Cong., 2nd Sess., Vol. IV, No. 7, pp. 333–336.

[189] Annual Report of British Consulate in Galveston, 1858, MS, p. 58, F.O. The Galveston *Civilian* of October 19, 1858, reported that the ship *Thomas Watson* and the barque *Lucerne* had arrived from the Canary Islands with "89 camels consigned to Isaac G. Williams and Co. They are private property, having been imported on the account of Mrs. Watson of Washington City."

[190] Lynn to Malmesbury, December 4, 1858; Lynn to Hammond, April 20, 1859, MSS, F.O.

[191] Lynn to Lyons (British Minister, Washington), March 23, 1859; Howard to Clarendon, April 7, 1857, MSS, F.O.

inconvenience at the northern city of Liverpool, the lack of a clean bill of health denied the vessel the privilege of a port-of-call at the tropical harbor of Havana, where the authorities would not have welcomed a vessel entering from the fever-laden city of Galveston without a health clearance.[192]

Upon being thwarted, Mrs. Watson demanded a clean bill, threatening to file a protest with the United States Department of State if it were not forthcoming. Lynn's policy during the epidemic was to refuse to grant a clean bill to any vessel scheduled to sail to a British port if the vessel had entered Galveston harbor prior to November 14th, the date of the last fever death in the city. He suggested to the lady that, since the lack of the document would cause her no difficulty in Liverpool, it was an open question as to what the real purpose of the *Thomas Watson's* next voyage might be.[193]

Thus the good lady and the consul were locked in a conflict from which neither would back down. Mrs. Watson sent a complaint against Lynn to the American Secretary of State. She also sent an urgent message to J. A. Machado of New York City, the nominal agent, but actually the owner of the vessel, urging him to come to Galveston at once.[194]

As soon as practicable, Lynn insisted upon making an investigation of the *Thomas Watson* and her consort, the American barque *Lucerne,* also detained at Galveston. The *Lucerne* was a sailing vessel of light draft, capable of crossing the sand bars on the Texas coast. The *Watson* was registered at 348 tons, the *Lucerne* at 199 tons; this cargo capacity was much more than would have been needed to carry 89 camels. An inspection of the two vessels showed that they carried the usual equipment needed for the transportation of slaves and also that the vessels bore the odor of the slaver.[195] Lynn insisted that the United States attorney in Galveston also inspect the vessels. The attorney admitted

[192] Lynn to Hammond, April 20, 1859, MS, F.O.

[193] Mrs. T. J. Watson to Lynn, December 13, 1958 and Lynn to Mrs. Watson, December 13, 1858, MSS, F.O.

[194] Howard to Clarendon, April 7, 1857, Lynn to Hammond, April 20, 1858, MSS, F.O.

[195] Lynn to Malmesbury, December 21, 1858, MS, F.O.

that the deck load of camels had been "merely a cloak for slaves" and that all the equipment necessary for carrying slaves was found on the boat. Nevertheless, since no slaves remained on board, "the cargo had been taken off by coasters,"[196] the federal attorney was without the concrete evidence he needed to take action.[197]

In the meantime the eighty-nine camels had been unloaded on the Island and were wandering about the city streets creating a general nuisance. The city fathers met and passed an ordinance making it a violation of the Municipal Code to allow camels to wander unattended in the city streets.[198] Galveston youths and ne'er-do-wells made a sport of pelting the strange, ungainly animals with stones, thereby frightening the camels into further behavior unbecoming to the peace and quiet of the port city.[199]

Eventually the British Foreign Office had received and digested the various reports concerning the camels imported into Galveston by a ship sailing under British registry. Lord Lyons, British Minister in Washington, had relayed to George Hammond of the Foreign Office the complaint Mrs. Watson had filed with the American Secretary of State and, in due time, the Earl of Malmesbury referred the matter of the ship *Thomas Watson* and the Galveston camels to the Lords of the Committee of the Privy Council for Trade. Her Majesty's Lords "were pleased to express the opinion that Consul was justified in withholding a clean bill of health . . . in regard to the town," but the Lords were "not without apprehension from the tenor" of Lynn's dispatch that his withholding of the clean bill of health from the vessel might have been inspired "unconsciously" by the consul's personal distaste for slave traders.[200] Lynn vigorously denied this suggestion by the "Lords," asserting, in a voluminous correspondence, that all of his

[196] Philip C. Tucker, "History of Galveston, 1543–1869," MS.

[197] Lynn to Malmesbury, December 21, 1858, MS, F.O.

[198] Houston *Telegraph,* December 24, 1858; Ordinance Book, 1857–1865, MS, Office of Galveston City Secretary, p. 34.

[199] Galveston *Civilian,* October 19 and 26, 1858; Houston *Telegraph,* December 24, 1858.

[200] Malmesbury to Lynn, April 18, 1859, MS, F.O.

actions had been guided solely by Her Majesty's trade regulations.[201]

In the meantime Mrs. Watson and J. A. Machado, who had by that time arrived in Galveston from New York, had been making life as unpleasant as possible for Consul Lynn in order to show him their distaste for his meddling in the operation of their mercantile enterprise.[202]

Into this ungracious and bickering situation, "the mariner's fate" thrust the little English schooner *Commerce,* the only ship owned by a compatriot of Consul Lynn named Samuel Parsons, an impecunious trader who operated a small mercantile establishment in Kingston, Jamaica. The *Commerce* had been forced into the port of Galveston because of a leaking bottom. All of the crew members on the vessel, except the master, J. S. Pearce, were "free persons of color." As Texas Law made it a criminal offense for a ship master to introduce free colored persons into the State, the crew members, in compliance with the law, were confined in the county jail.[203] Since the port was at that time suffering from the fever epidemic and because confinement in the close and unhealthy quarters of the jail amounted to a virtual inoculation with the dreaded fever, Consul Lynn made a personal plea before the County Judge of Galveston to permit the crew to be confined under arrest on board the schooner *Commerce* rather than in the "unhealthy gaol of this county." The judge agreed to permit this procedure "as a special favor to Her Majesty."[204]

Unfortunately there were no vacant berths at the wharves in Galveston at the time the *Commerce* arrived. The harbor-master had ordered the schooner to "make fast" to the vessel *Thomas Watson* lashed to a wharf. On the 31st of October, a sudden gale "had sprung up from the North" and, as a result of being thrust against the *Commerce,* the "'copper plates" on the bottom of the *Thomas Watson* were damaged. The fenders of the *Watson* failed to provide the usual protection for the ship "because, by that time, she was riding high, being

[201] Lynn to Hammond, April 20, 1859, MS, F.O.

[202] *Ibid.*

[203] Lynn to Samuel Parsons, February 21, 1859, and Lynn to Lyons, April 27, 1859, MSS, F.O.

[204] *Ibid.*

without her ballast" of either camels or slaves. Because of the circumstances involved, Mrs. Watson did not accept this incident in a gracious manner.[205]

Upon Lynn's suggestion, the master of the *Commerce* had already gone to New Orleans to secure funds with which to repair the leak in his vessel as it was impossible to raise the needed funds by a "bottomry award" due to the precarious condition of the *Commerce*. Being cognizant of both maritime law and the rules concerning the admissibility of testimony by free persons of color in Texas courts, Mrs. Watson, on the 4th of November, "libeled the British schooner Commerce for damages alleged to have been caused by the latter during a severe gale." The claim was filed in the United States District court in Galveston.

Since the only testimony which could have been produced in favor of the *Commerce* was inadmissible as evidence inasmuch as the testimony would have been that given by free persons of color, the case was decided in favor of Mrs. Watson solely on the basis of ex parte evidence. In accordance with the law, the vessel (valued at $1200) was sold to her to settle a $300 claim to which, under other circumstances, she would not have been entitled.[206]

Lynn had secured the legal services of State Senator M. M. Potter to protect the interest of the owner of the *Commerce*, but no legal redress to this miscarriage of justice was available under the law. Lynn had the crew of free Negroes sent under his protection by a British vessel to the care of British Consul Mure in New Orleans, as the free Negroes could not be legally put ashore long enough to permit their being assigned to a crew of an outgoing British vessel.[207]

The feud between the "owner" of the camel-carrying slaver and Consul Lynn attracted public notice when the *Civilian* published a "telegraphic dispatch" from Washington under the headline "The Camels With Their Backs Up." The dispatch noted that 'a complaint

---

[205] Parsons to Lynn, January 28, 1859 and Lynn to Lyons, March 23, 1859, MSS, F.O.

[206] Lynn to Parsons, February 21, 1859; Lynn to Mure, November 6, 1858; Lynn to Lyons, March 23, 1859; Lynn to Hammond, April 20, 1859, MSS, F.O.

[207] Lynn to Parsons, February 21, 1859 and Lynn to Mure, November 6, 1858, MSS, F.O.

had been lodged in the State Department against the British Consul at Galveston" alleging that Lynn's course in regard to the *Thomas Watson* had been actuated "by a feeling of petty malice." The owners of the vessel had preferred a claim of $10,000 against the British government on account of "damages sustained by this dereliction of duty on the part of the Consul."

By way of local comment, Hamilton Stuart, editor of the *Civilian,* referred "once more" to "The Camels":

We think we are safe in assuring our readers that the friendly relations between Her Brittanic Majesty and the Sovereigns of America will not be suddenly ruptured by the complaints of the Camels, as reported in the telegraphic dispatch from Washington. Whether that $10,000 will be paid without some evidence of actual wrong or damage, we are not precisely prepared to say; but we rather think it won't.[208]

Machado and Mrs. Watson were not only burdened with the hostility of Her Majesty's agent in the city, but were encumbered also with the embarrassing necessity of disposing of the now irrelevant camels. Fortunately Lieutenant Governor Lubbock happened to arrive in Galveston at that time. During the decade of the fifties Lubbock and his associates were not only engaged in importing various breeds of cattle but were also engaged in importing "choice breeds of fowls from Asia" as well;[209] as president of the Texas Stock Importing Company he had at his command the experience and the facilities required for the importation and care of live stock. The manner in which Lubbock relieved Mrs. Watson of the encumbering camels may be illustrated by an excerpt from his memoirs:

In the fall of 1858 a couple of ships, presumably British, anchored at Galveston under suspicious circumstances. They were first thought to be slavers watching for an opportunity of secretly landing their human freight. But the ships turned out to be laden only with camels; at least no evidence ap-

[208] Galveston *Civilian,* March 19, 1859.

[209] Francis Richard Lubbock, *Six Decades in Texas: or Memoirs of Francis Richard Lubbock, Governor of Texas in War Time, 1861–1863: A Personal Experience in Business, War and Politics,* edited by C. W. Rains, p. 236. Hereafter cited as Lubbock, *Memoirs.*

peared that they had any African Negroes aboard to sell as slaves. Happening to be in Galveston at the time, I went to see the camels (about forty in number), after they had been landed and penned. Mrs. Watson, an English lady, owner of the herd, was hunting some reliable person to whom she might intrust its care until finally disposed of by sale or otherwise. I was introduced as a proper person to the lady and her agent, Senor Machado. A few preliminaries once settled as to the extent of my obligations for their safety, I contracted with Senor Machado on satisfactory terms to assume the custody and maintenance of the camels when delivered at my ranch. Accordingly, a steamboat was chartered, on which Machado brought the animals to the mouth of Sim's Bayou for delivery . . . Machado, with his outlandish servants, Turks or Arabs or unpronounceable names, conducted the camels to my ranch, a few miles distant. Here, they were easily corraled in the pasture prepared for them.[210]

Two months prior to the actual landing of the animals, Stuart, writing in the *Civilian,* had commented upon "the camel speculation" attracting interest in some quarters. "Commercial arrangements," it was said, were being made with some point in Africa affording the best facilities for purchasing camels. "Who are the 'citizens of Texas' that have gone into this traffic in the ships of the desert?" inquired the editor. He did not venture to identify them, but observed that "a slight doubt sometimes passes over our minds, when we see accounts of the extensive preparations, by private enterprise in Texas, for the importation and rearing of camels."[211]

One of the firms interested in the importation of camels was the Texas Stock Importing Company of Galveston, whose president so obligingly helped Mrs. Watson and Senor Machado solve the problem of their superfluous camels. The secretary was Edward Riordan, a major domestic slave dealer who maintained large stocks of slaves in both Houston and Galveston, Riordan had slave-trading arrangements with Ennis and Company and the firm of Van Alstyne and Taylor, two large domestic slave dealers in Houston. The directors of the Texas Stock Importing Company were Francis Lubbock, Benjamin F. Terry, John H. Herndon, J. D. Waters, George Guinan, John A. Wharton,

---

[210] *Ibid.,* pp. 238–239.
[211] Galveston *Civilian,* August 31, 1858.

and Stephen S. Perry.[212] All of these men gave aid to the Nicaraguan filibusters and advocated measures which would lead to a reopening of the African slave trade.

As the year 1859 opened, Hamilton Stuart recognized that, due to the natural demand for cheaper slaves induced by the persistent agitation which he had helped to promote, an actual, if not a legal, revival of the trade was now almost an accomplished fact. Stuart was faced with the political consequences riding in the wake of the slave trade. On the strength of it the radical wing of the Democratic party in Texas was threatening to take the state out of the Union if the North refused to accept the new situation arising out of the gradual reopening of the slave trade. It was at this time that Stuart, after discussions with such moderates as Ferdinand Flake, Lorenzo Sherwood, Judge Gray, Senator M. M. Potter, James Love, William Pitt Ballinger, and Oscar Farish, decided to change his position on the slave-trade issue and to try to quiet the movement he had helped to launch.

It was a particularly trying time for Stuart. As Customs Collector, he had been badgered by the somewhat self-righteous Arthur Lynn over the problem of Mrs. Watson and her cargo of camels, as well as over several irritating incidents in which Lynn had accused Stuart of failing to lend proper protection to English sailors of color who were occasionally kidnapped off British vessels lying in the harbor and sold as slaves.[213] In a public reply to Lynn and to British criticism, Stuart printed an article on the slave trade in which he pointed out that, although the African traffic was making some Britishers rich, the English were continually complaining that their seamen were enduring great suffering while serving on the unhealthy African "slave watch." This righteous complaining, declared Stuart, was gross hypocrisy, for the facts indicated that the young British naval men "sought after" African duty. Individual British officers divided the profits made in the

[212] See papers concerning stockholders' meeting of the Texas Stock Importing Company, held at Galveston April 5, 1860, in The Ballinger Papers, MS (folder covering year 1860). Also see Houston *Telegraph*, December 7, 1858 and Lubbock, *Memoirs*, p. 139.

[213] Lynn to Mure, January 25, 1860, MS, F.O.; Galveston *Civilian*, June 23, 1857.

traffic with those who were in the trade. The going price paid to naval officers to allow an accosted ship to continue its voyage, said Stuart, was $25 per slave. There were indications, he implied, of collusion between British naval officers and the Gulf Coast slavers.[214]

During the late fifties several hundred Africans were imported into Southern states.[215] Stephen A. Douglas said at the time that more Africans had been imported into the United States during the year 1859 "than had ever been imported during any one year before, even when the trade was legal."[216] Some proponents of the trade felt that perhaps such openness was not altogether wise. That same year, an advertisement was printed in an Eastern Gulf Coast weekly newspaper stating that William S. Price and seventeen others would pay "three hundred dollars per head for one thousand native Africans, between the ages of 14 and 20 years (of sexes equal) likely, sound, and healthy, to be delivered within twelve months from this date, at some point accessible by land, between Pensacola, Florida and Galveston, Texas." The contractors wanted to be given thirty days' notice in advance of delivery.[217] The Richmond, Texas, *Reporter,* in the spring of the same year, carried an advertisement stating that 400 likely Africans recently landed on the Texas coast were offered for sale on reasonable terms. The agents identified themselves only by initials.[218] This trade was carried on with a surprising lack of subterfuge. E. H. Cushing, the editor of the Houston *Telegraph,* objected to the ill-advised publicity sometimes printed concerning the importation of labor. In one case in particular he criticized the Galveston *News* for implying that the brig *West* was in with a load of slaves.[219]

There were some Texans who advocated even more drastic measures to secure the much needed labor force than the importation of Africans. Dr. Francis Moore,[220] writing in the *Telegraph* in 1859, pointed

214 Galveston *Civilian,* February 29, 1859.

215 U.S. *House Exec. Docs.,* 36th Cong., 2nd Sess., Vol. IV, No. 7, p. 614.

216 DuBois, *Slave-Trade,* p. 181.

217 Enterprise, Mississippi, *Weekly News,* April 14, 1859.

218 Quoted in Allan Nevins, *The Emergence of Lincoln,* II, 34.

219 Houston *Telegraph,* March 11, 1859.

220 Dr. Francis Moore, Jr., at one time served as surgeon in the Texas army. In 1837, he founded the Houston *Telegraph;* he served as state senator from

out that a source of labor existed nearer at hand than Africa. "There are 30,000 free Negroes in Maryland," he wrote, "why can't they be seized, they are closer than Africa and are acclimated." Dr. Moore pointed out that a planter residing near Huntsville had purchased "five wild Africans" for $2000. Four of them had died a few weeks after they had reached the plantation. "The survivor was so wild that he would chase lizards and bugs when he saw them and was so unmanageable that he was little better than an idiot." This "cheap" Negro had actually cost $2000. Thus it was plain, Moore reasoned, the the best source for Texas cotton labor was not to be found in Africa, but rather in the free Negroes of such places as Maryland if some means could be found to "seize" them.[221]

The importation of Africans into the Galveston and Texas Gulf Coast area continued during the year 1860. During June African Negroes were landed on the coast off Galveston.[222] In August United States authorities at Galveston acknowledged that Negroes had been landed on the Texas coast but the customs officials took no action because they were unable to secure evidence which would legally implicate those engaged in the transactions.[223] Consul Lynn was told by "trusted friends" that Negroes had been landed recently at Indianola. In fact, one planter, whom Lynn knew as a personal friend, told him in confidence that he was on his way to Indianola to buy Africans from Mrs. Watson. "The interest or the timidity of those cognizant of the landing of Negroes," wrote Lynn, "has been sufficient to cause them to suppress information of the fact."[224]

1830–1840, and 1841–1852, as well as mayor of Houston for several terms. From 1859 through 1860, he was chief geologist for the State of Texas. "He was a fine orator, an intelligent and moderate newspaper editor, and a man of unusual ability along many lines of learning. In private life, as well as in business, he is said to have been one of the purest men in early Texas history; being a Presbyterian of the Old School persuasion, he lived up to his faith." (Quotation and details from Williams, *Writings of Sam Houston*, VIII, 125, notes.)

[221] Houston *Telegraph*, August 11, 1859.

[222] Lynn to Lyons, June 18, 1860, MS, F.O.; Russell to Lynn, July 18, 1860, MS, F.O.

[223] Lynn to Russell, August 31, 1860, MS, F.O.   [224] *Ibid.*

A merchant who had recently traveled along the Galveston Gulf Coast stated that

within his own personal knowledge there had been landed at Corpus Christi from slavers not less than nine hundred native Africans, all of whom had been disposed of to planters residing in the interior. Not the slightest notice of the matter was taken by the federal officials there, and the business was transacted as if it was of a perfectly legitimate character.[225]

The federal officials in control of customs offices at some points along the Texas Gulf Coast may not have taken "the slightest notice" of the Africans being imported, but Howell Cobb of Georgia, who became Secretary of the Treasury in 1857, occasionally attempted to intercept slavers moving into the Galveston area. The other secretaries in Buchanan's cabinet who might have taken an interest in stopping the clandestine slave traffic actually took more interest in protecting American merchantmen from over-zealous British naval officers who were stopping and searching American vessels suspected of being slavers[226] than they did in taking measures to curtail the trade. Howell Cobb, however, mobilizing a few revenue cutters and coastal survey vessels, attempted to see to it that the Customs House collectors along the Galveston coast did not lend illegal accommodations to the slave traders. In March, 1858, Cobb telegraphed instructions to F. H. Hatch, his collector in New Orleans, directing him to intercept the *E. A. Rawlins* expected to attempt to land a cargo of Africans on the coast of Texas. Prompt action was needed. "You will send the cutter at your port in search and use every possible exertion to intercept the landing," the secretary declared. He further instructed Hatch to order Stuart in Galveston "to do everything in his power to intercept the vessel."[227] A short while later the same "cutter fleet" was chasing the sloop *Fairy* en route to the Texas coast with slaves.[228] As "Cobb's Navy" failed to overtake the swift sailing slavers, the secretary detached the fast

[225] *Ibid.*

[226] Bailey, *Diplomatic History*, p. 801.

[227] Howell Cobb to F. H. Hatch, March 2, 1858, U.S. *House Exec. Docs.*, 36th Cong., 2nd Sess., IV, No. 7, p. 632. There was no telegraph wire to Galveston at that time.

[228] Cobb to Hatch, August 12, 1858, *Ibid.*, pp. 639–640.

steamer *Harriet Lane* from the customs fleet at New York City and sent the vessel to Galveston waters "to aid in curbing the slave trade moving there." Cobb issued orders to "prepare her for a long cruise, detail boat crews to visit inlets, [and] keep her assigned duty secret."[229] Just before the *Harriet Lane* sailed, Cobb wrote special instructions to the vessel's commander, Captain John Faunce, to emphasize that his assignment "to watch the trade" along the Texas Gulf Coast was "a great responsibility." Keep a sharp eye, wrote the secretary, for "small vessels hovering on the coast."[230] On the same day, the Secretary directed that "guns and reinforcements" be sent to Hamilton Stuart at Galveston and "inform him, at once, when they will arrive."[231]

A few weeks later, Cobb sent an urgent dispatch to Stuart at Galveston stating that African Negroes were being "smuggled on board mail steamers on the Gulf at Cedar Keys and are to be mixed up with a number of negroes purchased in Florida very recently and thence shipped to Texas." Stuart was told that on the arrival of these steamers at Galveston he was to examine the vessels. If he found African Negroes on board he was to "seize the steamer, and report to this department for further instructions."[232] For some reason the Customs House at Galveston failed to respond to these instructions. About a week later, Jacob Thompson, the "staunch Southern Rights man" from Mississippi who headed the Department of Interior, lent Cobb some of the Coastal Survey vessels to aid the "slave patrol" in the Gulf.[233]

Since the combined mobilization of the craft available to Cobb and his fellow Southerner failed to achieve an effective blockade against the slavers, it might be contended that their actual interest was not in a slave-trade blockade but rather in the transfer of as many craft and as much equipment as possible into Southern waters as a foresighted measure in anticipation of possible secession hostilities. It is a matter of record that the vessels and men of the treasury service at Galveston

[229] Cobb to Augustus Schell, Customs Collector, New York City, October 26, 1859, *Ibid.,* pp. 641–642.

[230] Cobb to John Faunce, November 2, 1859, *Ibid.,* p. 642.

[231] Cobb to Schell, November 2, 1859, *Ibid.,* p. 643.

[232] Cobb to Stuart, January 10, 1860, *Ibid.,* p. 644.

[233] Cobb to Jacob Thompson, January 18, 1860, *Ibid.,* p. 644.

and other Gulf ports formed an important part of the initial Confederate Navy. Considering the fact that the regular Navy practically ignored the slave traffic, however, it seems fair to hold that both Cobb and Thompson maintained more vigilance than might reasonably have been expected of them under the circumstances. In any case, the trade fell off in Texas as the approach of the Civil War convinced planters that, for the time being, it might be wise to delay plans for more cotton expansion.[234]

[234] Ballinger Papers, folder for 1860, MS; Lubbock, *Memoirs,* pp. 138–139.

PART
THREE

The Climax

7. SECESSION IN GALVESTON

THERE WERE EMOTIONAL and purely political factors pushing Texans toward secession in the late 1850's. Many of these were of profound psychological origins which may have been in the making for twenty years. The outstanding drive for secession, however, seems to have been economic, the drive for the expansion in cotton production. By then the railroads were well on their way to becoming a reality. Transportation was at hand to serve over 7 million acres of rich potential cotton land. Only the cheap African Negro labor, remained to be secured to realize the wealth from the land. Slaves were necessary. Only with an abundant supply could the land be worked. Yet the Lincoln government in the North not only took a position in opposition to the reopening of the African slave trade (and most Texans agreed that the slave trade was the only logical solution to their labor shortage), but it gave indications of wanting to eliminate the institution altogether. This, then, was one of the prime factors inducing Texans to vote for leaving the Union in 1861.

Powerful economic motives, therefore, lay behind the secession movement. However, the unusual complexity of the political situation which prevailed on the Gulf Coast exercised a profound influence upon the course of the movement in Texas. Although both the Whigs and the Democrats had held an occasional convention in Texas prior to that time, political organizations had usually coalesced around individual politicians. At about the time when the Whig party commenced to fade out of the national picture the Democratic party in Texas began to form a more definite organization.

During this same time the issue of whether the Kansas-Nebraska territories should be slave or free territories caused the division of the newly formed Democratic party into a states-rights versus a moderate or conservative faction—the latter eventually providing a base for the pro-Union wing of the party. The African slave-trade dispute and the related filibuster activities accentuated this division.

The two sides of the railroad and bank disputes further complicated the political situation by tending to draw adherents from both sides of the rising secession dispute. However, with the exception of Willard Richardson, the State plan advocates for railroad construction were more likely to belong to the conservative-minded faction than to the states-rights groups.

Still further complicating the political alignments was the appearance of the Know-Nothing movement in Texas during the years 1854 to 1857.[1] This faction, which received a tacit blessing from Sam Houston, attained a large popular following because of the resentment harbored by native American labor toward the large number of Ger-

[1] Galveston *News*, February 2, 1848 and October 30, 1855.

man immigrants who were then entering Texas through the port of Galveston.[2]

When it became apparent that this faction was gathering considerable political strength, Sam Houston, in need of a weapon to use against his opposition within the Democratic party, openly joined forces with the Know-Nothings. This alliance rested solely upon expediency since the allies held practically no common principles.[3] In fact, some of Houston's strongest supporters in the Democratic party were the Germans, who certainly had nothing in common with the Know-Nothings, and Houston himself later repudiated the nativism advocated by the Know-Nothings.[4] Thus, in 1857, as the division over the issue of secession was taking shape, the pro-Union Germans and Sam Houston's personal machine united into a political faction with the Know-Nothings against the states-rights, proslave-trade, secession wing of the Democratic party. In 1861 the issue was finally decided in favor of the states-rights faction because that group eventually won back their natural allies, the native American laborers. As the crisis was reached, the conservatives and the Germans remained as a pro-Union group, which may possibly have possessed a numerical majority, but which did not possess the aggressive and dynamic leadership necessary to harness the emotional aspects of the issues which were the ready instruments of the secession faction.[5] In this rapidly changing and fluid situation those leaders who merely wished to retain the *status quo* labored under a fatal disadvantage and therefore, in a closely balanced conflict, they were doomed to failure.

Early in 1857 Sam Houston, aware that he would not be returned to the Senate by the next legislature, announced that he would run for the governorship against the incumbent Hardin R. Runnels, a wealthy

[2] Arthur T. Lynn to J. F. Crampton, October 14, 1855, MS, F.O.; Houston *Telegraph,* September 6 and August 19, 1859; Galveston *News,* June 23 and February 5, 1856; Galveston *Die Union,* July 7, 1859.

[3] Anna Irene Sandbo, "Beginnings of the Secession Movement in Texas," *Southwestern Historical Quarterly,* XVIII (July, 1914), 51–73.

[4] Galveston *News,* November 27, 1855; Galveston *Die Union,* July 7, 1859.

[5] Galveston *News,* May 19, 1857; Houston *Telegraph,* September 6, 1856; Otto Hawn, *True Democracy Battles Not For Men But For Principles,* pamphlet, pp. 1–14.

planter, a proslave-trade advocate, and the regular nominee of the State Democratic Party. In this contest Runnels and his states-rights organization won by a large majority. This was the victory which emboldened this faction to press for the reopening of the slave trade, to encourage participation in filibustering expeditions, and to consider the possibility of secession in the event others might interfere with the "destiny" of Texas.[6] The boldness of this faction of the Democratic party frightened such leading Galvestonians as Stuart, Sherwood and Flake.[7] In association with other conservatives in Galveston and elsewhere they began to form a pro-Union wing of the Democratic party.[8] Their candidate for the 1859 contest was again Sam Houston, and on this occasion the pro-Union faction won the election, reversing the results of 1857. This defeat, which caused the proslave-trade faction to sharpen its attacks on the conservatives, gravely heightened the bitterness of the campaign practices. This rising acrimony compounded the combustible aspects of politics in Texas as the secession crisis reached a conclusion during the year 1860.[9]

The impact of the political conflict in the state as a whole had a marked effect upon the social and political scene on the smaller stage of Galveston Island. The conflicting interests cut across all the normal affiliations. For example, Sherwood and Richardson agreed upon railroad matters but were diametrically opposed to each other on the slave-trade and secession issues; Ballinger, who engineered the move to force Sherwood out of the legislature on the railroad issue, agreed with the New Yorker in his support of the Union and in opposition to slave trade; men such as Flake and Stuart, who deplored the xenophobic nativism of the Know-Nothings, nevertheless ardently supported Sam

[6] Houston *Telegraph,* July 11, 1859.

[7] *Ibid.,* July 13, 22, and August 3, 1859.

[8] Galveston *Union,* July 7, 1859; Dallas *Herald,* July 6, 1859.

[9] Charles W. Ramsdell, "Reconstruction in Texas," *Columbia University Studies in History, Economics and Public Law,* XXXVI, No. 1, Whole No. 95, pp. 1–20; Sandbo, "Beginnings of Secession," pp. 51–73. For an important study of the economic status of the members of the Secession Convention in Texas see Ralph A. Wooster, "Analysis of the Membership of the Texas Secession Convention," *Southwestern Historical Quarterly,* LXII (January, 1959), 322–335.

Houston who owed much of his strength to the rise of nativism. Senator Potter, who had pilloried Sherwood as an abolitionist in 1856 during the railroad battle, in 1859 went along with the New Yorker to the city of Houston to make some addresses in support of moderation, addresses for which he "was greatly slandered for want of Southern principles" and from which he returned to Galveston "thoroughly disgusted."[10]

Except for the surprising incident of the election of a Know-Nothing candidate for mayor of Galveston in 1855, neither radical secessionism nor nativism became a serious matter on the Island until the end of the decade approached. There were times, however, when such men as Consul Lynn were much disturbed by the "acrimony" and the "most seditious articles" which were published by the various journals devoted to these "causes"; but Lynn, at least, took comfort in the fact that despite the dangerous "talk" nothing serious happened.[11] Stuart and Ballinger too were often concerned about where the disturbing editorial policies trumpeted by such men as Richardson and Cushing might lead.[12] But Cushing, who visited the Island every now and then, observed calmly that Galveston was a hotbed of abolitionists as well as a center of "strong Southern men." He appeared to view political conflict as but an interesting aspect of public life.[13] All during the late fifties Richardson and Sam Houston maintained a continuing battle of words which provided much entertainment for Galvestonians. Only the old general himself seemed unable to keep his sense of humor.[14] Further excitement was added to the scene during these later years, when the grandiose schemes of the filibusters were being deflated, by a new company of empire builders, the Knights of the Golden Circle, which appeared on the streets and in the saloons, oft-

[10] Ballinger Diary, May 30, 1859, MS.

[11] Lynn to Crampton, October 14, 1855; Lynn to Lord Russell, January 15, 1861, MSS, F.O.

[12] Ballinger Diary, April 2 and 14, 1860, MS.

[13] Houston *Telegraph*, April 6, 1856 and July 22, 1859.

[14] *Congressional Globe*, 1858–1859, 35th Cong., 2nd Sess., February 28, 1859, 1433–1438; Richardson *Texas Almanac*, 1860, pp. 18–35, 36–89; Galveston *News*, November 2, 1858; Ballinger *Diary*, MS, May 6, 1859.

times aided and abetted by the colorful enthusiasts for a return to a "Lone Star" status.[15]

Many of the responsible Galvestonians had come to look upon "spectacular" politics as an amusing as well as a disturbing aspect of the passing scene. Few, it seemed, expected that Texas would ever be called upon to decide the grave issue of whether or not to leave the Union. Thus when the actual issue faced them, the secessionists were trapped by the grand statements which they had been making and the conservatives were overwhelmed because they had failed to organize effectively. Up to the very hour of the crisis conservative persons had totally underestimated the gravity of the circumstances which the "talk" of the fifties had fastened upon Texas and upon their Island.[16]

As the critical election campaign of 1859 reached its concluding phase during the hot weeks of July and August, the tempers of some leading Galvestonians were strained to the breaking point and old friendships were gravely threatened. On the afternoon of August 22nd, Oscar Farish, Senator Potter, Stuart, Tom Guinan, Guy Bryan and several other Islanders "argued for several hours" in Ballinger's office. There was much disagreement. Some threatened to pull up stakes and "go north." The next evening, a Saturday, the Democrats held a meeting at the Market. "Nearly all the old leaders, Stuart, Farish, Joseph and Andrews, were for Houston." The younger men and Richardson were for Runnels. Ballinger went home that night and read the works of Edmund Burke in a search for comfort and wisdom. On the next evening the "Bolters," Runnels' men—Hartly, Franklin, Tom Jack (Ballinger's law partner and brother-in-law), Guy Bryan and others—held a public meeting in the Market. It was "a larger and more enthusiastic" gathering than the regular Democratic meeting held a few days before.[17]

At both of these gatherings old friends came very close to insulting each other gravely in public. Hamilton Stuart felt that Tom Jack had impugned his honor at the Saturday night meeting; thus on Sunday

[15] Lynn to Lord Lyons, December 4, 1860, MS, F.O.

[16] Lynn to Russell, January 15 and March 11, 1861; Lynn to Lyons, December 4, 1860 and February 5, March 11 and 14, 1861, MSS, F.O.

[17] See Ballinger Diary, for July and August, 1859, MS.

morning the usually mild mannered Stuart called upon Jack to inquire if the latter had called "him a liar last night." A very serious verbal exchange passed between the two men. Fortunately, however, after a series of written communications had been carried between the two men by their friends, a duel was avoided. Ballinger admitted that "Tom was too much excited to weigh his words accurately."[18]

The German voters in Galveston were likewise in a difficult position. On the one hand their pro-Union sentiment caused them to favor Sam Houston and on the other hand the old general's previous nativism affiliations made the Germans wary. The Know-Nothing leaders were "seducing the Germans" with the assertion that the slave-trade Democrats "wanted to run out the German labor and bring in slaves."[19] As the campaign developed, however, and it became clear that the pro-slave-trade secession men had won over most of the native mechanic classes, the Germans decided to support Houston. Flake, who was using all his influence to move German sentiment in this direction, induced Houston to repudiate the former Know-Nothing movement in a letter which Flake immediately translated into German and printed in *Die Union*. Stuart also gave the English version of the letter circulation in the *Civilian*.[20] The imminent loss of the powerful German vote aroused some anger on the part of the Runnels supporters. Cushing proclaimed that Sam Houston was the "captive" of Flake and Galveston Germans. Others saw the situation as the other way around: "It is Sam's Flakey or flunky who is to help him pull the wool over the eyes of the Galveston German voters. Alas! Poor Flake!"[21]

In a letter delivered to Cushing and published in the *Telegraph*, a Galvestonian German, probably George Schneider, Sr., replied to these remarks and explained why the Germans were ardent supporters of the Union. "We came here, Sir," he wrote,

with an intense desire for freedom. We have long sought for the country which guarantees us that full share of political and religious liberty denied

[18] *Ibid.*   [19] Houston *Telegraph*, June 3, 1859.

[20] Galveston *Union*, July 7, 1859; Galveston *Civilian*, July 6, 1859.

[21] Houston *Telegraph*, July 11, 1859; see also an important exchange of letters regarding Flake, Lubbock, and Runnels printed in the July 6, 1859 issue of the Dallas *Herald*.

to us at home. We found that blessed country in this great Union, and this imposing confederacy of several states, and we will cling to it forever. Do not talk to us of dissolution of the Union. We do not believe in a Northern and Southern confederacy, but we do know that if this Union is dissolved the great bulwark of liberty will be destroyed.[22]

When the election was held in September, Ballinger, typical of the moderate-minded conservatives on the Island, refused to take a stand on either side of the unpleasant issue which was dividing old friends. He simply refused to vote at all.[23]

When the Galveston ballots were counted, it was learned that Runnels had received 403 votes and Houston only 307. The defeat of the conservatives was made even more apparent by the 456 votes cast for the ardent secessionist Lubbock for the office of lieutenant governor. In the state as a whole, however, the results of the polling put Houston in the governor's office.[24]

Since the concluding year of the decade and the opening of the next included a state election, a national election, and a popular referendum on the momentous question of secession, these months were marked by uneasy times on the Island. Friends tried to forget politics and regain the old unity, but this proved to be impossible because the various factions had of necessity to try to bolster their positions. Some relief from dissension was garnered, as the autumn days approached, from the appearance of an old enemy common to all, the fever. And in November, the Christmas season opened with an "ice storm," exciting the children and reviving talk of "old times" on the part of elder Galvestonians, and pleasantries which in former times had graced streetside conversations began to return to the city.[25]

As the critical decade of the sixties began, worried Galvestonians of a conservative turn of mind urged their political leaders to search for an honorable compromise; but when these leaders searching for an

[22] "Letter from a German," Houston *Telegraph*, July 13, 1859.

[23] Ballinger Diary, September 1, 1859, MS.

[24] Richardson, *Texas Almanac, 1861*, p. 215; Ballinger Diary, August 23 to September 1, 1859, MS; Houston *Telegraph*, August 3, 8, and 17, 1859.

[25] See Ballinger Diary, September–December, 1859, MS.

amicable solution, consulted Senator Louis T. Wigfall, they were told that further efforts in the direction of compromise would amount to nothing; "The North will not yield an inch," said the Senator.[26]

The Democratic State Convention met in Galveston on April 2, 1860 and wrote a platform which aimed at secession. With the active assistance of Willard Richardson in formulating and printing proposed resolutions, the delegates of the Convention resolved that Texas possessed the "full right, as a sovereign State to annul the compact and to resume her former place among the powers of the earth"; and that the people of the State of Texas ought to cooperate with their sister States to secure their mutual rights.[27] One delegate named Leland "was refused admission on the grounds that he was very recently a Black Republican. They refused to hear him before the convention," although he was allowed to defend himself before the admitting committee.[28] The treatment given Leland made it apparent that the secession-minded men now controlled the affairs of the Democratic party in Texas.

Conservative Galvestonians were, at that juncture, very concerned about the "darkening clouds" both at home and on the national horizon. A group of friends went to the boat landing on Saturday night, April 14, to get the latest papers from New Orleans. Stephen Douglas' speech on the "Protection of the States from Invasion" reported in latest journals, was studied carefully as they enjoyed the cool evening breeze off the Gulf. "I haven't any faith in Douglas," said Ballinger to his friends after a perusal of the latest intelligences; "never have had. I think him a bold, restless, and ambitious Democrat, but I believe he is the truest prominent Democrat north of the Mason-Dixon Line on the slavery question and that the Democrats' war on him is supremely foolish and suicidal."[29]

The next morning, a bright April Sunday in Galveston, found most

[26] Francis Richard Lubbock, *Six Decades in Texas: or Memoirs . . . A Personal Experience in Business, War and Politics,* pp. 303–304.

[27] Galveston *News,* April 10, 1860; *Proceedings of the Democratic State Convention of Texas Held in Galveston,* April 2, 1860, pamphlet.

[28] Ballinger Diary, April 2, 1860, MS.

[29] *Ibid.,* April 14, 1860.

of the "responsible families" having "strawberries and cream at Taylor's" as a part of the "proceedings" of the Episcopal Convention then in session on the Island. In the evening the Reverend Mr. Eaton delivered a sermon at Trinity Church which had the virtue of being a contribution to the lessening of tension without being "doctrinaire or argumentative."[30]

During the month of May, news of the "Bell-Everett ticket" reached the Island. This combination did not arouse enthusiasm, but at least it gave "gentlemen" a ticket they could "cordially" support. When the "intelligence" that Lincoln had been nominated reached the city, a meeting was held in the Market at which many Galvestonians expressed vigorous secession sentiments.[31]

Political affairs dominated the social scene as summer came to the Island. "Wasted all morning in political discussion which amounted to nothing," said Ballinger. "Same all over town."[32] Since the Galvestonian Democrats who favored secession were well organized in Breckinridge clubs, the conservative citizens early in August organized a formal Bell and Everett Club of the Constitutional Union Party which held regular weekly meetings. In addition to Love, Ballinger, and Farish, such men as Doctor Levi Jones, George A. Peck, Colonel A. C. McKeen, Andrew Neill, A. C. Crawford, E. O. Lynch, and R. H. Howard were active members in this *status quo* organization.[33] Most of these meetings were held in Colonel McKeen's office. The gentlemen attending were convinced that the best strategy for reasonable men to follow in both the South and the North was to unite on a ticket which could defeat Lincoln. Unfortunately, the gatherings were "rather slim affairs" at which the participants struggled to display "a good deal of enthusiasm." On August 23rd, however, attendance was large, for the weather was fine and Galvestonians wanted to hear Bal-

[30] Ballinger Diary, April 15, 1860, MS; Lynn to Lyons, December 10, 1860, MS, F.O.

[31] Galveston *News*, May 22, 1860; Doctor Dyer's "History of Galveston," MS, p. 56.

[32] Ballinger Diary, May 13 through May 24, 1860, MS.

[33] San Antonio *Alamo Express*, September 3, 1860.

linger's "constitutional speech." The speech was a success. "The Unionists all seemed delighted." Ballinger, however, was worried about
the impression he had made. He admitted in his diary that he knew that
the position he had taken would be likely to hurt his law practice. He
decided to be more discreet in such matters on future occasions.[34]

Ferdinand Flake did not endorse either the Breckinridge-Lane or
the Bell-Everett tickets; he remained a regular Union Democrat. To
assert his views he wrote a phamphlet which he printed in both the
German and English languages "setting forth that Douglas was the
only real and regular candidate of the Democracy," and he then endeavored to give this document wide distribution.[35]

On September 1st the Breckinridge-Democrats held a big rally in
Galveston. The old party functionary, Hamilton Stuart, made the opening address. He said that he would support Breckinridge even though
his candidate could not be elected; the Southern Democrats should have
supported Douglas but it was too late to argue such matters now. Most
of all he hoped that "the quarreling between Southern men would
cease." Charles McCarthy then took the platform and "gave Stuart the
very devil; said he had better join the enemy if he had no better comfort to give his friends. The crowd cheered."[36] It was a very effective
meeting in support of the secessionist point of view, and it sent the
old Democrat Hamilton Stuart home with a heavy heart. As the autumn days passed and the electioneering continued, the approaching
victory of the secessionist wing of the Democratic party appeared certain. On October 23rd Lubbock made a speech at an evening rally in the
Market. An experienced political observer noted that Lubbock was "a
very promiscuous and scattering talker, who made some strong points
especially with the foreigners."[37]

A few weeks later, on November 6th, when the votes were counted,

[34] Ballinger Diary, August 13 through August 23, 1860, MS; *The Constitutional Party of Texas: Addresses of the Union Executive Commitee of the
People of Texas,* 4 page pamphlet.
[35] Austin *State Gazette,* October 20, 1860.
[36] Ballinger Diary, September 2, 1860, MS.
[37] Ballinger Diary, October 23, 1860, MS.

it was learned that the election balloting in Galveston had produced 684 votes for Breckinridge, 205 votes for Bell, 65 votes for Douglas and none for Lincoln.[38]

When the news that Lincoln had won the national election became known on the Island, it "produced a deep sensation" in the city: "Many wise and good men" immediately suggested dissolution.[39] Richardson's reaction was that the "election of a Black Republican president" had determined that the "hour of waiting was past." The time for "a bold and decided Stand" had arrived. The editor "earnestly" recommended the holding of "precinct, ward, town, or county meetings, at which citizens of all political opinions should attend, and all the sentiments of the people be frankly expressed." Richardson recommended that committees of safety for each precinct be formed and a general committee for the county. The tone of Richardson's editorials carried a steady and responsible note. The agitating sharpness disappeared and was replaced by a somber comment and recommendations for deliberate action. The editor was sobered by the seriousness of events, but his actions were also prompted by the fact that a more reasonable attitude was necessary to win over the middle-of-the-road citizens of the county.[40]

On November 12th a public meeting was convened in Galveston to consider what action should be taken. F. R. Lubbock informed the gathering that in his opinion secession was the only honorable course to take. A committee of safety was formed to organize a unit of "Minute Men," and one of the speakers in support of the committee was "Colonel McKeen, an organizer of the much-abused Bell and Everett Club." Colonel McKeen's action in joining the Secessionists illustrated the shift of moderate minded men in Galveston toward secession after the election of Lincoln. The Colonel, in his address to the gathering, said that he thought the time for differences in the South had passed: ". . . a great danger [is] upon us. We should all unite hand and heart." He explained that he was a Southerner by birth, education and feeling; he would have rejoiced, he said, "to have seen this

[38] Galveston *News,* November 13, 1860.

[39] Ballinger Diary, November 8, 1860, MS.

[40] Galveston *News,* November 13, 1860.

THE MORGAN PIER, 1861

From a contemporary photograph in the Historical Collection, John
Winterbotham Room, Rosenberg Library, Galveston, Texas.

government in the hands of John Bell." He believed that Bell could have preserved the Union, "but that is past discussing, and a new duty awaits us." He refused to "submit" to "Black Republican Rule." He would do his best to assist in organizing any companies proposed by the Committee. Another Moderate, Judge Thompson, took a stand along side of Colonel McKeen. He foresaw, he said, resistance from Governor Houston. The old gentleman ought to be given time to fall in line. Should he prove obstinate, his power should be taken from him. Thompson had previously supported Houston. Hamilton Stuart and some of his followers were not willing to join the swing toward secession.[41]

"The fire eaters are counselling about what to do," wrote Ballinger. "They are clamorous for disruption, but how to bring it about is the great trouble." On Sunday, November 11th, few men went to church; they remained "to wait for news from the boat" concerning the result of election returns in other parts of the nation. On Monday it was announced that a public meeting would be called to "memorialize the government to assemble the legislature to call a convention to declare Texas out of the Union." Ballinger wrote a letter to the *Civilian* suggesting Judge David G. Burnet as president of the meeting; a great deal depended upon having a reasonable man in the chair.[42]

On Wednesday evening, November 14th, "the largest public meeting" ever seen in Galveston up to that time assembled. A contest immediately began to determine whether the conservative Judge Burnet or the secessionist William T. Austin should preside. The issue was decided by John S. Jones, the temporary chairman, when he arbitrarily placed Austin in charge. From that time on, according to Hamilton Stuart, "the proceedings were a cut and dried" affair.[43]

Many Galvestonians spoke at the meeting. It appeared that the conservatives neglected to state their case. "Colonel James Love and Oscar

[41] Galveston *News,* November 13, 1860.

[42] Ballinger Diary, November 14, 1860, MS.

[43] Lynn to Lyons, December [no date], 1860, MS, F.O.; Ballinger Diary, November 14, 1860, MS; Galveston *News,* December 8, 1860; Galveston *News,* November 22, 1860.

Farish took half way ground." The secessionists "went all the way." Ballinger, noting that the disunionists were "a much larger majority" than he had supposed, gave up the attempt to force his way through the crowd to the platform in order to express his convictions.

When Ballinger reached his home that night and had time to reflect, he felt ashamed that his courage had failed him. In his diary he wrote: "I passed a sleepless night. I feel low spirited. I cannot disguise from myself the deep apprehension, if not the positive conviction that our government will be overthrown and the Union dissolved. Several Southern states will secede. The employment of force to subdue them is so opposed to the spirit of our government that it will be worse than even disunion." He turned once more for comfort to Burke's *Reflections on the French Revolution.*[44]

On December 3, 1860, Stuart said that while he would not absolutely condemn secession, he advised "caution." He acknowledged that "all political power is inherent in the people and that they have at all times the inalienable right to alter, reform, or abolish this form of government"; however, should the Republicans prove moderate, the crisis might pass. "It is easy," he continued, "to talk of our wrongs and of revenge; but it will be hard to institute better governments or a happier order of things that we have hitherto enjoyed."[45]

Even though the battle for secession was almost won, Richardson continued to stress the fact that Lincoln was an enemy of the South. Richardson printed excerpts from various speeches made by Lincoln to show that the President-elect was not "moderate." Lincoln's Leavenworth, Kansas, speech was analyzed in detail; it was pointed out that Lincoln proposed to deal with "traitors as old John Brown had been dealt with." In Lincoln's view, said Richardson, secession was treason. "If any of our readers," said the editor, "are exercised in their own minds as to what course of federal treatment Mr. Lincoln" would prescribe for those who seek Southern rights, this speech "ought to settle that doubt."[46] This presented a grim outlook from either point of view.

[44] Ballinger Diary, November 14–16, 1860, MS.
[45] Galveston *Civilian,* December 3, 1860.
[46] Galveston *News,* December 8, 1860.

Conservative Galvestonians looked toward the future with some fear and much frustration.[47]

Faced as they were with the relentless movement of events that appeared to portend unpredictable developments, some fearful Galvestonians looked to their clergy for guidance, but they received no firm assurances. Even such godly men as Eaton seemed uncertain of the future as the year 1860 ended. No clergyman on the Island was willing to assert with certainty what the Divine Will might be in this situation. The only concrete statements forthcoming were to the effect that "events were in the hands of God"—an intelligence which added little new light to the situation.

In order to bring in some ray of Divine Light, the Committee of Safety and Correspondence in Galveston wrote to the Reverend Mr. J. E. Carnes, a well-known clergyman in Texas, requesting him to address the city "upon the duty of the Southern states in the present crisis." The Committee noted that many men of God had so far refrained for taking active sides on the issue; they pointed out to the clergyman that it was his patriotic duty to perform this service—that his motives "could not be mistaken inasmuch as the impending danger threatened to subvert religion, as well as government and society, and involve all in common ruin—and called, therefore, upon all to join in the effort to avert calamity." The Reverend Mr. Carnes replied that "a sense of duty" compelled him to agree to the request. On December 12th he delivered an address to the city. This "reasoned analysis" of the crisis warmed the hearts of "Southern men" but brought no comfort to moderate or Union-minded men.[48]

[47] Jonnie Lockhart Wallis, *Sixty Years on the Brazos: the Life and Letters of Dr. John Washington Lockhart, 1824–1900,* pp. 193–194; Noah Smithwick, *The Evolution of a State: or Recollections of Old Texas Days,* pp. 331–333.

[48] H. McLeod, F. Sims, E. B. Nichols, W. M. Armstrong, W. R. Smith, A. P. Lufkin, E. S. Wood, W. Richardson, J. P. Cole, and Guy M. Bryan to Rev. J. E. Carnes, December 5, 1860; Carnes to the Committee, December 8, 1860 (the above printed in Galveston *News,* December 8, 1860); J. E. Carnes, *Address on the Duty of the Slave States in the Present Crisis: Delivered in Galveston, December 12, 1860, by Special Invitation of the Committee of Safety and Correspondence, and Many of the Oldest Citizens of Galveston,*

On the brighter side, the men familiar with the affairs of commerce were optimistic. Trade was excellent. A Boston correspondent who had recently visited the Island wrote to a friend in Galveston that "much Northern gold is moving South due to post election panic." Eastern security prices were falling, boot and shoe manufacturers were laying off their hands. "Thirty days from now there will not be a specie paying bank in New England. The South will be flooded with gold . . . every steamer that leaves Boston for a Southern port goes out laden with precious metal." The correspondent said that the Merrimack Manufacturing Company had sent out, during the week, $450,000 in gold to southern ports such as Galveston to pay for cotton; in his opinion the Islanders could look to the future with confidence.[49]

A gentleman from Philadelphia who was visiting Galveston on business attended a meeting held in the city, at which citizens had expressed their views on the election of Mr. Lincoln. The Philadelphian said he was glad to learn that Texans were going to take a decided stand for their rights. "The stand your people are taking will open their [the North's] eyes to the grand mistake they have made" and perhaps would open the way to a compromise. Richardson remarked that he was gratified for "our Philadelphia visitor's views as to the good effect of a firm stand," but the editor foresaw no reasonable compromise. He noted, gratuitously, that the Keystone State had already "sold her birthright" for the "protective tariff held out to them by the Chicago platform."[50]

Lincoln's election aroused many Galvestonians to prepare for all "eventualities." Almost at once "nearly a hundred men joined the Lone Star Rifle Company." Companies of Lone Star Minute Men and Lone Star Flag Clubs were organized in Galveston and neighboring counties. The officers of these companies addressed crowds whenever possible. On these "patriotic and arousing" occasions "many came forward and enlisted."[51] On December 8th "twenty men met in a saloon on Market

---

a copy of this pamphlet is preserved in the Texas History Center, Austin, Texas.

[49] Letter from a "Recent Visitor," Galveston *News,* November 20, 1860.

[50] Galveston *News,* November 20, 1860.

[51] *Ibid.,* November 20 and 22, 1860.

Street and organized the Wigfall Guards." Another "saloon company" was the Island City Rifles. These early companies were usually organized and financed by "committees of safety."[52]

"So many 'Lone Stars' were never before seen in this city, not even in the days of the Republic." The election of Lincoln was the cause of this flourish. A Mr. J. M. Conrad, "a most accomplished printer," had prepared "a most beautiful" cut of the Lone Star from which he crested letter heads and envelopes. "We now see them in the hands of almost everybody."[53] Commercial-minded men lent their "valuable" assistance in the effort to arouse the "martial spirit." R. T. Allen, director of the Bastrop Military Institute, at Bastrop, Texas, ran advertisements in the *News* offering courses in military science. Since the purpose was to train soldiers, not scholars, those enrolling were not expected to conform to previous academic requirements.[54] Other patriots, in an effort to assist both the "cause" and commerce, engaged in merchandising operations demonstrating their readiness to supply "arms for the South! Buy a musket with bayonet for $10.00." Galveston agents for D. Kernaghan and Company of New Orleans placed "400 percussion Minie Muskets" at the disposal of Island patriots at $10.00 per weapon. Hatters, tailors, and clothing merchants lent their skill and energy to the cause of commerce as well as secession by outfitting several companies with "Lone Star" hats and other "regalia" at prices which were not unreasonable considering the fact that the rising demand had created a seller's market.[55]

Meanwhile the secessionist leaders and the rank and file of the faction grew increasingly irritable because Governor Houston delayed in taking positive action toward taking Texas out of the Union. Hamilton Stuart, still acting as customs collector in the city for the federal government, tried to allay the general anger by intimating from time to

[52] Ben Stuart, Galveston's Early Military Companies, MS, III, 39–40.

[53] Galveston *News,* November 22, 1860.

[54] *Ibid.,* January 22, 1861.

[55] Ben Stuart, "Galveston's Early Military Companies," MS, III, 39–40; Galveston *News,* November 22 and December 11, 18, and 22, 1860; Ben Stuart, "History of Galveston," MS, Bundle XXIII.

time through the medium of his newspaper that the governor was planning to visit the city in order to address the populace.[56]

An irate citizen, commenting on the possible appearance of Sam Houston in Galveston, said that

while we will listen with due consideration to the Governor's address, it would be well to hint to the old "faithful public servant" how indecorous it is to oppose the will of the unanimous voice of all parties. The people of the city have a right to expect a due consideration which so far he has not shown.

He calls himself the "servant" of the people, said this irate Galvestonian, "but ruler he would like to be . . . the people of Texas will not submit to the dictation of one man . . . and acquiesce in his submission doctrine."[57]

On December 20th, General Bradford of Alabama addressed a large gathering in the city. He spoke of General Houston and expressed sympathy with the General's "political aspirations." He regretted, nevertheless, that the Governor was "being laggard . . . in this crisis." He feared that "there were promises being held out to Governor Houston from quarters that the people were not apprised of, and that doubtless" this was the cause of his failure to convene the Legislature for the purpose of taking Texas out of the Union.[58]

In mid-December the secessionists in Galveston, impatient over Governor Houston's delay in the calling of a state convention, assembled a meeting of Islanders on December 16th and elected Judge R. C. Campbell, General E. B. Nichols, and John Muller to represent Galveston at a state convention when one was called. "The three agreed to pledge themselves to a policy of taking Texas out of the Union."[59] Lynn reported that only those persons who favored immediate secession or the revival of the old Lone Star Republic had ventured to risk

[56] Galveston *News,* December 22, 1860.

[57] Ben Stuart, "History of Galveston," MS, Bundle XXIII; Galveston *News,* December 8, 1860.

[58] *Ibid.,* December 22, 1860.

[59] *Ibid.,* December 18, 1860.

taking part in the election of the Galveston delegates.[60] R. B. Kingsbury, who was then in Galveston, wrote that the secessionists told him "they wanted no abolition speeches. They gave me a friendly warning by patting their revolvers." The Germans and Northern men were being carefully "watched."[61] It was at this same time that organizers for "The Secret Order of the Knights of the Golden Circle" appeared in Galveston. Their purpose was to unite the spirits of secession, advocates of revival of The Lone Star Republic, and remnants of the fading filibusters into a new movement to colonize and develop a new empire in lands they planned to take from Mexico. The gentlemen of this order graciously extended their assistance to the leaders of secession on the Island.[62]

Under the leadership of Oscar Farish, several moderate-minded men formed their own "Lone Star Association" which argued that Texas ought to stand alone against both the Union and the Southern Confederacy. They were "Unionists at heart, their views being to some extent mere antagonism to the Secessionists and the fire eating states." Ballinger refused to join this group because his "supreme desire" was still the "preservation of the Union" if it could be saved; if not, he was for "the largest possible confederacy" that could be formed. "I am no Lone Star Man," he wrote, "I think it a chimera."[63] Ballinger's nearest relatives, Tom and Nannie Jack, Guy and Laura Bryan, and John Hutchings and his wife, were all secessionists. Even so, the family gathered together on Christmas day, 1860, at Ballinger's house—"had a fine dinner and a pleasant time." Doctor Knox "remained late." The two men engaged in a long though guarded talk. Ballinger was convinced that Knox was a "thinking man"; although he sounded like a

[60] Lynn to Lyons, December 17, 1860, MS, F.O.

[61] R. B. Kingsbury Papers, TS, II; North, [*Journal.*] *Five Years in Texas: or What you Did Not Hear During the War from 1861 to January 1866. A Narrative of His Travels, Experiences, and Observations in Texas and Mexico,* p. 72.

[62] Lynn to Lyons, November 16 and 30, 1860 and Lynn to Lord Napier, April 25 and December 5, 1860, MSS, F.O.; C. A. Birdges, "The Knights of the Golden Circle: A Filibustering Fantasy," *Southwestern Historical Quarterly,* LXIV (January, 1941), 286–302.

[63] Ballinger Diary, December 21, 1860, MS.

"free soiler" it was hard to tell for certain because even amicable persons were now careful not to commit themselves firmly to unwelcome convictions in a friend's house.[64]

During the Christmas week Guy Bryan, in his capacity of chairman of the Island's Committee of Safety and Correspondence, published a pamphlet addressed to the people of Texas urging them to emulate Galvestonians and elect a slate of delegates which could be sent to a state secession convention. This revolutionary action was necessary, declared Bryan, because Governor Houston continued to refuse to convene the legislature in a special session.[65] Most observers now agreed that "unless extraordinary measures were adopted" Texas would secede. The Unionists, by their failure to express their convictions, had completely lost control of the situation in Galveston and very likely in the rest of the state as well.[66]

As the year ending the decade moved through the last days, those who had loved the old Union were resigned to its approaching "destruction." "We are doing an unwise and fatal thing," wrote Ballinger. "I have no heart in the cause. Its glory and responsibility I leave to others."[67] Thomas Harrison wrote Ballinger that "the children of those not in the front of the present secessionists would be ashamed of their fathers." Ballinger replied that he was "willing to bide the test of time on that subject." The disruption of the Union, he wrote, without first exhausting every effort to prevent the disaster was "treason to humanity." He was most fearful of the future; these were "evil times." Once more he expressed regret that he had not found the courage at the large public meeting on November 14th to state forcefully his "Union sentiments" and his opposition to "recklessness" which had guided public policy on the Island in this crisis. Ballinger felt himself "more than ever excommunicated from public affairs and politics"; he hoped that he would find the courage hereafter to continue "to think

[64] *Ibid.,* December 25, 1860.
[65] Guy M. Bryan, *Galveston Committee of Safety and Correspondence: An Address to the State of Texas,* pamphlet.
[66] Lynn to Lyons, December 30, 1860, MS, F.O.; Austin *Southern Intelligencer,* January 23, 1861.
[67] Ballinger Diary, December 30, 1860, MS.

for himself" and to speak frankly. One had to face the fact that "secession was revolution; I submit to it in preference to civil war and shall do my part of a loyal citizen to the State. I put these words here on the record," he concluded, "for the eyes of my children in after times."[68]

The predicament in which Ballinger found himself was typical of most of the moderate-minded persons living on the Gulf Coast.[69] James Love, for many years clerk of the federal court in Galveston and the "Uncle James" under whose guidance Ballinger had read law, was concerned about the fact that "popular rule" had become a "despot" in Galveston. He recently had seen votes being "sold back and forth" like merchandise. The rapid "deterioration" apparent in democratic practices on the Island in his opinion presented the prospect of rule by the mob and the demagogue.[70]

The position of the Germans was a particularly sensitive one; they were being "watched" for evidences of "treason" by the native mechanic classes who now had recovered their rightful place. It was asserted by some persons that "the infidel German" ought to be the most despised of all men on the Island. "Even the African Negro" was "superior" to the German in matters of patriotism.[71]

After the electrifying news of the secession of South Carolina reached Galveston, Ferdinand Flake, on January 5, 1861, published an editorial on the secession of the first southern state in *Die Union* under the explosive caption "Poor South Carolina." The critical tone of the story aroused much excitement among the "fire-eating" secessionists in Galveston. Toward evening, a mob collected in the streets and began shouting "poor South Carolina" as a derisive "war cry," taunting the position taken by the editorial in *Die Union*. As darkness deepened, the mob moved down the street to the office of *Die Union*,

[68] *Ibid.,* December 31, 1860.
[69] Wallis, *Sixty Years on the Brazos,* pp. 193–194; Smithwick, *The Evolution of a State,* pp. 331–333.
[70] James Love to Ballinger, January 1, 1861, Ballinger Papers, MS.
[71] William Simpson Oldham, *Speech on the Resolution of the State of Texas* (pamphlet), 13, Texas History Center; R. B. Kingsbury Papers, II.

and, during the night, employing the ruse of a "fake fire alarm," they broke into the newspaper's office, wrecked the press and scattered the type in the alley. Flake, who had been expecting such an eventuality for some time, had taken the precaution to set up duplicate equipment in his home. Using these facilities he defiantly continued publishing *Die Union* until he was able to repair his office press. A few of the more responsible secessionists in the city collected a fund to repay Flake for the cost of the damage done by the mob which had claimed to be acting for the "cause."[72]

One leading speaker of the secessionists remarked later that the "destruction of Mr. Flake's printing office by a mob at Galveston" expressed the sentiment that "we must treat our German fellow-citizens to a slight dose of the reign of terror, by turning them over to the gentle persuasion of the Minute Men." Willard Richardson noted the general opinion that "our German fellow-citizens" ought "to look out for gentle persuasion." "Of course," he continued, "no allusion can be intended to the German voters of Galveston county. They all voted for secession." As for the mob, it was "generally understood here that the 'destruction' was the work of some of Mr. Flake's own countrymen. How true this general belief is we cannot say, of our own knowledge, but such was and is the impression."[73]

Papers such as the San Antonio *Herald*, the LaGrange *True Issue*, and the Austin *State Gazette* echoed the report that "the outrage" was the work of Germans who determined to "demolish" *Die Union* because it was an "abolition concern." Friends of Flake called the act "lynch spirit" on the part of native mechanics who wanted to settle old economic grievances against the Germans. One of Flake's friends stated that "*Die Union* was no abolition concern, but a Union paper, and that the editor, Mr. Flake was an old Texan, a slave holder, and a better Southern man" than his critics. This observer pointed out that if "the destruction of life, liberty, and property for opinion's sake"

[72] Galveston *News*, January 22, 1861; San Antonio *Alamo Express*, February 4, 1861; "Galveston Sketches," MS, pp. 302–307; Ben Stuart, "Necrology," MS.

[73] Galveston *News*, January 22, 1861.

was condoned, Galveston might soon witness "coercion with a venge-ance."[74]

On the state level also events were moving toward a climax. On December 3, 1860, a group of secession leaders at Austin formally had called for an election of delegates to a secession convention. This election was scheduled to be held on January 8, 1861; the resulting convention was to meet in Austin on January 28th.

In order to provide Island delegates to this convention, James P. Cole, Chief Justice of Galveston County, on January 8th set up a formal election mechanism to provide the voters of the county with the means to elect representatives. R. C. Campbell, E. B. Nichols and John Muller, the candidates previously nominated by the county convention, presented themselves to the voters as prosecession candidates. Out of 1,022 votes cast Campbell received 601, Muller 508, and E. B. Nichols 900 votes.[75] The only choice allowed voters in this election was from among Galvestonians who favored secession.[76]

During the critical opening days of the year 1861, unrest prevailed in all parts of the state. Faced with the prospect of the forthcoming secession convention, Governor Houston was forced to act. In an effort to retain control of the legal government of Texas, he called the legislature to meet one week before the convention. At this same time South Carolina, Georgia, Florida, Alabama and Mississippi were on the way out of the Union. When the legislature met, Houston spoke to the body recommending that the state remain in the Union. The lawmakers were not in sympathy with the governor's views. They passed a resolution recognizing the constituent authority of the forthcoming convention. When this organization met on January 28th, the governor sparred with the delegates trying a delaying tactic, but he was not successful. On February 1st, the convention voted 166 to 7 for secession.[77]

As soon as news of the passage of the Ordinance of Secession

---

[74] San Antonio *Alamo Express,* February 4, 1861.

[75] Ernest William Winkler (editor), *Journal of the Secession Convention of Texas, 1861,* pp. 426–427.

[76] Lynn to Russell, January 15, 1861, MS, F.O.

[77] Winkler, *Journal of the Secession Convention,* pp. 252–261.

reached Galveston, both the *Civilian* and the *News* published one-page extras announcing the event as a fact indicating the certainty of eventual secession.[78] Arthur Lynn was astonished to note that the feeling of the majority of the Galvestonians "was not one of regret that a strong and vigorous nation was overthrown by a deplorable political schism, but rather one of joy and congratulation that they can now free themselves from a connection which had been injurious to their interests."[79]

The Ordinance of Secession provided that the voters of Texas were to be given an opportunity to accept or reject the decision of the convention by means of a popular referendum which was to be held on February 23rd.[80] During the interim preceding the referendum, a state Committee on Public Safety acting in the name of the convention and headed by J. C. Robertson, assumed quasi-governing power. The Galveston merchant General E. B. Nichols, a leading member of the committee, was appointed to the post of chief financial agent for the committee, and was assigned the task of procuring and organizing the military potentialities available on the Texas Gulf Coast into an instrument which could serve the state secession government then taking shape. An important part of this operation was the effort to acquire the military and naval equipment then in the hands of the federal troops and customs authorities in Texas.[81]

At various times in February and March General Nichols mobilized about 825 men from Galveston militia companies and employed them to wrest material from federal troops in Brazos Santiago, Indianola, and Brownsville.[82] At the same time he began to negotiate for the transfer of the United States revenue cutter the *Henry Dodge* to the control of the Texas Committee of Safety. Lieutenant W. F. Rogers and the crew of the *Dodge*, nominally under the local control of the customs collector Hamilton Stuart, agreed to resign from that service in a body and place themselves under Nichols' control as soon as they

[78] Galveston *Civilian*, February 2, 1861; Galveston *News*, February 2 and 4, 1861.
[79] Lynn to Lyons, February 5, 1861, MS, F.O.
[80] Winkler, *Journal of The Secession Convention*, p. 254.
[81] *Ibid.*, pp. 262–404.
[82] *Ibid.*, pp. 255–258 and 333–351.

had received their March 1st pay allotments. The general promised the lieutenant and his men the same rank and pay which they were enjoying in the federal service. When it became apparent that Lieutenant Rogers and his men planned to turn the *Dodge* over to Nichols, Hamilton Stuart refused to honor the lieutenant's requisitions for the supplies and the payroll funds needed to keep the vessel in operation. In these circumstances the Committee of Safety assumed this obligation at once.[83]

Most other federal activities and facilities were also taken over by the Committee during the months of February and March. For one thing, it assumed the obligations of the federal government in regard to mail service contracts in effect in Texas.[84] Perhaps more important, it also acquired control of such federal installations as light houses and harbor facilities in Galveston. A threat of force applied through orders from General Nichols implemented by the defected customs cutter the *Dodge* was sufficient to bring about the transfer.[85]

In other areas of the state similar activities on the part of the Committees on Public Safety occurred during the last two weeks of February. Realizing that the momentum of the secession faction was too strong to resist short of a resort to civil war in Texas, the Unionists and the moderates gave up their positions by default. Agents of the federal government tried to encourage Sam Houston to make a fight for a control of the state or at least to attempt to keep Texas out of the Southern Confederacy and to persuade it to take a neutral position under a revived Lone Star Republic. Some of these improvisations might possibly have been developed into countermovements which could have harnessed the quite considerable but by then intimidated Union sentiment in Texas. In any case, this possibility caused the Committee of Safety much worry during the anxious weeks in February and March. All of these improvisations, however, evaporated in the face of the determined and fast-moving secessionist leadership. When Gover-

[83] *Ibid.*, pp. 181–182 and 389–395; *The War of the Rebellion, Official Records of the Union and Confederate Armies*, Series I, Volume I, pp. 535–536 and IV, p. 113; hereafter cited as *Official Records*.

[84] Winkler, *Journal of the Secession Convention*, pp. 150–151 and 241.

[85] *Ibid.*, pp. 394–396.

nor Houston bowed to the superior weight of his opponents, the opposition to secession disintegrated.[86]

Galvestonians taking part in the popular referendum to ratify or to reject the Ordinance of Secession which took place in Galveston on February 23rd were profoundly influenced by the dominating success achieved in the city and on the Gulf Coast by the Committee of Safety under the able direction of General Nichols. Not only the display of organized military companies and the sudden prosperity resulting from the unusual expenditures arising from this new activity, but also the apparently easy victories which the local forces were enjoying in acquiring the stores and equipment from the retiring federal forces gave the secessionists an advantage which completely overwhelmed the few staunch Unionists who still refused to join the "band wagon." On the evening of February 23rd the officials conducting the referendum announced that 765 Galvestonians had voted for secession and only 33 had opposed it.

When the state convention reassembled on March 2nd to tally the state-wide results, it was learned that 46,129 Texans had voted for secession and 14,697 had voted against it. Immediately thereafter, the convention formally announced that Texas was from that day onward no longer a member of the Union. A few days later, when Sam Houston and others in the old regime refused to take the "test oath" of allegiance the general was forced out of the governorship and the Lieutenant Governor Edward Clark took over the reins of the new state government.[87]

As soon as the word of these official acts reached the Island, Hamilton Stuart turned the keys and the resources of the Customs House over to the state authorities. Clearances of ships in the port, some of whose status had been in some doubt, could now be granted, with the necessary papers made out in the name of the State of Texas. The foreign

---

[86] See the following: J. W. Moore to Governor Clark, April 13, 1861 and T. M. Joseph (Mayor of Galveston) to Governor Clark, April 13, 1861, Governors' Letter Books; *Official Records, Armies,* Ser. I, Vol. I, pp. 551, 573, 598–599 and 625–626; Walter Prescott Webb, *The Texas Rangers,* pp. 197–216.

[87] Winkler, *Journal of the Secession Convention,* pp. 252–261.

trade consuls adjusted their official documents accordingly. Arthur Lynn wrote that he "looked for a peaceable adjustment between the two separate nations." A low-tariff or free-trade situation between Galveston and Britain, in Lynn's view, would result in a large, direct exchange of Texas cotton for manufactured goods.[88] Trade and life in the city proceeded in the "usual way; except for the large display of volunteer companies there was nothing to indicate that a revolution had occurred."[89]

On April 19th, seven days after the opening of the attack on Fort Sumter, a dramatic incident occurred on Galveston Island which thrust a disturbing and ominously prophetic note into the exciting events which were adding exhilaration to life in the city during this historic period of transition. Sam Houston—sullen and angry because he had been shouldered aside by new leaders and because some newspapers were accusing him of making treasonous contacts with agents of Abraham Lincoln—determined to deliver a public address to the Islanders in an effort to clarify his position in the secession crisis.

When word of Houston's intention reached the city, responsible citizens from both sides of the secession issue were fearful that a harangue by the old warrior would end in a scene of mob violence. Therefore when the general arrived by steamboat, he was met at the wharf by a committee composed of four Galvestonians—Sydnor, Stuart, Nichols, and McLean—men who represented both sides of the controversy. These men told the general that he ought not to attempt to speak because the city was filled with newly organized troops which had been assembled to make a demonstration against the United States forces at Fort Brown.[90] "Old Sam," said an eyewitness to this exchange, "rose up"; he could look very large. He said to the committee: "Gentlemen, if I should go back home, as you suggest, it would go all over Texas that Sam Houston was scared out of making a speech. No, I can't do it."

[88] Lynn to Lyons, March 11 and 14, 1861, MS, F.O.

[89] Lynn to Lyons, March 30 and April 2, 1861 and Lynn to Russell, March 11, 1861, MSS, F.O.

[90] Houston Telegraph, April 23, 1861; Brazoria *Texas Republican,* May 4, 1861.

With a few friends, Houston walked up the street which was full of soldiers. Some of them were threatening. There were also armed civilians in the streets.

When they came to the door of the court house they found that it was locked. Someone said: "Go to the balcony of the Tremont Hotel." It was necessary to go up the back way to reach the balcony. As they went up the stairs a man from the crowd that had been following said: "Let's hang the damned old scoundrel!" He made a lunge forward, but a friend of General Houston turned about and kicked the assailant in the stomach; he rolled back down the wooden stairs. The party kept on and General Houston began his speech from the wooden balcony.[91]

A traveler named Thomas North was in Galveston that day. The danger of a riot was so great that he had been advised by his host not to leave his hotel. However, when the noise of the crowd died down, Thomas North ventured out upon the street and gazed up at Sam Houston standing upon the wooden balcony addressing a silent and unfriendly gathering.

There he stood, an old man of seventy years, on the balcony ten feet above the thousands assembled to hear him, where every eye could scan his magnificent form; straight as an arrow, with deep set and penetrating eyes, looking out from heavy and thundering brows, a high open forehead, with something of the infinite intellectual shadowed there.

Thomas North heard his "deep basso voice which shook and commanded the soul of the hearer." Added to this, the observer noted the powerful manner of the speaker, "made up of deliberation, self-possession and restrained majesty of action leaving the hearer impressed with the feeling that more of his power was hidden than revealed."

The following is North's account of Sam Houston's speech to the secessionists in Galveston:

The drift of Houston's speech was—*the inexpediency and bad policy of secession.*

He told them they could secure without secession what they proposed to

91 Lynn to Lyons, April 20, 1861, MS, F.O.; Ben C. Stuart, Scrapbook, MS, pp. 71–72.

secure by it. He gave the greater force to his declarations by appealing to them to know if he had not generally been right in the past history of Texas, when any great issue was at stake. Told them he made Texas and they knew it, and it was not immodest for him to say so; that the history of old Sam Houston was the history of Texas and they knew it; that he fought and won the battle of annexation, and they knew it; that he originally organized and established the Republic of Texas, and they knew it; that he wrested Texas from the despotic sway of Santa Anna; that he commanded at San Jacinto, where the great Mexican leader was whipped and captured, and they knew it.

"Some of you," he continued, "opposed the annexation of Texas to the United States, and I suppose have never forgiven me, even to this day, but I appeal to your sober judgments if, as it were, the very next day after annexation became history, Texas did not enter upon a career of fortune she had never realized before. I appeal to you for the frank confession that you have always prospered most when you have listened to my counsels. I am an old man now. I knew you in infancy, took you and dandled you on my knee, nursed you through all your baby ailments, and with great care and solicitude watched and aided your elevation to political and commercial manhood. Will you now reject these last counsels of your political father, and squander your political patrimony in riotous adventure, which I now tell you, and with something of prophetic ken, will land you in fire and rivers of blood.

"Some of you laugh to scorn the idea of bloodshed as a result of secession, and jocularly propose to drink all the blood that will ever flow in consequence of it! But let me tell you what is coming on the heels of secession. The time will come when your fathers and husbands, your sons and brothers, will be herded together like sheep and cattle at the point of the bayonet; and your mothers and wives, and sisters, and daughters, will ask, Where are they? and echo will answer, where?

"You may," said he, "after the sacrifice of countless millions of treasure, and hundreds of thousands of precious lives, as a bare possibility, win Southern independence, if God be not against you; but I doubt it. I tell you that while I believe with you in the doctrines of State rights, the North is determined to preserve this Union. They are not a fiery impulsive people as you are, for they live in cooler climates. But when they begin to move in a given direction, where great interests are involved, such as the present issues before the country, they move with the steady momentum and perserverance of a mighty avalanche, and what I fear is they will overwhelm the South with ignoble defeat, and I would say, amen, to the suffering and defeat I have pictured if the present difficulties could find no other solution, and that too by peaceable means. I believe they can. Otherwise I would say, 'Better die freemen than live slaves.'

"Whatever course my State shall determine to pursue my faith in State supremacy and State rights will carry my sympathies with her. And as Henry Clay, my political opponent on annexation said, when asked why he allowed his son to go into the Mexican War, 'My country, right or wrong,' so I say, my State, right or wrong."

We noticed several times the very men applauding the speech who had opposed the speaker and the speaking in the morning. The power of General Houston over a Texas audience was magical to the last degree, and doubtless well understood by himself; hence he feared no mobs.[92]

The speech was "listened to quietly, with now and then some cheers and laughter." At the end Colonel Sydnor "called for three cheers"; a part of the audience responded.[93] When the general came down again into the streets there was no one who wanted to "make trouble." The old warrior's magnetism and his logic had achieved a sobering effect.

However, "one blustering officer" had previously made threats that Sam Houston would not be permitted to make the speech. The general "inquired after this man." He kept demanding of the crowd that "they produce the officer, but they were quiet." The officer's friends "had got him out of the way, for if General Houston had found him, there would have been trouble." General Houston's friends finally persuaded him to leave the city before some incident occurred.[94]

The uneasy public order, the divisive spirit illustrated by the Houston incident, characterized the early secession days on the Island. The old cohesive unity of the Islanders did not begin to return until some weeks later when the harsh events of war began to take their toll. When however, the excitement of political conflict and the exhilaration of vocal defiance gave place to the grim reality of economic pressure and the humiliation of military occupation, then the Islanders

[92] Thomas North, *Journal,* 88–95.
[93] Houston *Telegraph,* April 23, 1861.
[94] Ben Stuart "Scrapbook," MS, pp. 71–72; Lynn to Lyons, April 20, 1861 and Lynn to Russell, April 20, 1861. MSS, F.O.

were drawn together not only in the face of a common enemy, but also in the face of a callous disregard on the part of friends. First, the Yankee blockaders closed off the city's trade with the ports of the world; and shortly thereafter, the Texas and Confederate military authorities decided to abandon the Island to the Yankees as an undefendable outpost. To add to the injury the mainland-oriented authorities insisted that the Island City should be burned to the ground and its wells filled with ashes as a gesture of inhospitality to the Yankees. Faced with abandonment and desertion on their rear, the federal gunboats at their harbor entrance, and the severe hardships of war time, the Islanders defiantly refused to allow their Queen City to be destroyed.

The surrender of Galveston to an insignificant federal force in October, 1862, aroused political repercussions sufficient to require the authorities to remove Paul O. Hebert, the Confederate general commanding in Texas.[95] Shortly afterwards General John B. Magruder, the new commander of Southern forces on the Gulf Coast, wishing to regain a military reputation he had but recently lost in Virginia, organized a hasty expedition and recaptured the Island from the federals during the morning hours of January 1st, 1863.

Although Magruder made a great public show of fortifying the Island's earthworks, he did not choose to commit his best artillery in a defense of the Island. Like Hebert before him, Magruder decided to make Houston rather than Galveston the stronghold of his command. If the federals had chosen to make a serious effort at any time during the remaining war years they could have retaken the Island.[96] The Galvestonians, being cognizant of this fact as well as of the Northern gunboats blockading the port, were constantly aware of the immediate presence of the enemy. Their threatened position was in sharp contrast to the security enjoyed by persons living in the interior, and this

[95] Galveston *News,* October 16, 1862; Houston *Telegraph,* November 10, 1862.

[96] Thomas E. Taylor, *Running the Blockade: A Personal Narrative of Adventure, Risks, and Escapes During the American Civil War,* pp. 152–157; Ballinger Diary, January 10, 1864, MS.

fact tended to impair friendly relations between the Galvestonians and Texans living on the mainland.

During the years 1863 to 1865 the Island was used as a garrison housing a part of the thousands of idle troops that remained in Texas. The large number of Texas troops kept west of the Mississippi for political and strategic reasons, were garrisoned on the Island in an effort to discourage an attempted federal reoccupation. The Confederate military authorities apparently decided to use men rather than artillery to defend the city because this plan provided the Gulf Coast with a mobile reserve and, in the event that the Island had to be surrendered again to the federal forces, the troops could be evacuated, whereas heavy artillery could not be removed under battle conditions. At all times during the war Galveston was written off as expendable.[97]

The large numbers of idle troops stationed on the Island were an economic asset to the Galvestonians; however, as the months passed and the fortunes of the Confederacy waned, serious disturbances arose between the soldiers and the civilians.[98] In the early period of the blockade the economy of the Island depended upon servicing the needs of the military. Later, when the seafaring Galvestonians and their associates the blockade-runners developed techniques which enabled them to outwit the federal war vessels, a thriving sea trade arose between Galveston and the ports of Europe and of the West Indies.[99] This was particularly true during the latter part of the year 1864 and 1865 because by that time the Southern seaports east of the Mississippi had been closed and the contraband trade at Matamoros had been curtailed by the federals.

Facing an almost desperate military, economic and social situation

[97] *Official Records,* Armies, Ser. I, Vol. IV, pp. 130–131; Ballinger Diary, January 16, 1863 and January 10, 1864, MS.

[98] San Antonio *Semi-Weekly,* February 12, 1863; Lynn to J. C. Massie, April 11, 1862, MS, F.O.; Taylor, *Running The Blockade,* pp. 159–160; Oscar Farish to Ballinger, April 30, 1864, Ballinger Papers, MS.

[99] William Watson, *Adventures of a Blockade Runner: or Trade in Time of War,* 188–314; *Official Records,* Navy, Ser. I, Vol. XXI, p. 720; J. P. Austin, *The Blue and the Gray,* pp. 183–190.

those Galvestonians who either had not the money to leave the Island or did not wish to abandon their property interest there began to accent their old seafaring, mercantile tradition; after all the maritime pursuits of smuggling, bartering and trading had all been a part of the Island's history.

The first two years of the War had convinced the Islanders that they had been virtually abandoned not only by the Confederate military but by the Texas mainlanders, as well. They realized also that on the first approach of a strong federal force the soldiers stationed on the Island would be removed to more secure inland fortifications. Understanding these facts the Galvestonians determined to make the best of their own situation. As inhabitants of a seaport city they had always been skilled at utilizing a variety of ways to extract money from persons temporarily residing in the port. They not only combined their resources and set up small enterprises to exploit to the utmost the Confederate payroll sent to the soldiers and officers stationed on the Island, but also the larger entrepreneurs combined with European and West Indian mercantile adventurers to inaugurate a substantial blockade-running trade.[100]

Once the ports of Mobile, Alabama and Wilmington, North Carolina had been closed, Galveston was the one remaining source for cotton to the very experienced blockade runners from Europe and the West Indian ports. In the last month of the War this trade showed signs of a remarkable growth with hundreds of bales accumulating on the wharves waiting for shipment. All of this came to nought as the War ended and the federals came in to acquire the cotton waiting export from Texas.

Thus, while the beleaguered Islanders were still loyal to Texas and to the Southern cause they had learned that their survival during this

[100] Watson, *Adventures of a Blockade Runner,* p. 258; *Official Records, Navy,* Ser. I, Vol. XXI, p. 720; Austin, *The Blue and the Gray* pp. 183–190; Houston *Telegraph,* June 20, August 12, 1864; Thomas E. Taylor, *Running the Blockade,* pp. 252–276; Ballinger Diary, January 10, 1864, MS; X. B. Debray, *A Sketch of the History of Debray's (26th) Regiment,* p. 11; *Official Records, Navies,* Ser. Vol. XIX, I, p. 261.

war depended solely upon their own devices. In these circumstances those who were required to remain in the city during the conflict recovered their old social unity which had been so badly damaged by the divisive effects of the secession crisis and aided each other in exploiting the few commercial opportunities arising from the war.[101]

[101] The author is at present engaged in writing a second volume which will cover the Civil War on the Gulf Coast.

A COMMENTARY ON SOURCES

Manuscripts

Valuable manuscript material for students interested in the history of the Galveston Gulf Coast during the fifties is available in various collections. The following comment concerning these collections of material is arranged in alphabetical order, but that does not necessarily imply the same order of evaluation as to their importance as source material on the history of the Texas Gulf Coast; all the collections mentioned are valuable.

William Pitt Ballinger's diary and his business and personal papers are of prime interest. Ballinger, who later attained a position of eminence in the Texas bar, was a rising young lawyer during this period. His practice included the handling of the legal affairs of many of the largest estates in the area as well as the legal business of many of the most important business and political leaders; for this reason his legal and personal papers as well as his voluminous diary provide a remarkable fund of information concerning the early history of the Texas Gulf Coast.

The papers of the British consular officer in Galveston, Arthur T. Lynn, are also of prime importance. Lynn, a Cambridge University educated Britisher, who was in a position to make numerous nonprovincial evaluations and comments regarding many aspects of affairs on the Texas Gulf Coast, presents an insight into three decades of Texas history which is unique indeed. In fact, it would appear that one of the neglected sources of interesting commentary upon the American scene by foreign observers who actually understood the affairs they were evaluating lies in the vast and so far untapped material in the files of the correspondence sent to their respective foreign offices by the many consular officers serving in the seaport and also the inland cities of the United States during the nineteenth century.

The papers of Guy M. Bryan, politician and member of a leading Texas family, contain some valuable material; however, as in the case of the Ballinger papers, the researcher must bring with him considerable knowledge of the personalities and events involved to gain much understandable information from the collection.

The R. B. Kingsbury papers and the Joseph Kleiber papers held by the Texas History Center in Austin are valuable for information concerning the African slave trade and for items pertaining to Texas trade with Union merchants during the Civil War period. Thomas F. McKinney's papers are of minor significance as far as the 1850's are concerned, are very important for the Civil War period, particularly in connection with the cotton trade in Texas.

The Lorenzo Sherwood collection of clippings is valuable inasmuch as it is the most complete file of information concerning Sherwood's important contribution to the political and economic thought on the Texas Gulf Coast during the critical fifties.

The various collections of papers and manuscript books and articles written by Ben C. Stuart are very useful for an understanding of the early history of Galveston. His observations are of particular interest because he was the son of Hamilton Stuart, who was the port's Customs Collector and also the publisher-editor of the Galveston *Civilian*. Since Ben was in his early teens during the late fifties, his observations are of primary value.

The private collection of Captain John Grant Tod's papers are valuable for the student interested in the history of Texas railroads during the 1850's.

Samuel May Williams was an important merchant and banker in Texas during the days of the Republic and also during the fifties. The Rosenberg Library has a large collection of his business papers. An examination of this collection, however, leads one to believe that important parts of Williams' papers have either been lost or are still in unknown private hands. Speaking of missing papers, one might mention the deplorable lack of any collection worth mentioning of the correspondence of the three important editor-politicians Willard Richardson, Hamilton Stuart and Ferdinand Flake.

The manuscript records of Galveston, Harris, Seguin, and Bexar counties as well as the minutes of the Galveston City Council and the voluminous manuscript records of the Galveston city and port ordinances were useful in this study. Also in the same category, the records of the correspondence between the Customs Collector of Galveston and the Treasury Department in Washington were very helpful as background material for an understanding of the economic and political activities in Galveston during the fifties. The records of the Customs Collector for the years between 1845 and 1865 were taken to Washington at the end of the Civil War; consequently, these records in their original form are available only in the Treasury Archives collections in Washington or on microfilms provided for research students by the Library of Congress. An examination of the existing film record leads one to believe that large portions of the Galveston records must have been lost or mislaid during the transfer of these documents to Washington following the close of the war; or perhaps the microfilms are incomplete. The best record, therefore, of trade statistics for the port of Galveston between 1845 and 1861 are to be found in the British consular reports and in the files of the Galveston *Civilian*. The records of Trade Statistics for the port of Galveston printed in the *Eighth Census* reports are, for some reason, not in accord with other existing records and appear to be untrustworthy.

Court Records

The reported or printed records of the Texas Supreme Court not only contain much useful material concerning the banking and railroad controversies of the fifties but also contain revealing details about the various persons and business houses involved in the reported law suits. Much more valuable, however, are the innumerable files of the many cases and litigations which were tried in the District Court at Galveston and at Houston. The minute detail found in these files is perhaps the largest single source of information concerning Galveston during the fifties. It is necessary, however, to possess a fair working knowledge of the Island's social and economic life and of the personalities and events of the period in order to make worthwhile use of this vast source of detail.

Printed Public Documents

The Journals of the Texas Legislature, the Session Laws, and departmental reports were useful in this study; the summary nature of these printed proceedings, of course, leaves much to be desired. The various reports issued by the United States Senate and House were also very useful, particular so concerning the filibustering and African slave-trade activities in Texas; the same may be said concerning the *British and Foreign State Papers* and *Hansard's Parliamentary Debates.*

Pamphlets, Directories and Newspapers

The several city directories and gazettes printed in Galveston and Houston contain much minute detail difficult to find elsewhere. A record of many of the political party conventions and related activities can be found in the pamphlets listed in the following bibliography. The four newspapers, three in Galveston and one in Houston, published as these organs were by able journalists, provide the researcher with an excellent and varied newspaper coverage of Texas Gulf Coast affairs during the fifties. Fires and floods, however, destroyed many of the collected files of Gulf Coast newspapers during the nineteenth century. There is no complete file of the four important papers in existence. Nonetheless, by working the holdings of the Rosenberg Library, Houston Public Library, San Antonio Public Library and the University of Texas Library it is possible to read a very large number of these important newspapers.

Magazines and Serial Publications

The volumes of *De Bow's Review* and *Blackwoods' Magazine* were useful in this study. The various national serial publications printed in the interest of the railroad industry during the fifties were of little use in a study of Texas railroads because the material printed concerning Texas was seldom factually accurate and was almost always of a promotional nature. As regards to modern serial articles, those printed in the *Southwestern Historical Quarterly* listed in the bibliography were all useful; the titles cited by the following authors were of particular assistance: Eugene C. Barker, Abigail Curlee, Andrew Forest Muir, Anna Irene Sandbo, and Harold Schoen.

Four significant studies dealing with Texas in the fifties have recently appeared in the *Quarterly*. Andrew Forest Muir, "The Railroads Come to Houston, 1857–1861," in Vol. LXIV (July, 1960), 44–63, is an excellent study of this subject in addition to being a close examination of other economic and social aspects of the city of Houston during the years immediately preceding the Civil War. Larry Jay Gage, "The City of Austin on the Eve of the Civil War," in Vol. LXIII (January,

1960), 428–438, is most useful. Ellen Bartlett Ballou, "Schudder's Journey to Texas, 1859," in Vol. LXIII (July, 1959), 1–14, is an interesting study of life in the interior of Texas, especially of the Texas Germans living in the area around San Antonio. Ralph A. Wooster, "Analysis of the Membership of the Texas Secession Convention," in Vol. LXII, (January, 1959), 322–335, gives a valuable examination of the economic and social status of the members of the Texas Secession Convention based upon the 1860 Census returns.

General Works—Primary

Captain Richard Drake's *Revelations of a Slave Smuggler* was of value in the examination of the African slave trade; however, this work was in part written almost as a work of fiction and therefore must be used with great care and only as corroboration of already established facts. James Fremantle's diary was valuable, particularly for its picture of slavery in Texas and for the causes of secession; his travels in Texas, of course, occurred after the Civil War had already begun. F. R. Lubbock's *Memoirs*, presenting the version of his part in affairs which he wanted put into the record, is more useful for what he left out than for what he wrote. The book, written long after most of the events described, is not accurate as to facts or dates—and his interpretation of events is also open to question. James D. Lynch's *Bench and Bar of Texas* is valuable biographical work and has some valuable details concerning major legal and constitutional controversies which occurred during this period. The biographical data is of limited use because the essays omit facts which might not be flattering to the subject under discussion. The accounts of travelers and the memoirs of the blockade runners were useful for their descriptions of the Island and the Gulf Coast; some of the more interesting accounts include those by Martin Maris, Thomas North, Frederick Law Olmsted, Thomas E. Taylor, William Walker, and William Watson.

General Works—Secondary

Many special works of a secondary nature were examined in this study; several general histories of this period of Texas history and of the national scene were used. Most of these are listed in the bibliography. There has been, however, no general annotated work written by a historian which records the history of the Texas Gulf Coast. The books which have been written concerning the Coast and Galveston Island in particular are of a popular nature and therefore are of little value to the historian. No adequate monograph has yet been written concerning such important items as the financial history of the state or the history of the Texas railroads. Likewise, no monograph has been written regarding the important merchant and trading houses of the Texas Gulf Coast with the single exception of the scholarly book on Gail Borden written by Professor Joe B. Frantz.

In the area of church history the outstanding works for Galveston are William Manning Morgan's *Trinity Protestant Episcopal Church, Galveston* and William Stuart Red's *History of the Presbyterian Church in Texas.* All the others in this category are of a popular nature and are often inaccurate.

In the matter of politics there is no comprehensive political history of Texas nor of the Gulf Coast for the pre-Civil War period; Anna Irene Sandbo's article in the *Southwestern Historical Quarterly,* previously mentioned, is very helpful. W. E. Burghardt DuBois' study of the African slave trade was very useful in this examination of the same trade in Texas. The monographs dealing with the related subject of filibustering were useful but they almost completely ignored the important part Texans played in these adventures.

Regarding the foreigner in Texas during this period, the works by Rudolf L. Biesele and Ella Lonn mentioned in the bibliography were very useful. Biesele's work, however, deals primarily with the Germans in the interior and only incidentally with the Galveston Germans.

In the matter of the professions Pat Ireland Nixon's history of medicine in Texas was very helpful; and Lynch's work mentioned earlier was a useful reference for data concerning the legal profession.

This brief comment merely mentions the major sources which were helpful in this effort to examine the history of Galveston during the fifties. Speaking in general terms, however, it was necessary to base this study mostly upon primary material. Galveston and the adjacent Texas Gulf Coast area have not attracted much interest among Texas historians who have apparently found the Great Plains, the cattle ranches, and the vast inland empire of the state a more fruitful area for research. It seems, nevertheless, that the not inconsiderable sea-orientated history of the varied area encompassed in the Texas land mass might also be worthy of closer examination.

BIBLIOGRAPHY

Manuscript Sources

Ballinger Papers, MSS. Barker Texas History Center, University of Texas, Austin.

Ballinger, William Pitt. Diary, MS. Rosenberg Library, Galveston.

Borden, Gail. Papers, MSS. Rosenberg Library, Galveston.

British Consulate Papers. Annual Reports of the British Consulate, Galveston, on Shipping, Navigation, Trade, Commerce, Agriculture, Population, and Industries to the British Foreign Office, 1850–1861. British Public Record Office. Some of this material is also contained in the Galveston British Consular Collection held by the Library and Archives of the San Jacinto Monument Commission.

British Foreign Office Papers. Consular Reports and Letters. British Public Record Office, London.

Bryan, Guy M. Papers, MSS. Texas History Center, Austin.

Census Reports for 1850 and 1860, MSS. Texas State Library, Austin.

District Court of Galveston, Minutes, 1856–1861, MSS. Galveston County Court House, Galveston.

Dyer, Joseph Osterman. "History of Galveston," MS. Rosenberg Library, Galveston.

Flake, Ferdinand. "Register of 1864 of the Male and Female Inhabitants of Galveston City," MS. Rosenberg Library, Galveston.

Galveston County Commissioners Court, Minutes, 1856–1870, MS. Galveston County Court House, Galveston.

"Galveston Sketches." Typescript Collection in the Texas State Archives, Austin.

Governors' Letter Books. Texas State Archives, Austin.

House, T. W. Papers, MSS. Texas History Center, Austin.

Kingsbury, R. B. Papers, TS. Texas History Center, Austin.

Kleiber, Joseph. Papers, MSS. Texas History Center, Austin.

"Lutheran Church Rolls in Galveston," MS. The John Winterbotham Collection. Rosenberg Library, Galveston.

McKinney, Thomas F. Papers, MSS. Texas History Center, Austin.

Mills, Robert. Papers, MSS. Texas History Center, Austin.

Proceedings of the Mayor and Board of Aldermen of the City of Galveston, 1849–1855, MSS. Office of the Galveston City Secretary.

Ordinance Book, 1857–1865, MS. Office of Galveston City Secretary.

Railroad Papers. Report of Tipton Walker to James B. Shaw, October 31, 1855, MS. Texas State Library Archives, Austin.

Seguin County Commissioners Court Record, Volume A (1858), MS. Seguin County Court House, Seguin, Texas.

Semi-Annual Trade Reports and Returns of Galveston Assessor and Collector, MSS. Rosenberg Library, Galveston.

Sherwood Collection, a collection of newspaper and magazine writings of Lorenzo Sherwood. Rosenberg Library, Galveston.

Stuart, Ben C. "Brief Chronology," MS. Rosenberg Library, Galveston.

—— "Galveston's Early Military Companies," MS. Rosenberg Library, Galveston.

—— "History of Galveston," MS. Rosenberg Library, Galveston.

—— "Necrology," MS. Rosenberg Library, Galveston.

—— "Scrapbook," MS. Rosenberg Library, Galveston.

Tax Assessor's Rolls, MSS. Comptroller's Department, Austin.

Tod, John Grant. Papers, MSS. A private collection owned by Mrs. Rosa Tod Hamner and John Tod Hamner of Houston.

Trinity Church, Galveston. Vestry Minutes, 1857–1888. MSS.

Tucker, Philip C. "History of Galveston, 1543–1869," MS. Texas History Center, Austin.

Williams, Samuel May. Papers, MSS. Rosenberg Library, Galveston.

Source Material Extracted from Federal and Texas
Courts of Law

James Baldridge v. *Robert and D. G. Mills*, District Court of Galveston,
March 31, 1857.

John Burnett v. *The Union Marine and Fire Insurance Company*, District
Court of Galveston, January 13, 1860.

Warren W. Buel v. *Galveston, Houston, and Henderson Railroad*, District
Court of Galveston, June 21, 1859.

Commercial and Agricultural Bank v. *Simon L. Jones and another*, 18 Texas
Reports, 811–831.

William Cook v. *Willard Richardson*, District Court of Galveston, November 23, 1860.

Henry Francis Fisher and Burchard Miller v. *William Smith Todd*, District
Court of Fredericksburg, January 17, 1856.

Galveston City Company v. *Benjamin Franklin and Henry A. Cobb*, District Court of Galveston, January 16, 1857.

The Galveston Wharf Company v. *Laurence Frosh*, District Court of Galveston, January 2, 1861.

Robert Mills and another v. *Fletcher C. Howeth*, 19 Texas Reports, 257–259.

Robert Mills v. *Alexander S. Johnston and another*, 23 Texas Reports, 309–331.

Robert Mills v. *Alexander S. Johnston and David Dewbury*, District Court
of Galveston, January 17, 1857.

Robert Mills v. *John Nooman*, District Court of Galveston, January 2, 1857.

Robert Mills and others v. *The State*, 23 Texas Reports, 295–308.

Robert Mills and another v. *Thomas J. Walton*, 19 Texas Reports, 271–273.

Robert and David Mills v. *Galveston, Houston, and Henderson Railroad*,
District Court of Galveston, July 1 and July 13, 1859.

C. A. Muller v. *Joseph Landa*, *Joseph Landa* v. *C. A. Muller*, 31 Texas Reports, 265–276.

The Peterhoff, 72 United States Reports, 28–92.

Robert Pulsford v. *Galveston, Houston, and Henderson Railroad*, District
Court of Galveston, June 30, 1859.

State of Texas v. *Adolph Flake*, District Court of Galveston, January 9,
1860.

State of Texas v. *Ferdinand Flake*, District Court of Galveston, October 7,
1848.

State of Texas v. *Theophilus Freeman,* District Court of Galveston, January 6, 1857.

State of Texas v. *Robert Mills, et al,* District Court of Galveston, January 12, 1857.

State of Texas v. *Robert Mills, John W. Jockusch, and David G. Mills,* District Court of Galveston, January 12, 1857.

State of Texas v. *Thomas B. Chubb,* District Court of Galveston, January 24, 1857.

State of Texas v. *Samuel May Williams and others,* 8 Texas Reports, 255–267.

State of Texas v. *Samuel May Williams, et al,* District Court of Galveston, January 20, 1857.

S. H. Summers v. *Robert Mills and others,* 21 Texas Reports, 78–92.

Betzy Webster v. *T. J. Heard,* 32 Texas Reports, 686–712.

Samuel M. Williams and others, v. *The State,* 23 Texas Reports, 264–292.

Printed Public Documents

BRITISH

British and Foreign State Papers. H. M. Stationery Office, London, 1841–1860.

Hansard, T. C. *et al* (editors). *Hansard's Parliamentary Debates.* Series 3. London, 1848–1860.

UNITED STATES

Congress. *Congressional Globe, Containing the Debates and Proceedings, 1833–73.* 46 vols. in 109. Washington: The *Globe* office, 1834–1873.

The Eighth Census of the United States, Population. Washington: Government Printing Office, 1864.

House Documents, 26th Congress, 2nd Session, V, No. 115. Washington: Government Printing Office, 1840.

House Executive Documents, 33rd Congress, 2nd Session, No. 93.

House Executive Documents, 35th Congress, 1st Session, No. 24. Washington: Government Printing Office, 1857.

House Executive Documents, 36th Congress, 2nd Session, IV, No. 7. Washington: Government Printing Office, 1860.

House Miscellaneous Documents, 47th Congress, 2nd Session, XIII. Washington: Government Printing Office, 1882–1883.

House Reports, 36th Congress, 1st Session, I, No. 74. Washington: Government Printing Office, 1859.

Official Records of the Union and Confederate Navies. 31 vols. Washington: Government Printing Office, 1894–1927.

Senate Executive Documents, 34th Congress, 1st Session, VI. Washington: Government Printing Office, 1855.

Senate Executive Documents, 35th Congress, 2nd Session, I, No. 13. Washington: Government Printing Office, 1858.

United States Engineering Department, Report of the Secretary of War in Relation to the Fortification and Defense of Galveston. Published in *Senate Executive Documents*, United States 34th Congress, 1st Session. Washington: Government Printing Office, 1855.

The War of the Rebellion: Official Records of the Union and Confederate Armies. 130 vols. Washington: Government Printing Office, 1880–1901.

TEXAS

Gammel, H. P. N. *The Laws of Texas, 1822–1897*. 10 vols. Austin: The Gammel Book Co., 1898.

Hartley, Oliver C. *A Digest of the Laws of Texas*. Philadelphia: Thomas, Cowperthwait and Co., 1850.

Texas *House Journals*, 1850–1860. Published variously by Texas State Gazette Office, Cushney and Hampton, J. W. Hampton, Marshall and Oldham, John Marshall and Company. Austin, 1850–1860.

Texas *Senate Journals*, 1850–1860. Published variously by Texas State Gazette Office, Cushney and Hampton, J. W. Hampton, Marshall and Oldham, John Marshall and Company. Austin, 1850–1860.

Texas *Session Laws*, 1845–1860. Published variously by Texas State Gazette Office, Cushney and Hampton, J. W. Hampton, Marshall and Oldham, John Marshall and Company. Austin, 1850–1860.

Winkler, Ernest William (editor). *Journal of the Secession Convention of Texas, 1861*. Austin: Austin Printing Co., 1912.

Pamphlets and Broadsides

A Brief History of the Galveston Wharf Company. Galveston: Galveston Wharf Co., 1927.

Bryan, Guy M. *Galveston Committee of Safety and Correspondence: An Address to the State of Texas*. Galveston: n.p., 1860.

By-laws of the Galveston, Houston, and Henderson Railroad Company.Galveston: Civilian Book and Job Establishment, 1860.

Carnes, J. E. *Address on the Duty of the Slave States in the Present Crisis: Delivered in Galveston, December 12, 1860, by Special Invitation of the Committee of Safety and Correspondence, and Many of the Oldest Citizens of Galveston.* Galveston: News Book and Job Office, 1860.

Charter and Bylaws of the Galveston Wharf Company. Galveston: Civilian Book and Job Printing Company, 1861.

Charter and Revised Code of Ordinances of City of Galveston Passed in Years 1856–57. Galveston: Civilian Book and Job Office, 1857.

The Constitutional Party of Texas: Addresses of the Union Executive Committee to the People of Texas. Austin: n.p., 1860.

Galveston Gas Company. A broadside explaining how to read a meter. Galveston: Civilian Steam Book and Job Press, 1860. A copy is to be seen at Eugene C. Barker Texas History Center, Austin, Texas.

Haun, Otto. *True Democracy Battles Not for Men but for Principles.* Galveston: Union Book and Job Office, 1858.

O'Rielly, Henry. *The Slave Aristocracy against Democracy: Statements Addressed to Loyal Men of All Parties; Antagonistic Principles Involved in the Rebellion.* New York: Baker and Godwin, Printers, 1862.

Oldham, Williamson Simpson. *Speech on the Resolution of the State of Texas.* Galveston: Civilian Job Press, 1861.

The Port of Galveston, U.S.A. New Orleans: Lykes Bros. Steamship Co. Inc., 1907.

Proceedings of the Democratic State Convention of Texas Held in Galveston, April 2, 1860. Galveston: News Book and Job Establishment, 1860.

Proceedings of the State Convention of the Democratic Party of the State of Texas, Which Assembled at Waco, Monday, May 4th, 1857. Austin: John Marshall and Co., State Printers, 1857.

A Report and Treatise on Slavery. Austin: John Marshall and Co., State Printers, 1857.

Sherwood, Lorenzo. *Memorial to Congress, January 3rd, 1866: As Regards to the New Railroad to be Constructed from Galveston to Kansas.* Galveston: Thomas Ewbank, Esq. and Others, 1866.

———. [Broadside issued by Sherwood explaining to the Citizens of Galveston why he would not deliver a scheduled address on the railroad question.] Galveston: Civilian Press, July 7, 1856.

Wall, E. L. (editor). *The Port Situation at Galveston.* Galveston: Galveston News Co., 1928.

Newspapers

Alamo Express. San Antonio, Texas.
Allgemeine Zeitung. Berlin, Germany.
Civilian. Galveston, Texas.
Daily Morning Call. Matamoros, Mexico.
Flag. Marshall, Texas.
Flake's Bulletin. Galveston, Texas.
Globe-Democrat. St. Louis, Missouri.
Herald. Galveston, Texas.
Herald. Dallas, Texas.
Herald. New York, New York.
Ledger. Philadelphia, Pennsylvania.
Mercury. Seguin, Texas.
News. Galveston, Texas.
Picayune. New Orleans, Louisiana.
San Antonio Texan. San Antonio, Texas.
Southern Intelligencer. Austin, Texas.
Standard. Clarksville, Texas.
State Gazette. Austin, Texas.
Semi-Weekly. San Antonio, Texas.
Telegraph. Houston, Texas.
Texas Republican. Brazoria, Texas.
True Delta. New Orleans, Louisiana.
True Issue. La Grange, Texas.
Die Union. Galveston, Texas.
Zeitung. Galveston, Texas.
Weekly News. Enterprise, Mississippi.

General Works

PRIMARY

Allen, William Youel. "Allen's Reminiscences," edited by W. S. Red, *Southwestern Historical Quarterly*, XVIII (January, 1915).

Austin, J. P. *The Blue and the Gray.* Atlanta: The Franklin Printing and Publishing Co., 1899.

Bartlett, Franklin Gray. "Expedition of the Alamo Rangers," *Overland Monthly*, New Series XXI (May, 1893).

"The City of Galveston," *De Bow's Review*, III (April, 1847), 348–349. Written by an unidentified European traveler.

"Commerce of Galveston," *De Bow's Review*, XXIX (December, 1860), 783.

Cushing, E. H. *The New Texas Reader: Designed for Use in the Schools.* Houston: E. H. Cushing, 1864.

Downs, Edward C. *Four Years a Scout and Spy.* Zanesville, Ohio: H. Dunne, 1866.

De Bow, J. D. B. *Statistical View of the United States . . . Being a Compendium of the Seventh Census.* Washington: Beverly Tucker, Senate Printer, 1854.

De Bow's Review. New Orleans: 1855–1867. *Passim.*

Debray, X. B. *A Sketch of the History of Debray's (26th) Regiment.* Austin: E. von Boeckmann, 1884.

Drake, Richard. *Revelations of a Slave Smuggler: Being the Autobiography of Capt. Richard Drake, an African Trader for Fifty Years, from 1807–1857.* New York: R. M. DeWitt, 1860.

"Education in Texas," *De Bow's Review*, XIX (December, 1855), 685–696.

Fenner's Southern Medical Reports. New Orleans: II (1851).

Fremantle, James Arthur Lyon. *The Fremantle Diary: Being the Journal of Lieutenant Colonel James Arthur Lyon Fremantle, Coldstream Guards, on His Three Months in the Southern States.* Edited by Walter Lord. Boston: Little, Brown and Co., 1954.

"Galveston Sugar and Trade Statistics," *Hunt's Merchant's Magazine*, XXXIX (October, 1858).

Gouge, William M. *The Fiscal History of Texas.* Philadelphia: Lippincott, Grambo and Co., 1852.

Gregg, Josiah. *Diary and Letters of Josiah Gregg.* Edited by Maurice Garland Fulton. 2 vols. Norman: University of Oklahoma, 1941.

Hobart-Hampden, Augustus Charles. *Sketches from My Life.* New York: D. Appleton and Co., 1887.

House, Edward Mandell. *The Intimate Papers of Colonel House.* Edited by Charles Seymour. 4 vols. Boston and New York: Houghton Mifflin Co., 1926.

Houston, Sam. *The Writings of Sam Houston, 1813–1863.* Edited by Amelia W. Williams and Eugene C. Barker. 8 vols. Austin: University of Texas Press, 1942–1943.

Hutchinson, W. F. "Life on the Texan Blockade," *Soldiers and Sailors Historical Society of Rhode Island: Personal Narratives.* Third series, No. 1. Providence: n.p., 1933.

Kennedy, Joseph C. G. *The Population of the United States in 1860: Compiled from the Original Return of the Eighth Census* . . . Washington: Government Printing Office, 1864.

Leonard, W. A. (compiler). *Houston City Directory for 1866.* Houston: Gray, Strickland and Co., 1866.

Linn, John Joseph. *Reminiscences of Fifty Years in Texas.* New York: D. and J. Sadlier and Co., 1883.

Lockhart, John Washington, *Sixty Years on the Brazos: the Life and Letters of Dr. John Washington Lockhart, 1824–1900.* Edited by Jennie Lockhart Wallis. Los Angeles: Dunn Brothers, 1930.

Lubbock, Francis Richard. *Six Decades in Texas: or Memoirs of Francis Richard Lubbock, Governor of Texas in War Time, 1861–1863. A Personal Experience in Business, War and Politics.* Edited by C. W. Raines. Austin: B. C. Jones and Co., Printers, 1900.

Lynch, James D. *The Bench and Bar of Texas.* St. Louis: Nixon-Jones Printing Co., 1885.

Malmesbury, James Howard Harris. *Memoirs of an Ex-minister.* 3rd edition. London: Longmans, Green and Co., 1884.

Maris, Martin. *Souvenirs d'Amerique: Relations d'un Voyage au Texas et en Haiti.* Bruxelles: M. J. Poot et Compagnie, 1863.

Morphis, J. M. *History of Texas.* New York: United States Publishing Co., 1874.

North, Thomas. [*Journal.*] *Five Years in Texas: or What You Did Not Hear during the War from 1861 to January 1866. A Narrative of His Travels, Experiences, and Observations in Texas and Mexico.* Cincinnati: Elm Street Printing Co., 1871.

"Notes on Texas," *Western Monthly Magazine,* I (September, 1858).

Olmsted, Frederick Law. *A Journey Through Texas: or a Saddle-Trip on the Southwestern Frontier with a Statistical Appendix.* New York: Dix, Edwards and Co., (London: S. Low, Son and Co.), 1857.

Richardson, Willard, *et al* (editors). *Galveston Directory, 1856–57.* Galveston: Galveston News Book and Job Office, 1857.

——, *et al* (editors). *Galveston Directory, 1859–60.* Galveston: Galveston News Book and Job Office, 1859.

——, *et al* (editors). *Texas Almanac.* Galveston: Richardson and Co., 1859–1860.

Schmitz, Joseph (editor). "Impressions of Texas in 1860" (an anonymous journal of a trip to Texas during 1859–1860), *Southwestern Historical Quarterly,* XLII (April, 1939).

Sherwood, Lorenzo, "Agencies to be Depended upon in Constructing Internal Improvements," "No. 1. Statesmanship—What is it?" *De Bow's Review,* XIX (July, 1855), 81–88.

——. "Agencies to be Depended on in the Construction of Internal Improvements, with Reference to Texas, by a Texan, No. 2." *De Bow's Review,* XIX (August, 1855), 201–205.

——. "Texas Railroads," *De Bow's Review,* XIII (October, 1852), 523–525.

Smith, Edward. *Account of a Journey through Northeastern Texas Undertaken in 1849.* London: Hamilton, Adams and Co., 1849.

Smithwick, Noah. *The Evolution of a State: or, Recollections of Old Texas Days.* Compiled by his daughter Nanna Smithwick Donaldson. Austin: The Steck Co., 1935.

Sterne, Louis. *Seventy Years of an Active Life.* London: Chiswick Press, 1912.

Taylor, Thomas E. *Running the Blockade.* 3rd edition. London: J. Murray, 1897.

"Texas," *De Bow's Review,* XXIII (August, 1867), 113–132.

Thrall, Homer S. *Pictorial History of Texas.* St. Louis: N. D. Thompson and Co., 1879.

"Trials of a Filibuster," *Harpers Weekly,* I (January 10, 1857), 23–24.

Walker, William. *The War in Nicaragua.* Mobile, Alabama, and New York: S. H. Goetzel and Co., 1860.

Watson, William. *The Adventures of a Blockade Runner: or Trade in Time of War.* London: T. F. Unwin, 1898.

Williams, R. H. *With the Border Ruffians.* New York: E. P. Dutton and Co., 1907.

SECONDARY

Acheson, Sam. *35,000 Days in Texas.* New York: The Macmillan Company, 1938.

Adams, Ephriam A. (editor). "Correspondence from the British Archives Concerning Texas, 1837–1846," *Southwestern Historical Quarterly,* XVII (October, 1913).

Alexander, De Alva Stanwood. *A Political History of the State of New York.* 2 vols. New York: Henry Holt and Co., 1906.

Bailey, Thomas A. *A Diplomatic History of the American People.* 2nd edition (?). New York: F. S. Crofts and Co., 1944.

Ballou, Ellen Bartlett. "Schudder's Journey to Texas, 1859," *Southwestern Historical Quarterly*, LXIII (July, 1959).

Bancroft, Hubert Howe. *History of the North Mexican States and Texas*. 2 vols. San Francisco: A. L. Bancroft and Co., 1889.

Barker, Eugene C. "The African Slave Trade in Texas," *Texas Historical Association Quarterly*, VI (1902).

Biesele, R. L. *The History of the German Settlements in Texas, 1831–1861*. Austin: Von Boeckmann-Jones Co., 1930.

——. "Prince Solms' Trip to Texas, 1844–45," *Southwestern Historical Quarterly*, XL (July, 1936).

Bonham, Milledge L. "The British Consuls in the Confederacy," *Columbia University Studies in History, Economics and Public Law*, XLIII, No. 3; whole No. 111 (1911).

Bridges, C. A. "The Knights of the Golden Circle: A Filibustering Fantasy," *Southwestern Historical Quarterly*, XLIV (January, 1941).

Briggs, Herbert W. *The Law of Nations*. New York: F. S. Crofts, 1946.

Carlson, Avery Luvere. *A Monetary and Banking History of Texas from the Mexican Regime to the Present Day, 1821–1929*. Fort Worth: The Fort Worth National Bank, 1930.

Carroll, H. Bailey. "Texas Collection," *Southwestern Historical Quarterly*, XLVIII (July, 1944), 87–125.

Catholic Youth Organization, Diocese of Galveston. *Centennial: The Story of the Development of the Kingdom of God on Earth in that Portion of the Vineyard Which Has Been the Diocese of Galveston*. Edited by Rev. John F. Lane. Houston: Catholic Youth Organization Centennial Book Committee, 1947.

Cohen, Henry, David Lefkowitz, and Ephraim Frisch. *One Hundred Years of Jewry in Texas*. Dallas: Jewish Advisory Committee for the Texas Centennial Religious Program, 1936.

Curlee, Abigail. "Robert Mills," *Dictionary of American Biography*, XIII edited by Dumas Malone. New York: Charles Scribners' Sons.

Cushing, E. B. "Edward Hopkins Cushing," *Southwestern Historical Quarterly*, XXV (April, 1922).

Donovan, Herbert D. A. *The Barnburners*. New York: New York University Press, 1925.

Deussen, Alexander. "The Beginnings of the Texas Railroad System," *Transactions of the Texas Academy of Science*, IX (1906), 42–74.

Dow, George Francis. *Slave Ships and Slaving*. Salem, Massachusetts: Marine Research Society, 1927.

DuBois, W. E. Burghardt. *The Suppression of the African Slave-Trade of the United States of America, 1638–1870.* New York: Longmans, Green and Co., 1896.

Eby, Frederick. *Education in Texas: Source Materials.* Austin: University of Texas, 1919.

Fields, F. T. *Texas Sketchbook: A Collection of Historical Stories from the Humble Way.* Illustrated by E. M. Schiwetz. Houston. The Humble Oil and Refining Company, 1956.

Fornell, Earl W. "Confederate Seaport Strategy," *Civil War History*, II (December, 1956).

Fornell, Martha and Earl W. "A Century of German Song in Texas," *American-German Review*, October–November, 1957.

Frantz, Joe B. *Gail Borden: Dairyman to a Nation.* Norman: University of Oklahoma Press, 1951.

Gage, Larry Jay. "The City of Austin on the Eve of the Civil War," *Southwestern Historical Quarterly*, LXIII (January, 1960).

Galveston Historical Society. *Historic Galveston Homes.* Galveston: n.p., 1951.

Hannemann, Max. "Die Seehöfen von Texas, ihr geographischen Grundlagen, ihre Entwicklung und Bedeutung," *Frankfurter Geographische Hefte*, Zweiter Jahrgang, Hft. 1 (1928).

Hansen, Marcus Lee. *The Atlantic Migration, 1607–1860.* Edited by Arthur M. Schlesinger, Cambridge, Massachusetts: Harvard University Press, 1940.

Havins, T. R. "Administration of the Sequestration Act in the Confederate District Court for the Western District of Texas, 1862–1865." *Southwestern Historical Quarterly.* XLIII (January, 1940), 295–322.

Kisch, Guido. "The Revolution of 1848 and the Jewish 'On to America' Movement," *Publications of American Jewish Historical Society*, XXXVIII (March, 1949), 185–237.

Kopp, Frederick. *Aus und Über Amerika: Tätsachen und Erlebnisse.* 2 vols. Berlin: F. Braunschweig, 1876.

Lonn, Ella. *Foreigners in the Confederacy.* Chapel Hill: University of North Carolina Press, 1940.

Mathieson, William Law. *Great Britain and the Slave Trade, 1839–1865.* London, New York: Longmans, Green and Co., 1929.

McGregor, Stuart. "The Texas Almanac," *Southwestern Historical Quarterly*, L (April, 1947).

Morgan, William Manning. *Trinity Protestant Episcopal Church, Galveston, Texas, 1841–1953.* Houston and Galveston: Anson Jones Press, 1954.

Muir, Andrew Forest. "The Destiny of Buffalo Bayou," *Southwestern Historical Quarterly*, XLVII (October, 1943).

———. "The Railroads Come to Houston, 1857–1861," *Southwestern Historical Quarterly*, LXIV (July, 1960).

———. "Railroad Enterprise in Texas, 1836–1841," *Southwestern Historical Quarterly*, XLVII (April, 1944).

Nevins, Allan. *The Emergence of Lincoln.* 2 vols. New York: Charles Scribner's Sons, 1950.

Nichols, Ruth G. "Samuel May Williams," *Southwestern Historical Quarterly*, LVI (October, 1952).

Nixon, Pat Ireland. *A History of the Texas Medical Association, 1853–1953.* Austin: University of Texas Press, 1954.

Ousley, Clarence. *Galveston in Nineteen Hundred.* Atlanta: W. C. Chase, 1900.

Owsley, Frank Lawrence. *King Cotton Diplomacy.* Chicago: University of Chicago Press, 1931.

Pierce, Harry H. *Railroads of New York: A Study of Government Aid, 1826–1875.* Cambridge, Massachusetts: Harvard University Press, 1953.

Ramsdell, Charles W. "Reconstruction in Texas," *Columbia University Studies in History, Economics and Public Law*, XXXVI, No. 1; whole No. 95 (1910).

Red, William Stuart, *A History of The Presbyterian Church in Texas.* Austin: Steck Co., 1936.

Reed, S. G. *A History of the Texas Railroads and of Transportation Conditions Under Spain and Mexico and the Republic and the State.* Houston: St. Clair Publishing Co., 1941.

Roberts, Rev. Edward Howell (compiler). *Princeton Theological Seminary Biographical Catalog, 1815–1932.* Princeton, New Jersey: The Trustees of the Theological Seminary of the Presbyterian Church, 1933.

Sandbo, Anna Irene. "Beginnings of the Secession Movement in Texas," *Southwestern Historical Quarterly*, XVIII (July, 1914).

Schoen, Harold. "The Free Negro in the Republic of Texas," *Southwestern Historical Quarterly*, XLIX (April, 1936) and XL (July, 1936).

Scroggs, W. O. *Filibusters and Financiers.* New York: The Macmillan Company, 1916.

Stuart, Ben C. "Hamilton Stuart: Pioneer Editor," Galveston *News*, June 3, 1917.

Stuart, Graham H. *Latin America and the United States.* 3rd edition. New York: D. Appleton-Century Co., Inc., 1938.

Smith, Harriet, and Darthula Walker. *The Geography of Texas.* Boston: Ginn and Company, 1923.

von Hinueber, Caroline. "Life of German Pioneers in Early Texas," *Southwestern Historical Quarterly,* II (January, 1899), 228. Prepared for publication by Rudolph Kleberg, Jr.

Walpole, Spencer. *Life of Lord John Russell.* 2 vols. New York: Longmans Green and Co., 1891.

Webb, Walter Prescott. *The Texas Rangers.* Boston and New York: Houghton Mifflin Co., 1935.

—— (editor-in-chief). *The Handbook of Texas.* 2 vols. Austin: State Historical Association, 1952.

Weeks, W. M. (compiler). *Debates of the Texas Convention.* Austin: J. W. Cruger, 1846.

Williams, Charles R. *Life of Rutherford Birchard Hayes.* 2 vols. Boston: Houghton Mifflin Company, 1914.

Winkler, E. W. (editor). "The Bryan-Hayes Correspondence," *Southwestern Historical Quarterly,* XXVII (July, 1924), 52–73.

Wooster, Ralph A. "Analysis of the Membership of the Texas Secession Convention," *Southwestern Historical Quarterly* LXII (January, 1959).

Wooten, Dudley G. (editor). *A Comprehensive History of Texas, 1865 1897.* 2 vols. Dallas: W. G. Scarff, 1898.

Works Projects Administration. *Texas: A Guide to the Lone Star State.* Compiled by . . . the writers' program of the Works Projects Administration in the State of Texas. American Guide Series. New York: Books Inc., 1940.

Yett, Tommy (comp.). *Members of the Legislature of the State of Texas from 1846 to 1939.* Austin: n.p., 1939.

Zucker, A. E. (editor). *The Forty-Eighters.* New York: Columbia University Press, 1950.

INDEX

Aberdeen, Lord: on African slave trade, 243

abolitionists: Hamilton Stuart on, 215–216

Accessory Transit Company: in Nicaragua, 198. SEE filibustering; transportation; Vanderbilt, Cornelius

African slave trade: attempts to legalize, ix, 215, 218; difficulties of, ix; federal position on, ix, 218, 218–219, 222, 223; and fiilbustering, ix, 194, 204; moral problems of, ix; the North in, ix, 250; profits from, ix, 216, 242, 247, 248; Texas laws on, ix, 218, 242–243; and Civil War, ix–x; and private banks, 50–51; Germans on, 135–136; Willard Richardson on, 145, 153–154, 177, 205, 216, 217, 218, 222–223, 223; Hamilton Stuart on, 148, 215–216, 221, 221–222, 223, 248 n, 249, 259; Ferdinand Flake on, 151, 221, 226–227; E. H. Cushing on, 153, 153–154, 216–217, 222, 222–223, 229; and cotton expansion, 157, 241–242; Arthur Lynn on, 158, 252–257, 261; newspapers on, 158, 194; Lorenzo Sherwood on, 171, 221; reasons for, 194, 241–242; Nicaragua as way station for, 194–195; John Henry Brown on, 200, 219; Quitman *Free Press* on, 204–205; Sam Houston on, 214, 227; conventions on, 215; scriptural support for, 215–216; and Britain, 216, 259–260; London *Times* on, 216, 217; and slaves, 216, 219, 245; French techniques for, 217; techniques for, 217, 247; laws on, 218; transportation for, 218; church support for, 220; *Civilian* on, 221, 250; M. M. Potter on, 221, 228; and Democratic party, 222, 224, 268; F. R. Lubbock on, 222, 258–259; Hardin Runnels on, 222; *Telegraph* on, 223–224; and Frank Bowden Chilton, 224; economic effect of, 224; C. C. Herbert on, 224; P. W. Kittrell on, 224; Dr. Thomason on, 224–225; M. Aycock on, 225; Thomas Palmer on, 225; James E. Shepherd on, 225; F. S. Stockdale on, 225; Peter W. Gray on, 227–228; conservatives on, 228; operation of, 229; and secession, 229–230; history of, 241, 242–243; Bowie brothers in, 242; Monroe Edwards in, 242, 243; J. W. Fannin in, 242; Jean Lafitte in, 242, Sterling McNeil in, 242; purposes of, 242; Lord Aberdeen on, 243; at Brazos River, 243; British Foreign Office on, 243, Cuba in, 243; Christopher Dart in, 243; at Havana, 243, 248–249; volume of, 243, 247, 248 n, 260, 261–262; John Barnes in, 244; at Caney Creek, 244; Charles Frankland in, 244; Richard P. Jones in, 244; Moro and Coigly in, 244; at Sabine River, 244; Richard Drake on, 245; Lord Palmerston, on, 246; on Texas coast, 246–247; vessels fitted out for, 247; R. B. Kingsbury on, 248 n; Lord Russell on, 248 n; from New Orleans, 250; and Benedict, Burr, and Benedict, 251; and Ellis and Cobb, 251; Bernardo José Machado in, 251; J. A. Machado in, 251; Thomas Watson in, 251; Mrs. Thomas Watson in, 251, 252–258, 261; Captain Dickey in, 251 n; Joao da Cunha Ferreira in, 251 n; Bradford Gibbs in, 251 n; Don Ramon de Guerediaga in, 251 n; and William Percher Miles, 251 n; Antonio Reiz Vieria in, 251 n; R. C. Welling in, 251 n; Captain Williams in, 251 n; and camels, 258; George Guinan in, 258–259; John H. Herndon in, 258–259; Stephen S. Perry in, 258–259; Benjamin F. Terry in, 258–259; J. D. Waters in, 258–259; John A. Wharton in, 258–259; Stephen A. Douglas on, 260; from Pensacola, Florida, 260; and William S. Price, 260; at Indianola, 261; attempts to stop, 261–263; and Howell Cobb, 262;

Hockley, Texas: railroad connection at, 184

Hogan, J. B.: in labor union, 101

homes: in Galveston, 92–93

Hooker, Ralph: in labor union, 101

Hopper, Seaborn: 105–106

hospital, Galveston: 67

hospital fee: for care of indigent persons, 65

House, Thomas William: activities of, 13; and Galveston-Houston power struggle, 13, 15, 59; operation of boats into Galveston by, 27; party given by, 93; and railroad controversy, 169

House of Representatives: John Henry Brown in, 219

Houston, Sam: feud of, with Willard Richardson: 145–146, 271; *Texas Almanac* on, 145–146; and E. H. Cushing, 146; on filibustering, 195, 213–214, 227; and Ferdinand Flake, 146, 225, 270–271; 273; and Know-Nothingism, 146, 224, 227, 268–269, 270–271; and Hamilton Stuart, 146, 215, 221, 225, 270–271, 273, 284–285; and African slave trade, 214, 227; and Dred Scott Decision, 214, 227; and Fugitive Slave Law, 214, 227; defeat of, by Hardin Runnels, 219, 269–270; as governor, 219, 229, 270, 274; as leader of moderate Democrats, 221, 225, 226; speeches of, 227, 294–297; and Germans, 269, 273; Galveston votes for, 274; Judge Thompson on, 280; on secession, 284, 285, 290, 292–293; General Bradford on, 285; proposed visit of, to Galveston, 285; Guy Bryan on, 287; forced out of office, 293; and Abraham Lincoln, 294; speaking ability of, 295; Thomas North on Speech of, 295–297

Houston, Texas: and Galveston, 10, 13, 14; and railroad controversy, 11, 12, 159, 162, 182–184, 184, 185, 186, 189; shift of commerce to, 11–12, 20; support of citizens of, 15; expansion of, 20; steamboats to, 29; medical society in, 39; attempts to establish medi-

cal school in, 39; filibustering from, 205, 208, 211: SEE ALSO Galveston-Houston power struggle

Houston and Texas Central Railroad: 159, 184; and Galveston, Houston and Henderson Railroad, 186–187

Houston Bachelor's Club: party given by, 95

Houston City Ice Company: 35

Houston-Galveston power struggle: SEE Galveston-Houston power struggle

Houston Public Library: xii, 306

Houston Tap and Brazoria Railroad: 159, 184

Houston *Telegraph*: SEE *Telegraph, Houston*

Howard, R. H.: in Bell and Everett Club, 276

Howard, Dr. W. H.: in Houston medical society, 39

Howard Association: care of indigent by, 68

Hoxey, General ——— : and Uncle Moses, 115

Huckins, James: background of, 84; Baptist church, 84

Hudson River: 182

Hudspeth, Chalmer Mac: xi

Hunchback, The: performance of, 109

Hurd, Captain ——— : kidnaping of free Negroes by, 232

Hutchings, John Henry: and Episcopalian church, 80, 81; and secession, 286

Hutchings, Sealy and Company, 52

Hutchings-Sealy National Bank: 52

Hutchins, William J.: and Galveston-Houston power struggle, 15, 59; and railroad controversy, 169

ice-importing business: of William Marsh Rice, 35

immigrants: number of, 129; use of *Texas Almanac* by 129

Leland, ——— : at Democratic convention, 275

levies, special: as taxes in Galveston, 58–59

Levy, I. C.: and Jewish church, 83

Lewis, Allen: as a director of Williams' bank, 53

Lewis, Stacy B.: and Galveston Wharf Company, 16

Lewis & Kemp's Ice Cream and Sherbet Saloon, 100

libraries: concern about, 102

library: of W. P. Ballinger, 102

Lieberman, L. and Jewish church, 83

Life Boat Company: 64

Lincoln, Abraham: election of, 276, 278; Willard Richardson on, 281; and Sam Houston, 294

Loan Plan: SEE Corporate Plan

Lockridge, Col. S. A.: filibustering by, 201, 202, 205, 206; to E. H. Cushing, 201; defeat of, 205, 206; and General Walker, 205–206, 210; in Galveston *News*, 210; Hamilton Stuart on, 210

Logan, Ada: performances by, 109

London *Times*: SEE *Times*, London

Lone Star, Order of: SEE Order of the Lone Star

Lone Star Association: organization of, 286; and Oscar Farish, 286

Lone Star Flag Clubs: organization of, 283

Lone Star Minute Men: organization of, 283

Lone Star Republic: revival of, 286

Lone Star Rifle Company: organization of, 283

López, General Narciso: as leader of filibustering, 194; invasion of Cuba by, 195; defeat of, 195, 196

Louie, Madame, & Troupe: performance by, 111

Louisiana: free Negroes in, 232

Louisiana: wreck of, 62; transportation of filibusters on, 230

Louisiana legislature: on railroad building, 185

Love, James: and W. P. Ballinger, 94; entertainment by, 94; and Democratic Party, 226; and Hamilton Stuart, 259; in Bell and Everett Club, 276; on secession, 280–281, 288

Lubbock, F. R.: and railroad controversy, 169; support of filibustering by, 200 n, 203, 204, 205, 258–259; and African slave trade, 222, 226-227, 258–259; at Democratic Convention, 224; and General Walker, 224; election of, as lieutenant governor, 229, 274; and camels, 257–258; and J. A. Machado, 258; and Mrs. Thomas Watson, 258; as director of Texas Stock Importing Company, 258–259; speech of, 277; on secession, 278

Lubbock, T.S.: and railroad controversy, 169

Lucerne: in African slave trade, 253

Lucretia Borgia: performance of, 109–110

lumber: importation of, 33. SEE ALSO timber

Lutheran church: SEE church, Lutheran

lyceums: development of, 102

Lydia Gibbs: in African slave trade, 251

Lynch, E. O.: in Bell and Everett club, 276

Lynn, Arthur T.: on cotton production, viii, 23; on grain production, 23; on charity of Galveston citizens, 65; on quarantine, 69; and Episcopalian church, 80,81; on life of Galveston aristocracy, 90–92; aid to British citizens by, 95; on land frauds, 106; on African slave trade, 158, 252–258, 261; on cotton expansion, 158; on railroad promoters, 188; on filibustering, 200, 214; Lord Palmerston to, 218, 231; on kidnaping of free Negroes, 231–232, 233, 239; and Hamilton Stuart, 232, 259; to mayor of Galveston, 234–235; rescue of Charles H. Thomas by, 234–235, 236–237; to Governor Elisha M. Pease, 235; to Earl of Malmesbury, 237; interest of,

Runnels, Hardin R.: and filibustering, 203; election of, as governor, 215, 219, 269–270, 274; defeat of, by Sam Houston, 219, 229; and African slave trade, 222, 226–227; at Democratic Convention, 224; and General Walker, 224; and Germans, 273

Rusk, General T. J.: on banks, 40

Russell, Lord: on African slave trade, 248 n

Rutersville Institute: 76

Sabin, C. B.: support of filibustering by, 205

Sabine, Texas: 232

Sabine and Galveston Railroad and Lumber Company: charter for, 185

Sabine Pass: and inland navigation, 5

Sabine River: African slave trade at, 244

safety, committee of: SEE committee of safety

St. Clair, Lotty: performance by, 108

St. Cyr, Henri de: on Galveston, 9; and Galveston Wharf Company, 16–18; as officer of Galveston Brazos Navigation Company, 30 n; on Galveston food, 36; support of Galveston Bay Bridge by, 190, 191

St. Joseph's Hall: school for boys at, 79

St. Louis, Missouri: as outlet for Texas trade, 171; on railroad routes, 185

St. Mary: rescue of General Walker by, 208

St. Mary's, University of: SEE University of St. Mary's

St. Mary's Cathedral: building of, 79

salaries: of city officials, 59; of workers, 101. SEE ALSO wage rate

Sampson, Henry: and Galveston-Houston power struggle, 15; and railroad controversy, 169

San Antonio, Texas: filibustering company from, 203–204

San Antonio and Mexican Gulf Railroad, The: railroad planned by, 159

San Antonio *Herald*: SEE *Herald*, San Antonio

San Antonio Public Library: 306

San Antonio River: recruiting for filibustering at, 211

sanitation: in Galveston, 66

San Jacinto Memorial Library: xii

San Jacinto River: inland navigation on, 5

San Juan River: 206

Sarah Barnes: in African slave trade, 244

Saunders, Mrs. T. C.: thefts from, 123

Sauter, J. A.: political power of, 135; knowledge of politics of, 138

Sauter, J. A., and Company: as private bankers, 41

Schmidt's Saloon: 99

Schneider, George Sr.: and German Lutheran church, 82; political power of, 135; on Germans in Galveston, 138–139; on secession, 273–274

school fund, state: 70

schools: lack of support for, 70–71; quality of, 70–71, 72, 73–76; in Galveston, 70–77; teacher shortage in, 76–77; establishment of, by churches, 79, 81, 82, 83; concern about, 102; subjects taught in, 103; E. H. Cushing on, 103–104

schools, medical: SEE medical schools

school teachers: SEE schools

school texts: published by E. H. Cushing, 73, 73 n

Schott, Justus Julius: political power of, 135

Schultze, Professor Joseph: performance by, 110

science: interest in, in Galveston, 111–114

scientific lectures: in Galveston, 112–113

Scroggs, W. O.: on Texas filibusters, 206

Sealy, John: and Galveston Wharf Company, 16, 18; and Episcopalian church, 80, 81; investiment of, in railroads, 187

secession: and cotton expansion, x, 267–268; and private banks, 50–51; Ger-

Suarez, Joseph Vincente: enslaving of, 237–239

sugar: export of, from Galveston, 24

Sugar Railroad: construction of, 182

Summers, Thomas O.: establishment of Methodist church by, 83

Supreme Court of Texas: 36; appeal of Robert Mills to, 56–57

Swearingen, Dr. R. J.: on Nicaragua, 199

Swenson and Swisher: as a private bank, 55

Sydnor, John S.: home of, 92; as slave dealer, 115, 151; and Ferdinand Flake, 150–151; support of Galveston Bay Bridge by, 190; support of filibustering by, 200 n; on Sam Houston's speech, 294, 297

Sydnor, Mrs. John S.: and Baptist church, 84

tailors: influence of Germans as, 130–131

Taliaferro, R. H.: as leader of Baptist church, 84

Taming of the Shrew: performance of, 109

Tatem & Reid: 25

tax assessor and collector: importance of, 58

taxes: in Galveston, 58

Taylor, E. W.: and Galveston-Houston power struggle, 15

teachers: SEE schools

Telegraph, Houston: on cotton production, viii, 157; and Galveston-Houston power struggle, 15, 20; on University of St. Mary's, 72; on spiritualism, 111–112; on Sam Houston, 146; E. H. Cushing as editor of, 152; on filibustering, 203, 211, 213; on African slave trade, 216–217, 220, 223, 260; on Hamilton Stuart, 222; on defeat of slave-trade ticket, 229; on Germans, 273. SEE ALSO Cushing, E. H.

temperance lectures: of Dr. Ross, 107

temperance societies: in Galveston, 107

Tennison, Lieutenant ——— : enslaving of free Negro by, 239

tensions: in Galveston, 114–115

Terry, Benjamin F.: and African slave trade, 258–259; as director of Texas Stock Importing Company, 258–259; and filibustering, 258–259

Texans: in filibustering, 193–215

Texas: passengers carried by, 29

Texas, East: SEE East Texas

Texas, University of: library of, vii

Texas Almanac: by Willard Richardson, 34–35, 145–146; use of, by immigrants, 129; attacks on Sam Houston in, 145–146

Texas & German Emigration Company, The: 128

Texas and New Orleans Railroad, The: 159, 185, 186–187

Texas & New York Line: operation of boats into Galveston by, 27

Texas constitution: on African slave trade, 218, 242–243

Texas district court: 36; records of, 305

Texas Gulf coast: SEE Gulf coast, Texas

Texas History Center in Austin: 304

Texas laws: on African slave trade, ix

Texas legislature: SEE legislature

Texas Railroad Convention: Lorenzo Sherwood at, 167

Texas Rangers: in Nicaragua, 202–203, 205, 206

Texas Revolution: McKinney and Williams in, 45

Texas Stock Importing Company: and importation of camels, 258

Texas Supreme Court: records of, 305

theatres: need for, 102

theatrical entertainments: in Galveston, 108–110

Thomas, Charles H.: kidnaping of, 233–237

Thomason, Dr. ——— : on African slave trade, 224–225

Vanderbilt, Cornelius: operation of passenger service from Galveston by, 27; and filibustering, 198, 199, 208, 215; and Garrison and Morgan, 198, 199

Vandiver, Frank E.: xi

van Sickle, Stephen: and Lorenzo Sherwood, 176

Velasco: kidnaping of Charles H. Thomas on, 233

Vesey, John: on African slave trade, 248–249, 249 n

Victoria, Texas: railroad from, 159

Vieria, Antonio Reiz: in African slave trade, 251 n

Virginia Point, Texas: railroad connection at, 186, 189; railroad party at, 191

vital records: SEE records, public

Vixen: capture of slaver by, 222

Waco, Texas: and Galveston, 10

wage rate: of printers, 101. SEE ALSO salaries

Walker, General William: and filibustering, 194, 195, 199–200, 201, 202, 205, 208, 213–214; in Nicaragua, 196, 198–208, 212–213, 213–214; on Pacific coast, 196; background of, 196–197, 198; character of, 198; and Francisco Castellon, 196; and Garrison and Morgan, 198; and Manifest Destiny, 198; as president of Nicaragua, 198; purposes of, 198, 214; first expedition of, 198–208; and E. H. Cushing, 199; Archibald Wynne on, 201; Quitman *Free Press* on, 205; disciplining of troops by, 205–206; defeat and execution of, 206–208, 214; military talents of, 208; compared to Moses Austin and Lafayette, 210; disagreement of, with Colonel Lockridge, 210; second expedition of, 212–213; removal of, from Nicaragua by Hiram Paulding, 212–213; in Mobile and New Orleans, 213; third expedition of, 213–214; and F. R. Lubbock, 224; and Hardin Runnels, 224; and A. P. Wiley, 224. SEE ALSO America, Central; filibustering, Nicaragua

warehousing: and cotton production, viii

Washington County, Texas: 206, 225

Watchman, Lockhart: on spiritualism, 111

Waters, Dr. H. W.: 208; in Houston medical society, 39; support of filibustering by, 203, 205

Waters, Col. John D.: 208; and filibustering, 202–208, 258–259; and African slave trade, 258–259; as director of Texas Stock Importing Company, 258–259

waterways, inland: SEE inland waterways; navigation, inland

Watson, Thomas: in African slave trade, 251

Watson, Mrs. Thomas: in African slave trade, 251, 261; and Arthur Lynn, 252–257; and J. A. Machado, 253; Earl of Malmesbury on, 254; Privy Council on, 254; and F. R. Lubbock, 258; and Hamilton Stuart, 259

weather conditions: on Galveston Island, 7–8

Welling, R. C.: in African slave trade, 251 n

Wells, C. G.: and Galveston Wharf Company, 16

Wells, J. H.: and railroad controversy, 170

Wendt, Reverend Mr. ——— : German Lutheran church led by, 82

Weser: immigrants brought in on, 129

West: in African slave trade, 260

West Bay: channel through, 30

West Indies: kidnaping of free Negroes from, 231; trade with, during Civil War, 300

Wharf Company. SEE Galveston Wharf Company

wharf facilities: operation of by various companies, 15–16

Wharton, John A.: and African slave trade, 258–259; and filibustering, 258–259; as director of Texas Stock Importing Company, 258–259

Wharton, Texas: railroad from, 159